AF805227

Indigenous Environmental Rights

This volume makes a legal theoretical contribution to the emerging regime of Indigenous environmental rights, drawing on the law, theory, and sociological and anthropological approaches. Firstly, it introduces key developments in the field of international human rights law and international environmental law, dealing with contemporary trends but also foundational principles and rights. It then addresses one of the most influential strands, that of (transformative) legal pluralism and its decolonizing effects on the law. And in a final part, it uncovers a known conceptual divide, distinguishing between anthropocentric and eco-centric approaches, thereby identifying key developments in the human rights field and rights of nature discourses. The book brings together experts in the field and also creates the space for scholarly dialogue, conceptually and beyond, which ultimately provides answers and directions in the field of Indigenous environmental rights, to newcomers and specialized scholars alike.

Jessika Eichler specializes in Indigenous peoples' rights, working with a dedicated interdisciplinary approach, combining the law with sociopolitical inquiry and theory. She coedits several prestigious writing projects, notably a Commentary on UNDRIPS (article-by-article), a Research Handbook of Collective Rights, and a forthcoming human rights book series.

Mario G. Aguilera is an international lawyer and scholar specializing in environmental and human rights law. He has worked with the Inter-American Commission on Human Rights and the Max Planck Institute for Social Anthropology. He is the author of *Environmental Human Rights* (2023), the first in-depth study of the emerging environmental human rights regime in Latin America and the Caribbean.

Transnational Environmental Law

TEL

SERIES EDITORS

Thijs Etty Amsterdam University College, University of Amsterdam, The Netherlands
Josephine van Zeben European University Institute, Italy

Transnational Environmental Law (TEL) is a series of books for the study of environmental law and governance beyond the state. It approaches legal and regulatory developments with an interest in the contribution of non-state actors and an awareness of the multi-level governance context in which contemporary environmental law unfolds. TEL has a broad disciplinary focus open to scholarly contributions covering a wide range of environmental issues and the evolving dynamics between environmental law and other legal disciplines. TEL strives for a new generation of environmental scholarship that will bridge geographical boundaries, scholarly styles and generations.

BOOKS IN THE SERIES

Jessika Eichler and Mario G. Aguilera, *Indigenous Environmental Rights: Towards a Holistic Regime*

Roger Merino, *Governing International Commons: From Polycentric to Plurinational Governance in the Amazon*

Annika Frosch, *Navigating the Souring Seas: The Global Experimentalist Governance of Ocean Acidification*

Agung Wardana, *Turning Defenders into Defendants: The Use of Lawfare against Environmental Activists in Southeast Asia*

Indigenous Environmental Rights

Towards a Holistic Regime

EDITED BY

Jessika Eichler

Max-Planck-Institut für ethnologische Forschung, Halle

Mario G. Aguilera

Max-Planck-Institut für ethnologische Forschung, Halle

CAMBRIDGE
UNIVERSITY PRESS

CAMBRIDGE
UNIVERSITY PRESS

Shaftesbury Road, Cambridge CB2 8EA, United Kingdom

One Liberty Plaza, 20th Floor, New York, NY 10006, USA

477 Williamstown Road, Port Melbourne, VIC 3207, Australia

314–321, 3rd Floor, Plot 3, Splendor Forum, Jasola District Centre,
New Delhi – 110025, India

Cambridge University Press is part of Cambridge University Press & Assessment,
a department of the University of Cambridge.

We share the University's mission to contribute to society through the pursuit of
education, learning and research at the highest international levels of excellence.

www.cambridge.org
Information on this title: www.cambridge.org/9781009646994

DOI: 10.1017/9781009647021

© Cambridge University Press & Assessment 2026

This publication is in copyright. Subject to statutory exception and to the provisions
of relevant collective licensing agreements, no reproduction of any part may take place
without the written permission of Cambridge University Press & Assessment.

When citing this work, please include a reference to the DOI 10.1017/9781009647021

First published 2026

A catalogue record for this publication is available from the British Library

Library of Congress Cataloging-in-Publication Data
Names: Eichler, Jessika editor | Aguilera Bravo, Mario editor
Title: Indigenous environmental rights : towards a holistic regime / Edited by Jessika Eichler,
Max-Planck-Institut für ethnologische Forschung, Halle; Mario G. Aguilera, Max-Planck-Institut
für ethnologische Forschung, Halle.
Description: Cambridge, United Kingdom ; New York, NY : Cambridge University Press, 2026. |
Series: Transnational environmental law | Includes bibliographical references and index.
Identifiers: LCCN 2026017341 (print) | LCCN 2026017342 (ebook) | ISBN 9781009646994 hardback |
ISBN 9781009647007 paperback | ISBN 9781009647021 ebook
Subjects: LCSH: Indigenous peoples (International law) | Indigenous peoples – Legal status,
laws, etc. | Environmental law, International | Environmental law | International law and human
rights | Customary law, International
Classification: LCC KI280 .I53 2026 (print) | LCC KI280 (ebook)
LC record available at https://lccn.loc.gov/2026017341
LC ebook record available at https://lccn.loc.gov/2026017342

ISBN 978-1-009-64699-4 Hardback

Cambridge University Press & Assessment has no responsibility for the persistence
or accuracy of URLs for external or third-party internet websites referred to in this publication and does not
guarantee that any content on such websites is, or will remain,
accurate or appropriate.

For EU product safety concerns, contact us at Calle de José Abascal, 56, 1°, 28003 Madrid, Spain, or email
eugpsr@cambridge.org

To Pope Francis and his Encyclical Letter Laudato Si'
and all environmental, human rights, indigenous defenders:
may they be protected from violence
Jessika Eichler

To my children, Lucas and Nicolas,
and to future generations –
may you inherit a Mother Earth as rich in cultural and ecological diversity
as the one your ancestors knew,
and a world guided by solidarity, justice, and care.
Mario Aguilera

CONTENTS

CONTRIBUTORS

Laura Calle-Alzate
Complutense University of Madrid, Madrid, Spain

Federica Cittadino
Institute for Comparative Federalism, Eurac Research, Bolzano/Bozen, South Tyrol, Italy

Nurys Esperanza Silva-Cantillo
Colombian Institute of Anthropology and History, Bogota, Colombia; National University of Colombia, Bogota, Colombia

Jonathan Liljeblad
College of Law, Governance, & Policy, Australian National University, Acton, ACT, Australia

Digno Montalván-Zambrano
Research Group on Law and Justice, Charles III University of Madrid, Madrid, Spain

Núria Reguart-Segarra
Faculty of Legal and Economic Sciences, Universitat Jaume I, Castello del la Plana, Castello, Spain

Ricardo Salas Astrain
Catholic University of Temuco, Temuco, Araucania, Chile

Cristian Pacheco Huaiquifil
Catholic University of Temuco, Temuco, Araucania, Chile

Isabel Wences
Research Group on Law and Justice, Charles III University of Madrid, Madrid, Spain; Complutense University of Madrid, Madrid, Spain

Tineke Lambooy
Nyenrode Business University, Breukelen, the Netherlands, and Airlangga University, Surabaya, Indonesia

Bart Jansen
University of Amsterdam, Amsterdam, the Netherlands, Nyenrode Business University, Breukelen, the Netherlands, and Airlangga University, Surabaya, Indonesia

FOREWORD: TOWARDS A PLURALISTIC FUTURE FOR INDIGENOUS ENVIRONMENTAL RIGHTS

The growing recognition of indigenous environmental rights has stirred long-overdue transformations in international law, pushing the boundaries of conventional legal theory and frameworks. In this incisive text, the authors offer a profound intellectual groundwork, positioning indigenous environmental rights not merely as a subcategory of environmental or human rights law, but as a *sui generis* legal regime in need of robust theorisztion, pluralistic accommodation, and decolonial restructuring.

At its heart, this contribution challenges the reader to reconsider foundational legal categories – rights, duties, subjecthood, justice – through the lens of indigenous cosmologies and legal orders. The authors traverse a vast legal and conceptual landscape, weaving together insights from environmental anthropology, international human rights law (IHRL), ecocentric and anthropocentric approaches, international environmental law, legal pluralism and indigenous justice approaches, critical legal approaches and legal theory, third world approaches to international law, legal anthropology, religious approaches, biocultural work, and decolonial theory. Their approach transcends the usual assimilationist paradigms in which indigenous participation is instrumentalized for State-centric environmental governance, instead advocating for recognition of indigenous peoples as full legal subjects – rights holders, guardians, knowledge-bearers, and sovereign decision-makers.

Framing the Concept: From Guardianship to Rights-Based Recognition

Opening with a discussion on Indigenous stewardship or guardianship, the authors assert the need to reconceptualize these roles within a genuine rights-based framework. Indigenous environmental rights, they argue, should not be subsumed under anthropocentric environmental rights or the emerging "rights of nature" (RoN) jurisprudence. Rather, these rights demand proper legal recognition as both individual and collective entitlements, grounded equally in international law and in Indigenous legal systems.

This positioning – of Indigenous peoples not as proxies for environmental claims but as autonomous legal actors – runs through the book's core. By placing Indigenous environmental rights at the nexus of third-generation (solidarity) rights, collective rights, and ecological rights, the authors invite a radical reconfiguration of legal doctrine that accommodates the communal, spiritual, and territorial dimensions of Indigenous life.

Decolonizing Dualisms: Conceptual Innovation in the Legal Landscape

One of the book's most intellectually generative moves is its deconstruction of several entrenched dualisms that often structure the discourse: human rights versus RoN, biodiversity law versus IHRL, individual versus collective rights, procedural versus substantive claims, and State-centered frameworks versus legal pluralism.

In addressing the human rights/RoN divide, the authors highlight the participatory and epistemic contributions of Indigenous peoples to both camps, rejecting the artificial separation between human and nonhuman rights. They demonstrate how RoN, often portrayed as ecocentric and posthumanist, in fact draws richly from Indigenous worldviews where nature and community are indivisible. The implication is clear: a decolonial legal order must cease to treat RoN and Indigenous rights as competing or mutually exclusive and, instead, recognize their convergence through Indigenous cosmovisions.

Similarly, the discussion of the biodiversity and climate regimes (Convention on Biological Diversity [CBD], Kunming–Montréal Global Biodiversity Framework [KMGBF], United Nations Framework Convention on Climate Change [UNFCCC]) vis-à-vis IHRL unpacks the piecemeal and often instrumental inclusion of Indigenous participation. Despite growing references to free, prior, and informed consent (FPIC), benefit-sharing, and knowledge protection, Indigenous agency is often limited to implementation roles without substantive decision-making power. The authors critically interrogate these "ad hoc" forms of inclusion, exposing their failure to embrace legal pluralism or address structural power imbalances.

International Mechanisms and Jurisprudential Openings

A detailed mapping of international legal developments adds doctrinal depth to the chapter. The discussion of the United Nations Declaration on the Rights of Indigenous Peoples (UNDRIPS), ILO Convention 169, Inter-American Court decisions (e.g., *Saramaka*, *Lhaka Honhat*), and contributions of the Human Rights Committee and Committee on Economic, Social and Cultural Rights demonstrates that Indigenous environmental rights are no longer marginal in global jurisprudence. Yet the authors rightly caution against conflating recognition with empowerment. Implementation deficits, fragmented protections, and the predominance of procedural over substantive safeguards persist.

The text's treatment of proceduralization – especially access to information, public participation, and access to justice – illustrates the need for treating Indigenous peoples' rights, both their procedural and substantive dimensions, in an integrated, holistic manner. Even where rights to consultation or FPIC exist, these may be co-opted by State-led development agendas or rendered ineffectual without enforceable mechanisms and respect for Indigenous governance institutions.

Legal Pluralism and the Epistemology of Environmental Law

Perhaps one of the book's most radical and promising claims is the call for transformative legal pluralism. Drawing from both theory and case law, the authors argue for the recognition of Indigenous law not as supplementary to State law but as coequal. This entails rethinking source hierarchies, interpretative authority, and procedural autonomy. The authors' engagement with hybrid spaces is especially compelling, suggesting a space in which plural legal systems coexist, contest, and potentially transform one another.

In this space, Indigenous legal concepts – such as land-as-law, kinship-based responsibilities, and *sentipensar* – challenge the positivist and anthropocentric logic of dominant legal systems. By centering affect, ancestry, and relationality, Indigenous laws reimagine the legal subject as embedded in community and environment, not abstracted from it. This epistemological opening is presented not only as a normative imperative but also as a response to ecological crisis, legal ineffectiveness, and colonial inertia.

Decolonial Potential and the Future of Indigenous Environmental Rights

A recurrent theme in the book is the decolonial potential embedded in the emergence of Indigenous environmental rights. Yet the authors avoid romanticizing this potential. They are attentive to the dangers of co-optation, symbolic recognition without redistribution, and the reification of indigeneity for global governance purposes. Decoloniality, in this framing, is not a rhetorical flourish but a programmatic demand: for epistemic justice, for Indigenous-led norm creation, and for legal transformation that reflects the lived realities of Indigenous communities.

The analysis of self-determination and alternative development paradigms (*Buen Vivir*, *Sumak Kawsay*, etc.) underscores the link between environmental justice and broader struggles for autonomy, cultural survival, and political transformation. The notion that Indigenous environmental rights may serve as an entry point for rethinking development itself – away from extractivism and toward plural economies – is both urgent and generative.

Conclusion: Toward a Holistic Regime

This book is truly interdisciplinary, critical, and forward-thinking. By refusing to isolate Indigenous environmental rights within narrow legalistic frames, it succeeds in offering a holistic and deeply contextualized understanding. Its contribution lies not only in clarifying complex legal intersections but also in reimagining law's foundations in light of Indigenous worldviews.

As the field of Indigenous environmental rights continues to evolve, this text will remain a touchstone for scholars, practitioners, and activists seeking to navigate its ethical, legal, and epistemological contours. Its commitment to legal pluralism, its insistence on Indigenous agency, and its decolonial horizon together make this much more than a mere introductory text, but rather an invitation – to think differently, and more justly, about the future of law and the earth.

Professor Damien Short Co-Director,
Human Rights Consortium (HRC)Professor,
Human Rights and Environmental Justice,
School of Advanced Study, University of London

PREFACE BY THE SERIES EDITORS

The recognition of Indigenous environmental rights has emerged as one of the most transformative – and contested – developments in contemporary environmental law and governance. At once legal, political, cultural, and ecological, the claims advanced under this banner question established assumptions about sovereignty, property, development, and even the nature of law itself. They open new spaces for reimagining humanity's relationship with the natural world, while also foregrounding the lived realities of Indigenous peoples who bear the brunt of environmental degradation.

Expertly curated by Jessika Eichler and Mario Aguilera, *Indigenous Environmental Rights: Towards a Holistic Regime* positions itself as a bridge-building project, responding to the complexity and fragmentation that mark this field. While rooted in legal theory and doctrine, the book engages deeply with anthropology, political science, sociology, and other cognate disciplines. This interdisciplinarity is not simply an academic gesture. Rather, it reflects the reality that Indigenous environmental rights are produced, contested, and redefined across multiple spheres: in courtrooms, legislatures, international forums, community assemblies, and the everyday negotiations of Indigenous peoples with State and non-State actors. By weaving together these insights, the book offers a multivariate perspective capable of doing justice to the layered and dynamic character of Indigenous environmental rights.

The volume takes as its starting point the recognition that Indigenous environmental rights are both conceptually novel and practically consequential. They resist easy categorization, demanding instead careful theoretical elaboration. To this end, the contributors explore how these rights are constructed and deconstructed in different legal and political contexts; how they challenge existing normative orders while contributing to legal pluralism and decolonial theory; how they broaden the horizon of environmental rights by embedding a specifically Indigenous dimension; and how they open new questions of representation and participation in multi-ordered spaces of negotiation. In this way, the volume not only expands the conceptual vocabulary of environmental rights, but also brings Indigenous perspectives into sharper focus within legal and governance debates.

What most distinguishes this collection from existing scholarship is that it moves beyond case study-driven approaches, which, although valuable, risk fragmenting analysis along jurisdictional or thematic lines. Instead, the editors and contributors embrace theoretical complexity while grounding their arguments in empirical realities. The empirical contributions serve as testing grounds for the theoretical constructs developed here, ensuring that conceptual innovations are informed by local experiences, diverse geographies, and practical struggles for recognition. This dialectic between theory and empirics provides the book with both rigor and legitimacy.

We are particularly pleased to include this edited volume in the Transnational Environmental Law book series. Its focus on Indigenous environmental rights remains an understudied but crucial area of transnational environmental law. Covering a wide range of jurisdictions – including several that have traditionally received less scholarly attention – the book demonstrates how these rights intersect with both environmental and Indigenous (human) rights, thereby contributing theoretically, philosophically, and normatively to both fields. The editors and contributors represent a diverse group of scholars, bringing together perspectives from multiple disciplines while preserving a central legal focus. Their combined voices enrich environmental law scholarship and strengthen the understanding of Indigenous environmental rights as a distinctive and growing area of transnational concern.

In aligning legal theory with empirical diversity and interdisciplinary perspectives, *Indigenous Environmental Rights* embodies the ambitions of the Transnational Environmental Law book series. It pushes the boundaries of established fields, interrogates foundational concepts, and offers a platform for voices and perspectives too often marginalized. In doing so, it contributes not only to scholarly literature, but also to the practical project of ensuring that Indigenous environmental rights find meaningful articulation and recognition in law and governance.

We commend this volume as an important resource for scholars, practitioners, policy-makers, and Indigenous communities alike.

Thijs Etty and Josephine van Zeben
Series Editors

Introductory Remarks

Indigenous Environmental Rights – Conceptual Considerations

Jessika Eichler and Mario Aguilera

It makes little sense to write about Indigenous peoples' rights without placing them in the post-pandemic context, and without articulating their distinct role in the climate crisis. Indeed, Indigenous peoples around the globe find themselves disproportionately affected by extractive operations but also so-called "development" or infrastructure projects – and this concerns, first and foremost, Indigenous peoples' immediate environment and livelihoods, as sources of subsistence and spiritual significance. Discrimination and marginalization are not new. Since the colonial era, Indigenous peoples have been exposed to external threats, including deadly diseases and systemic dispossession, while often lacking the institutional means to defend themselves. Today, this legacy persists in the form of environmental injustice, prompting sustained and organized forms of territorial resistance and socio-environmental defense on the ground. At the same time, the burden of protecting the planet's climate and biodiversity has increasingly fallen to the grassroots – particularly to Indigenous communities. Their knowledge systems, based on long-standing ecological stewardship and intergenerational knowledge transmission, are now gaining recognition, also beyond their own contexts. They are being brought to the forefront of global environmental governance, where Indigenous voices are playing a growing role in shaping the agendas of international climate and biodiversity forums.

As the title suggests, this book explores *Indigenous environmental rights* through both conceptual and theoretical lenses, while tracing the meanings these rights acquire in practice. In related debates, Indigenous peoples' contributions to multi-diverse societies, social cohesion, and plurilegality are often framed within utilitarian approaches that interpret Indigenous rights through integrationist or assimilationist paradigms. Within such frames, Indigenous environmental rights are frequently understood in terms of intergenerational stewardship (Page 2007; Winter 2022) or guardianship in relationship to nature (Barrit 2020; Fitzmaurice

2018) or otherwise as extensions of sustainable development discourse (Lightfoot 2016). This line of thinking tends to reproduce dynamics in which Indigenous representatives are positioned as translators, spokespersons, or even legal guardians or stewards of rivers, forests, and other nonhuman beings – roles that may occasionally reflect external expectations more than Indigenous self-understandings.

In contrast, this book adopts a predominantly rights-based and critical legal approach, one that affirms Indigenous environmental rights as possessing their own legal meaning – with substantive and procedural implications – within both State and Indigenous legal systems. These rights are recognized as both individual and collective in nature, grounded not merely in environmental or developmental utility, but in normative claims to legal standing, self-determination, jurisdiction over land, resources located therein, and biocultural relations. To situate Indigenous environmental rights within the broader framework of human rights, it is useful to begin with the evolving category of the right to a safe, clean, healthy and sustainable environment. This right, increasingly recognized in international normative discourses, often serves as an entry point for analyzing the environmental impacts that disproportionately affect Indigenous communities – particularly in the context of extractivism and climate change (e.g., Martin et al. 2015; Oluborode Jegede 2016). Closely linked are questions of environmental (in)justice, which have become a focal point for research in both legal and sociopolitical domains.

Much of the existing literature remains rooted in positivist interpretations of environmental law, examining the extent to which legal norms apply to indigenous claims. These analyses often underscore the persistent shortcomings of both international and domestic legal systems to provide effective protection of indigenous rights, especially in cases involving mining, deforestation, and other forms of environmental degradation (Westra 2011). In response, scholars have turned to spaces of global environmental governance as important arenas for understanding how Indigenous peoples engage with – and often challenge – dominant legal and policy paradigms, including right to nature narratives (Etchart 2022). These legal dynamics are increasingly analyzed through the lens of environmental anthropology, which offers critical tools for exploring the intersection between culture, law, and ecology. Anthropological perspectives help ground legal analysis in lived experience, highlighting the relational and place-based dimensions of Indigenous rights. Scholars such as Boyd (2012, 2017), Bryant (2015), Di Chiro (2016), Gabrielsen et al. (2016), Kopnina and Shoreman-Ouimet (2016), Martinez-Alier (2016), Merrills (2008), and Perreault et al. (2015) have contributed to a rich body of work that challenges universalist legal models and foregrounds the socioecological specificity of indigenous struggles.

Relatedly, Indigenous environmental rights can be situated within the broader trajectory of human rights evolution – specifically, within the discourse of so-called "third-generation rights." These follow the historical emergence of first-generation civil and political rights, and second-generation economic, social, and cultural rights (Tomuschat 2014; Vasak 1977): third-generation rights, often described as "solidarity rights," include the right to a healthy environment (Onazi 2026), the right to development (Onazi 2026), and the right to peace or humanity's rights (Corrias 2026; Gaillard 2026). They are typically collective in nature and frequently pose conceptual and practical challenges, especially in term of defining rights holders, attributing harm, or establishing duty bearers (Tomuschat 2014). Indigenous environmental rights resonate strongly with this logic. Like other third-generation rights, they are deeply collective, intergenerational, and tied to group identity and territory. Yet, precisely because of these characteristics, they often appear to sit uncomfortably with classical legal standards that favor individual claims, direct causality, and particularly defined State obligations. As a result, such rights may elude recognition, they may struggle with justiciability or be excluded from mainstream human rights frameworks altogether. This conceptual conflict underscores the need for a renewed theoretical engagement. Indigenous environmental rights challenge us to reconsider the architecture of human rights law – not simply by adding a new category, but by rethinking what rights can mean when grounded in relational ontologies, plural legal orders, and collective lifeways. As such, they demand to be understood simultaneously as a new legal category altogether, as environmental rights, collective rights, and third-generation rights – while also pushing the boundaries of each of these categories.

Another important turn in this debate emerges through the lens of legal pluralism and, more specifically, the recognition of Indigenous justice systems and philosophies. These frames foreground Indigenous cosmovisions that articulate environmental responsibility not as a matter of resource management, but as a spiritual and relational commitment to the Earth. Concepts such as *Buen Vivir, Vivir Bien, Pachamama* (discussed below) and other Earth-centered paradigms offer alternative ontologies in which human and nonhuman life are interconnected and mutually dependent (Acosta 2015; Altmann 2020; Escobar 2014; Gudynas 2011; Solón 2017). These worldviews challenge dominant legal models by recentering environmental ethics around reciprocity, interdependence, and balance. Such orientation is also reflected in emerging legal concepts such as biocultural rights, which aim to protect the intertwined nature of biodiversity and cultural identity. Although these approaches offer a more integrated and context-sensitive understanding of rights (Bavikatte 2014; Bennett & Bavikatte 2015; Girard, Hall, & Frison 2022; Macpherson, Torres Ventura, & Clavijo Ospina 2020; Rodríguez Caguana & Morales Naranjo 2020; Sajeva 2018), they differ in the extent to which they genuinely center Indigenous epistemologies, legal authority, and self-determination. Parallel to these developments is the growing recognition of the rights of nature (RoN) – a legal and philosophical movement that positions ecosystems as rights-bearing subjects in their own right (Boyd 2017; Rawson & Mansfield 2018; Rogers & Maloney 2017). While sometimes pursued independently from Indigenous agendas, these initiatives nonetheless resonate with Indigenous relational ontologies and offer a critical counterpoint vis-à-vis anthropocentric responses to environmental protection. In doing so, they initiate a broader reflection on the place of humans within ecological systems and the limitation of legal frameworks that prioritize human utility over ecological integrity.

As the preceding discussion suggests, this book seeks to move beyond binary framings that position Indigenous peoples either as passive victims of environmental harm or as symbolic stewards of nature. Instead, it centers Indigenous peoples as rights holders, legal actors, and epistemic authorities – as what Cornwall and Gaventa (2001) describe as "shapers and makers" of their own legal and political orders and as novel agents in international affairs. In doing so, the book responds to and builds upon existing positivist accounts, which offer valuable insights and points of reference but often remain confined within normative structures that struggle to accommodate Indigenous legal pluralism, relational worldviews, and the evolving nature of Indigenous environmental rights. These limitations are especially evident in scholarship that focuses narrowly on socioenvironmental impacts, typically through localized case studies that merely highlight Indigenous resistance to extractive projects (Cittadino 2019). Although such studies are vital, they often treat the environmental dimension, following an ad-hoc logic, as pertinent only when Indigenous livelihoods are threatened, rather than as constitutive of Indigenous legal and ontological orders. This book aims to shift that emphasis by positioning Indigenous environmental rights not merely as reactive claims, but as proactive, foundational frameworks through which relationships with land, water, flora, and fauna are governed. In this sense, the chapters that follow do not merely document violations or make advocacy efforts; they engage in the theoretical and practical work of reconceptualizing environmental rights from Indigenous standpoints. This debate invites reflection on some of the most persistent dualisms in the field – human/nature, neocolonial law/decolonial approaches, individual/collective, global/local, procedural/substantive, or environmental standards versus international human rights law (IHRL), as discussed at length in the following sections – while offering pathways for Indigenous environmental rights to enter into productive dialogue and negotiation with dominant legal and political paradigms.

I.1 The Origins of Indigenous Environmental Rights: Legal Pluralism, Legal–Epistemological Considerations, and Cosmovisionist Thinking

Given that Indigenous environmental rights are not easily attributable to or fully embedded within any specific legal framework, we must grapple directly with the question of legal sources. Almost inevitably, Indigenous environmental rights find at least partial anchoring within classical, State-centric legal systems, which continue to dominate at both domestic and international levels. Yet, by their very nature, these rights also reflect Indigenous legal traditions and worldviews, offering critical insights into the relational and often spiritual position the environment holds in Indigenous peoples' daily lives (e.g., Reguart-Segarra 2025). As it has often been emphasized, Indigenous peoples' specific claims, whether territorial, environmental, or cultural, are rarely separable or meaningfully studied in isolation. Empirical evidence consistently reveals the interwoven character of these dimensions, where environmental rights are intimately linked to cultural identity, territorial belonging, and modes of social and political organization. Complicating this further is the sheer diversity of Indigenous cosmovisions, which present a multiplicity of approaches to conceptualizing environmental relations and defining human–nature relationships. Nevertheless, some shared conceptual foundations can be identified, including paradigms such as earth-centered paradigms (Pachamama, Vivir Bien/Buen Vivir, etc., discussed below), human–earth balance models, as well as Indigenous critiques or other responses to ecocentric and post-development discourses (e.g., Álvarez 2020; Escobar 2014). Crucially, we must also contend with the emergence of mixed frameworks, where elements of Indigenous legal autonomy are interwoven with State law, producing what has been described as forms of integrated legal pluralism, especially visible in newly constituted plurinational States (Bolivia, Ecuador) that exhibit a degree of openness to Indigenous institutions and normative orders (e.g., Barrera 2012). However, the recognition of Indigenous justice systems and legal procedures remains highly fragmented and contested. Existing codes of competence and jurisdiction rarely confer absolute or full jurisdictional authority to Indigenous communities. Instead, such powers are typically constrained across dimensions such as *ratione personae*, *ratione materiae*, and *ratione loci*, leaving Indigenous legal orders with only partial or conditional authority. Critical scholars have rightly pointed to the piecemeal and ad-hoc nature of many of these legal pluralism arrangements, often characterizing them as "stand-alone" cases or judicial experiments that fall short of establishing robust, systemic pluralism. At best, these fragmented accommodations serve as illustrations of progressive developments in the law, rather than signaling a comprehensive transformation of legal systems to genuinely integrated and uphold Indigenous legal orders on equal footing with State-centric frameworks.

The entanglement of environmental concerns and indigenous agendas manifests in multiple, layered ways. Across diverse contexts, claims have been raised by or on behalf of Indigenous communities to secure legal protection for rivers, mountains, forests, or other natural entities, often advocating for these to be recognized as legal subjects vested with legal personality. These claims not only challenge anthropocentric legal traditions but also foreground Indigenous epistemologies that conceive of nature as relational, animate, and agentive. Importantly, the Inter-American Court of Human Rights (IACtHR) has recently engaged more explicitly with these concerns, particularly through its recognition of the rights to food and water, which the Court views as essential for safeguarding the survival and dignity of vulnerable groups. In the *Lhaka Honhat* decision, the Court emphasized that Indigenous peoples "essentially depend economically or for their survival on environmental resources (such as those associated with) the marine environment, forested areas and river basins" (*Lhaka Honhat* decision, para. 209). Environmental rights have also been derived from core Indigenous claims related to territories, lands, and natural resources, which necessarily generate protective obligations toward the ecosystems and nonhuman entities embedded within those territories. The spiritual dimension of land has become a particularly salient point of debate – not only among Indigenous claimants but also within judicial reasoning itself: for example, Colombian constitutional jurisprudence (e.g., *Atrato river* case) and Canada's *Grizzly Spirit* case have both engaged with Indigenous understandings of beings, places, and protective spirits, recognizing their profound influence on the relationships between peoples, territories, and nonhuman actors. Another critical dimension of Indigenous environmental thinking lies in the assertion of Indigenous knowledge systems, not only as rights claims in their own right but also as epistemic frameworks offering pluralistic, interdependent, and often more egalitarian conceptions of the human–environment relationship. Such perspectives challenge dominant Western legal paradigms and invite a rethinking of environmental law through relational, rather than extractive or utilitarian lenses.

Recognizing Indigenous knowledge systems generates effects that extend well beyond the legal domain in a strict sense, catalyzing important epistemological transformations that may ultimately contribute to what Bautista (2021) calls a form of "epistemological parity" and a "cognitive opening of the first world". As one of the distinguishing aspects of indigenous legal systems, indigenous authors have been referring to "ordering concepts" – one of them relying on the interrelation between indigenous peoples and the environment while understanding land as a source of the law (Gover 2020). Another key organizing principle drawn from Indigenous legal orders is the emphasis on learning from and observing the environment, generating forms of knowledge that can drive epistemic shifts and legal novelty (Gover 2020). Similar insights have been explored by Borrows (2013), who traces the sources of Indigenous law not only to sacred narratives but also to the physical world itself, a dynamic interplay that informs the development and drafting of Indigenous legal norms. The relationality inherent to Indigenous legal systems has also been described by Indigenous scholars as a kinship relation with the environment (Black 2011; Gover 2020; Morales 2018). This worldview underpins widely recognized concepts of guardianship or stewardship – the responsibility Indigenous peoples assume toward nature and its beings. Scholars working on these matters have highlighted the importance of Indigenous relational norms, which extend kinship ties beyond human communities to encompass ancestors, natural entities, and nonhuman actors. Critically, Coyle (2020) argues that failing to acknowledge the distinctiveness of these relational norms amounts to a fundamental misunderstanding and mistranslation between dominant legal frameworks and Indigenous legal orders. Such recognition inevitably calls into question the foundational assumptions of (Western) legal and philosophical traditions – particularly the notion that human beings exist separately from, and hierarchically above, the natural world, or that they are unbound by obligations to future generations and their needs (Coyle 2020).

Other scholarly accounts and research circles draw attention to the significance of narratives and storytelling in articulating the historical ethnography of Indigenous peoples and their deep connection to the natural world (Black 2011; Gover 2020). These oral histories and stories are often infused with spiritual dimensions, reflecting shared understandings of the natural order and anchoring Indigenous relationships to place and ancestry (Coyle 2020). Indeed, ancestral knowledge and intergenerational transmission play a central role in Indigenous ontologies, frequently cited in multilateral climate change negotiations and biodiversity debates, with sustainability thinking being a foundational element of Indigenous environmental rights approaches. Another salient dimension identified by scholars concerns the role of affect and emotional attachment to the immediate environment (Black 2011; Gover 2020), an aspect captured conceptually in *sentipensar* (con la tierra) – the blending of *sentir* (feeling) and *pensar* (thinking). This notion powerfully illustrates the intimate, embodied bond Indigenous peoples maintain with the natural world, a relationship that positions them not only as guardians or stewards, but also as spokespersons and translators of nonhuman voices within legal, cultural, and political arenas. Such interdependence between Indigenous communities and their environments is deeply embedded in the laws, customs, and practices that govern these relationships, serving not merely as regulatory mechanisms but as frameworks designed to ensure long-term stability, resilience, and continuity (Gover 2020).

We may also approach Indigenous environmental rights – as understood, articulated, and juridified by Indigenous peoples themselves – as undergoing a dynamic process of accommodation, whereby the former are gradually absorbed and reinterpreted within the frameworks of the dominant, State-centric legal order. Yet, the challenge of legal pluralism is not merely one of technical incorporation; it is fundamentally a question of negotiating the place, weight, and meaning of Indigenous law relative to State law. In this context, Indigenous legal orders occupy what Sousa Santos (1987) terms an "inter-legal space", where diverse interpretive standpoints, scales, and intersections interact and find articulation. Within such spaces, authority is not assigned exclusively to one system over another; rather, authority emerges from the recognition of a shared legal terrain. Crucially, this contrasts with models that treat law and legality as compartmentalized domains, which risk perpetuating the State's integrationist and assimilationist agenda under the guise of formal inclusion. Related sociolegal conceps, such as the notion of a "jurisprudence of hybridity" (Nursoo 2018), likewise highlight the enduring asymmetries between Indigenous law and neocolonial justice frameworks. According to Nursoo, mixed legal spheres emerge only through the critical work of "decolonizing the mind", which involves grounding legal authority in Indigenous law, destabilizing colonial legal hierarchies, and advancing a shift from monist pluralism – where one system dominates under a pluralistic veneer – to pluralist pluralism, where multiple systems coexist with genuine normative weight. Thus, debates around Indigenous environmental rights demand a legal pluralist imagination that extends beyond the mere pluralization of rights (i.e., embedding Indigenous rights within dominant legal codes). Instead, they require engagement with the structural transformations needed to introduce Indigenous legal orders into State systems in ways that honor legal pluralism (e.g., Salas Astrain & Pacheco Huaiquifil 2025) in its holistic, transformative sense – not as symbolic inclusion, but as meaningful power-sharing.

I.2 A Distinct Contribution to Common Dualisms and Rights Framing

As the preceding analysis has shown, Indigenous environmental rights have yet to find a clear and distinguished place in theoretical debates. They remain suspended between seemingly opposing interpretative poles: on the one side, framed primarily as collective or human rights claims; on the other, located within the expanding judicial discourse of environmental rights and the expansion of human rights protection to nonhuman subjects, for example, the "rights of nature" (RoN). Beyond the conceptual and jurisdictional implications of these classifications, such positioning presents a critical opportunity: it allows us to rethink the classical legal categories through which Indigenous environmental rights are commonly approached. In doing so, we may begin to decolonize the very frameworks of legal reasoning and classification that continue to shape these debates. This includes reconsidering the communitarian nature of many Indigenous claims, the sources of law considered authoritative, and the interrelatedness of claims as seen through holistic Indigenous cosmologies and environmental worldviews. The following sections engage with several key conceptual dualisms, seeking to clarify their implication and propose a more integrative and pluralistic way of understanding Indigenous environmental rights.

I.2.1 Rights of Nature versus Human Rights

The literature on the RoN has grown exponentially over the past decade, catalyzed by progressive legal developments in States such as Ecuador, Colombia, and New Zealand, where forests, rivers, and other ecosystems have been granted gal personhood (Calle-Alzate & Silva-Cantillo 2025; Jansen & Lambooy 2025; Montalván Zambrano & Wences 2025). Although these judicial decisions are often celebrated in isolation, they are, in some contexts, deeply entangled with indigenous worldviews and advocacy (O'Donnell et al. 2020) being success stories in their own regard. Rather than treating RoN and Indigenous rights as mutually exclusive or in opposition, a more nuanced, case-by-case approach reveals the extent to which RoN are informed by Indigenous philosophies grounded in spiritual traditions, ecological knowledge, and relational ontologies. It is in this light that RoN have been portrayed as an "intellectual triangulation between two legitimising philosophical categories," these latter categories referring to Indigenous cosmovisions and Western philosophies including Latour's Gaia writings, Naess' Deep Ecology or Morton's "object-oriented ontology" (Jansen & Lambooy 2025, p. 120).

In the Ecuadorian case, for example, Indigenous peoples have not only embraced RoN but have actively shaped its conceptual foundation. Their traditional legal systems – where rivers, mountains, animals, and plants are not mere natural resources, but kin, ancestors, and integral parts of communities' ways of life – offer a radically different basis from anthropocentric environmental protection. In this worldview, harm to the environment directly threatens territorial integrity and the related physical and cultural survival of Indigenous communities, particularly where access to clean water, food sources, and sacred spaces is compromised. In this light, when speaking about the RoN in indigenous contexts, these rights can often be viewed as derivatives of Indigenous rights – particularly their right to territory, understood as "*a* claim for the construction of meanings, for the exercise of the ontological and relational plurality of Indigenous peoples with their environment" (Montalván-Zambrano 2023; see also Montalván-Zambrano & Wences 2025). Although both RoN and Indigenous rights frameworks may differ in origin and scope, they frequently converge in their ecocentric ethical substance and legal implications, forming the foundations for mutual reinforcement. Importantly, this convergence does not diminish the legal weight of either framework; rather, it highlights their potential for strategic alignment, making Indigenous perspectives and structural vulnerabilities more visible and resisting fragmented conceptions of environmental harm that reduce it to a solely technical matter. Instead, environmental protection and harm must be understood as deeply intertwined with social justice, indigenous self-determination, and collective survival.

An important and closely related conceptual framework is the paradigm of Good Living (*Buen Vivir* or *Vivir Bien*), which originates from a diverse array of Indigenous traditions, particularly in the Andean region. Expressions of this paradigm include *Sumak Kawsay* (Quechua), *Suma Qamaña* (Aymara), *Ñande Reko* (Guaraní), and *Küme Mogen* (Mapuche), each of which embodies a holistic understanding of well-being rooted in reciprocity, balance, and harmony with nature. *Buen Vivir* codifies the spiritual and relational ties between Indigenous peoples and the(ir) environment, offering an alternative to dominant development models grounded in extractivism and anthropocentrism (Escobar 2014; Solón 2017). Significantly, *Buen Vivir* has been formally enshrined in the constitutions of both Ecuador and Bolivia as part of their State-building processes, marking a pivotal shift toward the legal recognition of "plurinational" frameworks that embrace Indigenous epistemologies. In Ecuador, in particular, RoN have been established as a foundational pillar of *Buen Vivir*, alongside the recognition of individual and collective rights and the promotion of a people(s)-oriented and solidarity-based economy (Ecuadorian constitution). Within the broader human rights framework, Indigenous peoples have been increasingly portrayed as guardians or stewards of the earth (Barrit 2020; Bennett & Bavikatte 2015; Page 2007; Winter 2022). In this context, Indigenous peoples are often seen as translators of nonhuman voices and as legitimate representatives of natural entities within legal and political arenas. These roles reflect intergenerational commitments to sustainability.

Similarly, and closely related, the concept of "biocultural rights" – defined as affirming the bond between Indigenous and local communities and their traditional lands and resources (Bennett & Bavikatte 2015) – has gained traction in international environmental circles (Rodríguez Caguana & Morales Naranjo 2020). However, these rights are oftentimes presented as distinct from indigenous rights per se, on the grounds that they lack explicit ties to political self-determination and are not necessarily grounded in ethnicity, religion, or minority status (Bennett & Bavikatte 2015); equally controversial is the concept of "earth jurisprudence". Others instead argue biocultural rights – alongside legal pluralism – allow for "recognizing the role of communities as interactive participants in their territories," also to be seen as an alternative for the decolonization of RoN (Calle-Alzate & Silva-Cantillo 2025).

A substantial body of theory on the expansion of rights protection to nonhuman subjects has evolved around the ideological divide between anthropocentrism and ecocentrism. Although these are often presented as opposing paradigms, it may be argued that such a binary can be transcended by engaging with Indigenous peoples' holistic and relational ways of engaging with the environment. Rather than adhering strictly to an either–or proposition on anthropocentric or ecocentric logics, many Indigenous ontologies embrace an integral perspective that acknowledges intra- and interspecies interdependence. Nonetheless, this conceptual dichotomy is a persistent rationale in legal reasoning. The Colombian Constitutional Court, in its landmark ruling T-622 – sixteen explicitly framed rights in opposition to one another – as anthropocentric versus biocentric or ecocentric, thus reinforcing the binary divide rather than challenging it. Similar patterns can be observed in other legal systems, where classical State law assumes an anthropocentric, dualistic role, while rooted in positivist traditions. Such legal paradigms call for a critical reorientation – one that foregrounds relationality and rethinks the very nature of legal subjectivity (Bagni 2022) based on justificatory legal pluralism.

If we are to consider Indigenous environmental rights as part of a human rights regime – albeit one of a distinct kind – it is essential to recognize their collective character and their intra- and interspecies dimensions, which deeply reflect relational understandings of the environment. These rights are further shaped by the particular vulnerabilities Indigenous peoples disproportionately face. Such vulnerabilities stem from, notably, a combination of historical and structural socioeconomic forms of discrimination, often rooted in their cultural identity; the persistent lack of recognition of Indigenous peoples as collective legal subjects; and the systemic barriers they encounter in exercising their collective rights. Moreover, due to their profound and place-based relationship with their territories, Indigenous communities are especially exposed to the adverse impacts of environmental harm – threats that not only affect ecosystems but also jeopardize their ways of life, cultural continuity, and survival (Aguilera 2023). Several interpretive approaches have been used to frame these rights. One widely discussed legal strategy is the concept of "derivative rights," such as the framing of environmental harm as a violation of the right to life. This approach seeks to protect Indigenous communities from environmental degradation, threatening their health and survival (Leib 2011). However, a frequent critique concerns the high evidentiary threshold required: legal recognition often depends on the harm being significant – typically life-threatening – which risks excluding more subtle but equally damaging forms of environmental injustice (Leib 2011). Another prevalent mechanism is the "socio-environmental impact assessment," where Indigenous environmental rights tend to be treated as ancillary or procedural concerns. These rights are often addressed sporadically and reactively, contingent upon the implementation of specific so-called "development" projects. As Cittadino (2019) notes, the environmental component of Indigenous peoples' rights tends to emerge "in the interplay between the rights of Indigenous peoples and the projects implemented at national level that may affect both Indigenous livelihood and the environment in which they live."

In contrast to these somewhat reactive frameworks, Indigenous agency has played a transformative role in shaping legal norms. Through global Indigenous movements, communities have asserted themselves as central actors in the progressive development of international law, notably contributing to the adoption of the United Nations Declaration on the Rights of Indigenous Peoples (UNDRIPS) (Charters & Stavenhagen 2012). Indigenous peoples have thus moved beyond the role of rights claimants to become rights holders, epistemic authorities, norm creators, and defenders – not only of collective rights but also of the natural world. Rooted in spiritual, cultural, and subsistence-based relationships with nature, Indigenous peoples thus have a legitimate and grounded claim to participate in shaping the contours of the emerging right to a healthy environment. And by virtue of being indigenous, as a rights holder group as such, indigenous peoples benefit from differentiated treatment, that is, rights only to be accessible for indigenous individuals and groups.

Recent jurisprudence, particularly from the Inter-American human rights system, reflects the importance of Indigenous laws to understand the contents of the right to a healthy environment. An evolutionary approach may be noted here, from a narrow focus on "environmental impacts" – as seen in the *Saramaka case* – toward an expanded recognition of the human right to a healthy environment that includes individual, collective, and nonhuman dimensions. This broader interpretation has informed both the *Inter-American jus commune* and recent constitutional developments in Ecuador, Colombia, and Guatemala, where the right to a healthy environment is increasingly understood in conjunction with the "integral development of their peoples" (*Lhaka Honhat Association* decision). As such, jurisprudence across domestic, regional, and international levels is coalescing around a more expansive and relational understanding of environmental and Indigenous rights – one that affirms their interconnectedness (Aguilera 2023) and contributes significantly to the construction of Indigenous environmental rights as a distinct and evolving legal category.

I.2.2 Biodiversity and Climate-Change Frameworks versus International Human Rights Law: A Legal Historiography and Institutional Overview

I.2.2.1 Pertinent Developments in the Specific Field of Indigenous Peoples' Rights

The adoption of the UNDRIPS marked a major achievement of the global Indigenous movement, following more than two decades of negotiation and active Indigenous participation (Burger 2012; Burger & Martín Castro 2006; Charters & Stavenhagen 2012). Foundational processes such as those initiated by the Working Group on Indigenous Populations (WGIP) and the Working Group on the Draft Declaration (WGDD) helped to reshape UN procedures, enabling Indigenous peoples to participate more directly in global decision-making (Burger 2012; Burger & Martín Castro 2006; Charters & Stavenhagen 2012) and eventually led to a further juridification of Indigenous rights at global level. We shall first look at some key institutional developments. Established in 2000, the UN Permanent Forum on Indigenous Issues (PFII) serves as an advisory body to ECOSOC, promoting awareness and implementation of Indigenous rights and UNDRIPS. Complementing the Forum are two expert bodies under the Office of the High Commissioner for Human Rights, the Special Rapporteur on the Rights of Indigenous Peoples (SR) and the Expert Mechanism on the Rights of Indigenous Peoples (EMRIP). The mandate of the SR, created in 2001 and renewed by the Human Rights Council (HRC), monitors violations, promotes best practices, and engages with United Nations (UN) and regional bodies to advance Indigenous rights. The Expert Mechanism on the Rights of Indigenous Peoples, with a strengthened mandate under HRC Resolution 33/25, provides guidance to States on implementing UNDRIPS and supports capacity-building efforts.

United Nations special procedures have increasingly contributed to jurisprudential developments in the field of Indigenous environmental rights. The PFII played a key role in this regard through its 2023 annual report, which focused on the special theme: "Indigenous Peoples, human health, planetary and territorial health and climate change: a rights-based approach." In this report, the Forum emphasized the intrinsic link between Indigenous health and the health of the planet, situating environmental degradation within a broader historical context of colonization and extractivism. It affirmed that Indigenous rights and the right to a clean, healthy, and sustainable environment are "interconnected and essential to an integrated planetary health governance framework" (para. 34). At a very general level, the Forum calls upon States to guarantee that indigenous peoples are offered "full and effective participation in all planning and policy development to address climate change" (para. 44). It specifically highlighted the need to respect free, prior, and informed consent (FPIC) in green technology initiatives, conservation measures, and the designation of protected areas. The report also called for meaningful Indigenous participation in programs addressing deforestation and land degradation, in the 2023 UN Water Conference, and in implementing and monitoring the Kunming–Montreal Global Biodiversity Framework. In 2024, the PFII deepened its engagement with the theme of environmental governance by convening the International Expert Group Meeting on "Indigenous Peoples in a greening economy". The meeting produced an extensive set of recommendations directed at Member States, UN bodies, Indigenous peoples, civil society, the private sector, and international organizations – underscoring the importance of inclusive and rights-based approaches in emerging environmental and economic transitions.

The Special Rapporteur on the Rights of Indigenous Peoples has contributed significantly to the normative and policy-oriented development of Indigenous environmental rights through two thematic reports, one on green financing and just transition (2023), and an earlier thematic study on the "impacts of climate change and climate finance on the rights of indigenous peoples" (2017). In the 2017 report, the Special Rapporteur issued a series of detailed recommendations to States, emphasizing the need to ensure that Indigenous peoples are meaningfully included in domestic climate change planning, monitoring, adaptation, and mitigation efforts. The report underscores the importance of obtaining FPIC at all stages of climate-related decision-making and calls for the active promotion of Indigenous self-governance structures within these processes. Moreover, the Rapporteur highlights the necessity of fostering equitable partnerships between government entities and Indigenous communities, including the allocation of financial resources to build capacity among all stakeholders engaged in climate finance. Gender considerations are also identified as essential to the design and implementation of climate adaptation and mitigation strategies (SR 2017). Directed at international donors and climate finance institutions, the SR calls for a rights-based approach: donors are urged to respect and promote Indigenous rights, enhance Indigenous peoples' capacity to participate in climate action, and ensure existing safeguards are being disseminated and operationalized. This includes establishing dedicated funding mechanisms that directly support Indigenous-led initiatives for climate change response and sustainable development. Lastly, the report stresses the need to strengthen mechanisms for monitoring and compliance, as well as to raise awareness of grievance procedures available to Indigenous peoples within the climate finance framework (SR 2017).

The SR emphasizes that green financing and the notion of a "just transition" must be understood through the lens of Indigenous peoples' distinct experiences and rights. In this context, a range of Indigenous environmental rights are invoked. The 2023 report calls on States to respect Indigenous rights as enshrined in IHRL and to protect communities from harm caused by businesses and financial actors operating within their territories or under their jurisdiction. It further urges the integration of Indigenous land, territorial, and resource rights, including the right to FPIC, into domestic legal frameworks governing the green economy (SR 2023). Specific obligations include ensuring Indigenous consultation and consent in all green finance initiatives affecting their territories, securing land tenure through demarcation, and preventing land-grabbing and unauthorized exploitation. States must also guarantee that Indigenous communities equitably benefit from green finance through access to employment, training, and capacity-building, as well as providing resources to strengthen their knowledge of financing mechanisms and support their participation by providing legal and technical assistance (SR 2023). Moreover, the report stresses the need for accessible, culturally appropriate, and independent grievance and remedy mechanisms, alongside robust monitoring and accountability systems to track the environmental and social impacts of green finance projects. Finally, the SR outlines corresponding responsibilities for donors, investors, and financial institutions, emphasizing the need for alignment with Indigenous rights and meaningful engagement throughout project lifecycles (see para. 78 of the 2023 report).

The UN's specialized procedures and organs operate in tandem with the core treaty monitoring bodies, which have come to play a foundational role in the protection of Indigenous peoples' rights. Among the earliest to address these issues were the Human Rights Committee (CCPR), the Committee on Economic, Social and Cultural Rights (CESCR), and the Committee on the Elimination of Racial Discrimination (CERD), each drawing on core treaty provisions – nondiscrimination (CERD), cultural rights (CESCR), and minority rights (CCPR). The Human Rights Committee, in particular, has progressively interpreted Article 27 of the International Covenant on Civil and Political Rights (ICCPR) – which guarantees ethnic, religious, and linguistic minorities the right to enjoy their culture, practice their religion, and use their language – to extend protection to Indigenous peoples. Recognizing the cultural specificity and territorial rootedness of Indigenous ways of life, the Committee has affirmed their rights as minorities in landmark cases such as *Ángela Poma Poma v. Peru*, linking cultural rights with land and resource access. In line with General Comment No. 23, the Committee emphasized that cultural rights would require States to adopt positive measures ensuring effective participation in decisions that affect Indigenous communities, particularly in the context of land use and development projects. Environmental considerations are often embedded within these decisions (see, e.g., Heinämäki 2010), as land- and resource-based livelihoods are deemed integral to Indigenous culture. Accordingly, the Committee examined whether State-authorized activities threatened culturally significant economic practices – such as reindeer herding or subsistence activities – central to community identity and survival. This approach is evident in a series of cases, including *Ilmari Länsman*, *Jouni E. Länsman*, *Kalevi Paadar*, and *Lubicon Lake Band*, where the Committee adopted a contextual and adaptive understanding of cultural practice, affirming that economic activities may fall within the scope of minority protection, closely tying these to traditional knowledge, spirituality, and cultural heritage (*Apirana Mahuika et al.*).

Noteworthy are the codification efforts that recognize Indigenous rights within the framework of the Convention on the Rights of the Child (CRC). Article 30 explicitly affirms the right of Indigenous children to enjoy their own culture, profess and practice their own religion, and use their own language. Complementary provisions such as Article 17(d) call upon mass media to respect the linguistic needs of Indigenous children, while Article 29 underscores the importance of education in fostering understanding and friendship among all peoples, including Indigenous communities. The Committee on the Rights of the Child further elaborates on these principles in its General Comment No. 11 (2009), "Indigenous Children and Their Rights under the Convention," which provides interpretative guidance tailored to the lived realities of Indigenous children. Similarly, the Convention on the Rights of Persons with Disabilities (CRPD) demonstrates a growing sensitivity to Indigenous issues. Indigenous identity is recognized as a ground of potential discrimination, particularly in the context of intersectional vulnerabilities. General Comment No. 3 (2016) on "Women and Girls with Disabilities" explicitly includes Indigenous status as a relevant category, whereas General Comment No. 6 on "Equality and Non-Discrimination" reaffirms the need for safeguards against multiple and intersecting forms of discrimination, including those faced by Indigenous persons with disabilities.

Indigenous environmental rights are frequently acknowledged within the context of natural resource exploitation, where international bodies have emphasized the need for independent assessment of socioenvironmental impacts and respective mitigation measures (e.g., CESCR, *Mexico's State report*). Across various jurisdictions, the CESCR has affirmed that issues related to land and natural resources not only require robust consultation and FPIC procedures, but must also guarantee the protection of environmental rights (see CESCR, *Concluding Observations on Ecuador's 4th report*; *Cameroon's 4th report*; *Mexico's 5th* and *6th reports*; *Colombia's 6th report*). Consistently, the Special Rapporteur on the Rights of Indigenous Peoples has elaborated on these obligations, referring to the codification of subsistence rights and the heightened vulnerability of Indigenous communities due to their profound dependency on their immediate environment (SR 2007).

Similar conclusions emerge from Inter-American human rights jurisprudence, which increasingly affirms the intrinsic interdependence between environmental protection and the exercise of human rights. As articulated in the *Lhaka Honhat* case, environmental degradation can severely compromise the enjoyment of fundamental rights, as the effective protection of the environment is shaped by the exercise of human rights (para. 244). The right to a healthy environment holds a prominent place within the Inter-American system: it is enshrined in Article 11 of the San Salvador Protocol, constitutionally recognized in at least sixteen States across the region, and reinforced by the adoption of the Escazú Agreement. The *Lhaka Honhat* judgment exemplifies how environmental concerns intersect with (other) substantive rights such as the right to food. The Court emphasizes the need for environmental policies that uphold food security for both present and future generations by establishing sustainability as a guiding criterion (para. 220). Importantly, it also introduces the criterion of cultural acceptability, explicitly recognizing that food-related rights must be interpreted beyond mere nutritional sufficiency, accommodating cultural and spiritual dimensions central to Indigenous identities (para. 220).

Relevant developments within the African human and peoples' rights system also warrant attention, particularly the landmark *Ogoni* case, which addressed the ecological and health-related consequences of oil exploitation in Ogoniland. The African Commission found that the Nigerian government had violated multiple rights of the Ogoni people, including through the contamination of waterways with toxic waste, leading to severe health impacts. Crucially, the ruling established that States bore obligations not only to refrain from harmful acts but also to protect Indigenous lands from environmental destruction by third parties (para. 58). Among the environmental duties highlighted was the obligation to conduct – or mandate – independent scientific assessments of ecological harm, with regular reassessment (para. 53). The decision further recognized indirect violations of the right to life, where State-sanctioned or tolerated ecological degradation had dehumanizing and life-threatening consequences for the Ogoni people, especially given their dependence on land and agriculture (para. 67). Similarly, forced evictions were examined through a human rights lens, with the Commission underscoring the devastating impacts of these, including physical and psychological harm, impoverishment, and the erosion of cultural survival (para. 63). In *Ogiek v. Kenya*, the African Court on Human and Peoples' Rights reaffirmed these concerns, noting that eviction policies threatened the Ogiek's ability to maintain a viable existence in the forest, which was essential for their housing, nutrition, and access to traditional medicine (para. 155).

I.2.2.2 Key Tendencies in the Field of International Environmental Safeguards

Having explored the contributions of international human rights bodies and regional jurisprudence, we now turn to the frameworks of protection established under international environmental regimes, most prominently global climate change and biodiversity governance. Unlike IHRL, where Indigenous-specific rights have been progressively codified, environmental treaties largely lack explicit provisions centered on Indigenous peoples. This absence renders the juridification of Indigenous environmental rights within these regimes an often fragmented and isolated process.

Within the biodiversity regime, Article 8(j) of the Convention on Biological Diversity (CBD) is particularly notable. It calls upon States to "respect, preserve and maintain knowledge, innovations and practices of indigenous and local communities embodying traditional lifestyles relevant for the conservation and sustainable use of biological diversity" and to promote their application alongside equitable benefit-sharing in terms of the use of such knowledge. However, the measures envisioned under Article 8(j) are expressly subject to domestic legislation and rely heavily on State discretion. As such, although the provision gestures toward participatory frameworks, it falls short of articulating a robust commitment to Indigenous-specific rights. This reflects in fact a broader pattern: international environmental law, even when acknowledging Indigenous contributions, often fails to embrace principles of legal pluralism, self-determination, or respect for Indigenous governance systems and customary practices. Although some State duties are spelt out in the provision in question, it remains largely for the State to preserve and maintain indigenous knowledge and practices, far from reflecting any legal pluralistic approach, a spirit of self-determination and autonomies, or respect for indigenous procedures, customs, and practices.

Recent years have seen notable progressive developments in the global biodiversity regime, particularly with the adoption of the Kunming–Montréal Global Biodiversity Framework (KMGBF) at COP15 and the formalization of implementation procedures at COP16 in Cali, Colombia. The KMGBF explicitly encourages State Parties to ensure the full and effective participation of Indigenous peoples at all levels of governance (para. 4) and calls on States to respect and give meaningful effect to Indigenous rights, especially as to the framework's implementation (para. 6). Importantly, the KMGBF includes a dedicated section titled "contribution and rights of indigenous peoples and local communities" (para. 7(a)), which rests on three core pillars:

1. Recognition of the unique roles and contributions of Indigenous peoples as custodians of biodiversity and partners in conservation efforts;
2. Respect, documentation, and preservation of Indigenous rights, knowledge, and traditional knowledge, ensured through FPIC and full participation in decision-making processes;
3. Assurance that the rights currently or prospectively exercised by Indigenous peoples will not be diminished or extinguished as a result of the framework's implementation.

Throughout the Framework, emphasis is placed on educational, communication and awareness-raising measures that explicitly refer to indigenous worldviews, values, and knowledge systems (paras. 7(o), 22). One of the framework's distinguishing features is the establishing of clear targets (for 2030) and long-term goals (for 2050). Notably, Goal C affirms Indigenous peoples' entitlement to a fair and equitable share of both monetary and nonmonetary benefits derived from the utilization of genetic resources, digital sequence information, and traditional knowledge – and mandates adequate protection thereof. Within the framework's targets, Indigenous peoples are assigned a central role in areas such as the reduction of threats to biodiversity (Targets 1, 3, and 5), the sustainable use of resources and equitable benefit-sharing (Target 9), and the development of tools and mechanisms for implementation and mainstreaming (Targets 19, 21, and 22). These elements, taken together, signal an evolving recognition of Indigenous peoples not only as stakeholders but as rights holders whose contributions are essential to achieving global biodiversity objectives.

Despite these progressive steps, several critical observations have been raised regarding the KMGBF. Scholars and practitioners have highlighted gaps in the framework's treatment of both direct and indirect drivers of biodiversity loss, its limited procedures for addressing business-related impacts on biodiversity, and its strong reliance on domestic and local-level implementation. These concerns touch on broader structural issues, such as the need for comprehensive policy reforms, the empowerment of Indigenous peoples, and the allocation of adequate budgetary resources to ensure effective action (Cariño & Berger 2024). At COP16, an important institutional development was witnessed with the transformation of the Working Group on Article 8(j) – which had been operating since 1998 – into a permanent supervisory body. This body is tasked with guaranteeing the full and effective participation of Indigenous peoples in all matters related to the Convention on Biological Diversity, with a particular emphasis on their knowledge systems and their essential role in biodiversity conservation (International Work Group on Indigenous Affairs [IWGIA] 2024). The new supervisory body will oversee the implementation of the KMGBF, the operationalization of Article 8(j), and the protection of Indigenous rights in biodiversity-related decision-making (IWGIA 2024). Alongside this institutional change, a new Program of Work on Article 8(j) was adopted, aimed at ensuring that States apply a human rights-based approach in all implementation steps under Article 8(j) and the KMGBF. Notably, this program seeks to align biodiversity governance with the principles and commitments articulated under the UNDRIPS (IWGIA 2024).

In the sphere of international climate governance, several notable developments may be noted, particularly under the auspices of the United Nations Framework Convention on Climate Change (UNFCCC). Adopted at the 1992 Rio Earth Summit, the UNFCCC laid the foundation for global climate cooperation, eventually leading to the landmark Paris Agreement in 2015, which set the specific objective of limiting global greenhouse gas emissions. Indigenous peoples have come to occupy a significant, although contested, position within international climate negotiations. Their formal participation has been organized through the International Indigenous Peoples' Forum on Climate Change (IIPFCC), which plays a key role in coordinating common positions, issuing joint statements, and engaging in lobbying and advocacy at UNFCCC events (Reed & Thorsell 2024). A pivotal institutional step was the creation in 2015 of the Local Communities and Indigenous Peoples Platform (LCIPP), later strengthened by the establishment of the Facilitative Working Group (FWG). This marked the first time Indigenous representatives achieved equal representation alongside State Parties within a UNFCCC-constituted body (Reed & Thorsell, 2024). However, structural challenges remain: the LCIPP continues to grapple with the entrenched State versus non-State actor binary of the UNFCCC system, which has been constraining its ability to fully realize its potential for genuinely influencing and participating in

Conference of the Parties (COP) negotiations (Reed & Thorsell 2024). Notably, at COP29, the mandate of the FWG under the LCIPP was renewed, solidifying its status as a formal constituted body within the UNFCCC framework (IWGIA 2024).

Yet despite these institutional gains, Indigenous representatives voiced sharp criticisms in their IIPFCC COP29 Closing Statement, calling it "unacceptable" that Indigenous rights were ultimately excluded from the New Collective Quantified Goal on Climate Finance (NCQG), with the conference instead prioritizing carbon market financing. The statement went further, condemning the "the unethical methods and even more unethical outcomes" of the COP29, underscoring the persistent marginalization of Indigenous knowledge systems, methodologies, and alternative problem-solving methods. As Indigenous delegates emphasized, these knowledge systems, practices, worldviews, or sciences could "provide a vital basis for effective adaptation strategies to climate change". Ultimately, COP29 proved to pursue an unambitious agenda, particularly given its failure to secure a meaningful transition away from fossil fuels. This failure carries disproportionate consequences for Indigenous peoples, who bear the brunt of the environmental and socio-cultural impacts of fossil fuel expansion and the ecological destruction thereby caused (IWGIA 2024).

Also noteworthy is the Indigenous Summit held in 2024 under the title "Just Transition: Indigenous Peoples' Perspectives, Knowledge, and Lived Experiences". The summit produced a set of eleven guiding principles for achieving a just transition that centers Indigenous rights and perspectives: these principles notably include the right to life; the right to self-determination and sovereignty; decolonization; reparations, including the return of lands and the full restoration of lands, territories, waters, and biodiversity; respect for Indigenous peoples' ways of life and livelihoods; transparency and accountability in governance processes; acknowledgment of historical injustices and the need for reparations; full protection of Indigenous peoples and their communities; formal recognition of Indigenous peoples' roles and responsibilities in environmental stewardship; commitment to maintaining the global temperature rise below 1.5°C; and the application of a rights-based approach to global and local supply chains.

I.2.2.3 Frameworks Compared: Juridification Processes, Negotiation Platforms, and Proceduralization

A number of critical observations need to be made when comparing the parallel institutional developments of international human rights law (IHRL) and international environmental law with respect to Indigenous rights, respectively. It would be far-fetched to understand these recent attempts of institutionalizing Indigenous rights under biodiversity and climate regimes (see Cittadino 2025) as anything resembling an entire legal code devoted to indigenous safeguards as it is the case with the UN Declaration on the Rights of the Indigenous Peoples and also the somewhat outdated ILO C169 convention (for a critical reading of IHRL in the environmental field, see Liljeblad 2025). Instead, what emerges is a pattern of ad-hoc recognition, where Indigenous agency is framed in largely utilitarian terms, often confined to specific environmental tasks, those that advance the immediate objectives of the respective regime – biodiversity conservation, knowledge transmission, and procedural participation in implementation practices. An enduring dilemma faced by indigenous peoples lies in the fragmented and inconsistent treatment of contexts, forms of violations, and normative levels at which their collective rights are infringed. For example, Indigenous knowledge is inherently tied to spiritual and cultural heritage rights (Reguart-Segarra 2025), and intersects with the rights to education, language, and cultural continuity. Additionally, the principles of FPIC must apply to all measures affecting Indigenous lives and livelihoods (see, e.g., Doyle 2017). These connections also open the door to more expansive rights claims, including self-governance, self-determination, and broader forms of collective autonomy – dimensions that remain unevenly recognized across legal systems. Notably, Indigenous participation in decision-making under these frameworks (for an institutional history in the field, see Burger 2012; Burger & Martín Castro 2006) remains poorly specified. The scope and nature of decision-making powers that should be attributed to Indigenous peoples within intergovernmental contexts are left largely undefined, raising critical concerns about the depth and substance of their involvement. The recent UNFCCC negotiations at COP29 are particularly revealing in this regard: they expose not only the limited space Indigenous peoples occupy in global climate governance but also the persistent failure to meaningfully accommodate Indigenous methodologies (see, e.g., Smith 1999), legal systems, and epistemologies. Despite rhetorical commitments to pluralism, the institutional architecture of environmental governance remains deeply State-centric, with little room for Indigenous legal pluralism or alternative decision-making frameworks.

Indeed, legal pluralistic approaches remain largely absent, as Indigenous laws, procedures and practices continue to be marginalized or overlooked in the context of COP negotiations and decision-making processes. Moreover, restricting Indigenous rights to the narrow sphere of environmental protection in a strict sense fails to address the broader, interconnected nature of rights violations Indigenous communities face in the context of environmental degradation: these include not only environmental and cultural harm but also violations of basic subsistence rights, physical integrity, health, and education – rights that arise from the multiple dependencies Indigenous peoples maintain with their territories. Legal responses such as benefit-sharing and knowledge protection, although valuable, offer only partial remedies; they do not address the systemic, multilevel infringements Indigenous peoples experience, nor do they fully recognize their claims to self-governance, self-determination, and broader collective autonomies. Indeed, IHRL in the field of environmental rights has been criticized for failing to articulate "potential avenues for legal action as well as the broader prospects for indigenous peoples within the prevailing international legal system" (Liljeblad 2025, p. 60).

With these hesitant steps toward institutionalization, the promise of global biodiversity and climate protection agreements risks remaining largely symbolic, offering little tangible improvement to the daily lives, rights, and futures of Indigenous peoples. While part of this disconnect can be attributed to recalcitrant States and their short-term political agendas, it also reflects the fragmented and incoherent voice with which international law speaks on Indigenous environmental rights. The prevailing legal landscape remains poorly integrated, with IHRL and international environmental law often operating in parallel, rather than in concert. Although treaty bodies and special procedures increasingly acknowledge progressive developments in adjacent regimes, and despite the emergence of a nascent common legal culture in environmental governance, instances of true interinstitutional coordination remain rare. This institutional disjuncture hampers the incorporation of human rights language into climate change discourse, and vice versa. Initiatives such as the Inter-Agency Support Group (IASG) on Indigenous Issues – pursuing the dedicated objective to support the mandate of the PFII – reflect a nascent effort toward bridging these regimes. Nevertheless, a genuinely integrated normative framework or common legal culture and jurisprudence at the intersection of IHRL and environmental law have yet to materialize. The reasons are manifold, namely structural limitations of international institutions, differentiated treaty membership, and the politically sensitive nature of environmental and collective rights all contribute to the lack of cohesion and commitment.

Measuring the recognition of Indigenous rights remains a complex undertaking – difficult to define in terms of starting points, scope, thresholds, normative criteria, levels of enforcement or tangible impact. Both IHRL and environmental law show increasing sensitivity toward Indigenous participation, cultural identity, and knowledge transmission. Yet, these developments often fall short of offering comprehensive responses to the enduring vulnerabilities faced by Indigenous communities. The juridification of Indigenous rights remains fragmented and selective, often invoked in a piecemeal fashion and constrained by the institutional mandates of the legal regimes within which they operate. Recognition processes, in this sense, tend to remain sporadic, ad hoc, and normatively incomplete. Legal frameworks frequently conceptualize Indigenous rights within the restrictive parameters of State sovereignty and territorial integrity, thereby limiting their transformative potential. As such, any effort to advance the juridification of Indigenous rights must be viewed critically in light of the structural limitations of existing legal systems and the prevailing political climate. Where progressive governments are in place, opportunities may emerge for indigenous decision-making and more inclusive normative development – yet these spaces remain contingent and unevenly distributed across jurisdictions.

An exclusive focus on intergovernmental dynamics or treaty-drafting language would render any analysis of Indigenous rights in international law incomplete. The placing of Indigenous concerns onto international legal agendas has not merely been a top-down institutional development but, more crucially, the result of sustained advocacy and mobilization by Indigenous peoples themselves, the global indigenous movement. The global indigenous movement – including the formation of caucuses and transnational networks – played a foundational role in the establishment of working groups within the United Nations and ultimately in the negotiation and adoption of the UNDRIPS. Crucially, mechanisms such as the EMRIP, composed predominantly of Indigenous experts, the mandate of the UN Special Rapporteur, and the establishment of the Permanent Forum on Indigenous Issues all reflect the influence of Indigenous agency in shaping international legal norms. These developments underscore the decisive role of bottom-up processes – not only in the creation of special procedures and institutions but also in norm development, rights interpretation, and legal implementation. From an epistemological standpoint, a narrow focus on classical legal principles and their State-centric genealogies, their governing legal principles, the origin of these and their continued influence, obscures the plural legal foundations of Indigenous rights, materializing in the current legal orders, rules of negotiation or institutional procedures. Especially in the post-UNDRIPS era, the boundaries between intergovernmental negotiations and Indigenous participation have become increasingly porous: as such, a more nuanced analysis – grounded in *travaux préparatoires* and meeting records – is essential to get a sense of Indigenous norm-setting in international law.

We are inevitably confronted with a recurring methodological challenge in assessing the success of juridification and normative negotiation processes – how to adequately accommodate legal and epistemic pluralism. This difficulty is not unique to the Indigenous rights context but reflects a broader critique of law as a system that tends to simplify complexity and often proves ill-equipped to engage with diverse realities – particularly vulnerability contexts that are, in practice, left to the courts to explore at depth. Given the multiplicity of Indigenous life-worlds – rooted in distinct cultural, spiritual, social, economic, and political frameworks – legal systems often struggle to respond adequately. However, this difficulty should not be framed as a fundamental incompatibility between classical legal systems and Indigenous legal orders. What is required instead is a systemic rethinking of lawmaking processes and institutional attitudes in international forums – one that embraces Indigenous legal conceptions not as supplementary or derivative, but as coequal systems of law. This implies not only a flexible institutional approach but also an ontological commitment to recognizing Indigenous legal systems as legitimate and integrated forms of justice and importantly, as occupying an equal position in the legal landscape. In the field of international environmental law, this requires moving beyond narrow commitments related to benefit-sharing, genetic resources, and traditional knowledge – it also means rejecting the superficial inclusion of Indigenous peoples merely as participants, without legal authority or enforcement capacity. The persisting failure of environmental regimes to meaningfully address Indigenous needs – subsistence, health, spirituality, and dignified living conditions – highlights the legal void that persists. The absence of robust individual or collective complaint mechanisms to address environmental harm further exacerbates this gap. Similarly, IHRL has yet to fully account for the multidimensional threats posed by environmental degradation, including both direct and indirect impacts. This also concerns a more specific conceptualization of the indigenous dimension of environmental human rights that is yet to be approached in detail by competent interpretative bodies. Failing to do so in fact also reveals its deficient understanding of indigenous rights with many indigenous communities having developed intimate relations with and dependencies on their ecological surroundings. Addressing this gap requires interpretative bodies to go beyond conventional framings and engage with Indigenous rights as inherently ecological and collective.

The "pluralism critique" may be regarded as one of the most significant shortcomings in the juridification of Indigenous rights. As previously noted, a conservative bias persists within international environmental regimes, often marginalizing or overlooking Indigenous justice systems – however, similar patterns of resistance can also be observed at the domestic and, to some extent, regional levels. Notably, while the Inter-American System has seen the gradual emergence of a more structured discourse on environmental rights – as exemplified by the Advisory Opinion 23/17 and the cases *Lhaka Honhat v. Argentina* (IACtHR) and *The Inhabitants of La Oroya v. Peru* – a less pronounced trajectory is evident within the European Court of Human Rights, despite recent rulings such as *Klimaseniorinnen v. Switzerland* (ECtHR). Nonetheless, climate litigation appears to mark a tipping point in the development of environmental rights (Tigre & Rocha 2025), both at the level of regional (see also the 2025 IACtHR's advisory opinion on climate issues) and international courts (e.g., the expected ICJ's Advisory Opinion on Climate Change). At the constitutional level, many States recognize environmental rights within their legal frameworks, often as enforceable guarantees (Daly & May 2018). Nevertheless, the effective realization of these rights frequently encounters significant obstacles: these include limited judicial independence, restrictive standing provisions, insufficient expertise among legal practitioners, and the economic precarity of affected individuals and communities. Moreover, interpretive practices may undervalue environmental claims, and judges often operate under political constraints or institutional disincentives that inhibit the full implementation of environmental protection at the domestic level (Daly & May 2018). By contrast, the explicit constitutional recognition of Indigenous environmental rights remains relatively rare (see, e.g., Articles 57 of the Ecuadorian Constitution and 30–31 of the Bolivian Constitution). States generally seem reluctant to elevate these rights to the highest level of the legal hierarchy, signaling a persistent unease with integrating Indigenous legal frameworks into domestic constitutional orders.

We may thus legitimately inquire to what extent we are witnessing a process of normative systematization, parallelism, or convergence in the field of Indigenous environmental rights – particularly when engaging in comparative constitutional analysis or examining developments at the regional level (e.g., the European *ius commune*, the Latin American *ius commune*, or judicial Pan-Africanism). It is widely accepted to conceptualize environmental rights, within a human rights framework, as carrying universal significance – whether framed as essential to the existence of humanity (as in *Lhaka Honhat*), as rights of future generations, or as inherently intergenerational. In contrast, the specific recognition of Indigenous rights to a healthy environment often remains subsumed under derivative frameworks, such as the rights to life, health, or cultural integrity. More recently, legal novelties such as the recognition of legal personality for natural entities (e.g., rivers or mountains) have opened new avenues for environmental protection. These nonhuman rights-bearing subjects frequently draw upon Indigenous cosmovisions and, in some cases, are managed by Indigenous authorities. However, critical perspectives caution that such recognition may marginalize Indigenous rights by linking their enforceability solely to the protection of nature, rather than affirming Indigenous environmental rights as autonomous and comprehensive – and as rights in their own sense. This dynamic tends to confine protections to cases where there is a direct, tangible connection between Indigenous communities and the natural entity in question – typically in the context of extractive industries or large-scale development projects that threaten sacred sites, subsistence resources, and collective survival.

Whereas the impacts of extractive industries on Indigenous lives and livelihoods have received considerable attention over the past two decades – particularly through the work of EMRIP and the Special Rapporteur on the Rights of Indigenous Peoples – Indigenous environmental rights have not yet achieved comparable visibility or systematic integration within the interpretative work or monitoring practices of international human rights mechanisms. Although treaty bodies increasingly acknowledge Indigenous peoples' vulnerabilities within broader discussions of inequality and discrimination, the development of a coherent, autonomous, and contextual interpretative framework for Indigenous environmental rights is yet to materialize. This gap may be partly attributed to a limited understanding or insufficient appreciation of the cultural, spiritual, and ontological significance that the natural world holds for many Indigenous communities. As a result, judicial and quasi-judicial bodies continue to rely predominantly on derivative rights approaches or the language of impacts. Addressing this deficiency requires a genuinely transformative shift: not merely the inclusion of new legal categories, but a profound engagement with Indigenous epistemologies, legal traditions, and worldviews. This similarly means for Indigenous legal orders to be recognized as valid sources of law, respecting Indigenous customs, practices and procedures, and institutions, and integrating culturally grounded understandings of environmental harm into human rights adjudication and environmental governance.

I.2.3 Individual versus Collective Rights

To deepen this debate, we must confront the colonial legacy embedded in legal systems – a legacy often reflected in the primacy of individual property rights that permeates contemporary legal orders, manifesting itself particularly in relation to land and natural resources (e.g., Watson 2018). This legacy has long marginalized Indigenous understandings of land tenure, which are grounded not in individual ownership but in communal relationships with their territories. A landmark moment came with the Inter-American Court of Human Rights' *Awas Tingni* judgment at the start of the twenty-first century, which embraced the notion of communitarian land ownership. The Court famously held:

> Given the characteristics of the instant case, some specifications are required on the concept of property in indigenous communities. Among indigenous peoples there is a communitarian tradition regarding a communal form of collective property of the land, in the sense that ownership of the land is not centred on an individual but rather on the group and its community. Indigenous groups, by the fact of their very existence, have the right to live freely in their own territory; the close ties of indigenous people with the land must be recognised and understood as the fundamental basis of their cultures, their spiritual life, their integrity, and their economic survival. (For indigenous communities, relations to the land are not merely a matter of possession and production but a material and spiritual element which they must fully enjoy, even to preserve their cultural legacy and transmit it to future generations.) (para. 149)

The legal notion of collective rights is most frequently invoked in relation to the right to land and its associated procedural corollary, the right to prior consultation and FPIC (e.g., Doyle 2017; Wright & Tomaselli 2019). However, collective rights remain exceptional within most prevailing legal systems, often categorized under the broader umbrella of "third-generation rights" (Vasak 1977), as discussed earlier.

It is indeed essential to examine the place and positioning of collective rights within the broader international human rights architecture. Here, we understand collective rights in the group-differentiated sense (Kymlicka 1995; Mitnick 2006; Tully 2008), recognizing that such rights address groups as collective entities. When engaging with treaty monitoring jurisprudence, however, we witness a conservative normative foundation rooted in the International Bill of Rights (UDHR, ICCPR, International Covenant on Economic, Social and Cultural Rights [ICESCR]), crafted in the mid-twentieth century, when the interpretative evolution of treaty bodies had been gradual. Article 27 of the ICCPR stands out as one of the few provisions to allow for substantial Indigenous claims to arise, offering protection under guarantees reserved for ethnic, religious, and linguistic minorities (as illustrated in cases such as *Ángela Poma Poma v. Peru* and *Ilmari Länsman v. Finland*). Notably, Article 27 frames minority rights in individualized terms, exercised "in community with" others – a phrasing mirrored in the European Framework Convention for the Protection of National Minorities. Both instruments construct minority rights as rights held individually by persons belonging to groups, rather than as collective entitlements held by the group itself. This individualized framing raises important questions of standing and rights-holding in the context of collective claims (e.g., Buchanan 1993; Jovanović 2012). Yet, when we shift the lens to Indigenous-specific contexts, the collective dimensions of rights become more explicit and substantive. Rights arising exclusively in Indigenous contexts include the right to prior consultation and FPIC; the recognition of Indigenous customs, procedures, and justice systems; self-determination and self-governance; alternative development models anchored in Indigenous worldviews; knowledge transmission practices; safeguards for cultural and spiritual identity; and the determination of membership criteria and community responsibilities.

With the emergence of a distinct regime of collective rights, it makes sense to ask how this framework also translates into a specifically collective understanding of Indigenous environmental rights. Such collectivization carries implications across multiple dimensions: it reshapes, inter alia, questions of subject or rights-holdership, the definition of corresponding rights and duties, the articulation of causal links between violation and harm, and the procedural and substantive dimensions through which these claims are adjudicated. A key question arising from this shift concerns whether Indigenous peoples are to be regarded primarily as victims of environmental harm or, alternatively, as (legal) guardians and representatives, or also as powerful translators of the natural world, acting on behalf of flora, fauna, and ecosystems (Eichler & Mora Navarro 2023). As discussed above, RoN – and this may also be said about environmental human rights – have not only been occupying a distinct place in academic debates (e.g., Jansen & Lambooy 2025; Montalván Zembrano & Wences 2025) but also as a legal category increasingly recognized in its own terms. This development is vividly reflected in the Inter-American Court of Human Rights' Advisory Opinion OC-23/17 on Colombia and reaffirmed in the Lhaka Honhat decision, both of which establish the right to a healthy environment as a "universal value", "a fundamental right for the existence of humankind", and an "autonomous right [with a nonhuman dimension that] protects the components of the environment, such as forests, rivers and seas, as legal interests in themselves, even in the absence of the certainty or evidence of a risk to individuals. This means that nature must be protected, not only because of its benefits or effects for humanity, but because of its importance for the other living organisms with which we share the planet" (para. 203). Although collectivity could, in principle, be expanded to include nonhuman rights holders, the present work argues for a distinctive human rights claim reserved for Indigenous peoples. This claim undoubtedly gives rise to derivative or relational rights, especially given Indigenous peoples' recognized role as stewards of the earth.

What, then, marks these environmental claims as specifically Indigenous in a collective sense? The collective right to cultural identity serves as the foundational condition for recognizing Indigenous and tribal peoples as distinct social and political actors entitled to collective rights. Without this recognition, discrimination and heightened vulnerability result. Importantly, this right acts as a cross-cutting principle shaping the scope of Indigenous human rights under IHRL. Building on this foundation, we argue that Indigenous environmental rights must likewise be understood as inherently collective, on grounds of their cultural identity, territorial ties, and the interdependence between land, livelihoods, and community physical and cultural survival. Indigenous peoples are consistently described as being disproportionately affected by extractive projects (e.g., Cahier 2022), land grabbing, forced displacement, and a host of related violations. These harms do not simply affect isolated individuals – they impact entire communities, often entire self-governed territories, generating collective harm that threatens, among many other aspects, the fabric of Indigenous social, political, and cultural life, including social cohesion.

At the heart of these collective harms lie Indigenous territorial rights and the intrinsic relationship between Indigenous peoples and their lands, creating a profound vulnerability context. Relatedly, this is further aggravated by the strong dependencies Indigenous peoples have on their territories and natural resources, not only for physical survival (e.g., as sources of subsistence) but also for broader dimensions of well-being, such as the need for guarantees of water quality, ecosystem health, and food sovereignty (e.g., Inter-American Commission on Human Rights [IACHR] 2010). Crucially, these dependencies are not merely material but cultural and spiritual. As underscored in the *Sarayaku* case, the Inter-American Court of Human Rights extended the understanding of physical integrity to encompass Indigenous cultural identity. Indigenous peoples' intimate connection with their environment is mediated through their spiritual practices, cultural traditions, and intergenerational responsibilities (e.g., Ksentini Report: Special Rapporteur on Human Rights and the Environment 1994).

Indeed, debates within Indigenous studies have long focused on traditional knowledge (TK), knowledge transmission, sustainable land practices, and the deep temporal ties connecting past, present, and future generations – constitutive elements of what is often termed "indigeneity" (see, e.g., Venkateswar & Hughes 2011). It is thus compelling to understand Indigenous environmental rights not merely as collective but as distinctively Indigenous collective rights: they reflect a specific group-differentiated orientation (Kymlicka 1999; Mitnick 2006; Tully 2008), often a form of positive differentiation that acknowledges the intimate web of dependencies and preconditions necessary for the fulfilment of other fundamental rights, including subsistence, health, and cultural rights. Importantly, Indigenous rights are widely portrayed as interrelated and interdependent (Sánchez-Lasaballett & González 2024), echoing Indigenous holistic views and methodologies that pervade not only their ontologies and epistemologies but also their environmental thinking. We are therefore led to conclude that Indigenous environmental rights provide a necessary, and often underestimated, response to a wide array of fundamental rights threats, addressing both the *jus cogens* nature of many of the violations perpetrated and the Indigenous-specific dimensions of these harms, which are deeply grounded in cosmovisions, collective identities, and cultural survival.

I.2.4 Procedural versus Substantive Claims: The Proceduralization of Indigenous Environmental Rights

Indigenous environmental rights encompass both procedural and substantive legal dimensions, with this latter category having been discussed earlier – notably finding articulation, emblematically, in "derivative rights approaches". However, contemporary developments in IHRL jurisprudence tend to overemphasize a narrow substantive communal property rights framework (Aguilera 2023). This focus often fails to engage meaningfully with the collective ontologies as well as the structural injustices that Indigenous communities continue to face. As a result, to address the complex legal and socioenvironmental challenges that define cases involving Indigenous peoples, there remains an urgent need to unpack the broader collective dimensions of Indigenous environmental rights. Moreover, failing to recognize a collective rights holder' legal personality where a clearly identifiable collective identity exists – such as the cultural distinctiveness of Indigenous peoples – undermines legal coherence and creates significant instability in the effective protection of human rights (Aguilera 2023). Indeed, for Indigenous peoples, the collective dimension of identity often takes precedence over individual identity, making the procedural capacity to claim and defend rights as an "organic group" (Wiessner 2011) a foundational element of Indigenous legal and political agency.

Complexities and normative pluralism in recognizing the collective environmental rights of Indigenous peoples are heightened when one considers that: first, Indigenous practices, procedures, and customs are not ancillary but foundational to the realization of their collective rights. In other words, rights implementation is inherently shaped by legal pluralism and necessitates alignment with Indigenous governance systems (see Gover 2020). Second, Indigenous cosmovisionist frameworks based on spiritual rights (e.g., Reguart-Segarra 2025) shape virtually every facet of Indigenous rights discourse. Illustrative here are paradigms such as *Buen Vivir* or *Vivir Bien*, which articulate a holistic, relational approach to human-environment interactions (see, e.g., Escobar 2014; Solón 2017). Debates increasingly focus on Indigenous knowledge systems (e.g., Nursoo 2018; Smith 1999) and cultural heritage (e.g., Xanthaki 2010), often characterized by intergenerational transmission and continuity. Third, Indigenous peoples still endure the legacies of colonial injustice in many forms – from the contested ownership of Indigenous material and intangible heritage (e.g., Lenzerini 2011) to the persistent colonial narratives in educational systems. Fourth, core claims to collective self-determination, autonomy, and alternative development models emerge as overarching demands. These are often contested in State-to-State horizontal relationships, revealing the persistent asymmetry in recognizing Indigenous peoples as political and legal actors.

A particularly significant regional development in the articulation of Indigenous environmental procedural rights is the Inter-American Court of Human Rights' Advisory Opinion OC-23/17. Building on its environmental jurisprudence developed in cases concerning indigenous and tribal peoples, the Court underscores the differentiated and often disproportionate impacts of environmental harm on Indigenous and tribal communities and focuses on the State's specific environmental obligations (para. 68). It emphasizes that States bear specific obligations under IHRL, particularly in relation to the general duty of prevention and under the procedural environmental guarantees of access to information and participation. Specifically, the Court identifies three key State duties:

1. Supervision and oversight: States must actively supervise and monitor activities that could cause environmental damage to Indigenous territories. This includes the development of independent mechanisms to prevent, investigate, and sanction environmental harm caused by both public and private actors (paras. 118–119, 151–152).
2. Environmental and social impact assessments (ESIA): any project affecting Indigenous lands must be preceded by an ESIA that includes an evaluation of social impacts and enables effective Indigenous participation through consultation (paras. 156, 164, 166, 169, 174).
3. Specific contents of the procedural guarantees alongside the general triple environmental protection obligations (access to information, public participation, access to justice) which are further defined here:
   i. Access to information: States must guarantee that Indigenous communities are informed about environmental impacts of activities that could potentially affect their territories, particularly concerning natural resource exploration and exploitation (paras. 214, 225).
   ii. Consultation and participation as autonomous obligations (not related to ESIAs): the Court reiterated the requirement that consultation and participation processes must respect the traditions and culture of indigenous communities, be realized at all stages of a project's lifecycle, ensure full awareness of potential risks and create sustained, effective and trustworthy channels for dialogue with the indigenous peoples, through their representative institutions (para. 227).

Despite the considerable advances articulated in Advisory Opinion OC-23/17, the Inter-American Court stopped short of clarifying the normative contours of the State's obligation to obtain FPIC from Indigenous and tribal peoples. While the Court consolidated the right to effective public participation and reiterated the procedural duties related to consultation, it conspicuously refrained from anchoring these obligations in a robust interpretation of FPIC. In particular, the Court noted that the purpose of ESIAs was to ensure that Indigenous communities were adequately informed of potential risks in order to assess "whether or not to accept the proposed development or investment plan" (para. 156). However, this language – although suggestive – falls short of clearly reaffirming consent as a necessary legal threshold, at least in cases of large-scale development or investment project which the Court establishes in *Saramaka* (para. 134). Instead, the Court's reasoning remains largely tethered to communal property rights and the related entitlement to consultation, thereby artificially alienating the interrelated rights to consultation, participation, and consent. It should be noted that, despite the meaning and scope of the right of access to justice as it is well-developed in the Inter-American Court's case law, the Court, while reaffirming such obligation, did not elaborate further criteria in the environmental context nor did it adapt the right to the specific legal, cultural, and institutional realities of Indigenous peoples. It should be noted that the colonial context and its neocolonial "remains" add necessity to the issue of appropriately remedying and redressing violations that are specific to indigenous peoples and their vulnerability situations. From a broader perspective, the Court missed the opportunity in its Advisory Opinion to synthesize its prior jurisprudence and articulate a comprehensive protective framework for the substantive and procedural environmental rights of Indigenous and tribal peoples – particularly with regard to the rights to a dignified life, life project, communal property, and physical and cultural integrity. Rather than advancing such a framework, the Court reiterates the derivative origin of the triple procedural obligations, treating them primarily as safeguards for other rights such as life or personal integrity (para. 211). This underscores the continuing need to disentangle and conceptualize the interrelations between these and other procedural guarantees in light of both collective self-determination and substantive environmental rights (see Aguilera 2023).

Indigenous environmental rights are further reinforced in the Escazú Agreement, a regional instrument that codifies the rights to information, participation and access to justice as constituent conditions to observe when implementing the right to a healthy environment, the protection of related human rights, and the promotion of sustainable development and environmental democracy across Latin America and the Caribbean. The Agreement recognizes that environmental human rights encompass both individual *and* collective dimensions; it further contributes to a more sophisticated understanding of vulnerability which it applies to Indigenous peoples. This facilitates the defining of conditions that give rise to State obligations. Moreover, the Escazú Agreement sets out detailed procedural standards designed to reduce structural barriers faced by vulnerable persons and groups. Notably, Article 7.15 explicitly requires Parties to respect and uphold their domestic and international obligations concerning the rights of Indigenous peoples. Yet, it should also be noted that the provision deliberately refrains from employing explicit rights-based language concerning the entitlements of Indigenous peoples, falling short of reflecting the normative content found in contemporary Indigenous rights instruments. In its known 2010 report "Indigenous and Tribal Peoples' Rights over their Ancestral Lands and Natural Resources", the Inter-American Commission adds to the debate on procedural guarantees; noteworthy here is the "effective protection of the natural resources in indigenous and tribal territories" (para. 197) while also referring to the importance of procedural rights in view of environmental protection more broadly, by stating that procedural rights "constitute necessary means to attain the ultimate objective of environmental preservation" (para. 197).

Indeed, procedural norms can also be identified within legal regimes specifically dedicated to the protection of indigenous peoples' rights. Particularly when examining international legal developments, however, we often observe a certain de-emphasis on procedural detail, with priority placed instead on substantive Indigenous claims: procedural demands tend to appear primarily in the form of participatory rights, which may carry both substantive and procedural dimensions: the most emblematic examples being the rights to prior consultation and FPIC (e.g., arts. 10, 11(2), 19, 28(1), 29(2), 32(2) UNDRIPS), as well as fundamental access-to-justice guarantees. This trend may be explained, at least in some regard, by the broad and often general nature of provisions in international law, which frequently delegate procedural specification to the domestic level. Yet, similar challenges arise domestically, where constitutional provisions alone rarely suffice, making it necessary for regulatory frameworks to define procedural detail. In practice, procedural rights in the Indigenous context are often reinvented or borrowed from other legal regimes: notably, this was the case for the jurisprudence of the Court of Justice of the European Union (CJEU), where procedural standing was attributed to Indigenous associations, the legal capacity to bring proceedings (*Inuit Tapiriit Kanatami* case), and where States were required to relax standing criteria for such associations (*Carvalho* case). The imperative for robust procedural safeguards is particularly salient in the Indigenous context, where rights are inherently grounded in strong organizational structures, collective decision-making bodies, and the assertion of group-based identities, and also by virtue of requiring necessary changes made to State institutions and decision-making powers for indigenous communities to gain a significant voice in these contexts.

And yet, we must recall that procedural standards in human rights law remain, to a large extent, individualized, generally permitting only individual rights to be claimed "in community with others" belonging to the same group (e.g., Jovanović 2012). This stands in stark contrast to the notion of the independent moral standing of a group, that is, the idea that a group exists as a normative entity distinct from its individual members (Jones 2016). Whereas some rights may actually only be exercised in community with others, these rights may constitute individual rights in the same way because some rights may be enjoyed individually without losing their collective character (Jovanović 2012). Scholars have offered various classificatory venues to capture this complexity. One important category involves so-called "dual standing" rights – rights exercisable by both individuals and groups (Buchanan 1993), which must be distinguished from "jointly exercised individual rights", often viewed as outward manifestations of collective rights. Indeed, if we were to concern ourselves with the way rights may be wielded, we could approach the question by referring to the "exercising criterion" (Jovanović 2012), which allows for collective rights to be understood as rights wielded in a collective form, also aligning with the category of "nonindividual standing rights" (Buchanan 1993). A final dimension of this debate touches on group responsibilities and membership criteria (Gover 2020), which necessarily involve collective decision-making processes and procedures. Importantly, these collective processes may generate even direct conflicts with individual rights, underscoring the need for careful procedural design and safeguards.

I.2.5 Uncovering Decolonizing Potential

Framing Indigenous environmental rights through a decolonial lens becomes compelling when we consider not only the place of Indigenous knowledge but also the positioning of Indigenous laws and institutions within dominant legal and governance systems. Such framing invites us to recognize Indigenous knowledge as an alternative valid epistemic source – offering distinct approaches to knowledge production, education, and science – and to understand Indigenous environmentalism as a critique of dominant extractivist paradigms and global processes that disproportionately harm the Global South. These are only a few of the rationales that underscore the urgency of this perspective. At least to some extent, recent international human rights developments have contributed to the juridification of Indigenous environmental rights, as seen in the adoption of instruments such as the UNDRIPS as well as biodiversity and climate change frameworks. However, it would be misleading to interpret these legal advancements as inherently decolonial. Critical legal scholarship, including Third World Approaches to International Law (TWAIL), has long emphasized the colonial roots embedded in international law and in many standards that ostensibly seek to regulate or protect Indigenous peoples' rights (e.g., Watson 2018). Other scholarly accounts highlight how Indigenous peoples have been systematically subjected to (neo)colonial practices – whether as objects of extractive research, through the marginalization of their knowledge systems, or via their positioning within educational hierarchies (Smith 1999). It hence becomes crucial to interrogate more carefully what Indigenous environmental rights actually entail in detail: what substantive changes do they bring to existing legal standards? And, perhaps most fundamentally, to what extent can Indigenous environmental rights frameworks be considered truly decolonial – rather than simply reformist adaptations within the prevailing legal and political order?

An important starting point for assessing the decolonial potential of Indigenous environmental rights (e.g., Salas Astrain & Pacheco Huaiquifil 2025) lies in examining the norm-drafting processes leading to the adoption of key legal frameworks, emblematically the UNDRIPS. The UN Declaration on the Rights of Indigenous Peoples emerged from over two decades of negotiations between Indigenous representatives and State actors, a process that not only vested the final instrument with enhanced legitimacy but also introduced important procedural transformations that enabled Indigenous peoples to formally participate in international norm-setting (Charters & Stavenhagen 2012) as discussed earlier.

At the constitutional level, significant efforts were likewise required to integrate Indigenous collective rights into domestic constitutional orders, particularly by recognizing legal pluralism and redefining the roles of Indigenous representatives within State structures. This process has been helpfully categorized in comparative analyses of Latin American constitutional developments, notably by Yrigoyen Fajardo (2015), who identifies four distinct phases:

- The first phase, "multicultural constitutionalism" (1980s), was marked by the rise of multiculturalism and the recognition of cultural diversity, without, however, fundamentally transforming the nature of the State or formally acknowledging legal pluralism or Indigenous jurisdiction.
- The second phase, "pluricultural constitutionalism" (1990s–early 2000s), signaled a shift toward a pluricultural State and the acceptance of internal legal pluralism, providing space for Indigenous movements and claims to be articulated – however, within a context shaped by the adoption of neoliberal policies, which often constrained social rights.
- The third phase, "plurinational constitutionalism" (2006–2009), moved explicitly toward decolonization by, for example, establishing the Plurinational State and embracing a more robust form of legal pluralism: this phase significantly advanced Indigenous self-determination, although some limitations on Indigenous jurisdiction persisted (Yrigoyen Fajardo 2015).
- The fourth phase, ecoconstitutionalism (2008–ongoing), makes the claim for nature to become a subject of rights (Yrigoyen Fajardo 2021).

We may also approach the decolonial potential embedded in Indigenous environmental rights by examining how these rights intersect with the principle of self-determination. Although frequently contested when framed in political terms, collective self-determination assumes a variety of meanings in Indigenous contexts, extending beyond claims to external sovereignty. Self-determination is commonly understood as encompassing both external and internal dimensions, with the latter shaping how Indigenous peoples govern their internal affairs and articulate their own normative frameworks. A particularly illustrative (and often overlooked) dimension here is the right to development, which itself invites critical reinterpretation. Rather than being confined to the dominant neoliberal paradigm with its narrow focus on economic growth, the right to development can manifest in multiple ways, accommodating pluralistic economic visions and alternative models of well-being. Indeed, constitutional reform processes in Bolivia and, to some extent, Ecuador have not only juridified Indigenous rights but have also demonstrated commitment to economic pluralism and alternative development paradigms that align with the degrowth discourse (see, e.g., Escobar 2014). Importantly, the right to development and the right to self-determination are often presented as interlinked, with their interrelation traceable to Common Article 1 of the ICCPR and the ICESCR. As a broad and open-ended legal concept, the right to development is particularly well-suited to accommodate the diverse ways of living, relational worldviews, and complex cosmovisions of Indigenous peoples – worldviews that, as we have seen, are intrinsically tied to their immediate environments and shaped by intergenerational thinking.

Coloniality, as scholars have shown, manifests itself in diverse and often disguised forms, notably through what has been termed the "coloniality of power" – a persistent structural condition that continues to affect Indigenous peoples until today. Its effects are multiple, shaping the "production, reproduction of knowledge, collective identities and subjectivities" (Gómez Isa 2018). In other words, the coloniality of power "implies that indigenous peoples are still in a situation of vulnerability and symbolic domination through the internalization of the logics of the coloniality of power" (Gómez Isa 2018). This critique extends beyond the political and social domains to encompass humanity's relationship with the environment. As Farget (2016) has argued, modern environmental regimes often perpetuate hierarchical positioning, placing human needs above ecological interdependence. In contrast, a communitarian perspective – as articulated by indigenous intellectuals like Choquehuanca (2021) – understands "living" in a spirit of reciprocity and relationality, where all beings are interdependent and human needs must never violate the rights of others.

Importantly, law itself is not neutral within these dynamics. Rather, it functions as a constitutive element of "this process of naturalisation of domination (in which) education and law play a remarkable role; they form a constitutive link to the coloniality of power" (Gómez Isa 2018; Walsh 2009). As scholars such as Gaventa (1980) and Comaroff and Comaroff (2008) have emphasized, the law often serves as an instrument of the powerful, a weapon wielded to secure and reproduce elite interests. While it would be an overstatement to present Indigenous environmental rights as a universal remedy to these structural conditions, we may cautiously hypothesize that they offer a unique entry point for opening epistemological debates, for reimagining the law toward a more plural and relational conceptualization, and for advancing a more holistic understanding of Indigenous peoples' collective rights. Crucially – and this is where their inherently decolonial potential lies – these processes place significant weight on the agency of Indigenous peoples themselves, particularly in their roles as decision-makers, negotiators, and authors of legal frameworks that define the contours of their self-determination and govern their lives and environments.

I.3 The Future of Indigenous Environmental Rights

1.3.1 Challenging Classical Legal Frameworks: Reinventing the Law and Reforming Institutions through Indigenous Environmental Rights

Critical legal scholarship and TWAIL have long highlighted the structural limitations inherent in international law when it comes to fostering meaningful agency for

Indigenous peoples. These limitations stem, in some regard, from the intergovernmental nature of international legal institutions and the Western legal traditions upon which they are historically founded. Despite the progressive momentum generated by Indigenous advocacy, particularly under the UN framework, there remain significant barriers to achieving substantive transformation. Institutions such as the EMRIP and the PFII, although symbolically important and operating with increasing Indigenous leadership, are still widely perceived as soft law mechanisms. Notwithstanding the advances reflected in Articles 41 and 42 of UNDRIPS, the outputs of these mechanisms largely lack binding legal force and remain unenforceable in practice, particularly in contexts where State cooperation is limited or absent. This underscores the urgent need to advance comprehensive reforms across all relevant human rights bodies, ensuring that Indigenous issues are not siloed within specialized institutions only but recognized as cross-cutting concerns. Moreover, Indigenous participation must extend beyond consultative roles toward genuine decision-making authority, an essential condition if international law is to move beyond symbolic inclusion and instead takes the route toward a truly decolonial paradigm.

Indigenous environmental rights present specific challenges to classical legal frameworks, which often lack the conceptual flexibility and cultural sensitivity needed to accommodate plural legal orders, religious diversity, and Indigenous worldviews. Indigenous environmental rights are frequently asserted in contexts marked by existential threats, ranging from violations of the rights to life, cultural identity, health, water, and subsistence, to broader infringements, concerning, emblematically, dignified living conditions. Without addressing these conditions and the structural nature of such violations, institutional and jurisprudential responses risk remaining superficial or ineffective. Alarmingly, institutional and academic inattention to the systemic and often violent dimensions of Indigenous life experiences still persists. Addressing this gap requires more than technical reform – it demands epistemic and methodological shifts. A potential starting point lies in initiatives such as the UN-declared International Decade of Indigenous Languages (2022–2032), which underscores the intrinsic interdependence of language, culture, and identity. This initiative reflects a broader normative ambition, namely to move beyond awareness-raising toward the consolidation of the UNDRIPS as part of customary international law, parts of which have actually been granted such status (Lenzerini 2019). In parallel, and as a similarly pressing issue, the academic community bears responsibility to follow pluralistic and decolonial approaches, embracing Indigenous research methodologies and respecting community-defined ethical standards when working with Indigenous individuals and knowledge systems. Without such shifts, efforts toward Indigenous environmental justice will remain superficial, incomplete and extractive.

Indigenous environmental rights also provide critical insights for rethinking global environmental and social justice. From a utilitarian perspective, diversity is increasingly valued across international legal treaties and discourses, with

Indigenous traditional knowledge and conservation practices recognized as essential not only for local sustainability but for securing the well-being of present and future generations, serving humanity. Over time, Indigenous concerns have gained visibility – and, to some extent, normative recognition – within international environmental justice frameworks, prompting a shift away from strictly Western development-oriented models. Indigenous environmental rights should thus be understood as sources of epistemological crafting, methodological pluralism, and normative transformation, offering a distinctly decolonial lens through which to critique and reimagine international environmental law and IHRL. Increasingly, indigenous environmental rights have come to be recognized as a missing ingredient in environmental justice agendas, with numerous reports and conferences reserving a space for indigenous-specific vulnerabilities – now, the extent to which these clauses and protocols develop legal teeth varies. Indigenous knowledge systems have increasingly been informing alternative, ecologically attuned strategies for environmental preservation and showing the normative force of context.

I.3.2 Indigenous Environmental Rights as a Proper Research Agenda

Research on indigenous environmental rights presumably gains increasing relevance in the coming years, as the global environmental crisis continues to disproportionately affect Indigenous communities. Future scholarship must foreground Indigenous vulnerabilities, particularly in the context of extractive industries and large-scale infrastructure projects that encroach upon ancestral territories and livelihoods – an area that has begun to receive legal attention, as seen in the *Saúl Luciano Lliuya v. RWE* case. Given the profound and multifaceted relationship Indigenous peoples maintain with their territories, it will be essential to further explore the temporal dimensions of environmental harm, including impacts on future generations and the transmission of Indigenous knowledge systems. This necessarily involves respecting the right to FPIC and recognizing Indigenous communities as knowledge holders alongside their participatory roles. Additionally, Indigenous positions as stewards or guardians of nature merit deeper legal inquiry, particularly regarding the potential for recognizing forms of legal standing or guardianship vis-à-vis nonhuman beings. Finally, there are numerous dimensions of vulnerability that warrant further examination on their own terms. These include, but are not limited to, Indigenous spiritualities as they relate to the environment, ancestral knowledge systems, intergenerational transmission processes, conservation practices, sustainability paradigms, culturally embedded environmental practices, and the agency of nonhuman beings.

Indigenous environmental rights are expected to gain further importance in light of the particular vulnerabilities Indigenous peoples face due to increasing external pressures. These include, inter-alia, threats rooted in neoliberal capitalist market logics (Svampa 2019), the global demand for natural resources and related forms of neocolonialism (Machado Aráoz 2013; Sousa Santos 2023), as well as systemic human failures related to the triple planetary crisis (climate change, biodiversity loss, and pollution) and global health emergencies. As such crises intensify and multiply, the risk of infringements upon Indigenous rights will only grow. In many cases, the geographical remoteness of Indigenous communities goes hand in hand with limited State presence, leaving them exposed to security threats posed by non-State actors and private entities, as well as to neglect in times of public health or environmental emergencies. These dynamics often detrimentally affect Indigenous livelihoods while creating dependencies that erode self-sufficiency and threaten cultural continuity. Traditional lifestyles and practices – central to Indigenous cultural identity – thus become increasingly undermined in contexts of heightened environmental and socio-economic stress, exacerbating with heightened natural resource demands. In this regard, it is crucial to examine the intersections between emerging international frameworks for the protection of environmental and human rights defenders and Indigenous environmental rights, illustrative being Article 9 of the Escazú Agreement. At the same time, alternative problem-solving methods are gaining more attention, with the first steps having been taken to recognize indigenous traditional knowledge systems, conservation methods and intergenerational thinking.

I.3.3 Indigenous Environmental Rights as a Field or Emerging Regime

Looking ahead, the development of Indigenous environmental rights requires the establishment of a distinct legal and conceptual field – one that cannot be reduced to isolated treaty provisions or occasional references within international law. This emerging field must be understood holistically, shaped by Indigenous epistemologies and collective experiences. However, its future will largely depend on prevailing political contexts. The global resurgence of far-right ideologies often coincides with environmental rollback, nationalist agendas, and hostility toward minorities, including Indigenous peoples. In Europe, for example, certain far-right parties have opposed renewable energy initiatives, denying or discrediting scientific predictions relating to global warming. Common to such platforms are anti-migration discourses and racialized stereotypes, which portray Indigenous peoples as "backward" or "uncivilized" – perpetuating dehumanizing tropes that undermine Indigenous dignity and other rights. Such conditions undermine efforts to advance pluralistic, genuinely democratic, diversity-oriented sociocultural–environmental frameworks. Yet, as the global environmental crisis deepens, the relevance of Indigenous conservation practices, ancestral knowledge systems, and relational methodologies are expected to grow. In the long term, these contributions may serve not only to strengthen environmental governance grounded in inclusive democratic participation but also sustain the transformative and decolonial aspirations embedded in Indigenous legal and political resurgence. As argued throughout this work, beyond their legal recognition and value in their own terms, the normative and epistemological weight of Indigenous environmental rights lies in their potential to reconfigure dominant legal orders through a decolonial lens: notably, by affirming Indigenous peoples as collective rights holders whose customary law, knowledge systems, and practices are pushing the frontiers of legal thought toward an ecosystemic paradigm and the recognition of nature's intrinsic value, grounded in principles of transformative social justice and equality.

What is proposed here should be understood as distinct from any understanding of a conventional legal framework. Indigenous environmental rights are already embedded across multiple legal regimes, including those concerning biodiversity; climate change; economic, social and cultural rights; and public health. The prospect of negotiating a new treaty – let alone a binding one – remains highly unlikely in the short run. Even a soft law instrument would require considerable political momentum and time, as evidenced by the protracted drafting process of the UNDRIPS, which took over two decades (Charters & Stavenhagen 2012). This difficulty is largely attributable to the politically sensitive nature of Indigenous rights, grounded in claims to sovereignty, territoriality, legal pluralism, and collective identity. Rather than aiming for a standalone legal regime, it may be more productive to conceptualize Indigenous environmental rights as a distinct legal field – one that highlights systemic vulnerability and extends the normative reach of nondiscrimination and equality with a view to inform jurisprudential developments. In contexts where environmental rights are undergoing juridification and are subject to interpretive oversight, Indigenous rights are increasingly assuming a central, not peripheral, role.

In other words, we speak of a proper legal regime not in the conventional sense – as constituting a legal order in its own terms – but instead as a distinct human rights concern that is continuously being considered and mainstreamed. Indigenous environmental rights are gradually gaining recognition across both hard law frameworks – such as ILO Convention No. 169, the UNFCCC, and the Convention on Biological Diversity – and soft law instruments, including the UNDRIPS and reports issued by the UN Special Rapporteurs and EMRIP. Although no dedicated legal instrument currently exists to specifically protect Indigenous environmental rights, the steady juridification of these norms and the growing attention they receive from courts, commissions, treaty bodies, working groups, and special procedures indicate progressive legal development. This trend reflects not only a broadening international consensus and wider recognition of Indigenous environmental rights but also signals an emerging normative will to consolidate their status within international, regional, and (potentially) constitutional legal frameworks.

Another important dimension concerns the connective potential between Indigenous environmental rights and broader frameworks of environmental human rights. In practice, a form of normative spill-over appears to be unfolding, whereby environmental human rights standards have drawn from the longstanding recognition and development of Indigenous rights (see, for example, IACtHR Advisory Opinion OC-23/17). The recently adopted Escazú Agreement – reflecting these normative trajectories – may, in turn, contribute significantly to the advancement and consolidation of Indigenous environmental rights, particularly by strengthening procedural guarantees and enhancing the protection of Indigenous communities engaged in the defense of their rights and territories, all within a binding regional legal framework. This dynamic appears to follow a logic akin to intersectionality or cumulative vulnerability, insofar as the disproportionate exposure of Indigenous peoples to environmental harm introduces a distinct dimension that enriches otherwise general human rights frameworks. Nevertheless, caution is warranted: the uncritical transplantation of conventional rights frameworks into the Indigenous context and juridification of normative concepts drawn from classical legal ontologies risks reproducing neocolonial logics. At the heart of Indigenous environmental rights lies their group-differentiated character – not only in the sense that certain rights are collectively held, but also in the substantive and procedural sense and with a distinct epistemological approach to be in place. This entails collective legal recognition and with it, collective standing, and also for Indigenous customs and decision-making processes to be respected, and for legal pluralism to be observed when interpreting and implementing rights.

We may thus envisage a range of institutional responses, including targeted institution-building efforts, to address the increasing environmental concerns articulated by Indigenous communities – particularly those whose livelihoods depend intimately on their surrounding ecosystems. However, the likelihood of securing a universally adopted, legally binding instrument in this field remains low. As noted above, this is largely due to the continued dominance of Western environmental paradigms and entrenched anxieties surrounding the recognition of Indigenous territorial rights and sovereignty claims. Moreover, a persistent Global North–Global South (with some exceptions) divide continues to constrain political momentum in favor of Indigenous agendas. This divide not only affects the political will, alliance forming and mobilization of international support but also reflects limited awareness among many Global North States. A more realistic intermediary pathway might involve the adoption of an additional protocol to an existing treaty, open to States willing to assume stronger commitments in support of Indigenous environmental rights. Greater normative traction may similarly be achieved through special procedures and thematic mandates – such as those led by the UN Special Rapporteur on the Rights of Indigenous Peoples, the EMRIP, and also relevant regional monitoring bodies such as the Committee to Support Implementation and Compliance of the Escazú Agreement. Alternatively, Indigenous environmental rights could be progressively developed through interpretative tools such as general comments by treaty monitoring bodies and jurisprudential novelties produced by human rights courts and commissions. Nonetheless, in the current intergovernmental legal landscape, Indigenous-led initiatives must still navigate the structural limitations imposed by State-centric procedures and norms, which continue to define the boundaries of indigenous participation and recognition in international law. Similar obstacles persist at the domestic level, where most State structures remain untransformed by decolonial principles and rarely engage with Indigenous peoples as equal political partners in constitutional reform or institutional reconstruction.

In envisioning institutional futures for Indigenous environmental rights, it is important to explore pluralistic models that enhance Indigenous participation also within existing judicial systems. One concrete pathway involves promoting Indigenous representation in domestic courts, including through the appointment of Indigenous judges – as seen in Bolivia, where Indigenous original justice has become constitutionally recognized, increasing indigenous representation in the judiciary. These experiences can foster pluralistic dialogue within conventional legal institutions, allowing Indigenous normative systems and their ecological governance practices to interact meaningfully with State law. Beyond institutional inclusion, the recognition of Indigenous knowledge holders as epistemic authorities in judicial and administrative processes is equally crucial. Their participation as expert witnesses (*peritos*) in cases concerning land, environment, and cultural heritage affirms the legitimacy of Indigenous knowledge practices and expands the evidentiary standards typically applied in environmental adjudication. Institutional designs that facilitate such plural forms of expertise signal a commitment to epistemic justice and reinforce Indigenous peoples' authority over matters that directly affect their lives, territories and spiritualities.

I.4 Sections and Chapters

I.4.1 Part I: Amidst International Human Rights Law and Environmental Legal Landscapes: International Orders Examined

This section explores the merits and challenges attributable to IHRL and international environmental law, respectively, in the way these establish effective safeguards for the exercise of indigenous environmental rights. The complex interplay of the two regimes in place allows further insights on the recognition but also the position of indigenous environmental norms in the global legal order. In that sense, new hierarchies emerge, the position of norms is (re-)negotiated, framework-specific norms may enter into conflict with each other, hence bearing the potential for further fragmentation of international law but also for a *sui generis* regime to emerge as a result.

The present section is also meant to fulfill an informative purpose for those not familiar with either IHRL, international environmental law, or legal studies generally, tracing key developments and moments in these legal spheres. Important technical including procedural debates are included in a dedicated space in this section, allowing the reader to get a sense of all pertinent judicial details as these concern the international level. Indigenous environmental rights are negotiated and eventually established in these frameworks, finding articulation either in the form of proper orders (e.g., UNDRIPS or ILO C169) in their own terms, as occupying an albeit limited space in an international treaty (e.g., CRC, CBD) or as a transversal issue, that is, a vulnerability issue to be considered when interpreting the law at a more general level (e.g., ICCPR, ICESCR, ICERD, ICRPD). International environmental developments have shown an increasingly open attitude toward indigenous agendas, their particular vulnerabilities and demands for appropriate representation in intergovernmental contexts. The section hence tries to convey a broader perspective of both relevant judicial detail and in situating indigenous environmental rights across major international legal frameworks.

The section initiates with **Jonathan Liljeblad**'s account of pertinent developments in the field of international human rights law and its key mechanisms that are created with the purpose of protecting indigenous peoples' rights. Liljeblad, however, addresses these developments with a critical and hegemony-sensitive view that understands indigenous representatives as dependent on a State-centric international order and its logics and also permits insights on ways to renegotiate such order to become more prone to indigenous environmental rights. It shows, more specifically, to what extent IHRL retains State authority and studies the resulting challenges for Indigenous peoples in their endeavors to use the specific channels of IHRL to make their environmental claims heard. The chapter also eventually uncovers strategies for Indigenous peoples to establish new hierarchies, ultimately to gain a better position in processes of promoting and implementing Indigenous environmental rights. **Federica Cittadino** then introduces the international biodiversity regime established with the Convention on Biological Diversity and its protocols in the way these reinforce and operationalize Indigenous peoples' rights. It discusses many pertinent safeguards reserved for Indigenous peoples under the biodiversity regime including benefit-sharing rights, FPIC, or the recognition of indigenous and community-conserved areas, but also more generally applicable rights such as self-determination, land and resource rights, or cultural rights. It also approaches the matter by studying to what extent CBD provisions may reinforce or put into effect established Indigenous rights by looking at recent rulings emitted by IHRL bodies and courts, and in a second attempt, how these rights expand on the substance of Indigenous rights, as illustrated by community protocols and mutually agreed terms. Cittadino finally presents to us the limitations of the framework, with particular attention paid to its implementation and in view of the recent developments around the Kunming–Montréal Global Biodiversity Framework.

I.4.2 Part II: Beyond the "Human" in Indigenous Environmental Law? Impressions from a Dualistic Debate

The section approaches Indigenous environmental law from a dualistic angle, that is, one of the most prominent diametrically opposed theoretical approaches adopted in the field, namely a human rights-based approach (HRBA) to the environment and the rights of nature (RoN). In other words, the former captures in essence what some may critically view as an "anthropocentric approach instead of," whereas the latter has generally become known as an "ecocentric" instead of perspective of rights. Now, Indigenous law seems susceptible to both "anthropocentric" instead of and "ecocentric" instead of approaches, hence opening the floor for foundational, conceptual debate and whether to maintain a discourse on instead of "centrisms." As mediators, translators, or guardians of earth, Indigenous people gain a prominent role in the spaces "in between", where legal gaps persist, where procedures are yet to be formulated for nature to gain a proper legal voice, or where Indigenous peoples themselves are being affected in their exercise of environmental rights. Indeed, disproportionate impacts may be noted in the case of Indigenous communities where extractive operations or "development" projects cause detrimental effects, affecting Indigenous peoples' lives and livelihoods to considerable extent. It seems a natural corollary to flow from the above that we shall reserve a proper legal space and category for an Indigenous right to an intact, safe environment – the form this ultimately takes is also disputed among Indigenous peoples, with many communities adopting a holistic environmental approach, understanding themselves as an integral part of the natural environment.

We hence add to the dualistic debates (HRBA versus RoN) on the matter, notably by adopting a dedicated, human rights-prone positioning while demonstrating awareness of the multiplicity of Indigenous relations with nature, either as proper claimants of their rights or as proponents and possibly spokespersons of or expert witnesses to flora and fauna, and the specific rights arising therewith. This may concern cases where the rights of flora or fauna are taken to the court by Indigenous peoples on behalf of nature. In fact, the debates around procedural rights including legal personality issues have been contributing to an understanding that considers these claims as autonomous rights existing independently from the human side of the law, a claim of universal interest and a fundamental right for human existence as argued by the Inter-American Court of Human Rights. The debates hence develop a certain sensitivity to indigenous perceptions vis-à-vis the environment, and therewith legal pluralism, while situating these and allowing these to enter into negotiation with classical environmental rights theories.

This theoretical section starts off with a comprehensive account on the "rights of nature" instead of by building on the ethnological semiology of Jean Baudrillard. **Bart Jansen** and **Tineke Lambooy** principally argue that RoN would challenge conventional anthropocentric legal paradigms by integrating Indigenous cosmovisions into Western jurisprudence. By examining legislative landmark cases such as the New Zealand Te Awa Tupua Act and Australia's Yarra River Protection Act, the chapter assesses to what extent these manifestations of recognition genuinely reflect Indigenous views or would instead merely adapt nature to pre-existing Western ontological (legal) philosophies. In fact, Jansen and Lambooy disclose that RoN frequently intersects with Indigenous cosmovisions and assume for RoN to assume a profound, metaphysical meaning beyond Western legal constructs; they notably attribute to the paradigm an evolving character, and draw on practical implementation challenges as well as its interplay with legal pluralism. The incorporation of RoN into Western legal systems unveils a dynamic where Indigenous knowledge is recognized but, at the same time, streamlined to conform with established legal structures. However, the chapter equally refers to the danger for RoN to merely codify Indigenous rights without capturing the full depth of Indigenous views, and also of risking to mispresent Indigenous knowledge as a mere extension of Western legal ontology. On the bright side, the authors view RoN as an endeavor to broaden the legal recognition of nature and its purported intrinsic values. The second chapter in this section then compares and contrasts RoN and Indigenous right to territory, also with the sufficient theoretical rigor: **Digno Montalván Zambrano** and **Isabel Wences** notably understand RoN as a framework having gained recognition across several jurisdictions as a response to the global ecological crisis, it is often to be derived from Western moral-philosophical foundations, supported by conservationist and scientistic debates. Rights of nature are then contrasted with "Iindigenous territorial rights", representing the struggle for the recognition of ontological and relational plurality arising with the Indigenous peoples–environment nexus. Basing itself on an analysis of multiple ecocentric frameworks and their legal application, the chapter assesses the extent to which the recognition of rights to nature does (not) align with Indigenous territorial claims. Montalván Zambrano and Wences also warn against the risks of imposing Western ecocentric categories onto Indigenous struggles, which bears the danger of replicating colonial logics underlying dominant ecocentric approaches. The authors eventually transmit to us an interpretation of RoN that embraces epistemic plurality while allowing for an appropriate representation of nature in courts, ultimately creating spaces for equitable dialogue and fostering a strategic alliance between indigenous territorial rights and RoN in the struggle against anthropocentrism. A final contribution tries to make sense of RoN and the biocultural approach by connecting to pertinent legal pluralistic debates and more particularly, Indigenous customary law. **Laura Calle-Alzate** and **Nurys Esperanza Silva-Cantillo** critically approach contemporary justice systems by offering alternative accounts beyond the anthropocentric view, finding its foundations in several accounts such as, emblematically, the RoN and that way reinforcing biocultural rights. In addition, the chapter places a specific accent here on the question of how nonhuman entities could be formally recognized as subjects of justice. By way of finding an answer to the question, Calle Alzate and Silva Cantillo rely on Indigenous justice systems that build on a dedicated nature–culture nexus that is nurtured by worldviews that transcend segmented anthropocentric perspectives. The chapter also tries to build bridges between State legal systems and Indigenous customary law. The chapter concludes biocultural rights and the recognition of legal pluralism allow us to recognize the role of Indigenous communities as interactive participants in their territories, hence promoting a view that strives for decolonizing the "rights of nature" instead of debate.

I.4.3 Part III: Decolonizing the Law: What Place for (Transformative) Legal Pluralism?

The field of Indigenous environmental rights necessarily opens the floor for a systemic questioning of the predominant law, its underlying principles, logics, or ideological orientation. Especially those familiar with Indigenous rights would be familiar with the widely known critique on the Western idea of individualized property permeating the law, the predominance of classical European decision-making structures, or the very idea of the State as the main and only sovereign entity. This may also concern the predominance of written legal codes and the uneasiness of dealing with Indigenous unwritten sources, customs, and procedures, ultimately laws that are yet to be fully recognized. By studying Indigenous rights, then, we necessarily come to adopt a critical legal approach, one that commonly assumes a decolonizing agenda – our work on Indigenous environmental rights is no exception to this.

The demand for legal pluralism in its transformative mission inherently bears such decolonizing potential; it could be seen as a bottom-up tool to break with predominant forms of law, commonly State law. Indigenous environmental rights prove emblematic here, by introducing, inter alia, Indigenous ontologies including proper customs and procedures; entire justice systems; and collective rights and spiritualities and cosmovisions into the common sense of the predominant legal sphere. The basic premises of the law, including not only issues relating to legal personality, subject-holdership, and legal representation, but also questions on the recognition of claims, are being critically approached and eventually reevaluated against the criteria established with Indigenous laws and orders.

In an attempt to uncover legally pluralistic thinking, **Ricardo Salas Astrain** and **Cristian Pacheco Huaiquifil** concern themselves with the transmodern function of Mapuche law, the *Az Mapu*. The chapter does so by building on two pertinent cases in Pewenche territory and gives us a general idea of *Az Mapu* as it arises in the specific context of indigenous environmental law. In that sense, it goes on to sociopolitically problematize the meanings inherent to Western law, its global outreach and imposition on the *Abya Yala* (American continent) and *Wallmapu* (Mapuche land). It importantly also approaches the matter from a legal-historical perspective, taking account of the histories of cruelty and violence in "Conquista" context and as these would affect Indigenous rights. Pacheco Huaiquifil and Salas Astrain further engage with contextual law, permitting us to understand the disentanglement of different dimensions of recognition in ancestral justice. Eventually, the chapter addresses RoN by giving it a decolonial reading of contextualized justice that, in turn, allows us to derive at a different understanding of nature–human relations, which also enables us to believe that the serious environmental crisis requires responses rooted in contextual law as it is the case for Mapuche law, the *Az Mapu* and its intrinsic relation with *Itrofillmogen* (nature). Finally, **Núria Reguart-Segarra** introduces the religious dimension of disputes over land and the environment: it departs from the assumption that Indigenous peoples' determination with which they protect their traditional territories from environmental encroachment is to be related back to their deepest spirituality and religious beliefs which also gives rise to indigenous collective identity/ies and their physical and spiritual well-being. Reguart-Segarra argues indigenous traditional knowledge is to be considered an inextricable and constituent element of their right to a healthy environment, and not only that, also their fundamental right to freedom of religion or belief – revealing how, according to their belief, traditional practices and knowledge systems are to be viewed in conjunction with spirituality. The chapter expresses concern about an apparent lack of understanding and realization of Indigenous peoples' freedom of religion or belief, which, in turn, also places in jeopardy the application of their environmental rights. In a practice-oriented fashion, the chapter explores different threats Indigenous religious identities and cultural survival are exposed to resulting from environmental degradation, and also fulfilling the purpose of providing guidelines for future scenarios.

References

Acosta, A. (2015). El Buen Vivir como alternativa al desarrollo: Algunas reflexiones económicas y no tan económicas. *Política y Sociedad*, 52(2), 299–330.

Aguilera, M. G. (2023). *Environmental Human Rights: New Thinking from Latin America and the Caribbean*. Brill/Nijhoff.

Altmann, P. (2020). The Commons as Colonisation – The Well-Intentioned Appropriation of Buen Vivir. *Bulletin of Latin American Research*, 39(1): 83–97.

Álvarez, Y. (2020). *Postdesarrollo, Pluralismo Jurídico y Derechos Indígenas: Alternativas al desarrollo y al Derecho*. tirant lo blanch.

Bagni, S. (2022). Los Derechos de la Naturaleza en la Jurisprudencia Colombiana e Indiana. *Revista Análisis Jurídico-Político*, 4(7), 99–123.

Barrera, A. (2012). Turning Legal Pluralism into State-Sanctioned Law: Assessing the Implications of the New Constitutions and Laws in Bolivia and Ecuador, in Schilling-Vacaflor, A. & Nolte, D. (eds.), *New Constitutionalism in Latin America: Promises and Practices*. Routledge.

Barrit, E. (2020). Global Values, Transnational Expression: From Aarhus to Escazú, in Heyvaert, V. & Duvic-Paoli, L. A. (eds.), *Research Handbook on Transnational Environmental Law*. Edward Elgar Publishing.

Bautista, R. (2021). Paper presentation. The Taller Internacional: Armonía, Con la Naturaleza en el Contexto Del Marco Global de Biodiversidad Posterior al 2020, FILAC, Ministerio de Relaciones Exteriores de Bolivia, Ministerio de Medio Ambiente y Agua, August 17.

Bavikatte, K. S. (2014). *Stewarding the Earth: Rethinking Property and the Emergence of Biocultural Rights*. Oxford University Press.

Bennett, T. & Bavikatte, K. S. (2015). Community Stewardship: The Foundation of Biocultural Rights. *Journal of Human Rights and the Environment*, 6(1), 7–29.

Black, C. F. (2011). *The Land Is the Source of the Law: A Dialogic Encounter with Indigenous Jurisprudence*. Routledge.

Borrows, J. (2013). *Canada's Indigenous Constitution*. University of Toronto Press.

Boyd, D. R. (2017). *The Rights of Nature – A Legal Revolution that Could Save the World*. ECW Press.

Boyd, D. R. (2012). *The Environmental Rights Revolution: A Global Study of Constitutions, Human Rights, and the Environment*. UBC Press.

Bryant, R. (2015). *International Handbook of Political Ecology*. Edward Elgar Publishing.

Buchanan, A. (1993). The Role of Collective Rights in the Theory of Indigenous Peoples' Rights. *Transnational Law and Contemporary Problems*, 3(1), 89–108.

Burger, J. (2012). Making the Declaration Work for Human Rights in the UN System, in Charters, C. & Stavenhagen, R. (eds.), *Making the Declaration Work: The United Nations Declaration on the Rights of Indigenous Peoples*. IWGIA.

Burger, J. & Martín Castro, D. (2006). Pueblos Indígenas en Naciones Unidas: Mecanismos de Protección, Agencias e Instancias, in Berraondo, M. (ed.), *Pueblos Indígenas y Derechos Humanos*. Universidad de Deusto.

Cahier, L. (2022). Environmental Justice in the United Nations Human Rights System: Challenges and Opportunities for the Protection of Indigenous Women's Rights Against Environmental Violence. *The George Washington Journal of Energy and Environmental Law*, 13(1), 37–57.

Calle-Alzate, L. & Silva-Cantillo, N. (2025). Rights of Nature: The Biocultural Approach and Indigenous Customary Law in Latin America, in Eichler, J. & Aguilera, M. G. (eds.), *Indigenous Environmental Rights: Towards a Holistic Regime*. Cambridge University Press.

Cariño, J. & Berger, D. N. (2024). Convention on Biological Diversity (CBD), in IWGIA (ed.), *The Indigenous World 2024*. The International Work Group for Indigenous Affairs.

Charters, C. & Stavenhagen, R. (2012). *Making the Declaration Work: The United Nations Declaration on the Rights of Indigenous Peoples*. IWGIA.

Choquehuanca (2021) Paper presentation. The Taller Internacional: Armonía, Con la Naturaleza en el Contexto Del Marco Global de Biodiversidad Posterior al 2020, FILAC, Ministerio de Relaciones Exteriores de Bolivia, Ministerio de Medio Ambiente y Agua, August 17.

Cittadino, F. (2025). Indigenous Rights under the Convention on Biological Diversity: Reinforcing and Expanding Human Rights Law, in Eichler, J. & Aguilera, M. G. (eds.), *Indigenous Environmental Rights: Towards a Holistic Regime*. Cambridge University Press.

Cittadino, F. (2019). *Incorporating Indigenous Rights in the International Regime on Biodiversity Protection: Access, Benefit-sharing and Conservation in Indigenous Lands. Legal Studies on Access and Benefit-sharing*. Brill Nijhoff.

Comaroff, J. & Comaroff, J. L. (2008). *Law and Disorder in the Postcolony*. Chicago University Press.

Committee on the Rights of Persons with Disabilities (2018). General comment N° 6 on 'Equality and Non-Discrimination'. OHCHR.

Committee on the Rights of Persons with Disabilities (2016) General Comment N° 3 on article 6 'Women and Girls with Disabilities'. OHCHR.

Committee on the Rights of the Child (2009) General Comment N°11 'Indigenous Children and Their Rights under the Convention (on the Rights of the Child)'. OHCHR.
Cornwall, A. & Gaventa, J. (2001). From User and Chooser to Makers and Shapers: Repositioning Participation in Social Policy. *IDS Working Paper*, 127, 1–28.
Corrias, L. (2026). Humanity and Intergenerational Rights as Manifestations of Collectivity, in Eichler, J. & Jovanović, M. (eds.), *Research Handbook of Collective Rights*. Edward Elgar Handbooks in Legal Theory. Edward Elgar Publishing.
Coyle, M. (2020). E Pluribus Plures: Legal Pluralism and the Recognition of Indigenous Legal Orders, in Schiff Berman, P. (ed.), *The Oxford Handbook of Global Legal Pluralism*. Oxford University Press.
Daly, E. & May, J. R. (2018). Learning from Constitutional Environmental Rights, in Knox, J. H. & Pejan, R. (eds.), *The Human Right to a Healthy Environment*. Cambridge University Press.
Di Chiro, G. (2016). Environmental Justice and the Anthropocene Meme, in Gabrielsen, T., Hall, C., Meyer, J. M., & Schlosberg, D. (eds.), *The Oxford Handbook of Environmental Political Theory*. Oxford University Press.
Doyle, C. (2017). *Indigenous Peoples, Title to Territory, Rights and Resources: The Transformative Role of Free, Prior and Informed Consent*. Routledge.
Eichler, J. & Mora Navarro, F. V. (2023). Proceduralising Indigenous Peoples' Demands: Indigenous Environmental Rights and Legal Pluralism in Contemporary Jurisprudence. *Legal Pluralism and Critical Social Analysis*, 55(1), 5–34.
Escobar, A. (2014). *Sentipensar con la Tierra: Nuevas Lecturas sobre Desarrollo, Territorio y Diferencia*. Ediciones UNAULA.
Etchart, L. (2022). *Global Governance of the Environment, Indigenous Peoples and the Rights of Nature: Extractive Industries in the Ecuadorian Amazon*. Palgrave Macmillan.
Farget, D. (2016). Colonialisme et pollution environnementale: prolongement et effets sur les droits des peuples autochtones. *Criminologie*, 49(2), 95–114.
Fitzmaurice, M. (2018). Indigenous Peoples and Intergenerational Equity as an Emerging Aspect of Ethno-Cultural Diversity in International Law, in Pentassuglia, G. (ed.), *Ethno-Cultural Diversity and Human Rights: Challenges and Critiques*. Brill Nijhoff.
Gabrielsen, T., Hall, C., Meyer, J. M., & Schlosberg, D. (2016), *The Oxford Handbook of Environmental Political Theory*. Oxford University Press.
Gaillard, E. (2026). Humanity and Intergenerational Rights as Manifestations of Collectivity, in Eichler, J. & Jovanović, M. (eds.), *Research Handbook of Collective Rights*. Edward Elgar Handbooks in Legal Theory. Elgar Publishing.
Gaventa, J. (1980). *Power and Powerlessness: Quiescence and Rebellion in an Apalachian Valley*. University of Illinois Press.
Girard, F., Hall, I., & Frison, C. (2022). *Biocultural Rights, Indigenous Peoples and Local Communities: Protecting Culture and the Environment*. Routledge Explorations in Environmental Studies. Routledge.
Gómez Isa, F. (2018). International Law, Ethno-Cultural Diversity and Indigenous Peoples' Rights: A Postcolonial Approach, in Pentassuglia, G. (ed.), *Ethno-Cultural Diversity and Human Rights: Challenges and Critiques*. Brill Nijhoff.
Gover, K. (2020). Legal Pluralism and Indigenous Legal Traditions, in Schiff Berman, P. (ed.), *The Oxford Handbook of Global Legal Pluralism*. Oxford University Press.
Gudynas, E. (2011). Buen Vivir: Today's Tomorrow. *Development*, 54(4), 441–447.

Heinämäki, L. (2010). The Right to Be a Part of Nature: Indigenous Peoples and the Environment. PhD thesis, Rovaniemi, University of Lapland.

Inter-American Commission on Human Rights (IACHR) (2010). *Indigenous and Tribal Peoples' Rights over Their Ancestral Lands and Natural Resources: Norms and Jurisprudence of the Inter-American Human Rights System, Thematic Reports*. IACHR.

International Work Group on Indigenous Affairs. (2024). IWGIA's reaction to the COP outcome. November 27, 2024. https://iwgia.org/en/news.html

Jansen, B. & Lambooy, T. (2025). Rights of Nature as Symbol and Ritual: Recognition of Indigenous Cosmovisions within Western Legal Ontology, in Eichler, J. & Aguilera, M. G. (eds.), *Indigenous Environmental Rights: Towards a Holistic Regime*. Cambridge University Press.

Jones, P. (2016). 'Group Rights', Stanford Encyclopedia of Philosophy. https://plato.stanford.edu/entries/rights-group/

Jovanović, M. (2012). *Collective Rights: A Legal Theory*. Cambridge University Press.

Kopnina, H. & Shoreman-Ouimet, E. (2016). *Routledge Handbook of Environmental Anthropology*. Routledge.

Kymlicka, W. (1995). *Multicultural Citizenship: A Liberal Theory of Minority Rights*. Oxford University Press.

Leib, L. H. (2011). *Human Rights and the Environment: Philosophical, Theoretical, and Legal Perspectives*. Brill Nijhoff.

Lenzerini, F. (2019). Implementation of the UNDRIP around the World: Achievements and Future Perspectives. The Outcome of the Work of the ILA Committee on the Implementation of the Rights of Indigenous Peoples. *The International Journal of Human Rights*, 23(1–2), 51–62.

Lenzerini, F. (2011). Intangible Cultural Heritage: The Living Culture of Peoples. *The European Journal of International Law*, 22(1), 101–120.

Lightfoot, S. (2016). *Global Indigenous Politics: A Subtle Revolution*. Routledge.

Liljeblad, J. (2025). Tracing Indigenous Environmental Rights: A Critical View of International Human Rights Law, in Eichler, J. & Aguilera, M. G. (eds.), *Indigenous Environmental Rights: Towards a Holistic Regime*. Cambridge University Press.

Machado Aráoz, H. 2013. Crisis ecológica, conflictos socioambientales y orden neocolonial: Las paradojas de NuestrAmérica en las fronteras del extractivismo. *Revista Brasileira de Estudos Latino-Americanos*, 3(1), 118–155.

Macpherson, E., Torres Ventura, J., & Clavijo Ospina, F. (2020). *Constitutional Law, Ecosystems and Indigenous Peoples in Colombia: Biocultural Rights and Legal Subjects. Transnational Environmental Law*. Cambridge University Press.

Martin, P., Bigdeli, S. Z., Daya-Winterbottom, T., du Plessis, W., & Kennedy, A. (eds.) (2015). *The Search for Environmental Justice*. Edward Elgar.

Martinez-Alier, J. (2016). Global Environmental Justice and the Environmentalism of the Poor, in Gabrielsen, T., Hall, C., Meyer, J. M., & Schlosberg, D. (eds.), *The Oxford Handbook of Environmental Political Theory*. Oxford University Press.

Merrills, J. G. (2008). Environmental Rights, in Bodansky, D., Brunnée, J., & Hey, E. (eds.), *The Oxford Handbook of International Environmental Law*. Oxford University Press.

Mitnick, E. J. (2006). *Rights, Groups and Self-Invention: Group-Differentiated Rights in Liberal Theory*. Aldershot.

Montalván Zambrano, D. (2023). Naturalezas y Derechos. La representación de lo no-humano en la política, la filosofía y el derecho. PhD thesis, Madrid, Universidad Carlos III de Madrid.

Montalván Zambrano, D. & Wences, I. (2025). The Rights of Nature and the Right to Territory of Indigenous Peoples: Decolonising Ecocentrism, in Eichler, J. & Aguilera, M. G. (eds.), *Indigenous Environmental Rights: Towards a Holistic Regime.* Cambridge University Press.

Morales, S. (2018). Locating Oneself in One's Research: Learning and Engaging with Law in the Coast Salish World. *Canadian Journal of Women of the Law*, 30, 144–168.

Nursoo, I. (2018). Indigenous Law, Colonial Injustice and the Jurisprudence of Hybridity. *The Journal of Legal Pluralism and Unofficial Law*, 50(1), 56–70.

O'Donnell, E., Poelina, A., Pelizzon, A., & Clark, C. (2020). Stop Burying the Lede: The Essential Role of Indigenous Law(s) in Creating Rights of Nature. *Transnational Environmental Law*, 9(3), 403–247.

Oluborode Jegede, A. (2016). The Environmental and Economic Implications of the Climate Change and Extractive Industry Nexus in Africa. *Environmental Economics*, 7(4), 95–103.

Onazi, O. (2026). Development and Alternatives to Development, in Eichler, J. & Jovanović, M. (eds.), *Research Handbook of Collective Rights.* Edward Elgar Handbooks in Legal Theory. Edward Elgar Publishing.

Page, E. A. (2007). Intergenerational Justice of What: Welfare: Resources or Capabilities? *Environmental Politics*, 16(3), 453–469.

Perreault, T., Bridge, G., & McCarthy, J. (2015). *The Routledge Handbook of Political Ecology*. Routledge.

Rawson, A. & Mansfield, B. (2018). Producing Juridical Knowledge: "Rights of Nature" or the naturalization of rights? *Environment and Planning E: Nature and Space*, 1(1–2), 99–119.

Reed, G. & Thorsell, S. (2024). UN Framework Convention on Climate Change (UNFCCC), in IWGIA (ed.), *The Indigenous World 2024.* IWGIA.

Reguart-Segarra, N. (2025). The Religious Dimensions of Indigenous Environmental Rights: Disputes over Land and Pathways Forward, in Eichler, J. & Aguilera, M. G. (eds.), *Indigenous Environmental Rights: Towards a Holistic Regime.* Cambridge University Press.

Rodríguez Caguana, A. & Morales Naranjo, V. (2020). Los Derechos de la Naturaleza en Diálogo Intercultural: Una Mirada a la Jurisprudencia sobre los Páramos Andinos y los Glaciares Indios. *Deusto Journal of Human Rights*, 6, 99–123.

Rogers, N. & Maloney, M. (2017). *Law as if Earth Really Mattered: The Wild Law Judgement Project.* Routledge.

Sajeva, G. (2018). *When Rights Embrace Responsibilities: Biocultural Rights and the Conservation of Environment.* Oxford University Press.

Salas Astrain, R. & Pacheco Huaiquifil, C. (2025). Mapuche Law (*Az Mapu*), Legal Pluralism, and Transmodernity: Possibilities and Limitations of Contextual Environmental Justice, in Eichler, J. & Aguilera, M. G. (eds.), *Indigenous Environmental Rights: Towards a Holistic Regime.* Cambridge University Press.

Sánchez-Lasaballett, E. & González, Y. (2024). Traditional Knowledge and Intellectual Property Rights in Latin America: Towards a Decolonial Approach. *Revista Direito GV*, 20, 1–28.

Smith, L. T. (1999). *Decolonising Methodologies: Research and Indigenous Peoples*. Zed Books.

Solón, P. (2017). *Systemic Alternatives: Vivir Bien, Degrowth, Commons, Ecofeminism, Rights of Mother Earth and Deglobalisation*. Fundación Solón, Attac France, Focus on the Global South.

Sousa Santos B. de (2023). *Law and the Epistemologies of the South*. Cambridge University Press.

Sousa Santos, B. de (1987). Law: A Map of Misreading. Toward a Postmodern Conception of Law. *Journal of Law and Society*, 14(3), 279–302.

Special Rapporteur on Human Rights and the Environment. (1994). Ksentini Report 'Human Rights and the Environment: Final Report' by Fatma Zohra Ksentini.

Special Rapporteur on the Rights of Indigenous Peoples (2023). Green financing – a just transition to protect the rights of indigenous peoples – report of the special rapporteur on the human rights of indigenous peoples, by José Calí Tzay.

Special Rapporteur on the Rights of Indigenous Peoples (2017). Impact of climate change and climate finance on indigenous peoples' rights – report of the special rapporteur on the human rights of indigenous peoples, by Victoria Tauli-Corpuz.

Special Rapporteur on the Rights of Indigenous Peoples (2007). Report of the Special Rapporteur on the situation of human rights and fundamental freedoms of indigenous people, by Rodolfo Stavenhagen.

Svampa, M. (2019). *Las fronteras del neoextractivismo en América Latina: Conflictos socioamientales, giro ecoterritorial y nuevas dependencias*. transcript Verlag.

Tigre, M. A. & Rocha, A. (2025). *The Role of Advisory Opinions in International Law in the Context of the Climate Crisis*. Brill | Nijhoff.

Tomuschat, C. (2014). *Human Rights: Between Idealism and Realism*. Cambridge University Press.

Tully, J. (2008). *Public Philosophy in a New Key: Volume I Democracy and Civic Freedom*. Cambridge University Press.

Vasak, K. (1977). A 30 Year Struggle: The Sustained Effort to Give the Force of Law to the Universal Declaration of Human Rights. *UNESCO Courir*, 3(11), 29–32.

Venkateswar, S. & Hughes, E. (2011). *The Politics of Indigeneity: Dialogues and Reflections on Indigenous Activism*. Zed Books.

Walsh, C. (2009). *Interculturalidad, estado y sociedad. Luchas (de)coloniales de nuestra época*. Universidad Andina Simón Bolívar.

Watson, I. (2018). *Indigenous Peoples as Subjects of International Law*. Routledge.

Westra, L. S. (2011). *Human Rights: The Commons and the Collective*. University of British Columbia.

Wiessner, S. (2011). The Cultural Rights of Indigenous Peoples: Achievements and Continuing Challenges. *European Journal of International Law*, 22(1), 121–140.

Winter, C. J. (2022). *Subjects of Intergenerational Justice: Indigenous Philosophy, the Environment and Relationship*. Routledge.

Wright, C. & Tomaselli, A. (2019). *The Prior Consultation of Indigenous Peoples in Latin America: Inside the Implementation Gap*. Routledge.

Xanthaki, A. (2010). *Indigenous Rights and the United Nations Standards: Self-Determination, Culture and Land.* Cambridge University Press.
Yrigoyen Fajardo, R. Z. (2021). Hacia la Descolonización del Derecho y la Justicia desde el Pluralismo Jurídico Igualitario y los Derechos de los Pueblos Indígenas. Conferencias introductorias para el evento intercontinental sobre Colonialismo, Descolonización y Neocolonialismo desde la Justicia y el Bien Común. Comité Panamericano de Juezas y Jueces por los Derechos Sociales y la Doctrina Franciscana y Pontificia Academia de las Ciencias Sociales.
Yrigoyen Fajardo, R. Z. (2015). The Panorama of Pluralist Constitutionalism: From Multiculturalism to Decolonisation, in Rodrigo Garavito, C. (ed.), *Law and Society in Latin America: A New Map*. Routledge.

PART I

Amidst International Human Rights Law and Environmental Legal Landscapes

International Orders Examined

1
Tracing Indigenous Environmental Rights
A Critical View of International Human Rights Law

Jonathan Liljeblad

1.1 Introduction

The present chapter seeks to contribute to ongoing discourses regarding international human rights approaches supportive of Indigenous peoples' environmental rights. Specifically, the analysis focuses on the movement within international human rights law (IHRL) to direct greater attention to the relationships between Indigenous peoples and the environment while identifying inherent complexities. The analysis allows critical Indigenous studies literature to be applied to and to develop a critique of international human rights approaches on Indigenous environmental rights.

The following sections shall guide audiences unfamiliar with Indigenous critiques of international law, with a particular attention to Indigenous environmental rights. The discussion begins with a background review that summarizes the progress in international law regarding Indigenous environmental rights and surveys the Indigenous critiques against it. The chapter then turns to focus on international human rights, with discussion that commences with an explanation of the promise offered by IHRL to Indigenous claims to environmental rights, and then proceeds with a presentation of Indigenous critiques that view human rights approaches as being problematic for Indigenous peoples. The discussion notes the prescriptive implications resulting from the aforementioned critiques, and in a last step identifies conciliatory perspectives.

1.2 Terms and Methods

A number of points regarding terms and methods should be noted with respect to the following sections. With respect to terminology, the present analysis frames discussion through a critical Indigenous studies approach, which applies critical studies concepts regarding epistemes and positionality. First, *epistemes* refers to forms of understanding in knowledge production, with critical studies highlighting the issue of epistemic injustice wherein legal discourses privilege some approaches in reasoning over others (de Sousa Santos 2014; Pohlhaus 2012). Indigenous legal scholars, in particular, highlight the tendencies of prevailing State-based legal systems to adhere to Western epistemes that differ from Indigenous systems of knowledge (Black 2011; Hokowhitu et al. 2021; Watson 2015). Second, *positionality* denotes an individual's background and experiences that drive their personal point of view (Chua & Massoud 2024). Indigenous critics direct attention to the role of positionality in law, in that legal institutions exercising Western legal approaches will address issues in ways that differ from Indigenous communities holding to Indigenous traditions (Black 2011; Watson 2015).

Third, the present analysis notes that critical Indigenous arguments for the existence of Indigenous law deviates from positivist perspectives that see law as a phenomenon associated with the State, and hence that there is a distinction between Indigenous conceptions of rights – including those regarding the environment – versus positivist interpretations of rights as legal protections held by the State (Black 2011; Newman 2023; Watson 2018). To avoid confusion, the present analysis differentiates Indigenous *rights* to the environment from Indigenous *relations* with the environment: the nomenclature of *rights* is used in connection with positivist orientations of law as a product of State-centric legal orders, such that rights are legal rights as prescribed by States; in contrast, the appellation of *relations* reflects critical Indigenous literature that directs attention to Indigenous perspectives that are distinct from State-based legal regimes. Last, critical Indigenous arguments feature holistic conceptions of Indigenous relations with the environment as permeating the totality of Indigenous existence (Black 2011; Harriden 2023; Watson 2018), and in keeping with such a scope the analysis focuses on the plural term *rights* to environment rather than a singular *right* to the environment.

With respect to method, the analysis reflects on theory through use of primary and secondary sources. Primary source materials encompass international instruments, jurisprudence of international courts, and documents from international institutions including human rights treaty bodies and United Nations (UN) special procedures. Secondary source materials consist of scholarly works regarding Indigenous peoples in international law. Last, the analysis uses a capitalized "Indigenous" in keeping with current UN practice in identifying peoples (UN 2023; United Nations General Assembly [UNGA] 2024).

1.3 Background

The present discussion provides context for analysis, providing insights in two subsections: (1) developments in international law to support Indigenous environmental rights and (2) Indigenous critiques of such efforts.

1.3.1 Indigenous Environmental Rights in International Law Outside of Human Rights: An Overview

The development of Indigenous environmental rights in international law has occurred within broader Indigenous movements in global politics and law, with a range of transnational Indigenous coalitions mobilizing Indigenous engagement with the international regimes that arose in the latter half of the twentieth century (Hall & Fenelon 2009; Lightfoot 2016; Poyer 2017; Xanthaki 2009). The outcomes of such efforts testify to their effectiveness, with prominent examples appearing in the UN thematic campaigns for the 1994 International Decade of the World's Indigenous Peoples and 2005 Second International Decade of the World's Indigenous Peoples (UN 2021a). Accompanying the aforementioned efforts were the creation of institutions such as the UN Permanent Forum on Indigenous Issues (UNPFII) to host Indigenous voices within the UN headquarters; the Expert Mechanism on the Rights of Indigenous Peoples (EMRIP) to serve as an advisory body to the UN Human Rights Council (HRC); and the Special Rapporteur on the Rights of Indigenous Peoples to research and clarify UN positions on Indigenous issues (EMRIP 2021a; UN 2021a, 2021b, 2021c).

In terms of international law instruments, the preceding developments were accompanied by the formation of dedicated Indigenous rights instruments in the form of the 1989 International Labor Organization (ILO) Convention Number 169 (ILO 169), which presents binding duties upon State parties toward Indigenous peoples, and the 2007 UN Declaration on the Rights of Indigenous Peoples (UNDRIPS), which expresses nonbinding provisions on norms of conduct in the treatment of Indigenous peoples (ILO 169 1989; UNDRIPS 2007). Relevant provisions in each will be discussed in a subsequent section on international human rights law, but the present point is that both instruments address Indigenous rights broadly, encompassing a holistic range of issues such as autonomy, governance, participation and consent, education, culture, and intellectual property (ILO 169 1989; UNDRIPS 2007). Environmental rights are included, with provisions in both ILO 169 and UNDRIPS covering various aspects of Indigenous relations to the environment (Liljeblad 2024), with direct examples including the rights to territories and lands (ILO 169 1989: Art. 14; UNDRIPS 2007: Preamble and Art. 26); rights to resources (ILO 169 1989: Art. 15; UNDRIPS 2007: Art. 26); rights to development (ILO 169 1989: Art. 7; UNDRIPS 2007: Arts. 3, 20, and 23); and rights to subsistence, health, and life (ILO 169 1989: Arts. 14 and 25; UNDRIPS 2007: Arts. 7 and 20–24). Wider rights beyond ownership and use also extend from the language in ILO 169 and UNDRIPS (Liljeblad 2024), with examples such as rights to conservation and protection of the environment (UNDRIPS 2007: Art. 29); cultural and spiritual aspects of the environment (ILO 169 1989: Arts. 5 and 8; UNDRIPS 2007: Arts. 11–13); and rights to Indigenous group identity that involve its relationship with the environment (ILO 169 1989: preamble and Arts. 1 and 2; UNDRIPS 2007:

Arts. 2 and 33). The extent of the aforementioned rights falls under accompanying rights of autonomy and governance, which include the rights of self-determination and self-identification (ILO 169 1989: Preamble and Arts. 1 and 2; UNDRIPS 2007: Arts. 3–4 and 33); rights to participation (ILO 169 1989: Arts. 5, 6, 15, 18, and 33; UNDRIPS 2007: Arts. 5, 18, and 27); and rights regarding consultation and consent (ILO 169 1989: Art. 16; UNDRIPS 2007: Arts. 10–11, 15, 17, 19, 28–29, 30, 32, 36, and 38). Collectively, the preceding assembly of rights reflects the wide scope of Indigenous connections to the environment, and so articulates the idea of a general Indigenous right to environment as encompassing an ensemble of procedural and substantive rights that relate to various aspects of Indigenous existence associated with the environment.

Within the global movements for Indigenous peoples, the progress on Indigenous rights was paralleled by complementary developments in international environmental law (Boyle 2018; Special Rapporteur on Human Rights and Environment [SRHRE] 2017). Notable milestones were the inclusion of Indigenous issues in the 1992 UN Conference on Environment and Development and later in the 2018 Framework Principles on Human Rights and Environment (HRC 2018; United Nations Conference on Environment and Development [UNCED] 1992). More issue-specific events also occurred, with major moments occurring in connection to climate change and biodiversity. With respect to climate change, under the 1994 UN Framework Convention on Climate Change (UNFCCC), the Conference of the Parties in 2008 established the International Indigenous Peoples' Forum on Climate Change (IIPFCC) and in 2015 created the Local Communities and Indigenous Peoples Platform (LCIPP) (IIPFCC 2024; LCIPP 2024). The IIPFCC serves as a caucus for Indigenous peoples in UNFCCC activities, and the LCIPP functions to promote exchange of Indigenous knowledge, capacity-building, and advising on climate change policies and actions (IIPFCC 2024; LCIPP 2024). With respect to biodiversity, the 1993 Convention on Biological Diversity (CBD) references Indigenous peoples in Article 8(j), which calls for States to "respect, preserve, and maintain knowledge, innovations, and practices of Indigenous peoples and local communities" (CBD 2024: Art. 8). In 1996, the 3rd Conference of the Parties to the CBD established the International Indigenous Forum on Biodiversity (IIFB), which serves the role of a caucus coordinating Indigenous engagement with CBD programs of work (IIFB 2024). The work of the IIFB led to the eventual creation of the 2010 Nagoya Protocol, which focuses on access and sharing of benefits arising from genetic resources and traditional knowledge with Indigenous peoples (Nagoya Protocol 2010). In 2024, the 16th Conference of the Parties to the CBD decided to create a permanent Subsidiary Body for Article 8(j) dedicated to expanding the full and effective participation of Indigenous peoples in the workings of the CBD (United Nations Environment Programme [UNEP] 2024).

The preceding developments in international environmental law accompanied articulations of Indigenous environmental rights that paralleled elements in ILO

169 and UNDRIPS. For the UNFCCC, the 16th Conference of the Parties (CoP) issued the Cancun Agreements, which acknowledging the rights of Indigenous peoples contained in UNDRIPS, including rights to full and effective participation (Osakada 2020; UNFCCC 2010). Later, the 21st CoP published language calling for considerations of Indigenous rights in actions to address climate change and encompassing traditional Indigenous knowledge in country-based actions for adaptation to climate change (UNFCCC 2015). The 23rd CoP, in its Decision 2/CP.23 on the LCIPP, noted the connection of the LCIPP to both the Paris Agreement and UNDRIPS; the need for parties to the UNFCCC to promote Indigenous rights; and the principles of the LCIPP in promoting Indigenous rights in supporting traditional Indigenous knowledge, particularly the rights of free, prior, and informed consent (FPIC) (Osakada 2020; UNFCCC 2017). Hence, the UNFCCC acknowledged the rights in UNDRIPS, with specific reference to its rights to participation (UNDRIPS 2007: Arts. 5 and 18) and consent (UNDRIPS 2007: Arts. 10–11, 19, and 28–29). In comparison, the CBD also referenced Indigenous rights, but differed from the approach of the UNFCCC. Specifically, the main text of the CBD expresses rights to protection of traditional Indigenous knowledge in the conservation and sustainable use of Indigenous territories and resources therein (Convention on Biological Diversity 1992: Arts. 8 and 10). In addition, the Nagoya Protocol articulates prior and informed consent, and so only partially overlaps with UNDRIPS' identification of free, prior, and informed elements of consent (Nagoya Protocol 2010: Preamble, Arts. 6–7, 10, and 13–17; UNDRIPS 2007: Arts. 10–11, 19, and 28–29). The Nagoya Protocol language differs from ILO 169's formulation, which only involves free and informed consent (ILO 169 1989: Art. 16). The Nagoya Protocol also mentions the need for effective participation of Indigenous peoples in the use of traditional Indigenous knowledge, which echoes the provisions on participation in both UNDRIPS and ILO 169 (ILO 169 1989: Arts. 5, 6, 15, 18, and 33; Nagoya Protocol 2010: Art. 12; UNDRIPS 2007: Arts. 5 and 18).

Alongside the aforementioned events in the global climate change and biodiversity regimes, there have been more global statements which have encompassed Indigenous rights in international environmental law, with a prominent recent example being the 2018 publication of the Framework Principles on Human Rights and Environment (Framework Principles), which draw upon both UNDRIPS and ILO 169 in identifying principles for Indigenous environmental rights. Specifically, in the Framework Principles, Principle 14 recognizes the need for heightened State measures to protect indigenous peoples, and Principle 15 expects States to promote the rights of indigenous peoples, including rights to resources; rights to FPIC; rights for the protection of traditional knowledge; and rights to fair and equitable sharing of benefits (UN Special Procedures 2018). Principle 15, in expressing its slate of rights, draws upon the provisions dedicated to each within UNDRIPS and ILO 169 (UN Special Procedures 2018: Principle 15).

Outside of legal instruments, international environmental law has also developed potential opportunities for Indigenous peoples in customary international law. In particular, James Anaya and Siegried Wiessner, in their comments on UNDRIPS, observed that as much as its status as a declaration renders UNDRIPS nonbinding, it is still possible to identify specific content within it that holds the character of customary international law (Anaya & Wiessner 2007). Their reasoning extends to other instruments such as ILO 169, in that their reasoning implies that while ILO 169 is only legally binding upon its twenty-four State parties, its language may also contain rights that exist as customary international law. Anaya and Wiessner, in their global surveys of jurisprudence across national jurisdictions, highlighted several Indigenous rights that have become a part of customary international law through State practice: right to cultural identity, right to self-determination, and right to traditional lands (Anaya & Wiessner 2007). The claim of Indigenous rights in customary international law has also been supported by international legal jurisprudence, with the decision of the Inter-American Court on Human Rights (IACtHR) in the case of *Mayagna (Sumo) Awas Tingni Community v. Nicaragua* (2001)[1] stating in its English language translation that "there is a customary international law norm which affirms the rights of indigenous peoples to their traditional land" (IACtHR 2001: para. 140[d]).

1.3.2 Indigenous Critiques of Indigenous Rights in International Law

Although the above summary may appear to mark a progression of Indigenous rights in international law, it is relevant to qualify such impressions with concerns raised by Indigenous critics. The critiques relate to the exercise of environmental rights by Indigenous peoples in terms of potential avenues for legal action as well as the broader prospects for Indigenous peoples within the prevailing international legal system.

To begin, the issues regarding the exercise of Indigenous environmental rights in international law can be understood through the framework of relationships involved in their implementation: horizontal, vertical, and diagonal. Horizontal relationships in international law refer to the relationships between States, such as the mutual duties of States to other States arising from international instruments or customary international law (Banda 2019; Boyle 2018; Knox 2008). Horizontal relationships pose the possibility of extraterritorial legal actions, with a prominent example in international environmental law being the *Trail Smelter* arbitrations involving Canadian smelting operations that harmed the environment within the United States (Banda 2019; UN 2006). Vertical relationships relate to the rights and duties between a given State and entities within its jurisdiction. Vertical relationships entail cases of non-State actors pursuing legal claims against States, which feature in human rights litigation wherein individuals and groups undertake legal actions against their host State for violating their human rights (Knox 2010). The

[1] Jurisprudence specific to human rights approaches to Indigenous environmental rights is highlighted in Section 1.4 addressing IHRL.

vertical aspects of human rights impact discussions over a right to the environment, with movements in international environmental law using human rights to frame a right to environment as a way of aiding individual legal claims for harms to the environment (Knox 2020). Cases involving individuals who seek legal actions outside their host State entail conceptions of diagonal relationships. Within international environmental law, diagonal scenarios would entail extraterritorial environmental harms, with arguments over the duties of a State to individuals and groups located within the territory of another State (Aguilera 2023; DeBellis 2024; Knox 2010). Phrased within the discourse of a right to environment, the issues would center around the duties of a State to ensure that activities under its control that cause environmental harm outside its territorial boundaries did not violate the human rights to environment held by individuals and groups outside its territories (DeBellis 2024; Knox 2010).

There is jurisprudence supporting diagonal rights, with the IACtHR issuing in 2017 an advisory opinion articulating a cause-and-effect approach toward extraterritorial jurisdiction that found a State's duties extend to the human rights of victims outside the State's territory who are impacted by the State's action (Aguilera 2023; IACtHR 2017). With respect to international environmental law, the European Court of Human Rights more recently addressed the possibility of diagonal climate change litigation in the case of *Duarte Agostinho and Others v. Portugal and Others* (European Court of Human Rights [ECHR] 2024a), in which the court denied arguments for extraterritorial jurisdiction tied to the general diffusion of greenhouse gas emissions, but left open the possibility of extraterritorial jurisdiction for cases involving transboundary pollutants that can be traced to specific installations (DeBellis 2024; ECHR 2024a).

The differentiation between horizontal, vertical, and diagonal axes functions as a means of organizing the types of legal strategies available for Indigenous actions to exercise environmental rights. Horizontal approaches would look to State-to-State engagements, and so would relate to cross-jurisdiction cases where an environmental issue by one State affected another State. In such scenarios, an Indigenous community seeking relief for a transboundary environmental harm would rely on its host State to advocate on its behalf, with the host State engaging with the State whose territory hosts the source of the environmental harm to take action against that source (Banda 2019; Ellis 2012). In effect, the host State would function as a patron acting on behalf of its Indigenous populations against other States. Vertical actions would encompass domestic cases in which an Indigenous community engages legal strategies against its own host State for violations of that community's environmental rights. Diagonal actions would describe transboundary situations wherein an Indigenous community engages courts to charge another State for violations of international legal duties affecting the community's environmental rights, with specific example of nuisance torts undertaken by communities for pollution originating in another State (Boyle 2005; Percival 2010).

A common feature across the three axes is their orientation relative to the State. Horizontal relations look to State-to-State interactions, such that States are the primary focus in deliberating issues of rights and duties in international law. Vertical relations open considerations to include individuals and groups, and hence enable space for Indigenous activism, but still position such activism in relation to the State, with Indigenous claims aimed at the State and Indigenous legal actions working through State institutions of law. Similarly, diagonal conceptions encompass actions by individuals and groups against other States, but in doing so maintain an orientation that situates them in connection with a State. In effect, across the different axes, the State holds hegemony vis-à-vis Indigenous peoples, with the State being (1) the locus of Indigenous rights claims as a patron acting on behalf of Indigenous concerns, as in cases of horizontal relations; (2) a target charged with Indigenous rights violations, as in situations of vertical or diagonal relations; or (3) a provider of legal mechanisms to pursue remedies against States, as in scenarios of litigation in courts undertaken in vertical or diagonal relations.

The hegemony of the State raises concerns for Indigenous peoples because it echoes Indigenous critiques of international law. In particular, the literature identified as Fourth World Approaches to International Law (FWAIL) argues that the prevailing international legal system is a product of Western imperial history, with the process of European colonization spreading a Westphalian legal order that privileged colonial powers and subordinated Indigenous peoples (Bruyneel 2007; Fukurai 2020; Macklem 2008). Fourth World Approaches to International Law align with the critical perspectives of Third World Approaches to International Law (TWAIL) in terms of their attention to the mutually constitutive ties between global power structures and international law, but differs in that TWAIL adheres to a State-centric focus whereas FWAIL seeks to go beyond the State to cover alternative entities reflecting diverse Indigenous political and legal orders (Fukurai 2020; Liljeblad 2022). In particular, although FWAIL and TWAIL share critical arguments that movements for independence transformed the historical world of European empires into the current era of State, FWAIL proceeds to assert that the international system of States continues to a legacy of hegemony in terms of a power structure wherein States hold dominant positions of sovereignty over Indigenous populations (Alfred & Corntassel 2005; Bruyneel 2007; Macklem 2008). The general tenets of FWAIL are, inter alia, the constituting of diverse Indigenous groups as autonomous political and legal entities; critiques of an international legal order that centers States as the dominant unit of legal personality; and opposition to ongoing colonial legacies of subjugation and disempowerment of Indigenous peoples in international law (see, for example, Beier 2009; Koot 2023; Liljeblad 2022; Watson 2018).

For critical Indigenous scholars, the hierarchy privileging States over Indigenous peoples is problematic because States, even if not monolithic, do not necessarily produce benign results. Scholars such as Irene Watson, Aileen Moreton-Robinson, Brendan Hokowhitu, and Linda Tuhiwai Smith argue that post-independence

States adapted colonial systems of administration to consolidate their powers, and in doing so maintained colonial legacies of domination over Indigenous peoples (Hokowhitu et al. 2021; Moreton-Robinson 2016; Smith 2021; Watson 2018). States sustained the political, legal, and economic marginalization of Indigenous communities, denying Indigenous sovereignty and inhibiting Indigenous capacities for resistance and autonomy (Ross 2006; Stark 2016; Watson 2018). In addition, they pursued assimilation of Indigenous cultures, advancing Eurocentric forms of understanding that suppressed the ontologies, epistemologies, methodologies, and axiologies comprising Indigenous knowledge systems (Hokowhitu et al. 2021; Merino 2023; Moreton-Robinson 2015). The consequence is not merely the destruction of Indigenous societies but also the erasure of Indigenous identities (Alfred & Corntassel 2005; Anghie 2005; Bruyneel 2007; Macklem 2008; Wilson 2021).

The three axes representing approaches for legal action for Indigenous environmental rights falls within the critiques of critical Indigenous literature. Specifically, the disposition of horizontal, vertical, and diagonal approaches relative to States incurs the concerns of critical Indigenous voices regarding the continued hegemony of States over Indigenous peoples. To a degree, scholars of international Indigenous movements such as James Anaya, Siegfried Wiessner, Mark McMillan, and Sophie Rigney look to the progress achieved by Indigenous peoples in advancing Indigenous interests within the international system (Anaya & Wiessner 2007; McMillan & Rigney 2016). More critical perspectives, however, emphasize the contestation in international legal discourses that have impaired Indigenous agendas (Davis 2008; Osakada 2020; Watson 2018; White Face & Wobaga 2013). Yuko Osakada, for example, details the work of States to constrain the ambitions for Indigenous representation in the respective regimes of the CBD, in connection with IIFB and the crafting of the Nagoya Protocol, and the UNFCCC, in relation to the scope of powers imbued in the IIPFCC and LCIPP (Osakada 2020). Comparable critiques appear against international Indigenous rights instruments, with Athanasios Yupsanis, Lez Malezer, and Tracey Whare noting features in ILO 169 that exclude Indigenous self-determination, restrict Indigenous monitoring of its provisions, and delimit the scale of Indigenous rights to those compatible with domestic legal systems (Malezer 2020; Whare 2020; Yupsanis 2011). Similarly, Megan Davis, Charmaine White Face, and Zumila Wobaga provide parallel research regarding UNDRIPS, highlighting the ways in which States imposed compromises in the drafting of the declaration to circumscribe the preferences of Indigenous representatives and ensure the integrity of State sovereignty (Davis 2008; White Face & Wobaga 2013). Collectively, the aforementioned works are consistent with the concerns of critical Indigenous literature regarding the prospects for Indigenous peoples in systems of State hegemony, as self-determined actors in international law. The resulting implications are that Indigenous actions for environmental rights vis-à-vis States, whether through horizontal, vertical, or diagonal strategies, will be challenged by the privileged positions held by States.

1.4 International Human Rights Law: Accommodating Indigenous Environmental Rights

The present section turns attention to the potential of IHRL to mitigate such critiques. The first subsection below observes the promise offered by human rights in responding to the concerns of critical Indigenous scholarship regarding State hegemony in international law. The second subsection then draws upon the commentaries of critical Indigenous scholarship about the international human rights system itself, with analysis reflecting on the cautionary implications that should be observed in pursuing international human rights approaches on behalf of Indigenous environmental rights.

1.4.1 The Promise of IHRL to Indigenous Peoples

The character of the international human rights system presents potential for addressing Indigenous critiques against a State-centric international legal system, including the concerns over the prospects for Indigenous activism in international environmental law. Specifically, in regards to the structural hierarchy imposing State hegemony, international human rights bear the potential of reversing the relation of State authority and non-State actors, transforming State discretion into State duties to protect the rights of individuals and groups (Lane 2018). Moreover, in prescribing State duties, international human rights discourses focus not only on a given State's delimitation of its own treatment of human beings under its jurisdiction but also on that State's efforts to promote the observance of human rights of groups and individuals under its jurisdiction toward each other (Banda 2019). In essence, IHRL operates to alter conceptions of State sovereignty away from absolutist extremes of State power toward a delimitation of State conduct (Donnelly 2004, 2014). For Indigenous populations, such constraints upon States pose a potential shift in the relative positioning of power between Indigenous peoples and States, and hence offer a promise of greater political space for indigenous peoples to advance their environmental rights (Graham & Wiessner 2012; Mende 2015).

The critique of IHRL against State power is manifest in various ways. For example, with respect to legal instruments, the core instruments encompass the 1948 Universal Declaration of Human Rights (UDHR), as a base expression of aspirations for rights, and a range of international instruments such as the 1966 International Covenant on Civil and Political Rights (ICCPR), 1966 International Covenant on Economic, Social, and Cultural Rights (ICESCR), and others, whose provisions prescribe expectations for State conduct (Office of the High Commissioner for Human Rights [OHCHR] 2024a). A central tenet in the implementation of international human rights is that status as a State party to a human rights treaty renders a State as legally bound to fulfill the provisions embedded in treaty texts (van Aggelen 2019; OHCHR 2024b). A State party's duties arising from a given convention include several obligations: an obligation to respect, an obligation to protect, and an obligation to fulfill (Committee on Economic, Social, and Cultural Rights [CESCR] 2000; OHCHR 2016, 2024b). The obligation to respect is a negative one, in that it requires a State to restrain itself from interfering with the enjoyment of human rights (CESCR 1999a, 1999b). The obligation to protect is positive, with a preventative component expecting States to issue laws and take actions to prevent violations of human rights – not only those committed by the State, but also those committed by third parties (van Aggelen 2019; OHCHR 2024b) – and a remedial component expecting States to enable access to remedies to victims of human rights violations (CESCR 1999a; OHCHR 2016). The obligation to fulfill is also positive (CESCR, 1999a), and requires a State to enable the realization of human rights by pro-actively working to improve people's access and use of human rights (CESCR 1999b) as well as fostering "the legal, institutional, and procedural conditions that rights holders need" to fully enjoy their rights (Kalin & Kunzli 2009: 112; OHCHR 2016). In essence, a decision to become a State party to a human rights convention incurs a commitment to surrender State discretion in the treatment of human beings and hence reflects a voluntary commitment to circumscribe State power.

Beyond these instruments, similar constraints on State conduct are apparent in international human rights institutions, with the particular examples of accountability mechanisms in the Human Rights Council and the various human rights treaty bodies. To begin, the HRC conducts a Universal Periodic Review (UPR), which is a process that periodically evaluates the performance of each member in the UN General Assembly in meeting its human rights obligations (HRC 2024b). UPR is a peer-reviewed process, wherein each State undergoing review is subject to the scrutiny of a working group comprised of Member States in the HRC (HRC 2024b). In addition, each of the various international human rights conventions is accompanied by protocols that establish treaty bodies with complaint procedures (OHCHR 2013). Treaty monitoring bodies examine the performance of State parties in meeting the obligations established under their respective treaties, compiling reports of State compliance with the terms of a treaty as well as producing general comments that provide advice on implementation of provisions in a treaty (OHCHR 2024d; UN Research 2024). In addition, treaty body complaint procedures allow for individual complaints, with either victims or entities representing victims to bring claims of human rights violations by States as they are articulated in a human rights convention (Creamer & Simmons 2020; OHCHR 2024c; Ulfstein 2012). Both UPR and treaty body complaint procedures reflect a delimitation of State power in the sense that a State by virtue of being subject to UPR or a complaint procedure is indicating a surrender of State freedom in the treatment of individuals and groups and an acceptance of external scrutiny.

For Indigenous peoples, the international human rights system presents potential benefits in terms of bolstering the provisions in international Indigenous rights instruments, both in terms of binding character and global reach. With respect to binding character, international human rights law offers instruments placing legal obligations upon State parties. As much as declarations like UNDRIPS and UDHR function to provide a normative basis for rights, the slate of international human rights treaties presents an assembly of provisions that are legally binding for State parties. With respect to global reach, international human rights instruments feature a wider range of State parties compared to ILO 169, which hosts merely twenty-four State parties located predominately in Latin America (UN Collection 2024). In contrast, the ensemble of international human rights instruments spans a wider geographic scope of State parties who have accepted their provisions as binding. For example, the ICCPR was ratified by 173 State parties and the ICESCR counts 171 State parties, which suggests that the rights expressed within them are supported by a broader reach of States compared to the rights contained in ILO 169 (UN Collection 2024). The implication is that, to the extent that Indigenous rights can find correlating provisions in international human rights instruments, there is a potential for Indigenous peoples to use international human rights to strengthen efforts on behalf of Indigenous claims to environmental rights.

Indigenous ambitions for an instrumental use of human rights requires a framing of Indigenous environmental concerns as a human rights issue. Such an association is feasible, in that as much as the fields of international environmental law and IHRL exist as distinct fields, there have been growing efforts in international law discourses to build bridges between the two in greater recognition of the holistic interconnections between humans and the environment (see, for example, OHCHR 2020; Pathak 2014; Springer 2016; UNGA 2012). Such discourses view both areas of international law as being mutually complementary, with the idea of a human right to a healthy environment encompassing a reciprocal arrangement wherein a healthy environment is a contributing factor to the realization of human rights while the presence of effective human rights serves to enable actions to protect the environment (Boyle 2012; Knox 2020; Knox & Pejan 2018; Springer 2016; UNGA 2018a, 2018b). The international legal discourses over the nexus between the environment and human rights extends to include Indigenous peoples, both in terms of recognizing rights specific to Indigenous peoples and in terms of rights more generally for groups of people (Corrin 2009; Engel 2012; UNGA 2017).

For examples illustrating the association between Indigenous rights and human rights, it is helpful to highlight some of the Indigenous rights to environment within ILO 169 and UNDRIPS raised in previous sections. Starting with rights to territories and lands (ILO 169 1989: Art. 14; UNDRIPS 2007: Preamble and Art. 26), the Human Rights Committee (HR Committee) of the ICCPR has maintained in its responses to State party submissions that Indigenous rights to territories and lands are inherent to the right to self-determination contained in ICCPR Article 1 and the right to culture contained in ICCPR Article 27 (Ulfstein 2004). In particular, in its observations to a Canadian submission during its 65th session in 1999, the HR Committee referenced ICCPR Article 1 in noting that "the right to self-determination requires … that all peoples must be able to freely dispose of their natural wealth and resources and that they may not be deprived of their own means of subsistence" (HR Committee 1999: para. 8; Ulfstein 2004). In addition, the HR Committee raises ICCPR Article 27's application to land in its General Comment No. 23, which states that for Indigenous peoples "culture manifests itself in many forms, including a particular way of life associated with the use of land resources" and goes on to add that cultural rights "may require positive legal measures of protection and measures to ensure the effective participation of members ... in decisions which affect them" (HR Committee 1994: para. 7). Similarly, the CESCR, in its General Comment No. 21 on the right to culture in the ICESCR, asserts that there is an Indigenous right to culture which includes a right to traditional lands and which consequently requires States to recognize and protect the rights of Indigenous peoples to "own, develop, control, and use their communal lands, territories, and resources" (CESCR 2009: para. 36; Liljeblad 2024).

Next, following the above, the right to resources contained in UNDRIPS and ILO 169 (ILO 169 1989: Art. 15; UNDRIPS 2007: Art. 26) finds parallels with the wording of "natural wealth and resources" in the right to self-determination, which appears in Article 1 of both the ICCPR and the ICESCR (Liljeblad 2024). Continuing further, the Indigenous right to development (ILO 169 1989: Art. 7; UNDRIPS 2007: Arts. 3, 20, and 23) likewise is expressed in the text on self-determination referencing the right to freely pursue "economic, social, and cultural development" in Article 1 of both the ICCPR and ICESCR, but also has additional support in the language of the right to work in Article 6 of the ICESCR which calls for training programs to help achieve economic, social, and cultural development (ICCPR 1966: Art. 1; ICESCR 1966: Arts. 1 and 6). The Indigenous right to subsistence (ILO 169 1989: Art. 14; UNDRIPS 2007: Art. 20) also appears in Article 1's statement "In no case may a people be deprived of its own means of subsistence" (ICCPR 1966: Art. 1; ICESCR 1966: Art. 1). The Indigenous right to health (ILO 169 1989: Art. 25; UNDRIPS 2007: Arts. 20–24) correlates to ICESCR Article 12's recognition of a right "to the enjoyment of the highest attainable standard of physical and mental health" (ICESCR 1966: Art. 12), which is clarified by CESCR General Comment No. 14's description of health as encompassing individuals, society, and relationships with land (CESCR 2000). The right to life (UNDRIPS 2007: Art. 7) similarly becomes relevant given its appearance in the text of ICCPR Article 6, which in turn is supported by the HR Committee's General Comment No. 36, which reasons that the right to life depends on the preservation of the environment (HR Committee 2018). Such rationalization incurs an overlap with the right to conservation of the environment (UNDRIPS 2007: Art. 29), in that it connects the realization of a right to life with the assurance of protection for the environment. The right to conservation of the environment, however, also ties into the right to culture, with the HR Committee noting in General Comment No. 23 that in cases where Indigenous peoples are minorities, Article 27 of the ICCPR expects State parties to protect "a particular way of life associated with the use of land resources, especially in the case of Indigenous peoples" (HR Committee 1994: para. 7).

Proceeding onwards, the right to cultural and spiritual aspects of the environment (ILO 169 1989: Arts. 5 and 8; UNDRIPS 2007: Arts. 11–13) is supported by the right to religion in ICCPR Article 18 and the right to culture articulated by ICCPR Article 27 for minorities and ICESCR Article 15 for all populations. For Indigenous peoples, the relationship with the environment is raised by CESCR General Comment No. 21's extension of the right to culture to include rights to land, territories, and resources (CESCR 2009). The Indigenous right to group identity involves a right of self-identification (ILO 169 1989: preamble and Arts. 1 and 2; UNDRIPS 2007: Art. 33), which facilitates Indigenous exercise of that right to reference its relationship with the environment. International human rights instruments do not explicitly assert a right to self-identification, but the right to self-determination in Article 1 of the ICCPR and ICESCR does reference political, economic, social, and cultural qualities and hence provides a given Indigenous group a means of addressing those aspects of its identity (ICCPR 1966: Art. 1; ICESCR 1966: Art. 1). To a lesser degree, Indigenous rights regarding participation, consultation, and consent (ILO 169 1989: Arts. 5–6, 15–16, 18, and 33; UNDRIPS 2007: Arts. 5, 10–11, 15, 17–19, 27–29, 30, 32, 36, and 38) have a measure of overlap with the right to participation in public affairs expressed in ICCPR Article 25 to the extent that Indigenous peoples seek engagement in broader societal decision-making (ICCPR 1966: Art. 25). The ICESCR does not have a comparable provision, but CESCR General Comment No. 25 notes that State parties must "must provide educational and technological means" for Indigenous peoples to "participate in a global intercultural dialogue for scientific progress" (CESCR 2020: para. 40).

Within international law there is affirmation for the use of human rights to support Indigenous environmental rights. Of particular note are the complementary works of the UN Special Rapporteur for Human Rights and Environment (SRHRE) and the UN Special Rapporteur on the Rights of Indigenous Peoples (SRIP). The SRHRE has highlighted the status of Indigenous peoples as among the vulnerable groups especially susceptible to environmental harms, and has subsequently argued for the heightened duties of States to protect Indigenous relationships with the environment as an essential dimension to be considered in States' efforts to promote human rights (SRHRE 2017, 2018). The SRHRE has provided guidance on human rights that are relevant for Indigenous relationships with the environment, noting that they include "rights to life, health, food, water, housing, and culture" alongside rights to participation, consent, traditional territories and natural resources, benefits from those territories and resources, and access to remedies (SRHRE 2017: paras. 50–51). Similarly, the UN SRIP has also noted the existence of human rights relevant for Indigenous peoples in regards to environmental topics such as climate change, biodiversity conservation, and land and natural resources (SRIP 2016, 2017, 2022). Specifically, drawing upon the provisions of international human rights instruments and the commentaries of various human rights treaty bodies, the Special Rapporteur on the Rights of Indigenous Peoples argues that key human rights for protecting Indigenous environmental rights encompass procedural aspects of self-determination, non-discrimination, consultation and consent, participation, and redress and reparations (SRIP 2016: paras. 20–32; 2017, 2020a, 2020b: para. 49). In addition, the SRIP identifies human rights related to substantive aspects that include land and natural resources, development, food, water, health and physical well-being, adequate standard of living, and culture (SRIP 2016: paras. 20–32; 2017, 2020a, 2020b: para. 49). Further, the SRIP asserts Indigenous environmental rights as supporting human rights, observing that human rights violations stem from a lack of effective protections for Indigenous rights to traditional territories, lands, and natural resources (SRIP 2020a: para. 69). In particular, effective access and ownership of land is critical for the realization of other Indigenous rights (SRIP 2020c).

Complementing the above activities are contributions from other rapporteurs of the UN Human Rights Council (HRC), who have extended discussions of human rights for Indigenous peoples to other environmental issues. For example, the reports of the Special Rapporteur on the Implications for Human Rights of the Environmentally Sound Management and Disposal of Hazardous Substances and Wastes has identified toxic exposure to hazardous substances as an interference to Indigenous rights of self-determination, development, culture, and land (HRC 2022a). Another example is the Special Rapporteur on the Human Rights to Safe Drinking Water and Sanitation, whose publications have recognized Indigenous rights as encompassing a right to water, which is a human right acknowledged by the UNGA, HRC, and CESCR (HRC 2022b). Adding to such considerations are the reports of the Special Rapporteur on Violence against Women and Girls, who has asserted that violations of rights to land frequently create disproportionate impacts on Indigenous women, and so result in intersectional violations of human rights (HRC 2022c).

The body of rapporteurs falls under the Special Procedures of the HRC (HRC 2025). The HRC, however, also hosts attendant contributions from the Expert Mechanism on Rights of Indigenous Peoples (EMRIP). EMRIP has addressed Indigenous rights to lands, territories, and resources throughout its mandate. A notable example is the 2020 EMRIP statement to the UN General Assembly (UNGA) directly addressing the Indigenous right to land (EMRIP 2020). In that statement, EMRIP asserts the significance of land for Indigenous peoples, not only as an economic asset but also a "defining element of their identity and culture and their relationship to their ancestors and future generations" (EMRIP 2020, para. 5), with unique customs, traditions, and land tenure systems tied to collective forms of ownership (paras. 6–7). In addition, the statement comments that the protection of lands, territories, and natural resources is necessary to guarantee other Indigenous rights such as rights to life, culture, dignity, health, water, food, adequate standards of living, and development (EMRIP 2020, para. 11). Another example subsequent to the 2020 statement is a 2021 report on self-determination to the UNGA, which affirms a "direct link between self-determination and Indigenous peoples' rights over their own lands and resources" (EMRIP 2021b: para. 39) that encompasses holistic relationships between Indigenous cultures and lands, territories, and resources (EMRIP 2021b: para. 54). In the same year, EMRIP also published a report regarding Indigenous children that links both the right to self-determination and the right to traditional lands, territories, and resources with the ability to enjoy other rights such as the right to health and culture (EMRIP 2021c: para. 13).

Parallel to the efforts of the preceding bodies of the HRC is the work of the UN Permanent Forum on Indigenous Issues (UNPFII). The UNPFII is situated under the UN Economic and Social Council (ECOSOC) but has issued reports that have raised human rights issues involving Indigenous links to the environment. For example, the UNPFII has published recommendations noting that free, prior, and informed consent requires the full disclosure of information on human rights impacts to environmental, social, cultural, and spiritual rights (ECOSOC 2009). In addition, the UNPFII has sought to express the right to development in terms of Indigenous approaches that follow holistic understanding of collective rights, security, and self-governance of lands, territories, and resources (ECOSOC 2010). Further, the UNPFII has highlighted the harms brought by infrastructure projects and extractive industries in Indigenous territories upon Indigenous human rights defenders (ECOSOC 2017), Moreover, the UNPFII has affirmed its call for recognition of collective rights of Indigenous peoples to land, territories, and resources (ECOSOC 2018).

Attendant with the broader leadership provided by the above UN bodies are the contributions of human rights treaty bodies, which through their decisions, comments, and communications have strengthened the application of international human rights law to address cases involving Indigenous peoples and the environment. For example, the HRC for the ICCPR decided in *Campo Agua'ẽ of the Ava Guarani People v. Paraguay* (2021) that environmental damage can produce consequences for Indigenous communities that violate the rights to privacy, family, and home in ICCPR Article 17 and the right to culture for minorities contained in ICCPR Article 27. Specifically, the HR Committee cites its General Comment 16 to clarify that Article 17's right to privacy, family, and home encompasses Indigenous ways of life on their traditional territories (HRC 1994; 2022: paras. 8.3–8.4), and references its General Comment 26 to argue that Article 27 "enshrines the inalienable right of Indigenous peoples to enjoy the territories and natural resources that they have traditionally used for their subsistence and cultural identity" (HRC 1988; 2022: para. 8.6). The HRC adds that the aforementioned protections are accompanied by rights of effective participation; free, prior, and informed consent; proportionality between activities that interfere with Article 27 and the survival of the community; and effective remedy (HRC 2022: paras. 8.7–10). More recently, in *Daniel Billy et al v. Australia* (2022), the HRC decided that climate change can damage Indigenous traditional lands to an extent that it impairs Indigenous subsistence and culture, incurring violations of the rights to privacy, family, and home in Article 16 and the right to minority culture in Article 27 (HRC 2022: paras. 8.12 and 8.14). For its part, the CESCR asserts in its General Comment 14 that the right to health in ICESCR Article 12 encompasses Indigenous relations to land, stating that "the displacement of indigenous peoples against their will from their traditional territories and environment, denying them their sources of nutrition and breaking their symbiotic relationship with their lands, has a deleterious effect on their health" (CESCR 2000: para. 27). Later, in its General Comment 26, the CESCR explains that the right of self-determination in ICESCR Article 1 is linked to Indigenous land, in that Indigenous abilities to pursue political, economic, social, and cultural development and dispose of natural resources requires "land or territory in which they can exercise their self-determination" (CESCR 2022: para. 11). ICESCR General Comment 26 proceeds to observe that the rights of non-discrimination in Articles 2 and 3 extend to protect the rights of Indigenous peoples to traditional land and territories, including their spiritual relationships to land and water (ICESCR 2022: para. 16),

Other treaty bodies have also contributed to the human rights discourse regarding Indigenous peoples and the environment. A notable example is the Committee on the Elimination of Racial Discrimination (CERD), which dedicated General Comment 23 to the status of Indigenous peoples, with a particular call for States to "recognize and protect the rights of Indigenous peoples to own, develop, control, and use their communal lands, territories, and resources" (CERD 1997: para. 5). The CERD continued its treatment of Indigenous land and territories as involving discrimination issues falling within the scope of the International Convention on the Elimination of All Forms of Racial Discrimination (ICERD), with the CERD's position apparent in its decisions in *Lars-Anders Ågren et al. v. Sweden* (2020), which finds that a lack of measures for free, prior, and informed consent for projects on Indigenous territories was a form of discrimination that violated their rights to territories, ancestral resources, natural territories, and identity (CERD 2020: para. 6.7); *Yaku Guartambel v. Ecuador* (2022), which likewise stated that a failure to respect and protect Indigenous rights to traditional territories based in Indigenous customary law is also a form of discrimination regarding property rights (CERD 2022a: para. 4.7); and *Concluding Observations on Suriname* (2022), which noted that lack of protections for Indigenous property rights "in line with their traditions, customs, and land tenure systems" (CERD 2022b: para. 23) was a form of discrimination. Different aspects of the environment are addressed by the Committee on Rights of the Child (CRC). For example, in its General Comment 11, the CRC finds that the right to life in Article 6 and the right to standard of living in Article 27 both call on States to direct elevated attention to protect Indigenous children and the use of traditional land to maintain Indigenous culture (CRC 2009: paras. 34 and 35). Later, in its General Comment 26, the CRC argues that environmental harms have discriminatory impact on Indigenous children in violation of the right to non-discrimination in Article 2; that particular attention should be directed to preserving the traditional lands of Indigenous children to uphold the right to standard of living in Article 27; and that environmental harms such as climate change have a disproportionate impact on Indigenous cultures, and so threaten the right to culture in Article 30 (CRC 2023: paras. 14, 49, and 58). In addition, the CRC's *Concluding Observations on Costa Rica* (2020) asserts that environmental projects such as hydropower and protected areas must include Indigenous children in processes of free, prior, and informed consent (CRC 2020: para. 43(2)). More recently, in *Chiara Sacchi et al v. Argentina et al* (2021), the CRC issued a series of communications to State parties, with each communication making the common recognition that climate change impacts an Indigenous child's rights in the International Convention on Rights of the Child (ICRC), including the right to life in Article 3 and the right to culture in Article 30 (CRC 2021: paras. 3.5, 3.7, and 10.13).

The work of the Special Rapporteurs, EMRIP, UNPFII, and human rights treaty bodies builds upon jurisprudence from regional courts in Africa and Latin America. Specifically, in Africa, jurisprudence comes from the African Commission on Human and Peoples Rights (ACHPR) and the African Court on Human and Peoples' Rights (ACtHPR). The ACPHR issued prominent decisions in *SERAC and CESR v. Nigeria* (2001) and *CEMIRIDE v. Kenya* (2003). In *SERAC and CESR v. Nigeria* (2001), the ACHPR found that petroleum operations impacting the lands of the Ogoni people had violated their human rights contained in the 1981 African Charter on Human and Peoples Rights (African Charter), and in *CEMIRIDE v. Kenya* (2003) the ACHPR determined that the Kenyan government's eviction of the Endorois people to create a game reserve violated their human rights under the African Charter (ACHPR 2001, 2017). The ACtHPR extended such reasoning to international human rights, with its ruling in *ACHPR v. Kenya* (2017) finding that the Kenyan government eviction of the Ogiek people from their traditional forest violated not only their human rights under the African Charter but also analogous human rights in international human rights law (ACtHPR 2017).

In Latin America, comparable jurisprudence comes from the Inter-American Commission on Human Rights (IACHR) and the Inter-American Court of Human Rights (IACtHR). In strict chronological order, in *Mayagna (Sumo) Awas Tingni Community v. Nicaragua* (2001), the IACtHR decided that the Nicaraguan State's failure to protect Indigenous communal lands from development concessions violated human rights contained in the 1969 American Convention on Human Rights (IACtHR 2001). Later, in *Maya Indigenous Communities of the Toledo District v. Belize* (2004) the IACHR found that timber and petroleum concessions by the Belize State endangered the human rights of affected Mayan communities (IACtHR 2004). The IACtHR continued such findings with *Case of the Yakye Axa Indigenous Community v. Paraguay* (2005), recognizing the importance of ancestral territories for sustaining the traditional lifestyles, culture, identity, and group cohesion of Indigenous communities (IACtHR 2005). The IACtHR related its jurisprudence to international law outside the Americas in *Case of the*

Sawhoyamaxa Indigenous Community v. Paraguay (2006) and again in *Kichwa Indigenous People of Sarayaku v. Ecuador* (2012), which situated Indigenous relations with the environment as within the scopes of protection provided by UNDRIPS and ILO 169 (IACtHR 2005, 2012). The trend continued in *Saramaka People v. Suriname* (2007), with the IACtHR reasoning that the Indigenous right to communal property, right to use and enjoy natural resources, and right to control territory could be drawn from the provisions of the ICCPR (IACtHR 2007), thereby connecting Indigenous environmental rights to international human rights instruments. More recently, in *Case of the Indigenous Communities of the Llaka Honhat (Our Land) Association v. Argentina* (2020), the IACtHR found that the right to a healthy environment can be construed as being among the rights protected by the ACHR, and that Indigenous peoples are among the groups with heightened vulnerability to violations of that right (IACtHR 2020). Collectively, the aforementioned cases from Africa and Latin America reflect a progression in international law toward an acceptance of human rights approaches in support of Indigenous environmental rights.

1.4.2 Indigenous Critiques of International Human Rights Approaches

Despite the promise of human rights presented in the previous subsection for Indigenous environmental rights, there is a body of critical Indigenous scholarship that expresses diverse concerns about the use of human rights on behalf of Indigenous peoples. Critical Indigenous literature is not monolithic, but rather contains a range of perspectives with different arguments. The diversity of perspectives is apparent in the nuances of Indigenous positions regarding human rights, or, in other words, internal diversity. For example, scholars such as James Anaya and Victoria Tauli-Corpuz reflect viewpoints that see Indigenous rights as an element of the international human rights system (Anaya 2013; Tauli-Corpuz 2007). They are supported by works that see Indigenous rights as a product of ongoing movements for more group-specific human rights protections that situate Indigenous peoples alongside other vulnerable groups that include women, children, migrant workers, and people with disabilities (Anaya 2013; Barelli 2010; Kulchyski 2011). In contrast, other scholars such as Fiona MacDonald, Ben Wood, and Janne Mende prefer to differentiate Indigenous rights and human rights, with human rights discourses overlapping with Indigenous issues either because human rights address the individual and group rights issues that may occur within Indigenous communities or because human rights protections for diversity foster spaces that may accommodate unique Indigenous identities (Anaya 2004; MacDonald & Wood 2016; Mende 2015).

More extreme voices in critical Indigenous discourse perceive a conflict between Indigenous rights and human rights, arguing that the international human rights system continues to accord a hegemonic position of power to States and that States are an extension of colonial legacies that sought to dominate Indigenous societies.

Notable examples are the works of Kristin Carpenter and Angela Riley, Shannon Speed and Jane Collier, Fiona MacDonald and Ben Wood, and Churchill Ward, who see States using their status as primary duty-holders under international human rights to legitimize the assimilation of Indigenous peoples into regimes of property and capitalism (Carpenter & Riley 2014), the acculturation of Indigenous communities into wider mainstream populations (Speed & Collier 2000; Ward 2011), and the suppression of Indigenous legal orders beneath the legal systems of the State and international community (Carpenter & Riley 2014; MacDonald & Wood 2016). In effect, the aforementioned critiques perceive States as claiming that their obligations under the international human rights system requires States to bring conflicting Indigenous cultures into alignment with international human rights norms. For such critics, States are manipulating their duties to human rights to justify the continuation of State sovereignty and attendant colonial legacies subordinating Indigenous peoples. Such arguments contradict conceptions of human rights as offering protection for Indigenous peoples against States. Rather, the implication of the aforementioned critiques is that Indigenous peoples have no opportunities for vertical or diagonal actions through human rights, since they see the international human rights system as being co-opted by States and hence as being an instrument of State interests against Indigenous peoples.

Other examples of critical Indigenous scholarship target the conceptual foundations of human rights as a whole. For example, Fiona MacDonald, Ben Wood, and Peter Kulchyski distinguish the aspirations of human rights and Indigenous rights, asserting that the international human rights system holds to normative ideals of universalism that drive efforts for equality while Indigenous rights hold normative ideals of distinctiveness which protect each Indigenous group's unique identity (Kulchyski 2011; MacDonald & Wood 2016). Peter Kulchyski and Ulf Dahre claim that there is little accommodation by human rights of Indigenous rights, arguing that rights discourses exhibit a hierarchy that privileges human rights over Indigenous rights whenever there is a conflict between liberal individualism and Indigenous group values (Dahre 2010; Kulchyski 2011). Jennifer Hendry and Melissa Tatum go further to question the appropriateness of rights-based approaches as such, reasoning that a framework centered on rights builds on the premise of a contestation between rights victims and rights violators, which they see as conflicting with Indigenous approaches which trend toward outcomes that are restorative not only for the affected parties but the larger community as a whole (Hendry & Tatum 2016). Underlying much of the aforementioned body of critiques is a concern that dealing with the social world through rights-based approaches is tied to Western-based forms of reasoning, and hence a continuation of colonial legacies that sought to suppress the existence of Indigenous knowledge systems (Carpenter & Riley 2014; Hendry & Tatum 2016). In essence, the collective argument of the preceding assembly of critiques reasons that human rights approaches are inappropriate for Indigenous peoples because human rights discourses make use of norms, meanings, and reasoning that are different from Indigenous cultures and thereby lead to outcomes divergent from Indigenous expectations.

The preceding arguments raised by Indigenous critics of human rights – both those opposed to the hegemonic position of States and those resistant to the conceptual foundations of human rights – echo the broader positions of critical Indigenous scholarship about the colonial legacies of international law, including international environmental law. Specifically, the critiques regarding the continued hegemony of States within IHRL parallel the commentaries of scholars such as Irene Watson, Heidi Kiiwetinepinesiik Stark, and Rupert Ross, who assert that the prevailing international system accords a dominant position to States at the expense of Indigenous sovereignty (Ross 2006; Stark 2016; Watson 2018). In addition, the critiques against the conceptual foundations of human rights evoke the works of scholars such as Roger Merino, Brendan Hokowhitu, and Aileen Moreton-Robinson, who charge the international system as benefiting from Eurocentric approaches that suppress the perspectives of Indigenous knowledge systems (Hokowhitu et al. 2021; Merino 2023; Moreton-Robinson 2015). As a consequence, the scholarship summarized in preceding paragraphs brings human rights under the umbrella of critiques held by critical Indigenous literature against international law and international environmental law.

1.5 Conclusion

The discussion of the sections above sought to highlight complexities in the use of human rights in the field of Indigenous environmental rights. The analysis focused on identifying the concerns raised by Indigenous peoples regarding the international human rights system, drawing upon perspectives in critical Indigenous literature. The more extreme arguments of critical Indigenous scholarship against the international human rights system might be construed as rejecting IHRL for Indigenous peoples. Such a position, however, incites a call for further inquiry regarding alternatives, with two potential directions for future research. First, the resistance to State hegemony incurs a question as to whether there can be a world without State hegemony – in particular, is it possible to have an international human rights system built on non-State actors, especially one whose power structure would accord Indigenous peoples status equal or greater to others? Second, the opposition to the conceptual formulation of human rights poses a challenge for articulating an Indigenous alternative. In essence, it points to the question of whether there can be an Indigenous construction of human rights consistent with Indigenous ways of understanding? Both questions present areas for discourse open to insights from future studies.

The tensions between human rights and Indigenous rights are not necessarily irreconcilable, with various Indigenous scholars asserting that despite related challenges, Indigenous peoples can still find utility in the IHRL system. For example,

Lillian Miranda, James Anaya, Kristen Carpenter, and Angela Riley explore ways by which Indigenous peoples can use the IHRL system to advance Indigenous agendas (Anaya 2013; Carpenter & Riley 2014; Miranda 2010). Classical human rights may not fully address the full gamut of Indigenous concerns (Carpenter & Riley 2014), yet they may supplement other strategies supporting Indigenous interests. Indigenous peoples, in effect, can integrate human rights strategies as an element within broader campaigns of action encompassing diverse activities advancing Indigenous agendas (Miranda 2010). The analysis undertaken in the preceding sections does not necessarily contradict such arguments and instead should be seen as complementing them by engaging more profoundly with the complexities facing Indigenous claims for environmental rights in the IHRL system. The analysis worked to denote nuances that both support and challenge the use of IHRL for Indigenous environmental rights, and thereby informs the agendas of Indigenous activists who follow the arguments of figures like Miranda, Anaya, Carpenter, and Riley. Developing such an understanding would be key for advocates for Indigenous rights to be able to formulate more sophisticated strategies to advance the interests of Indigenous peoples in the international legal system.

References

African Commission on Human and Peoples Rights (ACHPR). (2009). *Centre for Minority Rights Development (CEMIRIDE) and Minority Rights Group International on behalf of Endorois Welfare Council v. Kenya, Communication No. 276/2003, 27th Activity Report, June 2009–November 2009.* Available at: www.hrw.org/sites/default/files/related_material/2010_africa_commission_ruling_0.pdf.

African Commission on Human and Peoples Rights (ACHPR). (2001). *Social & Economic Rights Action Center (SERAC) and Center for Economic and Social Rights (CESR) v. Nigeria, Communication No. 155/96.* Available at: www.worldcourts.com/achpr/eng/decisions/2001.10.27_SERAC_v_Nigeria.htm.

African Court on Human and Peoples Rights (ACtHPR). (2022). *African Commission on Human & Peoples' Rights v. Republic of Kenya 006/2012 (Reparations).* Available at: www.african-court.org/cpmt/storage/app/uploads/public/62b/aba/fd8/62babafd8d467689318212.pdf.

African Court on Human and Peoples Rights (ACtHPR). (2017). *African Commission on Human & Peoples' Rights v. Republic of Kenya 006/2012.* Available at: www.african-court.org/cpmt/storage/app/uploads/public/5f5/5fe/9a9/5f55fe9a96676974302132.pdf.

Aguilera, M. (2023). *Environmental Human Rights: New Thinking from Latin America and the Caribbean.* Brill.

Alfred, T. & Corntassel, J. (2005). Being Indigenous: Resurgences against Contemporary Colonialism. *Government & Opposition*, 40(4), 597–614.

Anaya, J. (2013). The Human Rights of Indigenous Peoples: United Nations Developments. *University of Hawaii Law Review*, 35, 983–1012.

Anaya, J. (2004). International Human Rights and Indigenous Peoples: The Move toward the Multicultural State. *Arizona Journal of International and Comparative Law*, 21(1), 13–62.

Anaya, J. & Wiessner, S. (2007). The UN Declaration on the Rights of Indigenous Peoples: Towards Re-empowerment. *Juristnews*. Available at: www.jurist.org/commentary/2007/10/un-declaration-on-rights-of-indigenous-2/.

Anghie, A. (2005). *Imperialism, Sovereignty, and the Making of International Law*. Cambridge University Press.

Banda, M. (2019). Regime Congruence: Rethinking the Scope of State Responsibility for Transboundary Environmental Harm. *Minnesota Law Review*, 103, 1879–1959.

Barelli, M. (2010). The Interplay between Global and Regional Human Rights Systems in the Construction of the Indigenous Rights Regime. *Human Rights Quarterly*, 32, 951–979.

Beier, J. M. (2009). *Indigenous Diplomacies*. Palgrave Macmillan.

Black, C. (2011). *The Land Is the Source of the Law*. Routledge.

Boyle, A. (2018). Climate Change, the Paris Agreement, and Human Rights. *International & Comparative Law Quarterly*, 67(4), 759–777.

Boyle, A. (2012). Human Rights and the Environment: Where Next? *European Journal of International Law*, 23: 613–642.

Boyle, A. (2005). Globalising Environmental Liability: The Interplay of National and International Law. *Journal of Environmental Law*, 17(1), 3–26.

Bruyneel, K. (2007). *The Third Space of Sovereignty: The Postcolonial Politics of US–Indigenous Relations*. University of Minnesota Press.

Carpenter, K. & Riley, A. (2014). Indigenous Peoples and the Jurisgenerative Moment in Human Rights. *California Law Review*, 102(1), 173–234.

Chua, L. & Massoud, M. (eds.). (2024). *Out of Place: Fieldwork and Positionality in Law and Society*. Cambridge University Press.

Committee on Economic, Social, and Cultural Rights (CESCR). (2022). *General Comment 26 (2022) on Land and Economic, Social, and Cultural Rights, E/C.12/GC/26*. Available at: www.ohchr.org/en/documents/general-comments-and-recommendations/ec12gc26-general-comment-no-26-2022-land-and.

Committee on Economic, Social, and Cultural Rights (CESCR). (2020). *General Comment 14, The Right to the Highest Attainable Standard of Health, E/C.12/2000/4*. Available at: https://tbinternet.ohchr.org/_layouts/15/treatybodyexternal/Download.aspx?symbolno=E%2FC.12%2F2000%2F4&Lang=en.

Committee on Economic, Social, and Cultural Rights (CESCR). (2020). *General Comment 25 on Science and Economic, Social, and Cultural Rights, E/C.12/GC/25*. Available at: https://docs.un.org/en/E/C.12/GC/25.

Committee on Economic, Social, and Cultural Rights (CESCR). (2009). *General Comment 21, Right of Everyone to Take Part in Cultural Life, E/C.12/GC/21/REV.1*. Available at: https://tbinternet.ohchr.org/_layouts/15/treatybodyexternal/Download.aspx?symbolno=E%2FC.12%2FGC%2F21%2FREV.1&Lang=en.

Committee on Economic, Social, and Cultural Rights (CESCR). (2000). *General Comment 14, The Right to the Highest Attainable Standard of Health, E/C.12/2000/4*. Available at: https://tbinternet.ohchr.org/_layouts/15/treatybodyexternal/Download.aspx?symbolno=E%2FC.12%2F2000%2F4&Lang=en.

Committee on Economic, Social, and Cultural Rights (CESCR). (1999a). *General Comment 13, The Right to Education, E/C.12/1999/10*. Available at: https://tbinternet.ohchr.org/_layouts/15/treatybodyexternal/Download.aspx?symbolno=E%2FC.12%2F1999%2F10&Lang=en.

Committee on Economic, Social, and Cultural Rights (CESCR). (1999b). *General Comment 12, Right to Adequate Food (Art. 11), E/C.12/1999/5*. Available at: https://tbinternet.ohchr.org/_layouts/15/treatybodyexternal/Download.aspx?symbolno=E%2FC.12%2F1999%2F5&Lang=en.

Committee on the Elimination of All Forms of Racial Discrimination (CERD). (2022a). *Opinion Adopted by the Committee Under Article 14 of the Convention, Concerning Communication No. 61/2017, CERD/C/106/D/61/2017*. Available at: https://tbinternet.ohchr.org/_layouts/15/treatybodyexternal/Download.aspx?symbolno=CERD%2FC%2F106%2FD%2F61%2F2017&Lang=en.

Committee on the Elimination of All Forms of Racial Discrimination (CERD). (2022b). *Concluding Observations on the Combined Sixteenth to Eighteenth Periodic Reports of Suriname, CERD/C/SUR/CO/16–18*. Available at: https://tbinternet.ohchr.org/_layouts/15/treatybodyexternal/Download.aspx?symbolno=CERD%2FC%2FSUR%2FCO%2F16-18&Lang=en.

Committee on the Elimination of All Forms of Racial Discrimination (CERD). (2020). *Opinion Adopted by the Committee Under Article 14 of the Convention, Concerning Communication No. 54/2013, CERD/C/102/D/54/2013*. Available at: https://tbinternet.ohchr.org/_layouts/15/treatybodyexternal/Download.aspx?symbolno=CERD%2FC%2F102%2FD%2F54%2F2013&Lang=en.

Committee on the Elimination of All Forms of Racial Discrimination (CERD). (1997). *General Recommendation 23 on the Rights of Indigenous Peoples A/52/18 Annex V*. Available at: https://tbinternet.ohchr.org/_layouts/15/treatybodyexternal/TBSearch.aspx?Lang=en&TreatyID=6&DocTypeID=11&ctl00_PlaceHolderMain_radResultsGridChangePage=2.

Committee on Rights of the Child (CRC). (2023). *General Comment No. 26 (2023) on Children's Rights and the Environment, with a Special Focus on Climate Change, CRC/C/GC/26*. Available at: www.ohchr.org/en/documents/general-comments-and-recommendations/crccgc26-general-comment-no-26-2023-childrens-rights.

Committee on Rights of the Child (CRC). (2021). *Chiara Sacchi, et al v. Argentina, et al* (2021). Available at: https://tbinternet.ohchr.org/_layouts/15/treatybodyexternal/SessionDetails1.aspx?SessionID=1351&Lang=en.

Committee on Rights of the Child (CRC). (2020). *Concluding Observations on the Combined Fifth and Sixth Periodic Reports of Costa Rica, CRC/C/CRI/CO/5–6*. Available: https://tbinternet.ohchr.org/_layouts/15/treatybodyexternal/Download.aspx?symbolno=CRC%2FC%2FCRI%2FCO%2F5-6&Lang=en.

Committee on Rights of the Child (CRC). (2009). *General Comment No. 11 (2009) Indigenous Children and Their Rights Under the Convention, CRC/C/GC/11*. Available at: www2.ohchr.org/english/bodies/crc/docs/gc.11_indigenous_new.pdf.

Convention on Biological Diversity. (2024). *Article 8. In Situ Conservation*. Available at: www.cbd.int/convention/articles/default.shtml?a=cbd-08.

Corrin, J. (2009). From Horizontal and Vertical to Lateral: Extending the Effect of Human Rights in Post Colonial Legal Systems of the South Pacific. *International & Comparative Law Quarterly*, 58, 31–71.

Creamer, C. & Simmons, B. (2020). The Proof Is in the Process: Self-Reporting Under International Human Rights Treaties. *American Journal of International Law*, 114(1), 1–50.

Dahre, U. J. (2010). There Are No Such Things as Universal Human Rights – On the Predicament of Indigenous Peoples, For Example. *International Journal of Human Rights*, 14(5), 641–657.

Davis, M. (2008). Indigenous Struggles in Standard-Setting: The United Nations Declaration on the Rights of Indigenous Peoples. *Melbourne Journal of International Law*, 9, 439–471.

DeBellis, M. (2024). Transnational Climate Change Litigation. *Italian Journal of Public Law*, 16(2), 438–459.

De Sousa Santos, B. (2014). *Epistemologies of the South: Justice Against Epistemicide.* Paradigm Publishers.

Donnelly, J. (2014). State Sovereignty and International Human Rights. *Ethics & International Affairs*, 28(2), 225–238.

Donnelly, J. (2004). State Sovereignty and Human Rights. *Human Rights & Human Welfare*, 4(1). Available at: https://digitalcommons.du.edu/hrhw/vol4/iss1/38/.

Economic and Social Council (ECOSOC). (2000). Establishment of a Permanent Forum on Indigenous Issues, Resolution 2000/22, E/2000/22. Available at: www.un.org/esa/socdev/unpfii/documents/about-us/E-RES-2000-22.pdf.

Economic and Social Council (ECOSOC). (2018). Permanent Forum on Indigenous Issues, Report on the Seventeenth Session (16–27 April 2018), E/2018/43*–E/C.19/2018/11*. Available at: www.un.org/development/desa/indigenouspeoples/permanent-forum-session-reports.html.

Economic and Social Council (ECOSOC). (2017). Permanent Forum on Indigenous Issues, Report on the Sixteenth Session (24 April–5 May 2017), E/2017/43-E/C.19/2017/11. Available at: www.un.org/development/desa/indigenouspeoples/permanent-forum-session-reports.html.

Economic and Social Council (ECOSOC). (2010). Permanent Forum on Indigenous Issues, Report on the Ninth Session (19–30 April 2010), E/2010/43-E/C.19/2010/15. Available at: www.un.org/development/desa/indigenouspeoples/permanent-forum-session-reports.html.

Economic and Social Council (ECOSOC). (2009). Permanent Forum on Indigenous Issues, Report on the Eighth Session (18–29 May 2009), E/2009/43-E/C.19/2009/14. Available at: www.un.org/development/desa/indigenouspeoples/permanent-forum-session-reports.html.

Economic and Social Council (ECOSOC). (1996). *Report of the Working Group Established in Accordance with Commission on Human Rights Resolution 1995/32 of 3 March 1995, E/CN.4/1996/84*. Office of the High Commissioner for Human Rights. Available at: https://ap.ohchr.org/documents/alldocs.aspx?doc_id=780.

Ellis, J. (2012). Extraterritorial Exercise of Jurisdiction for Environmental Protection: Addressing Fairness Concerns. *Leiden Journal of International Law*, 25, 397–414.

Engel, D. (2012). Vertical and Horizontal Perspectives on Rights Consciousness. *Indiana Journal of Global Legal Studies*, 19, 423–455.

European Court of Human Rights (ECHR). (2024a). Grand Chamber, Duarte Agostinho & Others v. Portugal & Others, Application No. 39371/20, *Decision 9 April 2024.*

European Court of Human Rights (ECHR). (2004b). *Case of Ilascu & Others v. Moldova & Russia, Application No. 48787/99.* Available at: https://hudoc.echr.coe.int/fre#{%22itemid%22:[%22001-61886%22]}.

Expert Mechanism on the Rights of Indigenous Peoples (EMRIP). (2024). *Expert Mechanism on the Rights of Indigenous Peoples.* Office of the High Commissioner for Human Rights. Available at: www.ohchr.org/EN/Issues/IPeoples/EMRIP/Pages/EMRIPIndex.aspx.

Expert Mechanism on the Rights of Indigenous Peoples (EMRIP). (2021a). *Expert Mechanism on the Rights of Indigenous Peoples.* Office of the High Commissioner for Human Rights (OHCHR). Available at: www.ohchr.org/EN/Issues/IPeoples/EMRIP/Pages/EMRIPIndex.aspx.

Expert Mechanism on the Rights of Indigenous Peoples (EMRIP). (2021b). *Efforts to Implement the United Nations Declaration on the Rights of Indigenous Peoples: Indigenous Peoples and the Right to Self-Determination, A/HRC/48/75.* Available at: https://docs.un.org/A/HRC/48/75.

Expert Mechanism on the Rights of Indigenous Peoples (EMRIP). (2021c). *Rights of the Indigenous Child Under the United Nations Declaration on the Rights of Indigenous Peoples, A/HRC/48/74.* Available at: https://docs.un.org/A/HRC/48/74.

Expert Mechanism on the Rights of Indigenous Peoples (EMRIP). (2020). *Right to Land Under the United Nations Declaration on the Rights of Indigenous Peoples: A Human Rights Focus, A/HRC/45/38.* Available at: https://docs.un.org/A/HRC/45/38.

Fukurai, Hi. (2020). The Decoupling of the Nation and the State: Constitutionalizing Transnational Nationhood, Cross-Border Connectivity, Diaspora, and "National" Identity-Affiliation in Asia and Beyond. *Asian Journal of Law & Society*, 7(2020), 1–4.

Graham, L. & Wiessner, S. (2012). Indigenous Sovereignty, Culture, and International Human Rights Law. Suffolk University Law School Research Paper No. 12–04. Available at: https://papers.ssrn.com/sol3/papers.cfm?abstract_id=1980835.

Hall, T. & Fenelon, J. (2009). *Indigenous Peoples and Globalization.* Paradigm Publishers.

Harriden, K. (2023). Working with Indigenous Science(s) Frameworks and Methods: Challenging the Ontological Hegemony of 'Western' Science and the Axiological Biases of Its Practitioners. *Methodological Innovations*, 16(2), 201–214.

Hendry, J. & Tatum, M. (2016). Human Rights, Indigenous Peoples, and the Pursuit of Justice. *Yale Law & Policy Review*, 34(2), 351–386.

Hokowhitu, B., Moreton-Robinson, A., Tuhiwai-Smith, L., Andersen, C., & Larkin, S. (eds.). (2021). *Handbook of Critical Indigenous Studies.* Routledge.

Human Rights Committee (HR Committee). (2022). View Adopted by the Committee Under Article 5(4) *of the Optional Protocol, Concerning Communication No. 2552/2015, CCPR/C/132/D/2552/2015.* Available at: https://docs.un.org/CCPR/C/132/D/2552/2015.

Human Rights Committee (HR Committee). (2023). Views Adopted by the Committee Under Article 5(4) of the Optional Protocol, Concerning Communication No. 3624/2019, CCPR/C/135/D/3624/2019. Available at: https://docs.un.org/CCPR/C/135/D/3624/2019.

Human Rights Committee (HR Committee). (2018). General Comment No. 36, *Article 6: Right to Life, CCPR/C/GC/36*. Available at: https://documents.un.org/doc/undoc/gen/g19/261/15/pdf/g1926115.pdf.

Human Rights Committee (HR Committee). (1999). *United Nations Human Rights Concluding Observations: Canada, CCPR/C/79/Add.105*. Available at: https://documents.un.org/doc/undoc/gen/n99/099/27/pdf/n9909927.pdf.

Human Rights Committee (HR Committee). (1997). *Views: Communication No. 549/1993, CCPR/C/60/D/549/1993/Rev.1*. Available at: https://tbinternet.ohchr.org/_layouts/treatybodyexternal/Download.aspx?symbolno=CCPR%2FC%2F60%2FD%2F549%2F1993%2FRev.1&Lang=en.

Human Rights Committee (HR Committee). (1994). General Comment No. 23(5*)(Art. 27), CCPR/C/21/Rev.1/Add.5*. Available at: https://tbinternet.ohchr.org/_layouts/15/treatybodyexternal/Download.aspx?symbolno=CCPR%2FC%2F21%2FRev.1%2FAdd.5&Lang=en.

Human Rights Committee (HR Committee). (1988). *General Comment No. 16: Article 17, Thirty-Second Session*. Available at: www.ohchr.org/en/treaty-bodies/general-comments.

Human Rights Council (HRC). (2025). *Special Procedures of the Human Rights Council*. Available at: www.ohchr.org/en/special-procedures-human-rights-council/special-procedures-human-rights-council.

Human Rights Council (HRC). (2024a). *Sub-Commission on the Promotion and Protection of Human Rights (previously: Sub-Commission on Prevention of Discrimination and Protection of Minorities)*. Available at: www.ohchr.org/en/hr-bodies/sc/sub-commission#:~:text=The%20Sub%2DCommission's%20main%20functions,to%20carry%20out%20any%20other.

Human Rights Council (HRC). (2024b). *Universal Periodic Review*. Available at: www.ohchr.org/en/hr-bodies/upr/upr-home.

Human Rights Council (HRC). (2024c). *Universal Periodic Review: A Guide for Civil Society for the Fourth Cycle*. Available at: www.ohchr.org/sites/default/files/documents/hrbodies/upr/sessions/2022-10-24/UPR-4th-cycle-civil-society-guide.pdf.

Human Rights Council (HRC). (2024d). *4th UPR Cycle: Contributions and Participation of "Other Stakeholders" in the UPR*. Available at: www.ohchr.org/en/hr-bodies/upr/ngos-nhris.

Human Rights Council (HRC). (2022a). *Implications for Human Rights of the Environmentally Sound Management & Disposal of Hazardous Substances and Wastes, A/77/183*. Available at: https://docs.un.org/A/77/183.

Human Rights Council (HRC). (2022b). *Report of the Special Rapporteur on the Human Rights to Safe Drinking Water and Sanitation, Pedro Arrojo Agudo, A/HRC/51/24*, Available: https://docs.un.org/A/HRC/51/24.

Human Rights Council (HRC). (2022c). *Report of the Special Rapporteur on Violence against Women, Its Causes and Consequences, Reem Alsalem, A/HRC/50/26*. Available at: https://docs.un.org/A/HRC/50/26.

Human Rights Council (HRC). (2018). *Framework Principles on Human Rights and the Environment A/HRC/37/59*. Available at: www.ohchr.org/EN/Issues/Environment/SREnvironment/Pages/FrameworkPrinciplesReport.aspx.

Human Rights Council (HRC). (2016). *Expert Mechanism on the Rights of Indigenous Peoples, A/HRC/RES/33/25*. Available at: https://documents.un.org/doc/undoc/gen/g16/224/16/pdf/g1622416.pdf?token=xYrqWbeG1VdA9QcEtL&fe=true.

Human Rights Council (HRC). (2008). *Information and Guidelines for Relevant Stakeholders on the Universal Periodic Review Mechanism*. Available at: www.ohchr.org/sites/default/files/HRBodies/UPR/Documents/TechnicalGuideEN.pdf.

Human Rights Council (HRC). (2007). *Expert Mechanism on the Rights of Indigenous Peoples, Resolution 6/36*. Available at: https://ap.ohchr.org/documents/E/HRC/resolutions/A_HRC_RES_6_36.pdf.

Inter-American Commission on Human Rights (IACHR). (2004). *Maya Indigenous Communities of the Toledo District, Belize, Report No. 40/04, Case 12.053*. English translation available at: www.legal-tools.org/doc/1cef53/pdf.

Inter-American Commission on Human Rights (IACHR). (1999). Saldano v. Argentina, Report *No*. 38/99. English translation available at: https://cidh.oas.org/annualrep/98eng/Inadmissible/Argentina%20Salda%C3%B1o.htm.

Inter-American Court of Human Rights (IACtHR). (2020). *Indigenous Communities Members of the Lhaka Honhat Association v. Argentina*. English translation available at: www.corteidh.or.cr/docs/casos/articulos/seriec_400_esp.pdf.

Inter-American Court of Human Rights (IACtHR). (2017). *Advisory Opinion OC-23/17, The Environment and Human Rights*. English translation available at: www.refworld.org/jurisprudence/caselaw/iacrthr/2017/en/123157.

Inter-American Court of Human Rights (IACtHR). (2012). *Kichwa Indigenous People of Sarayaku v. Ecuador*. English translation available at: https://corteidh.or.cr/docs/casos/articulos/seriec_245_ing.pdf.

Inter-American Court of Human Rights (IACtHR). (2007). *Saramaka People v. Suriname (2007)*. English translation available at: www.corteidh.or.cr/docs/casos/articulos/seriec_172_ing.pdf.

Inter-American Court of Human Rights (IACtHR). (2006). *Case of the Sawhoyamaxa Indigenous Community v. Paraguay (2006)*. English translation available at: www.corteidh.or.cr/docs/casos/articulos/seriec_146_ing.pdf.

Inter-American Court of Human Rights (IACtHR). (2005). *Case of the Yakye Axa Indigenous Community v. Paraguay (2005)*. English translation available at: www.corteidh.or.cr/docs/casos/articulos/seriec_125_ing.pdf.

Inter-American Court of Human Rights (IACtHR). (2001). *Mayagna (Sumo) Awas Tingni Community v. Nicaragua No. 79/71*. Available at: www.corteidh.or.cr/docs/casos/articulos/seriec_79_ing.pdf.

International Covenant on Civil and Political Rights (ICCPR). (1966). Available at: www.ohchr.org/en/instruments-mechanisms/instruments/international-covenant-civil-and-political-rights.

International Covenant on Economic, Social, and Cultural Rights (ICESCR). (1966). Available at: www.ohchr.org/en/instruments-mechanisms/instruments/international-covenant-economic-social-and-cultural-rights.

International Fund for Agriculture and Development (IFAD). (2018). *Indigenous Peoples' Collective Rights to Lands, Territories, and Natural Resources*. IFAD. Available at: www.un.org/development/desa/indigenouspeoples/mandated-areas1/environment.html.

International Indigenous Forum on Biodiversity (IIFB). (2024). Available at: https://iifb-indigenous.org/.

International Indigenous Peoples' Forum on Climate Change (IIPFCC) (2024). Available at: www.iipfcc.org/.

International Labor Organization (ILO). (2024). *Ratifications of C169 – Indigenous and Tribal Peoples Convention, 1989 (No. 169)*. Available at: https://normlex.ilo.org/dyn/normlex/en/f?p=NORMLEXPUB:11300:0::NO::P11300_INSTRUMENT_ID:312314.

International Labor Organization (ILO). (1990). Leaflet No. 8: The ILO and Indigenous and Tribal Peoples. Available at: www.ohchr.org/sites/default/files/Documents/Publications/GuideIPleaflet8en.pdf.

International Labor Organization (ILO). (1989). *International Labor Organization Convention No. 169, Indigenous and Tribal Peoples Convention.* International Labor Organization. Available at: www.ilo.org/dyn/normlex/en/f?p=NORMLEXPUB:12100:0::NO::P12100_ILO_CODE:C169.

Kalin, W. & Kunzli, J. (2009). *The Law of International Human Rights Protection.* Oxford University Press.

Knox, J. (2020). Constructing the Human Right to a Healthy Environment. *Annual Review of Law & Social Science*, 16(4), 4–17.

Knox, J. (2010). Diagonal Environmental Rights, in Gibney, M. & Skogly, S. (eds.), *Universal Human Rights and Extraterritorial Obligations.* University of Pennsylvania Press.

Knox, J. (2008). Horizontal Human Rights Law. *American Journal of International Law*, 102, 1–47.

Knox, J. & Pejan, R. (eds.). (2018). *The Human Right to a Healthy Environment.* Cambridge University Press.

Koot, S. (2023). Articulations of Inferiority: From Pre-Colonial to Post-Colonial Paternalism in Tourism and Development among the Indigenous Bushmen of Southern Africa. *History and Anthropology*, 34(2), 303–322. https://doi.org/10.1080/02757206.2020.1830387.

Kulchyski, P. (2011). Aboriginal Rights are not Human Rights. *Prairie Forum*, 36(2011), 33–53.

Lane, L. (2018). The Horizontal Effect of International Human Rights Law in Practice. *European Journal of Comparative Law & Governance*, 5(2018), 5–88.

Lightfoot, S. (2016). *Global Indigenous Politics.* Routledge.

Liljeblad, J. (2024). Sea Peoples and Marine Plastic Pollution in Southeast Asia: An International Human Rights Approach in Support of Indigenous Rights to Environment. *UCLA Journal of International Law and Foreign Affairs*, 27(2), 59–113.

Liljeblad, J. (2022). *Indigenous Identity, Human Rights, and Environment in Myanmar: Local Engagement with Global Rights Discourses.* Routledge.

Local Communities and Indigenous Peoples Platform (LCIPP) (2024). Available at: https://lcipp.unfccc.int/homepage.

MacDonald, F. & Wood, B. (2016). Potential Through Paradox: Indigenous Rights as Human Rights. *Citizenship Studies*, 20(6–7), 710–727.

Macklem, P. (2008). Indigenous Recognition in International Law: Theoretical Observations. *Michigan Journal of International Law*, 30(1), 177–210.

Malezer, L. (2020). Perspective on the Convention 169: Its Significance to Aboriginal Peoples. *International Journal of Human Rights*, 24(2–3), 297–299.

McMillan, M. & Rigney, S. (2016). The Place of First Peoples in the International Sphere: A Logical Point for the Demand for Justice by Indigenous People. *Melbourne University Law Review*, 39(3), 981–2002.

Mende, J. (2015). The Imperative of Indigeneity: Indigenous Human Rights and Their Limits. *Human Rights Review*, 16(2015), 221–238.

Merino, R. (2023). Indigenous Knowledge and International (Anthropocentric) Law: The Politics of Thinking from (and for) Another World, in Chapaux, V., Megret, F., & Natarajan, U. (eds.), *Handbook of International Law and Anthropocentrism*. Routledge.

Miranda, L. (2010). Indigenous Peoples as International Lawmakers. *University of Pennsylvania Journal of International Law*, 32(2010), 203–262.

Moreton-Robinson, A. (ed.). (2016). *Critical Indigenous Studies*. University of Arizona Press.

Moreton-Robinson, A. (2015). *The White Possessive*. University of Minnesota Press.

Nagoya Protocol. (2010). Available at: www.cbd.int/abs.

National Resources Defense Council (NRDC). (2020). In Landmark Victory for Indigenous Communities, Dakota Access Pipeline Ordered to Shut Down. Available at: www.nrdc.org/bio/nrdc/landmark-victory-indigenous-communities-dakota-access-pipeline-ordered-shut-down.

Newman, D. (2023). Indigenous Rights and Decolonized Legal Positivism, in Dempsey, M. & Tanguay-Renaud, F. (eds.), *From Morality to Law and Back Again: A Liber Amoricum for John Gardner*. Oxford University Press.

Office of the High Commissioner for Human Rights (OHCHR). (2024a). *The Core International Human Rights Instruments & Their Monitoring Bodies*. Available at: http://www.ohchr.org/en/core-international-human-rights-instruments-and-their-monitoring-bodies.

Office of the High Commissioner for Human Rights (OHCHR). (2024b). International Human Rights Law. Available at: http://www.ohchr.org/en/core-international-human-rights-instruments-and-their-monitoring-bodies.

Office of the High Commissioner for Human Rights (OHCHR). (2024c). Individual Communications: Human Rights Treaty Bodies. Available at: http://www.ohchr.org/en/treaty-bodies/individual-communications.

Office of the High Commissioner for Human Rights (OHCHR). (2024d). Treaty Bodies. Available at: http://www.ohchr.org/en/treaty-bodies.

Office of the High Commissioner for Human Rights (OHCHR). (2024e). Complaints Procedures under the Human Rights Treaties. Available at: http://www.ohchr.org/en/treaty-bodies/human-rights-bodies-complaints-procedures/complaints-procedures-under-human-rights-treaties#:~:text=Details%20of%20the%20procedure%26text=If%20the%20State%20party%20comments,considered%20inadmissible%2C%20it%20is%20closed.

Office of the High Commissioner for Human Rights (OHCHR). (2024f). OHCHR and Business and Human Rights. Available at: www.ohchr.org/en/business-and-human-rights.

Office of the High Commissioner for Human Rights (OHCHR). (2024g). Business and Human Rights: Adopting the "Smart Mix." Available at: www.ohchr.org/en/stories/2024/12/business-and-human-rights-adopting-smart-mix.

Office of the High Commission for Human Rights (OHCHR). (2020). Special Rapporteur on the Human Right to a Healthy Environment. Available at: www.ohchr.org/en/Issues/environment/SRenvironment/Pages/SRenvironmentIndex.aspx.

Office of the High Commissioner for Human Rights (OHCHR). (2018). Framework Principles on Human Rights and the Environment. Available at: www.ohchr.org/sites/default/files/FrameworkPrinciplesUserFriendlyVersion.pdf.

Office of the High Commission for Human Rights (OHCHR). (2017). Reporting to the United Nations Human Rights Treaty Bodies Training Guides. Available at: www.ohchr.org/sites/default/files/Documents/Publications/PTS20_HRTB_Training_Guide_PartI.pdf.

Office of the High Commissioner for Human Rights (OHCHR). (2016). *Human Rights: Handbook for Parliamentarians Number 26*. Inter-Parliamentary Union. Available at: www.ohchr.org/sites/default/files/Documents/Publications/HandbookParliamentarians.pdf.

Office of the High Commission for Human Rights (OHCHR). (2013). Individual Complaint Procedures under the United Nations Human Rights Treaties. Available at: www.ohchr.org/sites/default/files/Documents/Publications/FactSheet7Rev.2.pdf.

Office of the High Commissioner for Human Rights (OHCHR). (2011). Guiding Principles on Business and Human Rights. Available at: www.ohchr.org/sites/default/files/documents/publications/guidingprinciplesbusinesshr_en.pdf.

Office of the High Commissioner for Human Rights (OHCHR). (2007). *United Nations Declarations on the Rights of Indigenous Peoples, A/RES/61/295*. OHCHR.

Osakada, Y. (2020). Indigenous Peoples as Actors in International Law-Making: Focusing on International Environmental Law, in Scott, K., Claussen, K., Cote, C.-E., & Kanehara, A. (eds.), *Changing Actors in International Law*. Brill.

Pathak, P. (2014). Human Rights Approach to Environmental Protection. *OIDA International Journal of Sustainable Development*, 7(2014), 17–24.

Percival, R. (2010). Liability for Environmental Harm and Emerging Global Environmental Law. *Maryland Journal of International Law*, 25(2010), 37–63.

Pohlhaus, G. (2012). Relational Knowing and Epistemic Injustice: Toward a Theory of Willful Hermeneutical Ignorance. *Hypatia*, 27(4), 715–735.

Poyer, L. (2017). World War II and the Development of Global Indigenous Identities. *Identities*, 24(4), 417–435.

Ross, R. (2006). *Returning to the Teachings: Exploring Aboriginal Justice*. Penguin.

Smith, L. T. (2021). *Decolonizing Methodologies*, 3rd ed. Bloomsbury.

Speed, S. & Collier, J. (2000). Limiting Indigenous Autonomy in Chiapas, Mexico: The Government's Use of Human Rights. *Human Rights Quarterly*, 22(4), 877–905.

Special Rapporteur on Human Rights and Environment (SRHRE). (2018). *Report of the Special Rapporteur on the Issue of Human Rights Obligations Relating to the Enjoyment of a Safe, Clean, Healthy, and Sustainable Environment, UN Doc A/HRC/37/59*. United Nations Human Rights Council.

Special Rapporteur on Human Rights and Environment (SRHRE). (2017). *Report of the Special Rapporteur on the Issue of Human Rights Obligations Relating to the Enjoyment of a Safe, Clean, Healthy, and Sustainable Environment, UN Doc A/HRC/34/49*. United Nations Human Rights Council.

Special Rapporteur on Rights of Indigenous Peoples (SRIP). (2022). *Rights of Indigenous Peoples, UN Doc A/77/238*. United Nations General Assembly.
Special Rapporteur on Rights of Indigenous Peoples (SRIP). (2020a). *Report of the Special Rapporteur on the Rights of Indigenous Peoples, UN Doc A/HRC/45/34/*. United Nations General Assembly.
Special Rapporteur on Rights of Indigenous Peoples (SRIP). (2020b). *Regional Consultation on the Rights of Indigenous Peoples in Asia, UN Doc A/HRC/45/34/ Add.3**. United Nations General Assembly.
Special Rapporteur on Rights of Indigenous Peoples (SRIP). (2020c). *Visit to the Congo, UN Doc A/HRC/45/34/Add.1*. United Nations General Assembly.
Special Rapporteur on Rights of Indigenous Peoples (SRIP). (2017). *Report of the Special Rapporteur on the Rights of Indigenous Peoples, UN Doc A/HRC/36/46*. United Nations General Assembly.
Special Rapporteur on Rights of Indigenous Peoples (SRIP). (2016). *Rights of Indigenous Peoples, UN Doc A/71/229*. United Nations General Assembly.
Springer, J. (2016). *IUCN's Rights-Based Approach: A Systemization of the Union's Policy Instruments, Standards, and Guidelines*. International Union for the Conservation of Nature. Available at: www.iucn.org/sites/dev/files/content/documents/iucn_rba_systematization_compiled.pdf.
Stark, H. K. (2016). Critical Empire: The Making of the Savage in a Lawless Land. *Theory & Event* 19(4). Available at: https://muse.jhu.edu/article/633282.
Tauli-Corpuz, V. (2007). Statement of Victoria Tauli-Corpuz, Chair of the UN Permanent Forum on Indigenous Issues on the Occasion of the Adoption of the UN Declaration on the Rights of Indigenous Peoples, 61st Session of the UN General Assembly. Available at: www.un.org/esa/socdev/unpfii/documents/2016/Docs-updates/STATEMENT-VICTORIA-TAULI-CORPUZ-IDWIP-2007.pdf.
Ulfstein, G. (2012). Individual Complaints, in Keller, H. & Ulfstein, G. (eds.), *UN Human Rights Treaty Bodies*. Cambridge University Press.
Ulfstein, G. (2004). Indigenous Peoples' Right to Land, in von Bogdandy, A. & Wolfrum, R. (eds.), *Max Planck Yearbook of United Nations Law, Vol. 8*. Kluwer Academic Publishers.
United Nations (UN). (2023). *Editorial Manual: Capitalization in English*. UN Department for General Assembly & Conference Management. Available at: www.un.org/dgacm/en/content/editorial-manual/capitalization.
United Nations (UN). (2021a). *Indigenous Peoples at the United Nations*. United Nations. Available at: www.un.org/development/desa/Indigenouspeoples/about-us.html.
United Nations (UN). (2021b). *Permanent Forum*. United Nations. Available at: www.un.org/development/desa/Indigenouspeoples/unpfii-sessions-2.html.
United Nations (UN). (2021c). *Special Rapporteur on the Rights of Indigenous Peoples*. Office of the High Commissioner for Human Rights. Available at: www.ohchr.org/EN/Issues/IPeoples/SRIndigenousPeoples/Pages/SRIPeoplesIndex.aspx.
United Nations (UN). (2016). Trail Smelter Case (United States, Canada). Reports of International Arbitral Awards, *Volume* III: 1905–1982. Available at: https://legal.un.org/riaa/cases/vol_iii/1905-1982.pdf.

United Nations Conference on Environment and Development (UNCED). (1992). *A/CONF.151/26*. Available at: www.un.org/en/development/desa/population/migration/generalassembly/docs/globalcompact/A_CONF.151_26_Vol.I_Declaration.pdf.

United Nations Declaration on the Rights of Indigenous Peoples (UNDRIPS). (2007). Available at: www.ilo.org/dyn/normlex/en/f?p=NORMLEXPUB:12100:0::NO::P12100_ILO_CODE:C169.

United Nations Environment Programme. (2024). *Decision adopted by the Conference of the Parties to the Convention on Biological Diversity on 30 October 2024 16/4, Programme of work on Article 8(j), CBD/COP/DEC/16/4*. Available at: www.cbd.int/doc/decisions/cop-16/cop-16-dec-04-en.pdf.

United Nations Framework Convention on Climate Change (UNFCCC). (2017). *Report of the Conference of the Parties on its Twenty-Third Session, Addendum, FCCC/CP/2017/11/Add.1*. Available at: https://unfccc.int/resource/docs/2017/cop23/eng/11a01.pdf.

United Nations Framework Convention on Climate Change (UNFCCC). (2015). Paris Agreement. Available at: https://unfccc.int/sites/default/files/english_paris_agreement.pdf.

United Nations Framework Convention on Climate Change (UNFCCC). (2010). *Report of the Conference of the Parties on Its Sixteenth Session, Addendum, FCCC/CP/2010/7/Add.1*. Available at: https://unfccc.int/resource/docs/2010/cop16/eng/07a01.pdf.

United Nations General Assembly (UNGA). (2024). *Annual Report of the Expert Mechanism on the Rights of Indigenous Peoples, A/HRC/57/64*. Available at: https://docs.un.org/en/A/HRC/57/64.

United Nations General Assembly (UNGA). (2018a). *Report of the Special Rapporteur on the Issue of Human Rights Obligations Relating to the Enjoyment of a Safe, Clean, Healthy, and Sustainable Environment, A/HRC/37/59*. Available at: https://undocs.org/A/HRC/37/59.

United Nations General Assembly (UNGA). (2018b). *Human Rights Obligations Relating to the Enjoyment of a Safe, Clean, Healthy, and Sustainable Environment, A/73/188*. Available at: https://undocs.org/A/73/188.

United Nations General Assembly (UNGA). (2017). *Report of the Special Rapporteur on the Issue of Human Rights Obligations Relating to the Enjoyment of a Safe, Clean, Healthy, and Sustainable Environment, A/HRC/34/49*. Available at: www.ohchr.org/en/documents/thematic-reports/ahrc3449-report-special-rapporteur-issue-human-rights-obligations.

United Nations General Assembly (UNGA). (2012). *Human Rights and the Environment, A/HRC/RES/19/10*. Available at: https://ap.ohchr.org/documents/dpage_e.aspx?si=A/HRC/RES/19/10.

United Nations General Assembly (UNGA). (1995). *Fact Sheet No. 9 (Rev.1), The Rights of Indigenous Peoples*. Available at: www.ohchr.org/sites/default/files/Documents/Publications/FactSheet9rev.1en.pdf.

United Nations Human Rights Special Procedures (UN Special Procedures). (2018). *Framework Principles on Human Rights and Environment*. Available at: www.ohchr.org/sites/default/files/FrameworkPrinciplesUserFriendlyVersion.pdf.

United Nations Research (UN Research). (2024). *UN Human Rights Documentation*. Available at: https://research.un.org/en/docs/humanrights/treaties.

United Nations Treaty Collection (UN Collection) (2024). Available at: https://treaties.un.org/Pages/ViewDetails.aspx?chapter=4&clang=_en&mtdsg_no=IV-4&src=IND.

van Aggelen, J. (2019). State Obligations Under Universal Human Rights Treaties, in Kadelbach, S., Rensmann, T., & Rieter, E. (eds.), *Judging International Human Rights.* Springer.

Ward, C. (2011). A Travesty of a Mockery of a Sham: Colonialism as "Self-Determination" in the UN Declaration on the Rights of Indigenous Peoples. *Griffith Law Review*, 20(3), 526–556.

Watson, I. (2018). Aboriginal Relationships to the Natural World: Colonial Protection of Human Rights and the Environment. *Journal of Human Rights and the Environment*, 9(2), 119–140.

Watson, I. (2015). *Aboriginal Peoples, Colonialism, and International Law: Raw Law.* Routledge.

Whare, T. (2020). Reflective Piece on the Maori and the ILO. *International Journal of Human Rights*, 24(2–3), 303–306.

White Face, C. & Wobaga, Z. (2013). *Indigenous Nations' Rights in the Balance: An Analysis of the Declaration on the Rights of Indigenous Peoples.* Living Justice Press.

Wilson, D. (2021). European Colonisation, Law, and Indigenous Maritime Dispossession: Historical Perspectives on the Construction and Entrenchment of Unequal Marine Governance. *Maritime Studies*, 20, 387–407. https://doi.org/10.1007/s40152-021-00233-2.

Xanthaki, A. (2009). *Indigenous Rights and United Nations Standards.* Cambridge University Press.

Yupsanis, A. (2011). The International Labor Organization and Its Contribution to the Protection of the Rights of Indigenous Peoples. *Canadian Yearbook of International Law*, 49(2012), 117–176.

2

Indigenous Rights under the Convention on Biological Diversity

Reinforcing and Expanding Human Rights Law

Federica Cittadino

2.1 Introduction

This contribution argues that the international biodiversity regime, established by the Convention on Biological Diversity (CBD)[1] including its Nagoya Protocol on access and benefit-sharing (ABS),[2] offers legal avenues to reinforce and operationalize the rights of Indigenous Peoples, both informing existing rights and complementing the international human rights' realm. The rights of Indigenous Peoples are well established under International Human Rights Law (IHRL), their recognition culminating with the adoption by the United Nations (UN) General Assembly of the UN Declaration on the Rights of Indigenous Peoples (UNDRIPS) in 2007 (Barelli 2016). This nonbinding instrument has systematized and consolidated the content of Indigenous Peoples' collective rights, which had already emerged in the jurisprudence and the decisions of human rights courts and treaty bodies (Åhrén 2016; Cittadino 2019; Wiessner & Lenzerini 2012).[3]

[1] Convention on Biological Diversity, Rio de Janeiro, June 5, 1992, in force December 29, 1993, 1760 UNTS 79.

[2] Nagoya Protocol on Access to Genetic Resources and the Fair and Equitable Sharing of Benefits Arising from their Utilization to the Convention on Biological Diversity, Nagoya, October 29, 2010, in force October 12, 2014, 3008 UNTS 3 (hereinafter Nagoya Protocol).

[3] Several key provisions of the UNDRIPS are considered customary international law. See Wiessner (2013), International Law Association, Conclusions and Recommendation of The Committee on the Rights of Indigenous Peoples, Resolution No. 5/2012, para. 2 (2012), and Supreme Court of Belize, *Aurelio Cal, et al. v. Attorney General of Belize* (Claims No. 171 and 172 of 2007), Judgement of October 18, 2007, paras. 127, 131, and 132. See also Cittadino (2019), pp. 144 ff, where I explain why the debate about the customary nature of Indigenous Peoples' rights is less crucial than expected for the purposes of incorporating Indigenous Peoples' rights in the CBD because CBD parties have also ratified, although to different extents, the main human rights treaties upon which Indigenous Peoples' rights are adjudicated.

Indeed, the main argument of this contribution is that Indigenous Peoples' rights are not only enshrined in IHRL but are indirectly protected also under the CBD regime. Some provisions of this treaty regime, described in Section 2.2, de facto operationalize the content of some rights of Indigenous Peoples in the context of biodiversity protection and ABS. The rights that may benefit from a human rights-friendly interpretation of the CBD are especially the right to self-determination, the right to land and natural resources, cultural rights, and the right to free, prior and informed consent (FPIC).[4] The way in which the CBD regime reinforces these rights is discussed in Section 2.3. This contribution also argues that the CBD regime lays out the foundations for Indigenous Peoples' rights that are additional to those protected under IHRL including the UNDRIPS, such as the right to fair and equitable benefit-sharing, the right to genetic resources, the right to traditional knowledge, and biocultural rights. The contours and limitations of these rights, their distinctiveness compared to similar rights protected under the UNDRIPS, and the extent to which they may contribute to the protection of Indigenous Peoples is explored in Section 2.4.

Overall, this chapter raises two main points. First, the rights of Indigenous Peoples as protected under the CBD constitute a "*sui-generis*" regime that does not perfectly coincide with IHRL. Those regimes complement and, in some cases, reinforce each other. The CBD is to be interpreted in light of the existing corpus of Indigenous Peoples' rights protected under IHRL pursuant to the principle of systemic interpretation in international law (Cittadino 2019). Further to that, the CBD specifies the ways in which Indigenous Peoples' rights are relevant and must be implemented in the context of the CBD, when it comes especially to the areas of ABS and conservation. Second, the CBD as an international environmental regime gives new meaning to the concept of Indigenous environmental rights. These are intended in this contribution not as human rights that protect the collective enjoyment by Indigenous Peoples of the environment, but instead as environmental provisions that give substance to Indigenous rights in some specific regimes. These new rights go beyond the existing categories of environmental rights to which the literature currently refers, namely rights to nature, the human right to the environment, and environmental participatory rights. Indigenous environmental rights under the CBD are mainly anthropocentric and not focused on the protection of the environment, although they incorporate holistic visions of nature complemented by culture. Differently from existing categories of environmental rights, Indigenous environmental rights are both substantive and procedural in nature. These claims will be discussed in more detail in the conclusion.

[4] On the content and legal status of these rights, see for example Cittadino (2019: 68–155).

2.2 Indigenous Peoples and Their Place in the Convention on Biological Diversity Regime

The CBD embraces three main objectives, namely the conservation of biodiversity, its sustainable use, and the fair and equitable sharing of benefits deriving from access to genetic resources (Art. 1). In this context, there are mainly two subregimes of the CBD that acknowledge Indigenous Peoples' contribution and/or affect Indigenous Peoples' rights: these are the ABS regime (Art. 8(j) CBD and Arts. 5(2), 6(2), 7, and 12 Nagoya Protocol) and that regulating conservation through the creation of protected areas (Art. 8(a)–(b) and relevant COP decisions below) (Cittadino 2019).

The CBD regime has to be read also in light of the newly adopted Kunming–Montreal Global Biodiversity Framework (GBF).[5] This has notably contributed to a reinforced human rights approach within the CBD (Parks & Tsioumani 2023). While earlier editions of the GBF had been criticized for both excluding Indigenous views on the unity of culture and nature and ignoring Indigenous Peoples' land tenure (systems) (Cariño & Farhan Ferrari 2021), the final version adopted in Montreal in 2022 refers to Indigenous Peoples' rights in its global targets. For instance, Target 21 considers seeking Indigenous Peoples' FPIC as a precondition for accessing traditional knowledge (TK). In addition, Target 3 mentions the rights of Indigenous Peoples while achieving the goal to have 30 percent of land and waters conserved through the establishment of protected areas.[6]

Before delving in the content of the CBD provisions concerning Indigenous Peoples and their rights, the following aims to provide some context, by elaborating on the history of Indigenous Peoples' involvement in the CBD as well as the reasons of their special consideration in this regime. The CBD's scope of application, focusing on biodiversity protection, sustainable use, and benefit-sharing, makes this regime overlap with the scope of some typical Indigenous Peoples' rights, such as the rights to land and natural resources. As most of existing protected areas conserving biodiversity globally are located on Indigenous lands, both the CBD and IHRL are applicable legal frameworks in those cases: Both regimes "concern the management of natural resources and raise the issue of which subjects can exercise powers over them" (Cittadino 2019: 2).

The special role of Indigenous Peoples within the CBD is anchored in the CBD's text itself, notably in its Preamble and Articles 8(j) and 10(c) that protect Indigenous

[5] COP dec. XV/4, CBD/COP/DEC/15/4 (December 19, 2022).

[6] This target is important considering that most protected areas are hosted on Indigenous lands and that Indigenous territories are usually the richest biodiversity hotspots still in existence. See Sobrevila (2008: xii) and Garnett et al. (2018). This reasoning is also included in the explanation of Target 3 available at: www.cbd.int/gbf/targets/3.

Peoples and local communities' TK and customary use of biological resources in the context of in-situ conservation[7] and sustainable use, respectively. As observed by Girard et al. (2022: 8), these provisions, initially thought to incentivize the use of TK, were used to "Trojan-horse" the involvement of Indigenous Peoples and local communities in international negotiations on benefit-sharing, genetic resources, and related aspects. Since the creation of the Working Group on Article 8(j) in 1998,[8] Indigenous Peoples' representatives have been involved as observers within it, therefore contributing to the interpretation and the evolution of Article 8(j). According to the CBD any "body or agency, whether governmental or non-governmental, qualified in fields relating to the conservation and sustainable use of biological diversity" may qualify as observer and participate without the right to vote in the meetings of the CBD Conference of the Parties (COP) concerning matters of their interest.[9] In addition, Indigenous Peoples were involved in the works of the COP and, later on, in the Working Group on ABS, drafting the text of the Nagoya Protocol. Very importantly, COP 16 established the Subsidiary Body on Article 8(j) and Other Provisions of the Convention on Biological Diversity Related to Indigenous Peoples and Local Communities, a consultative body similar to the Subsidiary Body on Scientific, Technical and Technological Advice (SBSTTA), mandated to advise the COP "on matters of relevance to indigenous peoples and local communities that are within the scope of the Convention and its Protocols."[10] The first meeting of this body took place in October 2025 in Panama City.

The involvement of Indigenous Peoples in the CBD can be explained with an increasingly developed understanding, materializing in the State practice and consolidated through COP decisions, of the link between cultural diversity and biological diversity, indirectly referred to in Article 8(j) of the CBD, and with it, an increasingly marked acknowledgment of Indigenous Peoples' contribution to the conservation of biological diversity (Girard et al. 2022: 11; Zurba & Papadopoulos 2023: 85). The engagement of Indigenous Peoples is also associated with the increasing acknowledgment of their rights in international law (Zurba & Papadopoulos 2023: 85). Finally, the involvement of Indigenous Peoples in the international biodiversity regime was made possible thanks also to their mobilization at the institutional level, with the creation of umbrella organizations such as the International Indigenous Forum on Biodiversity (IIFB), which groups all

[7] According to Art. 2 CBD, "'In-situ conservation' means the conservation of ecosystems and natural habitats and the maintenance and recovery of viable populations of species in their natural surroundings and, in the case of domesticated or cultivated species, in the surroundings where they have developed their distinctive properties."

[8] COP dec. IV/9, CBD/COP/DEC/IV/9 (May 4–15, 1998).

[9] See Art. 23(5) CBD and Rule 7 of the Rules of Procedure for meetings of the CBD COP, available at https://dev-chm.cbd.int/convention/rules.shtml.

[10] COP dec. 16/5, CBD/COP/DEC/16/5 (November 1, 2024). This decision was taken in addition to the adoption of a new Programme of Work on Article 8(j), COP dec. 16/4, CBD/COP/DEC/16/4 (October 30, 2024).

Indigenous-led organizations, and smaller ones like the Indigenous Women's Biodiversity Network (IWBN) (Osakada 2021; Parks & Tsioumani 2023).

2.2.1 Access and Benefit-sharing

Concerning ABS, the abovementioned Article 8(j) of the CBD constitutes the main textual reference in the framework treaty. According to this provision, State parties shall:

- "respect, preserve and maintain knowledge, innovations and practices of indigenous and local communities embodying traditional lifestyles relevant for conservation and sustainable use of biological diversity and promote their wider application with the approval and involvement of the holders of such knowledge"; and
- "encourage the equitable sharing of the benefits arising from the utilisation of" TK.

In other words, Article 8(j) protects TK and promotes its application under the condition of having some form of Indigenous Peoples' consent to the matter. Furthermore, the same provision establishes that benefits must be shared internally, within each contracting party ("intra-State benefit-sharing"), with Indigenous Peoples when utilizing their TK (Morgera & Tsioumani 2010: 34). Benefit-sharing is only foreseen as far as the utilization of TK is concerned, thus leaving unregulated those cases where genetic resources deriving from Indigenous Peoples' natural resources are utilized. In addition, the strong implications of this provision for Indigenous Peoples are weakened by the conditional language used: It is merely referred to "encourage" benefit-sharing, to do so "as far as possible and as appropriate," and "subject to national legislation." Further deficits may be found in the lack of adherence to more explicit human rights language. This is evident by the use of the term "indigenous and local communities," which seemingly does not borrow from the terminology "Indigenous Peoples," carrying clear implications for self-determination, as used under IHRL.[11] Another unprecise correspondence exists between the CBD and IHRL concerning the locution "with the approval and involvement" of Indigenous Peoples that is certainly less precise compared to the FPIC standard.[12]

Under IHRL, indeed, consultation must be conducted with the objective of obtaining FPIC in cases in which Indigenous Peoples' rights would be restricted otherwise. Consent is to be obtained in case of relocation (Art. 16(2) ILO

[11] Concerning this terminology, COP dec. XII/12 (UNEP/CBD/COP/DEC/XII/12, October 13, 2014) has established to use the term "indigenous peoples and local communities" in future decisions. On the implications of that, see Parks and Tsioumani (2023: 2) and Cittadino (2019: 168).

[12] It is interesting to note that in the GBF, the locution "free prior and informed consent" is indicated as referring to "the tripartite terminology of 'prior and informed consent' or 'free, prior and informed consent' or 'approval and involvement'."

Convention 169[13] and Art. 10 UNDRIPS), storage of hazardous materials in Indigenous lands (Art. 29(2) UNDRIPS), taking of Indigenous "cultural, intellectual, religious and spiritual property" (indirectly under Art. 11(2) UNDRIPS), confiscation, occupation or damage (indirectly under Art. 28(1) UNDRIPS), taking place of military activities with no relevant public interest (Art. 30(1) UNDRIPS), and by way of jurisprudential interpretation in case of large-scale development projects (Doyle 2015).[14] Furthermore, even in instances where consent is not mandatory, States need to comply with a lot of procedural requirements to make sure that participation is truly prior, informed, and noncoercive (Cittadino 2019: 102–120). Whenever Indigenous Peoples are affected by decisions of public authorities or private projects concerning their territories, FPIC serves as a *bona fide* objective that requires prior consultation with the objective of reaching consent (Eichler 2019; Wright & Tomaselli 2021).[15]

Challenges relating to the interpretation and implementation of Article 8(j) led to the creation in 1998 of a specific working group on the matter, the Working Group on Article 8(j), whose mandate is to facilitate the implementation of said provision (Cittadino 2019: 61).[16] The subsequent practice developed by the CBD COPs, as well as the adoption of the Nagoya Protocol have partially remedied the gaps inherent to Article 8(j), in the latter case exclusively as concerning State parties that have ratified the Protocol.[17] Reports of the Working Group on Article 8(j) and COP decisions have recognized the link between benefit-sharing deriving from the utilization of TK and the larger regime on ABS that includes also issues relating to

[13] International Labour Organisation Convention 169 Concerning Indigenous and Tribal Peoples in Independent Countries (hereinafter ILO Convention 169) (Geneva, June 27, 1989, in force September 5, 1991), 1650 UNTS 383.

[14] See Inter-American Court of Human Rights, *Case of the Saramaka People* v. *Suriname* (hereinafter *Saramaka* case), Judgment of November 28, 2007, paras. 134 and 137. The FPIC requirement, however, was not referred to explicitly in a later decision in the *Case of the Kichwa Indigenous People of Sarayaku v. Ecuador*, Judgment of June 27, 2012. See Aguileira (2023: 44).

[15] Arts. 6(1)(a), 7(1), 15, 17(2) ILO Convention 169. Arts. 18–19, 32(2) UNDRIPS. See also, for example, UN Human Rights Committee, *Ángela Poma Poma* v. *Peru*, Communication No. 1457/2006; UN Committee on the Elimination of Racial Discrimination, General Recommendation No. 23: Rights of Indigenous Peoples, UN doc. A/52/18 (August 18, 1997) (hereinafter General Comment 23), Annex V; UN Committee on Economic, Social and Cultural Rights, Concluding Observations of the Committee on the Third Periodic Report of Ecuador as approved by the Committee on the Third Periodic Report of Ecuador as approved by the Committee at its forty-ninth session, UN doc. E/C.12/ECU/CO/3 (December 13, 2012). On FPIC, see Doyle (2015). FPIC is also relevant in the context of corporate due diligence. See, for example, the World Bank's Environmental and Social Framework (2017) (specifically Environmental and Social Standard 7, at pp. 75–83), available at https://thedocs.worldbank.org/en/doc/837721522762050108-0290022018/original/ESFFramework.pdf. This framework "sets out the mandatory requirements of the Bank in relation to the projects it supports through Investment Project Financing" (at 3). See also, UN Committee on Economic, Social and Cultural Rights, General Comment No. 24 on State Obligations under the International Covenant on Economic, Social and Cultural Rights in the Context of Business Activities, UN doc. E/C.12/GC/24 (June 23, 2017). See Cantú Rivera (2021); Klein et al. (2024).

[16] In addition to that and as already reminded above, a subsidiary body on Article 8(j) was created in 2024 to recognize Indigenous Peoples' role in the interpretation and evolution of Article 8(j).

[17] The list of parties can be found here: www.cbd.int/abs/nagoya-protocol/signatories.

accessing genetic resources.[18] This interrelation was translated into the concept of "traditional knowledge associated with genetic resources" and then expanded further in the Nagoya Protocol.

Article 5(2) of the Nagoya Protocol regulates benefit-sharing deriving from the "utilization of genetic resources that are held by indigenous and local communities."[19] It creates an obligation for parties to adopt, "in accordance with national law" and "as appropriate," a domestic normative framework to ensure benefit-sharing with Indigenous Peoples, based on mutually agreed terms (MATs). These are private contracts that are to be concluded between Indigenous Peoples contributing with TK and those actors utilizing it, be they States or private actors, such as businesses and research institutions. Furthermore, Article 6(2) of the Protocol establishes that access to genetic resources held by Indigenous Peoples must be regulated in such a way that it is being enjoyed only after "prior informed consent or approval and involvement of indigenous and local communities is obtained." Important developments concerning benefit-sharing and genetic resources relate to the creation by the CBD COP of a global mechanism to share benefits related to the use of digital sequence information (DSI) on genetic resources.[20] DSI is particularly problematic in terms of benefit-sharing because it can be retrieved digitally with no need to physically access genetic resources that would be necessary to extract relevant genetic data, thus making prior consent empty letter. The global mechanism on DSI, recently operationalized through the creation of a global fund,[21] will therefore allow, if correctly implemented, to share monetary benefits accrued to pharmaceutical and agricultural industry from the use of DSI with Indigenous Peoples who are holders of relevant genetic resources.

A similar standard on prior consent is adopted in Article 7 of the Protocol concerning access to TK. In addition, the latter provision requires the establishment of MATs in case where access to TK is being sought. When it comes to TK, therefore, the Nagoya Protocol establishes the requirement of adopting MATs as a possible legal tool to operationalize both benefit-sharing and the consent-like requirement established in the context of ABS.

Another significant step taken by the Nagoya Protocol with reference to TK is the consideration given to Indigenous "customary laws, community protocols and procedures." These, according to Article 12 of the Nagoya Protocol, need to be taken into account when implementing obligations related to TK. The development of these protocols by Indigenous Peoples, as well as minimum requirements for

[18] Report of the Fifth Meeting of the Ad Hoc Open-Ended Working Group on Article 8(j) and Related Provisions of the Convention on Biological Diversity, UN doc. UNEP/CBD/COP/9/7 (November 13, 2007), paras. 81 ff; Report of the Sixth Meeting of the Ad Hoc Open-Ended Working Group on Article 8(j) and Related Provisions of the Convention on Biological Diversity, UN doc. UNEP/CBD/WG-ABS/8/2 (July 15, 2009); COP dec. VII/19, CBD/COP/DEC/VII/19 (April 13, 2004).

[19] Art. 5(1) Nagoya Protocol specifies the conditions of inter-State benefit-sharing in accordance with Art. 15(3) and (7) CBD.

[20] COP dec. 15/9, CBD/COP/DEC/15/9 (December 19, 2022); see also www.cbd.int/dsi-gr.

[21] COP dec. 16/2, CBD/COP/DEC/16/2 (November 1, 2024).

MATs and model contractual clauses for benefit-sharing, must be supported by State parties (Art. 12(3)). Community protocols are also referred to within the CBD framework outside the Nagoya Protocol (Parks & Tsioumani 2023: 5–6). The Mo'otz Kuxtal Voluntary Guidelines,[22] adopted in 2016, encourage the adoption of these community protocols as a way to operationalize FPIC.

Community protocols are legal tools elaborated directly by Indigenous Peoples, sometimes in reaction to external actors that demand access to their knowledge and resources. They constitute a way to formalize Indigenous Peoples' position on a number of issues, including who is entitled within the community to negotiate with external actors, the level of openness of that community vis-à-vis external interference, the modalities to engage with the community for external actors to observe, how consent should be sought, and the worldviews of the concerned communities, among other matters (Girard et al. 2022: 16, 18). These protocols are therefore intended as a way to operationalize Indigenous Peoples' self-determination because they represent a declaration of intent on the part of the communities concerning their priorities (Cittadino 2019: 247–250). They are also regarded as instruments for fostering broader participation and promoting recognition, particularly when consultation and consent are sought by external actors such as governmental bodies, corporate entities, or other external actors (Parks & Tsioumani 2023: 6).

Equally important for the purpose of recognition is the abovementioned acknowledgment, in both the Nagoya Protocol and in the Mo'otz Kuxtal Voluntary Guidelines, of the importance of Indigenous customary laws, which are expression of their self-determination and legal pluralism. Indigenous customary laws reflect Indigenous different epistemologies and worldviews and emerge from their traditional cultural practices (Tobin 2014: 29). The specific mention of Indigenous customary laws is a way to recognize and grant "epistemological parity" to Indigenous Peoples' conceptions and knowledge (Eichler & Navarro 2023: 13).[23] Furthermore, because Indigenous customary laws are essential for the identification of Indigenous land (Anaya & Williams, Jr. 2001: 43–47), recognizing them as sources of law reinforces the legal position of Indigenous Peoples within the CBD framework, given that their rights to genetic resources might be linked to their rights to land and natural resources.

Another important requirement established with the Nagoya Protocol is the provision mandating the COP to create a Compliance Mechanism (Art. 30), the latter being created in 2014[24] and displaying some noteworthy novelties concerning

[22] COP dec. XIII/18, CBD/COP/13/18 (December 17, 2016).

[23] This paper is in turn quoting a paper presented by Rafael Bautista at a conference by FILAC, the Ministerio de Relaciones Exteriores, and the Ministerio de Medio Ambiente y Agua in Bolivia on 17 August 2021.

[24] COP/MOP (Conference of the Parties to the Convention on Biological Diversity Serving as the Meeting of the Parties to the Nagoya Protocol on Access to Genetic Resources and the Fair and Equitable Sharing of Benefits Arising from Their Utilization) dec. NP-1/4, CBD/NP/COP-MOP/DEC/1/4 (October 20, 2014).

the involvement of Indigenous Peoples. The mechanism is run by the Compliance Committee, which is made of fifteen members nominated by State parties and two Indigenous members nominated by Indigenous Peoples and local communities acting as observers. Observers can participate in discussion but have no voting rights. At the same time, Indigenous representatives can be excluded from discussions if State parties consider that compliance needs brought to the attention of the mechanism are not relevant for Indigenous representatives: This potential exclusion certainly renders Indigenous Peoples' involvement arbitrary. Another mechanism through which Indigenous Peoples can make their voices heard concerning compliance with the Nagoya Protocol is established in the procedures to establish the Compliance Mechanism, which foresee that the Committee can activate itself autonomously on the basis of information received inter-alia from Indigenous Peoples. This means that the Compliance Mechanism allows for the monitoring of parties' compliance of the Protocol's obligations relating to Indigenous Peoples (Zheng 2021: 66).

2.2.2 Conservation through the Creation of Protected Areas

Regarding the creation of protected areas within the framework of in-situ conservation, the CBD is extremely parsimonious. Article 8(a) and (b) of the CBD limits itself to creating an obligation for parties to "establish a system of protected areas" or similar and to define guidelines to identify those areas. The modalities in which these protected areas are to be created, the subjects entitled to decide on the matter, and potential conflicts with existing rights are not addressed in the text of the Convention.

The CBD legal framework, however, has incredibly evolved through COP decisions,[25] and in particular with the adoption of the Programme of Work on Protected Areas (PoWPA) in 2004.[26] The PoWPA establishes the principle that "the establishment, management and monitoring of protected areas should take place with the full and effective participation, and full respect for the rights of, indigenous peoples and local communities."[27] This clearly identifiable human rights approach to participation in the context of protected areas is also complemented by additional COP decisions that explicitly refer to the UNDRIPS as a benchmark to determine the substance of Indigenous participatory rights in the context of the PoWPA.[28] A further historical development in the PoWPA is the recognition of Indigenous and Community Conserved Areas (ICCAs) as potentially contributing to conservation within the framework of the CBD. This is also a sign of legal pluralism within

[25] For a list of relevant COP decisions, see Cittadino (2019: 272), footnote 34.

[26] COP dec. VII/28, CBD/COP/DEC/7/28 (April 13, 2004).

[27] PoWPA, ibid., para. 22. A related requirement is that of impact assessment, that is discussed in more details in Cittadino (2019: 291–295).

[28] For example, COP dec. X/31, CBD/COP/DEC/X/31 (October 29, 2010), para. 1(i) and COP dec. X/2, CBD/COP/DEC/X/2 (October 29, 2010), para. 4.

the CBD legal framework that recognizes alternative and oftentimes not formalized forms of conservation[29] as comparable to formally recognized protected areas for the achievement of the protection objective of the Convention. The main limitation of the evolving legal interpretation of CBD-related conservation standards is that successive COP decisions have adopted contradictory requirements, with a resulting inconsistent approach throughout decisions concerning the incorporation of Indigenous rights into the CBD.[30]

2.3 How Convention on Biological Diversity Provisions Reinforce Existing (Collective) Rights

As asserted by Reyes-García et al. (2022: 84), "Indigenous peoples' and local communities' participation in biodiversity policy contributes to the recognition of human and Indigenous peoples' rights" while "engagement in biodiversity policy is essential for Indigenous peoples and local communities to be able to exercise their recognized rights to territories and resources." This claim applies also to the CBD regime.

The previous section has illustrated that the CBD and the Nagoya Protocol regulate situations where a number of Indigenous rights are at stake. Cultural rights are notably concerned when it comes to the protection of TK. Under IHRL, cultural rights are protected primarily through Article 27 ICCPR, which establishes the right to a distinct culture,[31] and Article 15 ICESCR, which includes the right to take part in cultural life and to intellectual property and has been interpreted to cover the protection of Indigenous cultural heritage and traditional knowledge.[32] The duty to protect Indigenous cultural manifestations is also widely protected under ILO Convention 169 (Arts. 5, 8, 23) and the UNDRIPS (Arts. 7–8, 11–13, 15–16, 24, 31).[33] Land and resource rights, protected under IHRL through property rights[34] and cultural rights,[35] lay indirectly at the basis of those provisions regulating access

[29] See CBD/COP/14/L.19, Annex II.

[30] See Cittadino (2019), chapter 4 and conclusion.

[31] On the scope of Art. 27 ICCPR, see General Comment 23. On the centrality of Indigenous cultural rights, see Wiessner (2011).

[32] UN Committee on Economic, Social and Cultural Rights (CESCR), General Comment No. 21, Right of everyone to take part in cultural life (art. 15, para. 1a of the Covenant on Economic, Social and Cultural Rights), UN doc. E/C.12/GC/21 (December 21, 2009), para. 37; General Comment No. 17: Right of Everyone to Benefit from the Protection of the Moral and Material Interests Resulting from any Scientific, Literary or Artistic Production of Which He or She is the Author, UN doc. E/C.12/GC/17 (January 12, 2006), para. 32. See Section 2.4 on why the scope of TK does not perfectly coincide with indigenous cultural rights.

[33] See Cittadino (2019: 97–102). Compared to ILO Convention 169, UNDRIPS significantly protect the right to live as distinct peoples and the right not to be forcibly assimilated (Arts. 7–8).

[34] Art. 14(1) ILO Convention 169, 26 UNDRIPS, and 21 American Convention on Human Rights (San José, November 22, 1969, in force July 18, 1978).

[35] General Comment 23, para. 7; CERD, Decision 1/68, United States, para. 8; Art. 13 ILO Convention 169; Art. 8 and 25 UNDRIPS. See Cittadino (2019: 73–75, 82).

and utilization of TK and genetic resources held by Indigenous Peoples; they also constitute important premises for the recognition of ICCAs as legitimate forms of nature conservation. Land rights, framed as collective property[36] recognized in accordance with Indigenous customs,[37] include rights of ownership, possession, and effective control on lands traditionally occupied, use of natural resources, restitution in case of dispossession (Art. 28 UNDRIPS), and require participation when restrictions affect traditional lands.[38] Participatory rights too are to be safeguarded when accessing TK and genetic resources and creating protected areas. These rights are framed as prior consultation (Art. 27 ICCPR),[39] participation in public decision-making (Art. 18 UNDRIPS) or FPIC (Arts. 19 and 31 UNDRIPS), but always entail a level of engagement with Indigenous Peoples that must be effective.[40] And ultimately the somewhat related right to self-determination of Indigenous Peoples (Art. 3 UNDRIPS),[41] intended mainly as the right to be protected as distinct peoples,[42] is foreseen to the extent that community protocols,

[36] Anaya and Williams Jr. (2001: 45). See Inter-American Court of Human Rights, Case of *the Mayagna (Sumo) Awas Tingni Community v. Nicaragua*, Judgment of August 31, 2001, para. 149; Case of the *Yakye Axa Indigenous Community v. Paraguay*, Judgment of June 17, 2005, para. 143; Case of *the Moiwana Community v. Suriname*, Judgment of June 15, 2005, para. 133; Case of *the Sawhoyamaxa Indigenous Community v. Paraguay*, Judgment of March 29, 2006, para. 120; Case of *Kaliña and Lokono v. Suriname* (hereinafter *Kaliña and Lokono* case), Judgment of November 25, 2015, para. 103. Inter-American Commission on Human Rights, *Mary and Carrie Dann v. United States*, Report No. 75/02 of December 2002, 27, para. 128; *Maya Indigenous Communities of the Toledo District v. Belize*, Report No. 40/04 of October 12, 2004, para. 114. See also Report of the Committee set up to examine the representation alleging non-observance by Peru of the Indigenous and Tribal People's Convention, 1989 (No. 169), made under article 24 of the ILO Constitution by the General Confederation of Workers of Peru (CGTP), para. 32(b); Supreme Court of Canada, *Delgamuukw v. British Columbia*, Judgment of December 11, 1997, paras. 194, 199, and 201; Constitutional Court of South Africa, *Richtersveld Community and Others v. Alexkor Ltd and Another*, Judgement of October 14, 2003, para. 62. See also Report of the Special Rapporteur on the right to food, UN Doc. A/65/281 (11 August 2010), para. 12: "Property, as protected under article 21 of the American Convention on Human Rights, is considered to constitute a collective right of indigenous people, since land ownership is often centred not on the individual, but rather on the group and its community," and para. 26. Collective ownership is also reflected in the declarations made by indigenous peoples. See, for example, Charter of the Indigenous and Tribal Peoples of the Tropical Forests (Penang, 15 February 1992), Art. 16; Indigenous Peoples' Earth Charter, Kari-Oca Conference (25–30 May 1992), para. 2; Indigenous Peoples' Plan of Implementation on Sustainable Development (Johannesburg, 2 September 2002), para. 6; Kimberley Declaration, International Indigenous Peoples Summit on Sustainable Development Khoi-San Territory (Kimberley, 20–23 August 2002), para. 7; Corobici Declaration (San José, 6–7 December 2004), General Principle 1; Output document, Indigenous Peoples International Conference on Sustainable Development and Self Determination (Rio de Janeiro, 17–19 June 2012), principle 2; Alta Outcome Document, Global Indigenous Preparatory Conference for the United Nations High Level Plenary Meeting of the General Assembly to be known as the World Conference on Indigenous Peoples (Alta, 10–12 June 2013), Theme 1 that reaffirmed indigenous land tenure systems.

[37] Art. 26(3) UNDRIPS.

[38] *Saramaka* case, paras. 115 and 128; CERD, Considerations of reports submitted by States parties under article 9 of the Convention, Suriname, UN doc. CERD/C/SUR/13-15 (April 11, 2014), paras. 13–19; Human Rights Committee, Concluding Observations on Suriname, UN doc. CCPR/C/SUR/3 (March 7, 2014), paras. 101–147). On related State duties, see Cittadino (2019: 84–87).

[39] Heinämäki (2010: 31–35).

[40] See Section 2.2.1.

[41] On the content of self-determination and the way this right is applied by human rights treaty bodies, see Cittadino (2019: 125–139).

[42] Cittadino (2019); Heinämäki (2010: 58–63).

customary laws, and ICCAs are considered legitimate legal tools to implement the CBD regime. Also, Indigenous participation in the CBD Working Group on Article 8(j), the Subsidiary Body on Article 8(j), and the Compliance Committee of the Nagoya Protocol confirms the view that the right to self-determination of Indigenous Peoples implies the participation of Indigenous Peoples in norm-making processes at the international level, given the extensive impact these may have on the enjoyment of Indigenous rights.[43] In this sense, if Article 8(j) of the CBD and the relevant provisions of the Nagoya Protocol were to be implemented in full, the CBD would offer to Indigenous Peoples a legal framework where their rights could specifically be exercised.[44]

The main mechanism through which the CBD framework reinforces Indigenous Peoples' rights is by incorporating them through systemic interpretation of its provisions read in conjunction with IHRL and UNDRIPS provisions. Pursuant to Article 31(3)(c) of the Vienna Convention on the Law of the Treaties,[45] any treaty must be interpreted, in addition to literal, teleological, and contextual interpretation, by taking into account "any relevant rules of international law applicable in the relations between the parties." Furthermore, Article 22 of the CBD establishes that rights and obligations deriving from other treaties shall not be affected, unless they pose a serious threat to biodiversity. Similarly, Article 4(3) of the Nagoya Protocol enshrines the principle of mutual supportiveness, according to which "the Protocol should be implemented in a mutually supportive manner with other international instruments relevant to" it. In this sense, the Preamble of the Nagoya Protocol also notes the UNDRIPS, thus explicitly acknowledging the centrality of this instrument in the legal framework of the Nagoya Protocol.

In line with that, when filling the interpretative gaps of both Article 8(j) of the CBD and the abovementioned provisions of the Nagoya Protocol that refer to Indigenous Peoples, rights to land, natural resources, participation, and the right and the principle of self-determination must be considered both to give full meaning to CBD provisions and to make them fully operational. In other words, the CBD framework must be interpreted and implemented in ways that not only do not negatively affect existing rights protected under IHRL, but also promote them in the context of the CBD. In particular, self-determination is intended as a teleological limit to avoid interpretations of the CBD and related treaties that may cause an infringement of Indigenous rights that affect their cultural distinctiveness (Cittadino 2019: 67 ff).[46] In addition, community protocols, references to

[43] Heinämäki (2010: 63).

[44] On the limits related to implementation, see Section 2.3.1.

[45] Vienna, May 23, 1969, in force January 27, 1980.

[46] The reports of the former Special Rapporteur on Human Rights and the Environment John Knox and John Boyd have recommended that States respect the rights of Indigenous Peoples when implementing the CBD. See Report of the Special Rapporteur on the issue of human rights obligations relating to the enjoyment of a safe, clean, healthy and sustainable environment, UN doc. A/HRC/34/49 (January 19, 2017); Report of the Special Rapporteur on the issue of human rights obligations relating to the enjoyment of a safe, clean, healthy and sustainable environment, David R. Boyd, UN doc. A/75/161 (July 15, 2020), paras. 72 and 92. The latter report also recommends to ratify the Nagoya Protocol in order to ensure benefit-sharing.

customary laws, and acknowledgment of ICCAs as accepted conservation measures, are concrete legal requirements to realize Indigenous Peoples' rights in the context of the CBD.

Another important contribution of the CBD regime to Indigenous Peoples' rights is also reflected in the case law of the Inter-American Court of Human Rights (IACtHR), in which infringements of Indigenous Peoples' rights are tested against participation and benefit-sharing requirements that are based, inter-alia, upon CBD-related standards. This means that the CBD legal framework is starting to be used by human rights treaty bodies to operationalize the proportionality requirement that permits to test the validity of restrictions on Indigenous Peoples' rights. In the *Kaliña and Lokono v. Suriname* case, notably, the IACtHR explicitly cited Articles 8(j) and 10(c), as well as the PoWPA, to reinforce the argument that participatory safeguards and benefit-sharing have to be implemented when creating a natural reserve within the communities' lands in order not to infringe upon Indigenous Peoples' participatory rights grounded in Article 23 of the American Convention on Human Rights (Aguilera 2023; Cittadino 2019: 289; Tomaselli & Cittadino 2021).[47]

In another recent case, *Lhaka Honhat v. Argentina*,[48] the IACtHR referred to Articles 8(j) and 10(c) of the CBD to define the scope of Indigenous Peoples' environmental rights, as enshrined in both Articles 20(1), 29(1), and 32(1) of the UNDRIPS and Article XIX of the American Declaration on the Rights of Indigenous Peoples.[49] In particular, this reference serves to reinforce the link between environmental protection of Indigenous lands and natural resources and the cultural distinctiveness of Indigenous Peoples, which, as argued by the Court, are highly interdependent (Aguilera 2023). In this sense, the CBD framework is used to substantiate this link, thus reinforcing the environmental dimension of Indigenous Peoples' rights.

Furthermore, the CBD contributes to enlarging the scope of Indigenous Peoples' rights as protected under IHRL. The scope of Indigenous rights within the CBD regime may in some cases be more extensive than in IHRL: the participation of Indigenous Peoples when accessing genetic resources and TK, as well as when creating protected areas, needs to be ensured even in the absence of a restriction to any other substantive rights of Indigenous Peoples (Cittadino 2019; Girard et al. 2022: 15). In contrast, in IHRL, FPIC is to be ensured as a procedural requirement to avoid the violation of Indigenous rights when their enjoyment is restricted.[50]

[47] Art. 23 of the American Convention protects the right to democratic participation. Aguilera (2023: 87) argues that in the *Kaliña and Lokono* case the Inter-American Court of Human Rights blurred the lines between general public participation and the right to consultation of Indigenous Peoples, which instead should be recognized by reason of their cultural distinctiveness and in order to preserve that.

[48] *Case of the Indigenous Communities of the Lhaka Honhat (Our Land) Association v. Argentina*, Judgment of February 6, 2020.

[49] See American Declaration on the Rights of Indigenous Peoples, AG/RES.2888 (XLVI-O/16) (June 15, 2016).

[50] See Section 2.2.4.

The CBD framework inter-alia reinforces the nature of Indigenous Peoples' rights as collective rights, as it also proves facilitating when recognizing Indigenous Peoples as collective rights-holders and collective subjects of rights. A case in point of the former is the Nagoya Protocol that, for establishing Indigenous Peoples' entitlement to TK, refers to traditional sources of law that are produced collectively, such as Indigenous customary laws and community protocols. An illustration of the latter point (collective subjects of rights) is the trigger procedure of the Compliance Mechanism of the Nagoya Protocol described in Section 2.2: The compliance committee can hear not only individual claims resembling the procedures followed by human rights courts, but also collective ones transmitted by groups that provide information on parties' non-compliance (Zheng 2021: 70). This means that complaints can be filed by groups and peoples, thus recognizing their collective subjectivity, vesting them with legal personality.

In this sense, the CBD contributes to transforming the dominant understanding of human rights as individual rights (Badger 2011). The collective conception of Indigenous rights promoted by the CBD might prompt human rights courts and treaty bodies both to acknowledge the collective nature of Indigenous rights, as for instance the IACtHR and the African Commission on Human and Peoples' Rights already did,[51] and to recognize the admissibility of complaints filed by groups, which is a quite underexplored frontier. Concerning the collective nature of Indigenous rights, the European Court of Human Rights (ECtHR), the Human Rights Committee (HRC), the Committee on Economic, Social and Cultural Rights (CESCR),[52] and the Committee on the Elimination of Racial Discrimination (CERD) so far have embraced the notion of individual rights that can be enjoyed collectively to protect minority rights (Cittadino 2019: 51). Indeed, also the IACtHR's collective conception of Indigenous Peoples' rights is limited to specific rights, such as inter-alia land and natural resources, cultural identity, consultation and consent, and could be expanded further in light of the CBD legal framework. A collective conception of Indigenous rights could be embraced by human rights

[51] The communitarian interpretation of Indigenous land rights was inaugurated in the Inter-American system, with the so-called *Awas Tingni* case, para. 149. On the *Awas Tingni* case, see Anaya and Grossman (2002). The orientation about collective land rights was confirmed in following jurisprudence, for example Case of *the Yakye Axa Indigenous Community v. Paraguay*, Judgment of June 17, 2005, para. 143; *Case of the Moiwana Community v. Suriname*, Judgement of June 15, 2005, para. 133; *Case of the Sawhoyamaxa Indigenous Community v. Paraguay*, Judgment of March 29, 2006; *Kaliña and Lokono* case, para. 103. Concerning the decisions of the African system, see African Court on Human and Peoples' Rights, *African Commission on Human and Peoples' Rights v. Republic of Kenya*, Judgment of May 26, 2017, paras. 123–131. African Commission on Human and Peoples' Rights, *The Social and Economic Rights Action Center and the Center for Economic and Social Rights v. Nigeria*, Decision of October 27, 2001, para. 63; *Centre for Minority Rights Development (Kenya) and Minority Rights Group International on behalf of Endorois Welfare Council v. Kenya*, Decision of February 4, 2010, para. 196.

[52] The HRC and the CESCR are the monitoring bodies of, respectively, the International Covenant on Civil and Political Rights (New York, December 16, 1966, in force March 23, 1976, 999 UNTS 171) (hereinafter ICCPR) and the International Covenant on Economic, Social and Cultural Rights (hereinafter ICESCR).

courts and treaty bodies also in view of the universal nature of the UNDRIPS that was almost universally adopted by the UN General Assembly.[53] Regarding the second aspect (admissibility of complaints filed by groups), the requirement that complainants must be individually affected by the infringement of protected rights might evolve for instance before the ECtHR in a way to consider Indigenous groups as admissible complainants.[54] This was the case for environmental organizations in climate litigation (see *Klimaseniorinnen* case)[55] and might be extended to Indigenous Peoples living in Europe, also in the case of other environmental impacts.

The CBD framework also contributes to identifying new ways through which Indigenous Peoples' rights might be implemented in a pluralistic way (Herencia Carrasco 2019: 169). This is the case, for instance, of community protocols and related customs (Cittadino 2019: 343) under Article 12(1) of the Nagoya Protocol that need to be considered when implementing participatory and benefit-sharing requirements in relation with TK.[56] This requirement is a new way to implement cultural and participatory rights, as community protocols live up to Indigenous Peoples' practices, procedures, and traditions also being co-drafted by Indigenous communities, and also reflect the extent to which and the modalities in which Indigenous groups are willing to engage with external actors. They could therefore represent a way for Indigenous Peoples to determine steps of Indigenous engagement where decisions on their land and resources are concerned. The reference to communities' customary laws in the same provision is furthermore a way to formalize legal pluralism in the context of the Nagoya Protocol, because issues of entitlement to TK and related participatory and benefit-sharing requirements must be determined with reference to Indigenous Peoples' customs. In addition, ICCAs are a pluralistic modality to recognize the conservation efforts made by Indigenous Peoples and their contribution to the biodiversity protection obligations of States. ICCAs constitute an example of Other Effective Area-based Conservation Measures (OECMs), defined in Article 2 of the CBD as "a geographically defined area other than a Protected Area, which is governed and managed in ways that achieve positive and sustained long-term outcomes for the in situ conservation of biodiversity."[57] In this sense, ICCAs may help CBD parties to achieve in-situ conservation objectives. In view of these

[53] Four States originally voted against, namely Canada, the USA, New Zealand, and Australia, but later they reversed their position. See https://social.desa.un.org/issues/indigenous-peoples/united-nations-declaration-on-the-rights-of-indigenous-peoples.

[54] This is already so before the IACtHR. See IACtHR, *Advisory Opinion OC-22/16 of February 26, 2016, Requested by the Republic of Panama*, Entitlement of Legal Entities to Hold Rights under the Inter-American Human Rights System (Interpretation and Scope of Article 1(2), in Relation to Articles 1(1), 8, 11(2), 13, 16, 21, 24, 25, 29, 30, 44, 46 and 62(3) of the American Convention on Human Rights, as well as of Article 8(1)(a) and (b) of the Protocol of San Salvador.

[55] *Case of Verein Klimaseniorinnen Schweiz and Others v. Switzerland*, Application no. 53600/20 (April 9, 2024).

[56] Under IHRL, indigenous customs are to be taken into account in the jurisprudence of the Inter-American system. See Heinämäki (2010: 35–36, 78).

[57] See also COP dec. 14/8, CBD/COP/DEC/14/8 (November 30, 2018).

provisions, the legal pluralism in accommodating Indigenous legal justice systems, customs, and procedures already present in the IHRL framework (Eichler & Navarro 2023: 9 ff) is therefore reinforced by the CBD legal framework.

2.3.1 Limitations of the Convention on Biological Diversity Regime

Notwithstanding the explicit recognition of the role of Indigenous Peoples within the CBD regime and the adoption of important legal tools (benefit-sharing, participatory rights, community protocols, ICCAs, and recognition of Indigenous customs) to support this role, the gap between the law in the books and law in action remains huge in the case of CBD Indigenous-specific provisions. As observed by Parks and Tsioumani (2023: 6), CBD and Nagoya Protocol provisions on Indigenous Peoples have rarely been transposed into domestic laws. Lack of implementation is therefore one of the main limitations of this regime in the sense of its concrete impact on the rights of Indigenous Peoples. The lack of a solid legal framework domestically is usually combined with abuses of rights perpetrated by private companies (Sangha et al. 2019).

The gap between abstract legal standards and how they are translated in practice is, broadly speaking, considerable in this field (Parks & Tsioumani 2023: 4).[58] For instance, regarding ABS standards, some authors highlight that the content of community protocols is hardly understandable for people outside the communities because these are "emanations of customary rules" and traditions expressed in different forms while difficult to isolate from the sociocultural context in which they are embedded (Girard et al. 2022: 16). The same authors add that interactions are problematic because they are usually driven by external stakeholders. Difficulties abound in practice also in the field of conservation: Champagne-Côté et al. (2023) have illustrated that creating Indigenous protected areas is daunted with both administrative hurdles and opposition by domestic governments.

Despite these limitations, the complementarity of the CBD and the human rights regimes could be considered bidirectional. Not only are Indigenous Peoples' rights protected within the CBD in a regime-specific way, but the lack of implementation of these rights within the CBD can be challenged before human rights courts and treaty bodies (Cittadino 2019; Zheng 2021). These legal avenues provide therefore at least some remedies, such as applications before domestic courts in the first place – and when domestic remedies are exhausted, to regional human rights courts, as happened in the *Kaliña and Lokono v. Suriname* case above. Misalignments or infringements of CBD standards could also come to the fore in the decisions on individual petitions[59] as well as general comments or

[58] On the implementation of ABS standards in the food sector, see Humphries et al. (2023).

[59] For this to be possible, the State party to which the petitioners belong must have ratified optional protocols to each of the abovementioned treaties that recognize the jurisdiction of the abovementioned monitoring bodies.

recommendations adopted by the HRC, the CESCR, the Committee of the Elimination of Racial Discrimination, and the Committee on the Rights of the Child.[60] Even the petition system of the ILO monitoring system in relation to the ILO Convention 169 might be a relevant quasi-judicial forum where the failed implementation of CBD-related standards could be used as an argument to assess the violation of Indigenous Peoples' rights as stipulated in C169. In a nutshell, if States continued to fail to implement the Indigenous-specific provisions of the CBD, this failure could be challenged before human rights treaty bodies, because application of the CBD with disregard of Indigenous Peoples is likely to affect Indigenous rights to land, natural resources, participation, and self-determination to name a few.

2.4 Novel Indigenous Peoples' Rights in the Convention on Biological Diversity

This section argues that the CBD gives rise to four new categories of collective rights of Indigenous Peoples that have hitherto not been protected or only partially protected under IHRL. These are (1) the right to a fair and equitable sharing of benefits or right to benefit-sharing, (2) the right to genetic resources, (3) the right to traditional knowledge, and (4) biocultural rights. The following describes the material substance of these rights and elaborates on their added value, while also discussing (potential) limitations.

The right to benefit-sharing arises every time the TK of Indigenous Peoples and the genetic resources held by them are utilized by external actors, be they States or private actors. Such right derives from Article 8(j) of the CBD and Articles 5(2) and 5(5) of the Nagoya Protocol. Article 15(2) of the ILO Convention 169 foresees the possibility for Indigenous Peoples to participate in benefits, but only in the case of mining activities affecting Indigenous Peoples' rights to natural resources. Benefit-sharing has also been referred to as a procedural condition, together with effective participation and previous impact assessment, for the preservation of Indigenous Peoples' land and resource rights (e.g., *The Saramaka People v. Suriname*; *Endorois v. Kenya*), cultural rights (Human Rights Committee, *Apirana Mahuika et al v. New Zealand*),[61] or when protected areas are created on Indigenous Peoples' lands (*Kaliña and Lokono Peoples v. Suriname*). The former UN Special Rapporteur on Human Rights and the Environment John Knox proposed sixteen principles concerning human rights obligations related to the enjoyment of a safe, clean,

[60] These bodies, respectively, monitor the implementation of the International Convention on the Elimination of All Forms of Racial Discrimination (New York, 7 March 1966, in force 4 January 1969) and of the Convention on the Rights of the Child (New York, November 20, 1989, in force September 2, 1990).

[61] Decision of November 15, 2000, para. 9.5.

healthy, and sustainable environment, which also include benefit-sharing (Zheng 2021). Indeed, the right to benefit-sharing has gained an autonomous standing within the CBD regime that is independent from the condition for other substantive rights to be restricted. In other words, benefit-sharing under the CBD and the Nagoya Protocol is triggered by the mere utilization of TK and genetic resources, even where land, resource, and other cultural rights have not been infringed upon. This means that the CBD legal framework does not establish benefit-sharing merely as a procedural requirement to safeguard other related substantive rights as it would be the case under IHRL but instead as a material right on its own.[62] According to Articles 5(2) and 5(5) of the Nagoya Protocol, however, the right to benefit-sharing is protected mainly through domestic laws establishing legal frameworks regulating benefit-sharing. The material content of benefit-sharing is therefore not defined within the Nagoya Protocol itself (Gottschalk 2022: 62). To understand the exact substance of benefit-sharing, we must refer to CBD COP decisions and the Annex to the Nagoya Protocol; these have actually elaborated extensively on the fact that benefits can be distinguished into monetary ones and non-monetary ones.[63] The latter include, for instance, the sharing of research results, social recognition, or initiatives for capacity-building. To come back to the enforceability of this right, the Compliance Mechanism of the Nagoya Protocol can, in principle, monitor the adoption of legal standards on ABS rights, although it cannot sanction noncompliance being a nonjudicial mechanism (Zheng 2021: 66). Domestic courts instead can find a violation of this right if a domestic legislative framework on ABS was adopted.

The right to genetic resources, cited by Morgera et al. (2014: 104), would emerge from a combined reading of Articles 5(2) and 6(2) of the Nagoya Protocol. These provisions indirectly foreshadow a right to property over genetic resources while establishing a right to obtain benefit-sharing when using them accordingly. Furthermore, States would bear a positive duty to create the conditions to seek consent when they access genetic resources or when these are accessed by other actors. As for the right to genetic resources, the conditions for the enjoyment of this right must be established by domestic legislation. The question arises whether this right should be autonomous from land and natural resource rights or if the latter constitute the underlying legal titles for establishing that genetic resources are "held" by Indigenous Peoples within the meaning of the Nagoya Protocol (Cittadino 2019). Indeed, separating the right to genetic resources from resource and land rights would open more avenues for protection, for instance, where the

[62] An alternative explanation could be, as Morgera et al. (2014, p. 104) argue, that Article 5(2) of the Nagoya Protocol is "implicitly underpinned by a substantive environmental right of indigenous and local communities to their genetic resources."

[63] See Bonn Guidelines on Access and Benefit-sharing, COP dec. VI/24, CBD/COP/DEC/VI/24 (May 22, 2002).

link between genetic resources and physical resources is not easy to prove or when Indigenous customs specifically relate to genetic resources, even outside Indigenous Peoples' lands. The creation of a global mechanism to share benefits related to the use of DSI on genetic resources takes the direction of recognizing rights to genetic resources independently from land and resource rights. Enforcement could again be ensured before the Compliance Mechanism of the Nagoya Protocol and before domestic courts if a domestic legislative framework was in place (Zheng 2023: 143).

The right to TK has emerged thanks to a cross-fertilization between the CBD regime and IHRL. The roots of this right are to be found in Articles 8(j) and 10(c) of the CBD (Heinämäki 2022: 189; Solntsev 2019: 408). However, the term "traditional knowledge" is not explicitly used in the text of the CBD;[64] it made its first appearance as a specific object of a right in Article 31 of the UNDRIPS in 2007. According to this provision, TK is articulated in the context of cultural heritage, and Indigenous Peoples have the right to maintain, protect, and develop it, inter-alia by exercising intellectual property rights over TK.[65] Articles 5(5), 7, and 12 of the Nagoya Protocol have contributed to articulating the right to TK in the context of the CBD framework in a more detailed way compared to the UNDRIPS framework. Now, according to the right to TK as protected under the CBD and the Nagoya Protocol, Indigenous Peoples should be able to hold and develop TK in an undisturbed and exclusive way and to share it subject to their consent. Another obligation arises, namely for States to preserve and maintain TK, take into account community protocols and Indigenous customary law, and to support indigenous peoples in freely developing these protocols in relation to the preservation and use of TK. Indigenous Peoples, furthermore, exercise related rights to benefit-sharing when their TK is used and are granted the right to consent when their TK is accessed by external actors.

The question may arise of whether this right could not be subsumed under the category of Indigenous Peoples' cultural rights (James 2020), deriving from the principle of nondiscrimination, and pursuant to Article 5(a) and (b) of the ILO

[64] Some authors observe the term TK is not employed by Indigenous Peoples that prefer to refer to "Indigenous and Local Knowledge" (Reyes-García et al. 2022: 86). The notion of TK in the CBD would seemingly be unfit to capture the complexities of Indigenous cosmovision and how it is being transmitted across generations (Whyte 2013: 9).

[65] Art. 31(1) UNDRIPS reads as follows: "Indigenous peoples have the right to maintain, control, protect and develop their cultural heritage, traditional knowledge and traditional cultural expressions, as well as the manifestations of their sciences, technologies and cultures, including human and genetic resources, seeds, medicines, knowledge of the properties of fauna and flora, oral traditions, literatures, designs, sports and traditional games and visual and performing arts. They also have the right to maintain, control, protect and develop their intellectual property over such cultural heritage, traditional knowledge, and traditional cultural expressions." Art. 31 is to be read in light of Arts. 11–12 UNDRIPS that protect the right of Indigenous Peoples to preserve, develop, and transmit their cultural and religious traditions. Intellectual property rights over TK are outside the scope of this chapter, but an important development has recently occurred in this field. The World Intellectual Property Organization (WIPO) has been working on developing a legal framework on intellectual property rights relating to TK and genetic resources for more than twenty years. WIPO has recently managed to adopt the text of a treaty on this topic. See WIPO Treaty on Intellectual Property, Genetic Resources and Associated Traditional Knowledge (Geneva, May 14, 2024, not yet in force).

Convention 169, which protects "social, cultural, religious, and spiritual values and practices" and their integrity.[66] The right to TK may further be derived from Articles 7 and 8 of the UNDRIPS protecting Indigenous Peoples' distinctiveness and preventing forced assimilation as ontological condition for the enjoyment of any other collective right (Aguilera 2023: 77). Indeed, none of these provisions capture precisely the notion of TK that is only protected indirectly through cultural rights. TK goes beyond the notion of cultural rights and might be defined as "the knowledge, innovations and practices of indigenous and local communities embodying traditional lifestyles relevant for the conservation and sustainable use of biological diversity"[67] also embodying lifestyles relevant for conservation. A specific right to protect TK would therefore improve the comprehensiveness of Indigenous Peoples' rights (Cittadino 2019: 185). Furthermore, when compared to the UNDRIPS (Arts. 11–13, 15, and 31), the right to TK as specified in the CBD legal framework contains specific participatory and procedural requirements that are not foreseen otherwise. Article 31(2) UNDRIPS for instance requires States "to take effective measures to recognize and protect the exercise of" the right to cultural heritage and TK, but it does not specify that utilization of this knowledge requires prior consent and implies benefit-sharing and other requirements about taking into account Indigenous customs, as specified in the CBD regime (do Vale Alves forthcoming). The novelty of TK in the CBD consists precisely in the fact that it contains – or may even consist of – Indigenous nonanthropocentric conceptions of nature. In this sense, TK requires an understanding of the protection of biodiversity that is enmeshed with culture and would, in turn, require a transformation of the very CBD regime in terms of how nature protection is conceived, thus challenging the Western notion that culture and nature are separated (Mazzocchi 2020).

When TK, is intended as accommodating both culture and nature, it corresponds to the notion of biocultural heritage[68] and therefore overlaps with biocultural rights (Bavikatte 2014; Mulrennan & Bussières 2020). These rights contain two equally important foundations, nature and culture, and are bound to environmental protection. In this sense, they also imply a duty to protect the environment for Indigenous Peoples – constituting an important source of subsistence, carrying spiritual significance and beyond – and can therefore also be described as "rights to environmental stewardship" (Sajeva 2018; 2022: p. 173). The advantage of these rights would therefore be that they incorporate a holistic vision of nature that is bound to culture, common to Indigenous Peoples' cosmovisions. At the same time, biocultural rights would protect Indigenous Peoples' culture and the practical

[66] See also Arts. 8 and 23 ILO Convention 169.

[67] Secretariat of the Convention on Biological Diversity (2019), Glossary of Relevant Key Terms and Concepts within the Context of Article 8(j) and Related Provisions (CBD Guidelines Series), p. 2. As stated in this publication adopted by the CBD COP with dec. 14/13, CBD/COP/DEC/14/13 (November 30, 2018), Annex, this definition is derived from Art. 8(j) CBD. For a definition of TK, see also Parks and Tsioumani (2023: 2), Heinämäki (2022: 187); Cardoso Rodrigues (2017: 152).

[68] See https://biocultural.iied.org/evolving-concept.

manifestations thereof only to the extent that these contribute to the protection of nature, thus limiting Indigenous Peoples' autonomy as to their future development (Sajeva 2022). This limitation, however, is somehow integral to the fact that if these arose specifically in the framework of the CBD, they would need to be in accordance with the aims and the scope of the CBD. Furthermore, as practice shows, Indigenous Peoples' groups and their organizations have often used the argument of a substantial alignment of their ways of life and cosmovision with nature protection to claim a bolder international acknowledgment of their role in the protection of the environment and related decision-making.[69] This argument has also been used by human rights treaty bodies to ascertain the violation of Indigenous rights based on environmental impacts of external activities on their lands (Aguilera 2023; Cittadino 2019). The recognition of rights bound to nature protection could therefore be seen as an indirect consequence of the strategy pursued by Indigenous Peoples at the international level. This recognition would furthermore be justified by the existing link between the integrity of Indigenous lands and the preservation of their distinct culture.[70] A domestic case where the dimension of stewardship of, inter-alia, Indigenous Peoples and local communities has clearly emerged is *Tierra Digna v. Colombia*, also known as *Atrato river* case, where the Constitutional Court of Colombia designated Indigenous Peoples as guardians of the Atrato river, which was hitherto considered a subject of rights (Villavicencio Calzadilla 2019).[71] Alongside the stewardship dimension, the positive substance of biocultural rights is understood by scholars as a combination of land, self-determination, and cultural rights (Sajeva 2018: 105–110). The right to TK described above seems, in comparison to biocultural rights, more specific as to its material content since it foresees explicit procedural requirements to ensure the protection of TK through FPIC and benefit-sharing, as well as through more specific State duties to protect the right to TK.

The new rights described in this section may contribute to reinforce the conceptualization of Indigenous Peoples' rights as collective rights. Biocultural rights are based on the entwinement of culture and nature that is typical of Indigenous cosmovisions developed and transmitted within the group. The right to TK is equally based upon collective customs; it is also enshrined in the UNDRIPS,

[69] For example, Forest Peoples Programme, Indigenous Peoples' Rights, State Sovereignty and the Convention on Biological Diversity (January 25, 2004): "given Indigenous peoples' fundamental and holistic relationship with their traditional lands, territories and resources"; Indigenous Peoples' Political Declaration, Prep. Com. IV, Bali, Indonesia (June 6, 2002); Kari-oca Declaration and Indigenous Peoples' Earth Charter, World Conference of Indigenous Peoples on Territory, Environment and Development, Kari-Oca (May 25–30, 1992). This link has the been formalized for the first time in Principle 22 of the Rio Declaration and in the case law and decisions of human rights courts and treaty bodies. See Aguilera (2023) and Cittadino (2019). The link between Indigenous Peoples' ways of life and nature protection has been emphasized also in the literature: See Cardoso Rodrigues (2017: 152), Eichler and Navarro (2023), and Heinämäki (2022).

[70] *Awas Tingni* case, para. 149; *Saramaka* case, para. 128; *Endorois* case, para. 154; General Comment 23, paras. 3.2 and 7; Art. 13 ILO Convention 169; art. 25 UNDRIPS.

[71] Colombian Constitutional Court, *Tierra Digna y otros v. Presidencia de la República y otros*, Judgment No. T-622, Judgment of November 10, 2016, Expediente T-5.016.242.

which has established collective Indigenous rights. The same reasoning could be extended to the right to benefit-sharing that is closely dependent upon the right to TK. Less clear-cut is the nature of the right to genetic resources, since these might be based upon Indigenous collective property rights but they might also be independent from them. In the case of genetic resources, it remains to be seen if and how this right would be adjudicated before domestic and international courts. What is clear is that the lack of fulfilment of the provisions establishing the presented rights can be challenged before the Compliance Mechanism of the Nagoya Protocol that can receive information submitted also by Indigenous groups. This, as argued, is a sign that Indigenous Peoples are starting to be recognized as collective subjects of rights. Another element that supports the framing of these rights as collective rights is the articulation of specific State duties, notably preserving TK, establishing domestic legal frameworks for benefit-sharing and FPIC when using or accessing TK and genetic resources, and taking into consideration community protocols and customs in relation to TK.

As emerges from the scope of the described rights (right to benefit-sharing, right to genetic resources, right to TK, and biocultural rights), these are both closely connected to and highly dependent on one another. For instance, the right to benefit-sharing would not arise without an established right to TK and/or genetic resources, being understood therefore as a derivative right. It is also likely that a right to genetic resources not clearly based upon established Indigenous land rights and resource rights would have to be ascertained through Indigenous customs instead and would therefore be closely connected to TK. If we turn to biocultural rights, these are by definition a combination of rights founded upon the connection of Indigenous Peoples with the environment in which they live, and therefore built upon a combination of rights, that is, to self-determination, land, natural resources, and culture. The overlapping of these rights establishes cumulative titles of protection, thus enhancing the opportunities for their effective protection, functioning as a protective umbrella. Their enforceability at the domestic level, however, depends on whether a domestic legislative framework has been put in place.

Another common characteristic of these newly arising collective rights is that they are based both on a strong link between culture and nature and on a vision of nature that is oftentimes sacred and therefore has a value on its own independently from its use by humans. Although this aspect can be seen as constituting a nonanthropocentric conception of nature, the rights that derive from such conception are not necessarily ecocentric in nature. Indeed, the right to benefit-sharing, the right to genetic resources, the right to TK, and biocultural rights are not primarily aimed at preserving the autonomous value of nature but at compensating Indigenous Peoples for the use of their knowledge and resources.

Finally, it is not possible either to draw a sharp line between the categories of substantive and procedural rights. On the one hand, it is true that the right to benefit-sharing exists independently from the violation of other substantive rights, but this does not make it automatically a substantive right on its own rather than being a procedural right. Indeed, most of the rights described above, except for biocultural rights, are mainly fulfilled through procedural requirements. However, there are other aspects, such as the need to preserve TK, the right to enjoy TK, and the complex nature of benefit-sharing that are substantive rather than procedural. Therefore, the picture remains nuanced.

2.5 Conclusion

This chapter has shown that the CBD as an international environmental regime gives new meaning to the concept of indigenous environmental rights. These are meant in this contribution not as human rights that protect the collective enjoyment by Indigenous Peoples of the environment, but instead as environmental provisions that give substance to indigenous human rights as they materialize in some specific regimes. The CBD and its Nagoya Protocol contain provisions that help implementing Indigenous rights to land, natural resources, cultural rights, FPIC, and self-determination, and complement protection thereof in the context of biodiversity protection and ABS. The provisions concerned are those on the protection of TK; those requiring benefit-sharing in case of the use of TK and genetic resources belonging to Indigenous Peoples; consent-like obligations where Indigenous TK and genetic resources are being accessed; those establishing a Compliance Mechanism within the Nagoya Protocol; those CBD COP decisions that require the participation of Indigenous Peoples while establishing protected areas; and those that acknowledge the recognition of ICCAs as suitable conservation schemes. These provisions build on existing Indigenous Peoples' *rights* and aim to complement them, as well as to facilitate their implementation in the CBD context. The rights at stake are Indigenous Peoples' cultural rights, land and resource rights, participatory rights, and ultimately the collective right to self-determination. The ways through which the CBD reinforces and expands on existing rights include the following, the incorporation of Indigenous rights in the CBD by means of systemic interpretation; the reference made to the CBD by international human rights bodies to ascertain the violation of Indigenous Peoples' rights; the broader scope of some Indigenous Peoples' rights, such as participatory rights, as protected under the CBD legal framework.

In this sense, this contribution has also demonstrated that the rights of Indigenous Peoples as protected under the CBD constitute a "*sui-generis*" regime that does not perfectly coincide with human rights. Notably, environmental rights in the CBD are informing existing human rights and complementing Indigenous Rights as protected under IHRL.

This contribution finally argues that the CBD regime gives rise to four new categories of collective rights of Indigenous Peoples that are not (fully) protected under IHRL. These are the right to benefit-sharing, the right to genetic resources, the right to traditional knowledge, and biocultural rights. These rights bear a good potential for additional protection because they apply to situations that would otherwise not be covered under IHRL, the entitlement to genetic resources being illustrative. At the same time, their applicability is limited only to cases where biodiversity protection or ABS are concerned. Furthermore, uncertainties and limitations arise when it comes to the recognition and implementation of these four new categories of rights: lack of implementation of CBD provisions at domestic level would mean that these "new" rights would not be well-founded in domestic legal systems and therefore hardly enforceable at that level. Enforceability may be ensured at the international level with the Compliance Mechanism of the Nagoya Protocol, which, however, as explained above, may only facilitate implementation rather than sanctioning lack of compliance. Enforceability could also be ensured before human rights treaty bodies, should these courts and quasi-judicial bodies be able to establish a link between the legal titles presented here and the rights of Indigenous Peoples that are already protected under their jurisdictions.

In terms of the theoretical contribution of these rights, this chapter has demonstrated that the CBD legal framework contributes to reinforcing legal pluralism, as it refers to and recognizes autonomous Indigenous legal sources, customs, practices, and procedures for assessing Indigenous Peoples' entitlements to TK and, indirectly, to genetic resources. Furthermore, the CBD framework contributes to reinforcing the category of Indigenous Peoples' collective rights and collective entitlement to rights, because not only does it reinforce existing collective rights, but it also creates new collective rights.

Finally, Indigenous Peoples' rights protected under the CBD framework, although carrying a strong environmental component, do not perfectly coincide with the categories of environmental rights to which the literature currently refers, namely rights to nature, human rights to the environment, and environmental participatory rights (Heinämäki 2010). As discussed in this chapter, Indigenous Peoples' environmental rights protected under the CBD are mainly anthropocentric and not focused on the protection of the environment: Although they embrace holistic visions of nature and are complemented by culture, the main purpose of Indigenous environmental rights (under the CBD) is not to protect the environment in which Indigenous Peoples live in but to compensate them for the use of their TK and genetic resources. Furthermore, these rights cannot completely be assimilated under the category of environmental participatory rights, because they go beyond participation and instead embrace more substantive rights.

References

Aguilera, M. G. (2023). *Environmental Human Rights: New Thinking from Latin America and the Caribbean*. Brill Nijhoff.

Åhrén, M. (2016). *Indigenous Peoples' Status in the International Legal System*. Oxford University Press.

Anaya, S. J. & Grossman, C. (2002). The Case of Awas Tingni v. Nicaragua: A new Step in the International Law of Indigenous Peoples. *Arizona Journal of International and Comparative Law*, 19(1), 1–15.

Anaya, S. J. & Williams, R. A., Jr. (2001). The Protection of Indigenous Peoples' Rights over Lands and Natural Resources under the Inter-American Human Rights System. *Harvard Human Rights Journal*, 14: 33–86.

Badger, A. (2011). Collective v. Individual Human Rights in Membership Governance for Indigenous Peoples. *American University International Law Review*, 26(2), 485–514.

Barelli, M. (2016). *Seeking Justice in International Law: The Significance and Implications of the UN Declaration on the Rights of Indigenous Peoples*. Routledge.

Bavikatte, S. K. (2014). *Stewarding the Earth: Rethinking Property and the Emergence of Biocultural Rights*. Oxford University Press.

Cantú Rivera, H. (2021). Towards a Global Framework on Business and Human Rights, Indigenous Peoples, and Their Right to Consultation and Free, Prior and Informed Consent, in Wright, C. & Tomaselli, A. (eds.), *The Prior Consultation of Indigenous Peoples in Latin America: Inside the Implementation Gap* (pp. 27–40). Routledge.

Cardoso Rodrigues, P. (2017). The Environmental Protection of Traditional Knowledge and the Active Participation of Indigenous Peoples in the Planning, Management and Decision-Making Processes as means of Improving the Effectiveness of Environmental Law, in Maljean-Dubois, S. (ed.), *The Effectiveness of Environmental Law* (pp. 149–170). Cambridge University Press.

Cariño, J. & Farhan Ferrari, M. (2021). Negotiating the Futures of Nature and Cultures: Perspectives from Indigenous Peoples and Local Communities about the Post-2020 Global Biodiversity Framework. *Journal of Ethnobiology*, 41(2), 192–208.

Champagne-Côté, R., Beaudoin, J.-M., Bélanger, L., St-Onge, M., Asselin, H., & Suffice, P. (2023). Indigenous Leadership in Creating a Protected Area: The Akumunan Biodiversity Reserve (Canada). *Global Ecology and Conservation*, 48(2), e02681.

Cittadino, F. (2019). *Incorporating Indigenous Rights in the International Regime on Biodiversity Protection: Access, Benefit-Sharing and Conservation in Indigenous Lands*. Brill Nijhoff.

do Vale Alves, A. (forthcoming). Article 31, in Eichler, J., Doyle, C., & Howard, S. (eds.), *United Nations Declaration on the Rights of Indigenous Peoples: Article-by-Article Commentary*. Beck • Hart • Nomos.

Doyle, C. M. (2015). *Indigenous Peoples, Title to Territory, Rights and Resources: The Transformative Role of Free Prior and Informed Consent*. Routledge.

Eichler, J. (2019). *Reconciling Indigenous Peoples' Individual and Collective Rights: Participation, Prior Consultation and Self-Determination in Latin America*. Routledge.

Eichler, J. & Navarro, F. V. M. (2023). Proceduralising Indigenous Peoples' Demands: Indigenous Environmental Rights and Legal Pluralism in Contemporary Jurisprudence. *Legal Pluralism and Critical Social Analysis*, 55(1), 5–34.

Garnett, S. T., Burgess, N. D., Fa, J. E., Fernández-Llamazares, Á., Molnár, Z., Robinson, C. J., Watson, J. E. M., Zander, K. K., Austin, B., Brondizio, E. S., Collier, N. F., Duncan, T., Ellis, E., Geyle, H., Jackson, M. V., Jonas, H., Malmer, P., McGowan, B., Sivongxay, A., & Leiper, I. (2018). A Spatial Overview of the Global Importance of Indigenous Lands for Conservation. *Nature Sustainability*, 1(7), 369–374.

Girard, F., Hall, I., & Frison, C. (eds.). (2022). *Biocultural Rights, Indigenous Peoples and Local Communities: Protecting Culture and the Environment*. Routledge.

Gottschalk, P. (2022). Taking Environmental Rights in the Anthropocene Seriously: The Case of Biodiversity and the Nagoya Protocol, in Baber, W. F. & May, J. R. (eds.),

Environmental Human Rights in the Anthropocene: Concepts, Contexts, and Challenges (pp. 52–69). Cambridge University Press.

Heinämäki, L. (2022). Indigenous Peoples Environmental Human Rights – From Objects of Protection towards Stewardship: Assessment of Current International Standards, in Newman, D. G. (ed.), *Research Handbook on the International Law of Indigenous Rights* (pp. 169–201). Edward Elgar Publishing.

Heinämäki, L. (2010). The Right to Be a Part of Nature: Indigenous Peoples and the Environment (Dissertation), University of Lapland.

Herencia Carrasco, S. (2019). The Rights of Indigenous Peoples in the Jurisprudence of the Inter-American Court of Human Rights: A 'Third World Approaches to International Law' Assessment to Advance Their Protection in the Inter-American Human Rights System, in Corradi, G., Desmet, E., Feyter, K. d., & Vanhees, K. (eds.), *Critical Indigenous Rights Studies* (pp. 160–177). Routledge

Humphries, F., Laird, S., Wynberg, R., Morrison, C., Lawson, C., & Kolesnikova, A. (2023). *Survey of Access and Benefit-Sharing Country Measures Accommodating the Distinctive Features of Genetic Resources for Food and Agriculture and Associated Traditional Knowledge*. FAO.

James, S. P. (2020). Legal Rights and Nature's Contributions to People: Is There a Connection? *Biological Conservation*, 241(Part A), 108325.

Klein, L., Muñoz-Torres, M. J., & Fernández-Izquierdo, M. Á. (2024). Free, Prior, and Informed Consent. *International Journal on Minority and Group Rights*, 31(5), 898–926.

Mazzocchi, F. (2020). A Deeper Meaning of Sustainability: Insights from Indigenous Knowledge. *The Anthropocene Review*, 7(1), 77–93.

Morgera, E., Buck, M., & Tsioumani, E. (2014). *Unraveling the Nagoya Protocol: A Commentary on the Nagoya Protocol on Access and Benefit-sharing to the Convention on Biological Diversity*. Brill Nijhoff.

Morgera, E. & Tsioumani, E. (2010). The Evolution of Benefit-Sharing: Linking Biodiversity and Community Livelihoods. *Review of European Community and International Environmental Law*, 19, 150–173.

Mulrennan, M. E. & Bussières, V. (2020). Indigenous Environmental Stewardship: Do Mechanisms of Biodiversity Conservation Align with or Undermine It?, in Turner, N. J. (ed.), *Plants, People, and Places* (pp. 282–312). McGill-Queen's University Press.

Osakada, Y. (2021). Indigenous Peoples as Actors in International Law-making: Focusing on International Environmental Law, in Scott, K. N. (ed.), *Changing Actors in International Law* (pp. 101–129). Brill Nijhoff.

Parks, L. & Tsioumani, E. (2023). Transforming Biodiversity Governance?: Indigenous Peoples' Contributions to the Convention on Biological Diversity. *Biological Conservation*, 280(4), 1–11.

Reyes-García, V., Fernández-Llamazares, Á., Aumeeruddy-Thomas, Y., Benyei, P., Bussmann, R. W., Diamond, S. K., García-Del-Amo, D., Guadilla-Sáez, S., Hanazaki, N., Kosoy, N., Lavides, M., Luz, A. C., McElwee, P., Meretsky, V. J., Newberry, T., Molnár, Z., Ruiz-Mallén, I., Salpeteur, M., Wyndham, F. S., Zorondo-Rodriguez, F., & Brondizio, E. S. (2022). Recognizing Indigenous Peoples' and Local Communities' Rights and Agency in the Post-2020 Biodiversity Agenda. *Ambio*, 51(1), 84–92.

Sajeva, G. (2022). The Legal Framework behind Biocultural Rights: An Analysis of Their Pros and Cons for Indigenous Peoples and Local Communities, in Girard, F., Hall, I., &

Frison, C. (eds.), *Biocultural Rights, Indigenous Peoples and Local Communities: Protecting Culture and the Environment* (pp. 165–181). Routledge

Sajeva, G. (2018). *When Rights Embrace Responsibilities: Biocultural Rights and the Conservation of Environment*. Oxford University Press.

Sangha, K. K., Maynard, S., Pearson, J., Dobriyal, P., Badola, R., & Hussain, S. A. (2019). Recognising the Role of Local and Indigenous Communities in Managing Natural Resources for the Greater Public Benefit: Case Studies from Asia and Oceania Region. *Ecosystem Services*, 39(4), 100991.

Sobrevila, C. (2008). *The Role of Indigenous Peoples in Biodiversity Conservation: The Natural but Often Forgotten Partners* [Online], International Bank for Reconstruction; World Bank. Available at: https://siteresources.worldbank.org/INTBIODIVERSITY/Resources/RoleofIndigenousPeoplesinBiodiversityConservation.pdf.

Solntsev, A. (2019). Indigenous Peoples and Environmental Rights, in May, J. R. & Daly, E. (eds.), *Human Rights and the Environment: Legality Indivisibility Dignity and Geography* (pp. 401–413). Edward Elgar Publishing.

Tobin, B. (2014). *Indigenous Peoples, Customary Law and Human Rights: Why Living Law Matters*. Routledge.

Tomaselli, A. & Cittadino, F. (2021). Land, Consultation and Participation Rights of Indigenous Peoples in the Jurisprudence of the Inter-American Court of Human Rights: The Cases of *Kichwa Indigenous People of Sarayaku v. Ecuador* and *Kaliña and Lokono v. Suriname*, in Villiers, B. de, Marko, J., Palermo, F., & Constantin, S. (eds.), *Litigating the Rights of Minorities and Indigenous Peoples in Domestic and International Courts* (pp. 149–177). Brill Nijhoff.

Villavicencio Calzadilla, P. (2019). A Paradigm Shift in Courts' View of Nature: The Atrato River and Amazon Basin Cases in Colombia. *Law Environment and Development Journal*, 15(1): 49–59 [Online]. Available at: https://eprints.soas.ac.uk/33081/1/19049.pdf.

Whyte, K. P. (2013). On the Role of Traditional Ecological Knowledge as a Collaborative Concept: A Philosophical Study. *Ecological Processes*, 2(7).

Wiessner, S. (2013). The State and Indigenous Peoples: The Historic Significance of ILA Resolution No. 5/2012, in Breuer, M., Epiney, A., Haratsch, A., Schmahl, S., & Weiß, N. (eds.), *Der Staat im Recht: Festschrift für Eckart Klein zum 70. Geburtstag* (pp. 1357–1368). Duncker & Humblot.

Wiessner, S. (2011). The Cultural Rights of Indigenous Peoples: Achievements and Continuing Challenges. *European Journal of International Law*, 22(1), 121–140.

Wiessner, S. & Lenzerini, F. (2012). *Rights of Indigenous Peoples*. Sofia Conference.

Wright, C. & Tomaselli, A. (eds.) (2021). *The Prior Consultation of Indigenous Peoples in Latin America: Inside the Implementation Gap*. Routledge.

Zheng, X. (2023). *The Complementarity between the Nagoya Protocol and Human Rights: Genetic Resources, Traditional Knowledge and the Rights of Indigenous Peoples and Local Communities*. Springer.

Zheng, X. (2021). Empowering Indigenous Peoples and Local Communities: A Human Rights-based Appraisal of the Compliance Mechanism of the Nagoya Protocol. *Review of European, Comparative* and *International Environmental Law*, 30(1), 61–72.

Zurba, M. and Papadopoulos, A. (2023). Indigenous Participation and the Incorporation of Indigenous Knowledge and Perspectives in Global Environmental Governance Forums: A Systematic Review. *Environmental Management*, 72(1), 84–99.

PART II

Beyond the 'Human' in Indigenous Environmental Law?

Impressions from a Dualistic Debate

3

Indigenous Law, Cosmovisions, and the Rights of Nature

On Semiotic Displacements of Legal Recognition

Bart Jansen and Tineke Lambooy

If the whole world becomes Western, where will the sun rise?

(Baudrillard 2006: 82)

3.1 Introductory Remarks

One of the primary tasks of legal philosophy is to peel away the layers of simplicity that veil legal phenomena, thereby unveiling their deeper complexity. Such endeavor assists in fostering a more comprehensive and nuanced approach to law and justice, which is essential for advancing legal systems that aspire to address the complexity of reality. This complexity has been exemplified (and also addressed) by a new legal phenomenon emerging since the early twenty-first century. On September 28, 2008, Ecuador became the first State in the world to recognize the "Rights of Nature" (RoN) in its domestic constitution (Articles 71–73), an initiative often understood as the first, if not the most striking, pluralizing constitutional endeavor: "Nature shall be the subject of those rights that the Constitution recognises for it" (Article 10 Constitution). This newly established legal subjectivity challenges the notion that humans are the sole agents of the earth's functioning, sparking contentious debates in legal philosophy and serving as a catalyst for action-oriented change for many. This chapter explores the intricate relationship between Indigenous law, on the one hand, and RoN, on the other. The often-stated assertion that Indigenous law and RoN align or are even synonymous is problematized through the lens of Jean Baudrillard's ethnological semiology.

Rights of Nature is frequently associated with a rupture from traditional human rights frameworks, as it recognizes nature as an autonomous subject of rights. Some theorists regard RoN as a paradigmatic shift that emphasizes ecocentric justice rather than the protection of human interests. Others, however, contend that the core principles of RoN are already embedded within existing human rights frameworks, such as the right to a safe environment, territorial rights, or spiritual rights. This tension is particularly pertinent to Indigenous peoples, for whom the relationship between humans and nature is often intrinsically interwoven with their legal and cultural traditions. Rights of Nature as a relatively new environmental ethical discourse presents an intellectual triangulation between two legitimizing philosophical categories and a wide array of RoN: the legitimizing philosophical categories are, on the one hand, Indigenous cosmovisions and, on the other, typically Western philosophies – for instance, the Gaia writings of the celebrated Bruno Latour (2015), representing the more spiritually inclined academics, the deep ecology ideas of Arne Naess (1973), and, of those with a greater capacity for abstraction, the object-oriented ontology of Timothy Morton (2013). These categories legitimize RoN because they would revolutionize the interaction between humans and nonhumans (Boyd 2017): academic contributions focusing on the normative foundations and procedural implications within environmental law are often "ornamented"[1] by such ontological explorations that envisage nature as a rights-holder (Bellina 2024: 322; González-Serrano 2024: 11–14). Therefore, in the RoN discourse, "recognizing" RoN holds significant ethical importance. The assumption is that rights and values are intrinsic to nature: thus, treating nature justly is synonymous with recognizing these rights. Rights of Nature, as it were, invokes what Claude Lévi-Strauss termed *La pensée sauvage* [*Wild Thought*] (1962) – a mode of thought in which classificatory systems are not merely functional, but are also imbued with moral and spiritual significance. Recently, a "second wave" of RoN literature has emerged, which, from the perspectives of legal implications and the two discussed philosophical foundations, problematizes the RoN discourse. Such a second wave is far from being an anti-RoN discourse; it regards the more-or-less assumed equality or complementarity between Indigenous cosmovisions and RoN as categorical errors, or at the very least, views such portrayal as highly problematic (Petersmann 2024).

In this contribution, we critically reflect upon the concept of "recognition" within RoN, a term frequently regarded as conventional in (legal) literature. We contend that this term unveils not only social and historical but also theoretical complexities, in the form of teleological and categorical errors, that should be acknowledged within the RoN discourse too, as it does within the discourse of Critical Legal Studies. It is for this reason that we examine the potential "performativity" of the term in this contribution. Performativity is a well-established concept in linguistic philosophy and social theory, focusing on how language exerts an effect on reality, that is, "how to do things with words" (Austin 1962). Performativity analyses how

[1] In his *Kritik der Urteilskraft* [*Critique of Judgment*] (1790: 70), Immanuel Kant regarded the tattoos of New Zealanders as forms of ornamentation, much like the adornment of churches. He appears to reduce the tattoos to mere embellishments, overlooking the possibility that they may have a functional role in an anthropological context (Danto 2003: 40–46).

language not only *de*-scribes reality but also *pre*-scribes it. Bourdieu refers to this as the "principle of magical efficacy" of the performative (Bourdieu 1980: 188). The performative brings about what it asserts through the declarations it makes. This magical efficacy does not reside so much in the language itself but in the group that authorizes and recognizes this language, and thereby authorizes and recognizes itself.

In this chapter, we use examples from Oceania owing to the unique cosmologies and traditional knowledge (TK) held by Indigenous peoples in this region, particularly in New Zealand and Australia, which offer profound insights into the significance of nature for these communities and its supposed intrinsic value. These perspectives can provide valuable insights for the concept of RoN generally, at a more abstract level. Additionally, Oceania hosts some of the most pioneering examples of the legal recognition of RoN. For instance, the Whanganui River in New Zealand has been granted legal personhood, setting a significant precedent for recognizing natural entities as legal subjects. These legal novelties can serve as case studies and inspiration for other jurisdictions globally (Willems et al. 2021: 11).[2] Moreover, the relationship between Indigenous peoples and their land in Oceania is imbued with cultural and historical significance. Examining these relationships enables proponents of RoN to appreciate the so-called ethical foundations upon which such rights may be established and defended, which we shall explore in greater critical detail in the following section of this chapter, specifically the question of whether a metaphysical understanding of RoN is possible. Through various performatives frequently discussed in RoN literature, such as Indigenous laws versus State-centric laws, legal colonialism, the metaphysical understanding of RoN, as well as legal pluralism, our contribution aims to fulfill the task of critical theory. By introducing these concepts as performatives, we hereby propose that their "vocal" usage within the RoN discourse is tantamount to action. This performativism is unbound by truth value; rather, it holds significance as a force (Derrida 1988: 13, 17). Specifically, we aim to highlight such realities that appear mediating but may (potentially) be colonizing by addressing the implications associated with the performativity of "recognition."

3.2 A Metaphysical Understanding of Rights of Nature

Rights of Nature within environmental ethics are often associated with (Harden-Davies et al. 2020) and legally related to (Kauffman and Martin 2017; O'Donnell *et al.* 2020), or even equated with, Indigenous cosmovisions and customary law (Cano Pecharroman 2018). In this way, RoN may be attributed a modest up to a fully fledged metaphysical status – at least when considered from a Western

[2] See also the granting of legal personhood to the Atrato River in Colombia based on *Corte Constitucional* [The Constitutional Court], *Sentencia* [Ruling] T-622/16, Bogotá, DC, 10 November 2016.

ontological perspective. Within this framework, the use of the term "recognition" erroneously gives the impression that a plurality of metaphysical approaches can coexist, a matter that we shall explore in greater depth later in this contribution. Many Indigenous ontologies, more specifically, hold a viewpoint where everything is interconnected, where actions and relationships are paramount, rather than just the material forms of things. Consequently, place spirits[3] and ancestors are not considered inferior to "nature" but rather are part of it, or even conditional to it (Tănăsescu 2020: 432).

In Western metaphysical thought, RoN are understood not simply as a human-made legal construct, but as something that emerges from nature itself; the rights and values are thus inherent and intrinsic to nature, that is, naturalistic as natural law (Nash 1989: 13–32). This particular ontological view is often confused with the instrumental description of RoN. In the instrumental description, these rights are defined in technical legal terms. Accordingly, RoN are seen as a legal fiction, established as a means to an end – the protection of nature. The technical–legal concept of RoN does not, and need not, depend on metaphysical assumptions about RoN (Gilbert et al. 2023: 365).

Recognizing rights for natural entities certainly entails legal complexity. It raises questions about how such rights should be defined, applied, and enforced. Different legal traditions and systems interpret these concepts in various ways, leading to discussions about the operationalization and effectiveness (in enforcement) of such rights. From a legal–philosophical perspective, this presents a contemporary version of the age-old distinction between legal naturalism and legal positivism.

Naturalism considers law as given by nature, based on a natural order. Throughout the history of thought on naturalism, whether anchored in religion or not, the fundamental idea has always been that a natural order exists independently of human minds. For this reason, proponents of a metaphysical view of RoN prefer to speak of "recognition" of RoN; RoN, they argue, are primordial: they exist, whether we acknowledge them or not and, therefore, RoN are an end in themselves (cf. Burdon 2012: 48; Hickman 1996: 56). Burdon, for instance, argues that RoN are not so much legal in nature, but of a universal ethical nature, deeply rooted in naturalism, which extends the moral sphere to nonhuman nature (Burdon 2011; 2013). Valenzuela argues that Aquinas' naturalism could be applied to environmental ethics by underpinning the value of natural beings and the moral responsibility toward nonrational beings through participation in the eternal law (Valenzuela 2017: 310).

Legal positivism, on the other hand, focuses not on the metaphysics of law but primarily on human-dependent legal norms that prescribe human behavior (Matthews 2019: 11). These legal norms are not primordial but are essentially a human product and thus variable in time and place. This legal constellation is

[3] In this context, "place spirits" specifically refer to the souls of the deceased, such as in Māori culture, who depart from a sacred location, "*hawaiki*," to the "*po*," the spiritual realm (Best 1923: 17–18).

therefore human-centered, or as the author of the famous essay "Should Trees have Standing?" (1972) described in his eponymous book: "an earth justice system will be unavoidably anthropocentric" (Stone 1972: 4).[4] The primary reason Stone brings up for changing the law and giving natural entities standing before a court of law is purely instrumental. The question is not whether rights have a metaphysical presumption but what behavior they juridify. Instead of "recognition" of RoN, we might better speak of "granting" or "attributing" RoN, it is suggested here. In this second perspective, RoN are a means to an end.

The notion of RoN as a differentiated form of naturalism (Cicoria 2022: 65, 84) opens the door to the idea that RoN deserve a modest or total equation with Indigenous cosmovisions and customary law. This metaphysical understanding of RoN, according to Petel, is a fundamental translative operation, wherein, at least as an assumption, "RoN express Indigenous cosmologies" (Petel 2024: 28). This understanding is verbally expressed in New Zealand's Te Awa Tupua Act (2017),[5] which has been described as a paradigm shift in legal, governance, and conservation terms (Cribb and Leberman 2021; Cribb et al. 2024). Article 12 of the Act "recognizes" the Whanganui River as "an indivisible and living whole, comprising the Whanganui River from the mountains to the sea, incorporating all its physical and metaphysical elements." Article 13 enshrines the intrinsic values representing the essence of Te Awa Tupua, known as "Tupua te Kawa." These values state that the river is a source of spiritual and physical nourishment, flowing as an indivisible whole from the mountains to the sea, consisting of interconnected streams. The Act requires that all relevant authorities and decision-makers uphold and respect these values.

Similarly, this metaphysical understanding of RoN can be observed in the Yarra River Protection (Wilip-gin Birrarung murron) Act of 2017 in the State of Victoria, which recognizes the Yarra River as a "living, natural entity" and emphasizes the responsibility of Australian Indigenous peoples with the motto "keep the Birrarung alive."[6] Unlike the comparable act of legislation in New Zealand, this Act does not grant legal personality to the river, nor does it establish rights of the river, or appoint a specific legal guardian. Instead, it establishes an independent Birrarung Council, appointed by the Minister for Environment, to act as "the Voice of the River."[7] The council, composed of various experts and Indigenous elders, provides independent

[4] Stone had already discerned the impossibility of a post-anthropocentric legal system. For a Heideggerian perspective, see Zimmerman (1983). The very notion of its possibility, as Baudrillard eloquently puts it, would result in an "anthropological deregulation": "And a simultaneous deregulation of ethics, of all the moral, juridical, symbolic rules which were those of humanism" (1992: 97). However lofty the pretensions of so-called Earth Jurisprudence may be, the many contemporary examples still reflect anthropocentric language. Matthee (2024) explores how Māori provisions and eco-poetry highlight the limitations of logocentric language in representing the natural world.

[5] Te Awa Tupua (Whanganui River Claims Settlement) Act 2017, No. 7 (New Zealand).

[6] Yarra River Protection (Wilip-gin Birrarung murron) Act 2017, No. 49 of 2017.

[7] Joseph Krutch demonstrates the connection between the phenomenon of the "Voice" of a natural entity and naturalism in his work *The Voice of the Desert* (1955).

advice to the minister on significant activities and plans concerning the Yarra River and its banks (Kahui 2024: 4). The role of the council is advisory, highlighting the competing needs of the river itself and its use as a resource by humans. In both New Zealand and Australia, initiatives have been established to recognize rivers as an indivisible and living entity, incorporating both physical and metaphysical dimensions – namely, nature itself, with its presumed intrinsic value.

The pressing question, mindful of the difference between the distinct forms of naturalism and positivism, is whether this recognition should simply be seen as a means to manage the river by subjecting it to legal, positivist, personification or guardianship (Petel 2024: 24, 29), that is, the law as a technique for a calculatable nature.[8] Examples such as the personification of the Whanganui River in New Zealand and the Yarra River in Australia as a proper subject can also unveil that the attribution of personality or stakeholder status to nature reinforces this juridical–technical *worldview*, the naturalization of rights (Rawson and Mansfield 2018), rather than implying an ontological shift or a paradigm shift – this often ostensibly pretended shift is a significant topic that we shall elaborate upon further in the fourth section of this chapter. Some argue that by formally incorporating nature as a rights-bearing subject into legal systems, Indigenous political movements gain access to State processes, which in turn channels both nature and Indigenous politics into established administrative and governance frameworks (Hanschel et al. 2022: 1024; Petel 2024). This development is described in the literature as the "juridification of Indigenous politics."[9] This, in other words means: the translation of Indigenous concepts into the Western State's liberal framework.[10]

3.3 The Colonization of Indigenous Law

The RoN discourse is far from unambiguous or monolithic (Tănăsescu 2022: 16). Although the paradigm of RoN is gaining popularity (O'Donnell et al. 2020: 403), practical challenges persist in its enactment (Bookman 2023). These challenges include questions about how RoN should be integrated into existing legal frameworks and enforced in practice. These practical considerations add a layer of complexity to such a paradigm. The increasing body of academic publications on this subject reveals a wide spectrum of approaches (e.g., Kahui et al. 2024): from the perspective of *environmental ethics*, RoN is often situated within the framework of

[8] For insights into the management of nature, refer to Heidegger (1962: 14), and for the presupposition of the calculated technique within the politico-juridical–ethical domain, such as RoN, consult Derrida (2003: 80).

[9] There are numerous academic references for this phenomenon. The most significant, in our view, are: Casagrande and Collin (2024), Fuenzalida (2024), Gregg (2020), Henrard and Gilbert (2018), Kirsch (2012), Sieder (2020), and Zoettl (2016).

[10] This is a highly distilled description of what can be found in the following references: Bellina (2024: 327), Gudynas (2011), Petel (2024: 28), and Tănăsescu (2022: 60, 67, 78).

ecocentrism, where natural entities, nonhumans, possess intrinsic value independent of human interests (Putzer et al. 2022b: 92; Vilkka 1997). Other perspectives, such as a *relational approach* that connects the rights of nature with human rights, or a *decolonial approach* that challenges Western concepts of nature and rights by integrating Indigenous knowledge, can also be considered. Additionally, a *holistic approach to rights*, in which nature and humanity are seen as complementary entities, may be explored. *Community rights*, which emphasize the protection of natural and cultural heritage, offer an alternative framework for understanding RoN, particularly from the perspective of Indigenous communities. *Ecocentric discourses* frequently discuss the interconnectedness with and the intrinsic natural value of Indigenous cosmovisions.

In the Australian context, RoN assume an interconnecting function between so-called "Earth Laws" and "First Laws" (Poelina et al. 2024: 83–126). "Earth Laws" are legal and ethical approaches that grant rights to nature and Earth itself, akin to those of human and legal entities. In a nutshell, this collection of approaches proposes that the rights of natural systems and other living beings should be recognized and protected within legal frameworks. The term "First Laws" in Australia refers to the traditional legal culture existing among Australian Indigenous communities and Indigenous Torres Strait Islander peoples. These First Laws are based on spiritual, cultural, and ecological knowledge passed down through generations, regulating the relationship between humans, nature, and spiritual life (Poelina et al. 2024: 28–31). In this relationship, nature is not merely a resource but a living entity (cf. Martuwarra Fitzroy River Council 2016). This view contrasts sharply with the dominant legal and economic systems of the Global North, where property rights and exploitation of natural resources are central (Putzer et al. 2022a). Wesche suggests that the future success of RoN will depend on the ability to integrate the "harmony with nature vision" into modern legal systems, necessitating a fundamental shift in thinking about ownership and rights (Wesche 2023: 15–16).

For millennia, the Indigenous peoples of Australia and the Torres Strait Islands have borne a fundamental, unique, and deeply rooted responsibility to care for the(ir) land according to their own law(s) (Marshall 2019). These First Laws differ significantly from the Western legal system. Evans (2002), following Derrida's idea that Western metaphysics is characterized by logocentrism – the primacy of "speaking" (Derrida 1967: 11) – argues that in Indigenous culture, narrative knowledge is a form of "writing."[11] Of course, we must not forget that Indigenous TK is often expressed and transmitted as "oral literature" (Barthes 1966: 21–22), and it is precisely for this reason that it is frequently marginalized, both in the academic realm and in public life generally. The concept of "speech," as Derrida employs it in his semiology, thus represents the western epistemological frameworks – something

[11] Jansen (2024a), in the context of Indigenous and Western ontologies, previously articulated a similar distinction between semiotics and semantics, wherein signs encompass the broader scope of semiotics, whereas words fall within the domain of semantics (174).

that harkens back to Plato's reverence for the spoken *logos*.[12] Derrida criticized Western logocentrism for creating a hierarchy between speaking and writing; writing is undervalued and considered inferior because it is seen as derivative or indirect. This cultural influence is evident in colonialism, as shown in the hierarchy created by the British. Written knowledge has been subordinated by the British government since the start of colonialism and reduced to "a marginalised language game" (Evans 2002: 134) within a "legal field" (Bourdieu 1986) that is thoroughly Western and colonial (Burke 2020: 100–101). Consequently, the British imposed their laws of land ownership, thereby, in line with the later doctrine of *terra nullius*, disregarding Indigenous customary and communitarian forms of land tenure as unrecognized and thus, inherently inferior. This resulted in widespread dispossession and exclusion of Indigenous people. From a metaperspective, the tension between oral and written traditions reflects a broader *epistemological* conflict – not merely between two *semiological* media: "writing" and "speaking" in reverse – but between Indigenous oral dynamic forms of relational knowledge, and the Western legal paradigm which privileges written documentation and contractual logic. This conflict is not only historical but continues to shape contemporary struggles over land, sovereignty, and recognition of Indigenous rights worldwide.

This existential difference in understanding the law and legal semiotics makes achieving justice within the Australian legal system challenging for Indigenous peoples. The Spinifex people (Pila Nguru), for example, who inhabit mainland Western Australia, claimed their land under the Australian legal system based on the Native Title Act 1993.[13] Previously, they were subject to Western Australian legislation and managed by local administrators while camping on Crown land and designated reserves.[14] To claim their land, they had to meet the criteria set out in the definition of "native title" as described in the Act. Thus, it is a legitimate question whether Australian law and courts are suitable institutions for addressing Indigenous issues.

Indigenous peoples face obstacles when filing cases in Australian courts – problems directly related to Western law and the linguistic and philosophical beliefs underlying the predominant legal system, that is, legal semiotics (Kendon 1988). For the Spinifex people, who do not possess an Anglo-Australian legal framework, but indeed have their own form of law, it was a formidable challenge to translate their legal principles into the concepts of the Anglo-Australian legal system (Higgins 2021: 733–734). Despite the scant recognition afforded to Indigenous

[12] Plato, *Phædrus*: "Indeed writing, Phædrus, doubtless has this feature that is terribly clever, and truly resembles painting. For the offspring of that art stand there as living beings, but if you ask them about something, they altogether keep a solemn silence" (275*d*).

[13] Native Title Act 1993 (Commonwealth), section 223.

[14] *Mabo v Queensland* (No. 1) [1988] HCA 69, (1988) 166 CLR 186; *Mabo v Queensland* (No. 2) [1992] HCA 23, (1992) 175 CLR 1.

law by the Australian legal system,[15] significant obstacles remain, including the lack of formal documentation, the stringent requirements for detailed testimonies that conflict with Indigenous oral traditions, and the mismatch between Indigenous conceptions of land as a communal and living entity and the Western notion of land as private property (Alexander et al. 2024). Nevertheless, the Spinifex people succeeded in claiming their land by performing their law through ceremonies, which involved "writing" – in the sand, with paint on boards, bark, bodies, and contemporary cloth with modern paint – as well as "reading" the land and recognizing its specificities (Schreiner 2007: 196; 2013: 170).

Moreover, Indigenous Australians find themselves in a cynical double bind, a "catch-22," as Western binary thinking expects them to be "irrational" and "uncultivated." However, if they do not meet this expectation and where an Indigenous person actually engages in legal negotiation and bridges the difference, they are dismissed as "inauthentic" and thus ineligible for compensation or land rights. Similarly, the ability to "speak" in the Western language game acquired by Indigenous people comes at the cost of their status as "Indigenous Australians" (cf. Fanon 1952: 14). "Urbanized Indigenous people thus lose their Indigeneity in the construction of their subjectivity (Butler 1991) when they exercise their ability to "speak" in legal institutions (Blichner and Molander 2008: 47; Evans 2002: 138–140) – a phenomenon called "semiotic whitening" by Mena (2024). It appears that Australian law is imposed on and applied to Indigenous people as a colonial construct (Krygier 2002); Western legal colonialism is perpetuated by the truth-producing power of (legal) language.

3.4 Legal Pluralism, a Critique

The phenomenon of legal translation and representation necessarily introduces the concept of "legal pluralism," which gained traction among legal anthropologists in the 1970s (Allott and Woodman 1985: 1–7) – not to suggest that it did not exist before (Tamanaha 2008). Griffiths (1986) defined legal pluralism as the existence of multiple legal systems within one geographic area or society. According to Griffiths, legal pluralism refers to the coexistence of different legal orders, such as State-centric law, religious law, customary law, and other forms of social regulation, which may operate independently or interact with each other. In this light, Galanter (1981) emphasizes that "justice" can take place in many "rooms," including private ordering and Indigenous law, which exist parallel to and often interact with liberal State's legal systems. Between liberal and Indigenous legal cultures, there has been much conflict, which can be traced back to the focus on the individual versus the group (Tamanaha 2008: 407–408), and relatedly, the concept

[15] Australian Law Reform Commission. (1986, June 11). *Recognition of Aboriginal customary laws (ALRC Report 31).*

of property. Liberalism emphasizes individual freedom, the rule of law, and limited government. John Stuart Mill's *On Liberty* (1859) articulates these principles, particularly through the harm principle, which justifies State intervention only to prevent harm to others. However, Mill's framework excludes certain groups, notably Indigenous peoples. While advocating self-governance, he justified colonial paternalism, exposing conflicts within the liberal State between universal freedoms and structural exclusions. In the discourse on pluralism, liberalism, according to Mouffe, posits that individuals inhabit a world replete with numerous perspectives and values, which, due to our epistemological limitations, we cannot fully assimilate. Nonetheless, when these perspectives are brought together, they are expected to coalesce into a harmonious whole (Mouffe 2005: 10). The literature on RoN that adopts this liberal perspective varies in form and scope (Jansen 2023: 46).

Not least, the distinction between liberal, that is, predominant, Western legal, and Indigenous legal cultures is of a semiotic nature; as previously discussed in this contribution, Western ontology is "logocentric" in essence. It privileges speaking and listening over drawing, writing, and reading. This implies that liberalism too upholds the belief that "for people of good faith, all of our political differences can be overcome if we only remain committed to speaking" (Kahn 2011: 156). Liberalism, therefore, fundamentally assumes the existence of entities with a "Voice" who take their place at the table and resolve their potential disputes in harmony and reason. When Indigenous law and liberal State-centric law, and relatedly, the concept of property exist in a relationship where they interact with each other, Teubner speaks of "legal irritants" (Teubner 1998: 31–32), wherein liberal law must be considered an "irritant" when applied to Indigenous communities, thereby putting Indigenous legal cultures under pressure (Schreiner 2013: 170). Thus, it may occur that a "Voice" of a natural entity, once "recognized" by a Western system, is expected to fully engage in the liberal discourse that gives the primacy to speaking and listening. Within the RoN discourse, similar to the Indigenous law discourse, an appeal is made to the possibilities of legal pluralism – as if RoN introduced a kind of new law into reality that competed for significance and jurisdiction with existing law (Cribb et al. 2024; Page and Pelizzon 2024: 5–8).

With Indigenous law being incorporated into Western law, therefore, this cannot be regarded as the sole form of legal pluralism. Even those who recognize a classical distinction between "weak" and "strong" legal pluralism cannot empirically witness the incorporation of Indigenous law into liberal law as such (Kleinhans and Macdonald 1997: 38–44). "Weak legal pluralism" hereby describes a situation in which multiple legal systems exist, but one system is dominant and the others are subordinate, whereas "strong legal pluralism" refers to a situation where multiple legal systems exist independently and operate without hierarchical subordination to a dominant system (Griffiths 1986). In other words, the incorporation of Indigenous laws into liberal legislation cannot be regarded as a genuine form of legal pluralism. This is because Indigenous laws do not operate independently; they are integrated into the dominant liberal legal system and may possibly also be subject to the procedures and customs of that system.

The concept of "recognition" is thus applied – in studies of legal pluralism – to the relationship between State and non-State legal orders (Harris 2024). The term is used inconsistently and can refer to various actions or omissions by the State, such as recognizing non-State orders without granting them legal status; considering their norms in judicial or administrative decisions; enforcing, incorporating, or integrating these norms and institutions into the State system; or even prohibiting certain practices. This process of juridification, where legal means are used to regulate social and political issues, seems to lead to depoliticization, where conflicts and power dynamics are transformed into legal issues, thus relegating the political aspects to the background, for example:

- in the Mabo Case (1992), the Australian High Court acknowledged the native title rights of the Meriam people, overturning the doctrine of *terra nullius*. However, this recognition was ultimately subordinated to Australian law, thereby transforming political struggles into legal matters. This meant that Indigenous sovereignty was not fully recognized – only a form of land tenure, subordinated to State authority;
- the Native Title Act (1993) acknowledged the land rights of Indigenous Australians yet simultaneously subjected these rights to the overarching legal framework of the Australian State, converting political and cultural claims into legal disputes and thereby depoliticizing the broader issues of sovereignty. This legal framing shifted the issue from one of political and cultural sovereignty to a technical legal dispute, thereby depoliticizing Indigenous claims; and
- in the Yorta Yorta Case[16] (2002), the native title claim of the Yorta Yorta people was dismissed due to the failure to demonstrate continuous adherence to traditional laws, thus exemplifying how State legal frameworks can effectively undermine Indigenous autonomy.

Being unaware of power relations implies a failure to recognize the specific circumstances in which Indigenous peoples find themselves, which may also have implications at a judicial level. Upon deeper examination, the fundamental issue when considering RoN from the perspective of legal pluralism is that RoN cannot be defined based on an autonomous logic, or as a self-contained system, due to its political entanglement with the broader situation in the respective State, region or community. As a result, the phenomenon of "legal pluralism" in the RoN discourse as it regards RoN initiatives in Australia and New Zealand remains, strictly speaking, a signifier devoid of its signified.

[16] *Members of the Yorta Yorta Aboriginal Community v The State of Victoria* [1998] 1606 (18 December 1998) – Federal Court Decision; *Members of the Yorta Yorta Aboriginal Community v State of Victoria* (Including Corrigendum dated 21 March 2001) [2001] FCA 45 (8 February 2001) – Full Federal Court Decision; *Members of the Yorta Yorta Aboriginal Community v Victoria* [2002] HCA 58 (12 December 2002) – High Court Decision.

3.5 Legal Pluralism and Neocolonialism

In the expansion of the Western legal system through RoN, we do not see a new legal paradigm shift taking place – as an apologetic liberal view of RoN often suggests (Calzadilla 2019) – but rather a homogenizing expansion of the existing State-centric horizon (Bellina 2024: 332), thereby confirming the existing, predominant legal paradigm within which "recognition" must take place (Povinelli 2002). In other words, the Western legal instrumentalist paradigm provides Indigenous peoples in Australia and New Zealand with a basic template which, by virtue of its colonialist origins, continues to determine the limits of what and how their law should be (Kuhn 1962: 50–51). The RoN discourse, after nature's evolution from matter to energy, now seeks to position it as an interactive subject, for example, a contracting party, as Serres prescribes (1990: 67–69). According to Baudrillard, this leads to a paradox wherein, by regarding nature as a subject, we force it into our own image, thereby disrupting an ecological balance that has always been rooted in a metaphysical equilibrium between object and subject (Baudrillard 1992: 80–81). Baudrillard identifies in this dynamic a subject centrism (1983):

> We have always lived off the splendor of the subject and the poverty of the object. It is the subject that makes history, it's the subject that totalizes the world. Individual subject or collective subject, the subject of consciousness or of the unconscious, the ideal of all metaphysics is that of world subject; the object is only a detour on the royal road of subjectivity. (141)

If the object is to rise in esteem, this is only the case where, in that master–slave dialectic, the object is elevated to the status of subject. Thus, we witness a false paradigm shift, because it is not that the *anthropos* must become part of nature (*physis*), but rather that nature must become part of the *anthropos*, not leading to postanthropocentrism, but to post-physiocentrism.[17] Yet, as Baudrillard questions: "Why privilege the position of the subject?" (142). As long as RoN do not entail the transformation of people to objects, but rather transform natural entities to subjects, the discourse, insofar as it claims to represent a paradigm shift, is manifestly in default. These RoN are then no "harmony with nature"; it is a "harmony with humankind."[18]

[17] Unless postanthropocentrism is not so much the erasure of the *anthropos* "like a face drawn in the sand at the edge of the sea" (Foucault 1966: 398) in favor of the environment within which that *anthropos* exists, then the subjectification of the lifeworld is indeed a humanization of nature (*physis*), rather than a naturalization of the human, that is, RoN is not postanthropocentric law, but rather post-physiocentric law.

[18] That such events – where the human being transforms to nature, that is, from subject to object – did indeed take place, or that at the very least earnest attempts were made, is how Friedrich Nietzsche described the transformation of man in the Dionysian festivals (1830): "Man is no longer merely an artist; he has become the very artwork itself, as ecstatically and gloriously transformed as he once beheld the gods transformed in dreams. It is now the artistic force of nature, transcending human hands, that unveils itself – a finer clay, a rarer marble is here moulded and chiselled: the human being. This human, fashioned by the artist Dionysus, stands in relation to nature as a statue does to the Apollonian artist" (47).

Baudrillard makes an interesting distinction between the *Law* and the *rule*.[19] The "Law" describes an (almost) universal system of meaning and values that always strives for objective recognition. Its foundation is transcendence (metaphysics), and it manifests itself as an institution that totalizes the real. The "rule," however, is immanent within a limited, bounded system, within which it is unyielding. Applying Baudrillard's anthropological distinction to legal pluralism in Australia quickly reveals that the limited domain of the rule is usurped by the universal domain of the "Law." "Law" and "rule" are Baudrillardian legal irritants, fundamentally incompatible. A ritual, such as initiations, corroborees, funerals, smoking ceremonies, songlines, decorations, will never become a Law (Baudrillard 1976: 71; 1983: 207) – a stark reality for the "Law," which can never accept that the world consists of sequences that do not fall under its jurisdiction (Baudrillard 1979: 179–209).[20] The ritual or ceremonial domain of Indigenous peoples in contrast to the domain of Western law leads to confusion. For Indigenous Australians, law and ritual are intertwined, as exemplified by the term "*rom*," which the Yolŋu (a collection of clan groups in the northeast of Arnhem Land) use to denote both law and ritual (Williams 1987: 108). Thus, there exists an Indigenous concept that "shows at the level of kinship, succession, ownership and the furnishing of proof that a ceremonial structure or rather a ceremonial figure appears where we expect a legal one" (Schreiner 2019: 38).

Perhaps one of the most elegant illustrations of this distinction is provided by Marcel Mauss in his *Essai sur le don* [*Essay on the Gift*] (1925), particularly in his account of the symbolic and ritual exchange among the Māori. Mauss described so-called "*taonga*" as spiritually imbued objects within Māori culture, which, through exchange, turn into social obligations and the power of "*hau*": "it is truly 'native': the *hau* follows every possessor" (Mauss 1925: 80). Unlike the "Law," the Māori do not engage in contractual agreements as the legal extension of subjectivity. Rather, their exchanges follow an invisible "rule" that obliges participants to reciprocity, although not in the form of bilateral or multilateral agreements. The exchange remains circular: retaining a *taonga* for personal use violates several taboos, such as the taboo on accumulating value, the taboo against hoarding, and the taboo on individualization. In contrast to Māori exchange, Western exchange, that is, "the economy," is founded upon equivalence and value. Thus, within the liberal framework of "Law," there is always a "residue" after an exchange – whether it be the value

[19] Incidentally, in Barthes' *Sade, Fourier, Loyola* (1971), we encounter a similar distinction when he writes about ritual: "Law, no. Protocol, yes" (Barthes 1971: 167).

[20] For a detailed account, see the excellent work *The Songlines* (Picador, 1987) by Bruce Chatwin, where the songlines are presented as a mythical map of Australia passed down through song and forming the basis for their walkabouts. A selection of literature that unveils Indigenous Australian ritualism definitely includes Thomas Keneally's *The Chant of Jimmie Blacksmith* (Angus & Robertson, 1972), Patricia Grace's *Mutuwhenua: The Moon Sleeps* (Cambridge University Press, 1978), Kim Scott's *Benang: From the Heart* (Freemantle Press, 1999), Alexis Wright's *Carpentaria* (Giramondo, 2006), Marie Munkara's *Every Secret Thing* (Abacus, 2009), and, again, Kim Scott's *That Deadman Dance* (Picador, 2011).

of the object or the subject's status as free and equal. The grand RoN discourse, which understands nature as possessing a greater or lesser degree of intrinsic value, is, from this Māori perspective, equally a noncircular value-accumulator. For the Māori, there is no "residue" or surplus value: the exchange is symbolic, ritualistic, and therefore circular (Mauss 1925: 77–82; cf. Schreiner 1990: 71–73).

If we once again take a step back to the concept of legal pluralism, Schreiner asserts that no unities can be discerned (cf. Gover 2020: 872–875) between the social role of Western legal institutions and the symbolic and ritualistic role of Australian Indigenous law through the lens of this profoundly Western concept (Schreiner 2004):

> [P]luralism is so absorptive as a concept that it can incorporate every existent plurality of all kinds, while at the same time liquidating them. It is the character of every pluralism to reduce the plurality that it aims for to a unity – a unity that creates order in a plurality of similarity and difference. Pluralism and Law may with a certain pride state that they can embrace a great deal; at the same time they have to admit that they are the only thing left at the end. In this sense the trap they set proves to be their own pitfall. (93)

There is thus no pretended mediation, or any reimagining of the law through symbol or ritual (Watts 2016), but to use Habermas' terminology, a "colonisation of the life-world." Habermas identified this transition, where mediation turns into its colonization, as the task of critical theory (1981: 318). This task of critical theory is increasingly taken up within the RoN discourse by legal scholars, starting from the (old) finding: "colonialism universalized European notions of nature as a commodity for human exploitation" (Gonzalez 2015: 411–412). Critical legal and Third World approaches to international law (TWAIL)[21] scholars have argued that international law, including international institutions and human rights, is rooted in colonial domination and the exploitation of Indigenous populations in Latin America, Asia, Africa, and Oceania. Indigenous communities were and are disproportionately affected by large-scale exploitation of natural resources and are threatened by environmental destruction and the criminalization of their resistance. In the debate on RoN, there is growing academic attention to this ongoing oppression of Indigenous peoples and their knowledge, as well as the ambivalences inherent in RoN (Bellina 2024; Petel 2024).

These ambivalences are unveiled by the term "recognition" (Sieder 2020: 5), for example, as recorded in the Yarra River Protection Act 2017: "This Act *recognises* the intrinsic connection of the traditional owners to the Yarra River and its Country and further *recognises* them as the custodians of the land and waterway which they call Birrarung" (Preamble, italics in original). Here, nature is politicized as a contestable space (cf. Latour 2004; Swyngedouw 2010) and made politically and socially neutral through the Act; in other words, the Yarra River is "juridified" (Lindt 2024: 21–25, 220–228). Although this process of recognition can provide the

[21] Notable works from these TWAIL scholars include *Human Rights: A Political and Cultural Critique* (University of Pennsylvania Press, 2002) by Makau Mutua and *Imperialism, Sovereignty, and the Making of International Law* (Cambridge University Press, 2005) by Antony Anghie.

State with an opportunity to strengthen its power by stabilizing legal frameworks and reducing political conflict, it may also create space for contestation. In cases where RoN are bottom-up invoked by Indigenous communities, juridification could serve as a double-edged sword: on the one hand, it might institutionalize the State's role as the ultimate protector of established legal orders; on the other, it could be a means through which Indigenous cosmovisions are legitimized, potentially transforming governance structures and introducing new forms of environmental stewardship (cf. Hanschel et al. 2022: 2020–2025).

The recognition within the modern Western legal system thus clashes with the "communitarian tradition" of Indigenous practices, where ownership of land and natural resources is not centered on the individual but rather on the community, and the collective "ownership" – to employ a Western legal term, for lack of a better expression – of natural resources.[22] According to Petel, this is because the homogenizing and compulsively forward-driving trajectory of the modern legal system marginalizes these traditional practices (cf. Hightower and Anker 2016: 3; Petel 2024: 29–30). By making a liberal–legal appeal to Indigenous cosmovisions in favor of RoN, the concept of "recognition" reveals a form of legal colonization, that is, the danger of the colonization of Indigenous cosmovisions, which brings us to the next section.

3.6 Indigeneity as Teleology

The ease with which academic publications deploy Indigenous cosmovisions to legitimize RoN, combined with Western philosophies as supporting evidence (Jagodzinski 2024: 248–249), has prompted an academic counterresponse, a second wave of RoN literature that rightfully points out the "ideological ambivalence of the discourse" (Petel 2024: 33).[23] Not only do RoN worldwide consist of a range of normative and procedural ambivalences, which are acknowledged by the first wave of RoN literature as well (Putzer et al. 2022b; Tănăsescu 2022: 16), but the ideological ambivalences comprise a combination of Eurocentric philosophical–anthropological teleologies (Baard 2023: 429–430; Holm 2017; Kurki 2022: 548–549; Nordlander 2021) and categorical errors (Whittemore 2011: 661) that punctuate these normative and procedural ambivalences. Conveniently, this overlooks the complexity that the term "recognition" unlocks in favor of the epistemological basis of State-centric law

[22] Cf. Inter-American Court of Human Rights. (2001, August 31). *Case of the Mayagna (Sumo) Awas Tingni Community v. Nicaragua* (Merits, Reparations and Costs), Judgment. Consideration 149: "Among indigenous peoples there is a communitarian tradition regarding a communal form of collective property of the land, in the sense that ownership of the land is not centered on an individual but rather on the group and its community."

[23] For examples see these publications: Cabanes (2023), Cano Pecharroman (2018), Harden-Davies *et al.* (2020), Kauffman and Martin (2017), McGregor and Sritharan (2023), O'Donnell *et al.* (2020), and Tarrdif *et al.* (2023).

(Sieder 2020: 11) and the potential negative implications it holds for Indigenous peoples and their law(s) (Akchurin 2015: 956; Guim and Livermore 2021: 1407–1048).

Indeed, the tendency to indigenize RoN can be viewed as a pragmatic strategy to garner more support for RoN, but also as a continuation of the age-old Western idealization of the "noble savage" that expresses the Western desire for nature and authenticity (Tănăsescu 2015: 119) – a dangerous latent[24] Western stereotype rife with racist assumptions (cf. Hames 2007; Lyotard 1974: 130). On the one hand, there are indeed compelling arguments for why Indigenous peoples are ascribed special roles as stewards of the forest, the river, and so forth. As custodians of knowledge, including ancestral wisdom, they lay claim to specific entitlements that only Indigenous peoples can assert (O'Donnell et al. 2020: 420–425). On the other hand, the strategic utilization of Indigeneity as a source of legal privilege to represent nature can lead to a deeply unsettling outcome, where communities may feel pressured to conform to such stereotypes, reminiscent of the colonial representations of savagery as historically described. This thus reinforces the colonial dynamics inherent in Indigenous empowerment within the framework of RoN, as illustrated by the compelling demand for "primitive authenticity" (Petel 2024: 31–33), plunging communities into a "simulacrum of pastness" (Rifkin 2017). Viewed in this way, the broad spectrum of RoN aims to catalogue environmental justice rather than being receptive to TK, at least only to the extent that it would contribute to environmental justice (Táíwò 2022).

Within this line of reasoning, the frequently made assertion in the RoN discourse according to which RoN emerge predominantly from a bottom-up process must also be considered in more detail (e.g., Talbot-Jones and Bennett 2022). In other words, Indigenous communities are said to independently advocate for RoN to protect the territories they inhabit. This often-repeated assertion is similarly teleological-strategic, if only because colonizers have historically transformed Indigenous territories into zones of exploitation, imposed their legal systems (entirely top-down), and left Indigenous tribes to navigate within the recyclable liberal leftovers of the colonial legal framework in an attempt to salvage what remains for the protection of nature (Baudrillard 1992: 27). This is what Sloterdijk coined as a form of cynicism inherent in "State and hegemonic power" (Sloterdijk 1983: 422, *et seq.*). Within this cynicism, one might question the validity of the bottom-up narrative by sharing the following observation (Kahn 2005): "No one asked the indigenous populations whether they preferred a French or British colonial master" (235). This is significant for the issue of "recognition" because, as H. L. A. Hart instructs us, only the official authority – that is, the colonial master – is

[24] Edward W. Said, in his *Orientalism* (1978), made a distinction between "Latent and Manifest Orientalism" (201–225), with "latent" referring to the deeply ingrained, often unconscious assumptions and attitudes about the Orient that are embedded in Western culture and thought. This form of orientalism manifests as an implicit attitude that remains consistent over time.

able to properly recognize the law, while those subject to that jurisdiction relate to the law through that official authority (1961: 97–106). Consequently, those upon whom the law is imposed remain detached from any assured knowledge of what governs them (Fitzpatrick 1992: 204).

The RoN discourse that appropriates Indigenous cosmovisions typically builds on the concept of "nature," much like Western philosophers tend to do (Tănăsescu 2022):

> Nature (or Earth) as Mother, the cliché often attributed to indigenous thought, is nothing but the obsession with totality dressed up as indigeneity. Nature as totality is featureless and abstract, the exact opposite of place-thought. (44).[25]

Totalizing examples of the previously mentioned Western philosophers are those who capture such totality with the term "Gaia" (Latour 2015), also understood as an intrinsic value (Naess 1973), or as "mesh" (Morton 2010: 28–33). This is not surprising, as Western thought inherently tends toward it, because these societies have lived "based on expansion and explosion at all levels, under the sign of the universalisation of the market, and of economic and philosophical values" (Baudrillard 1978: 87).

3.7 Recognition as a Narrative

Erroneously, some strands in the literature even suggest that Indigenous peoples essentially already have their RoN recognized, merely requiring codification (Skurky 2022; Ugwu 2025), rendering RoN ontologically indifferent to Indigenous cosmovisions (Jansen 2024a). In this light, RoN do not escape the paradox attributed to ethnology by Baudrillard: "For ethnology to live, its object must die" (Baudrillard 1981: 18). Comparable to those economists in the seventeenth century who began to account for nature as a mere "factor of production," a resource external to them (Latour 2017: 74), Indigenous cosmovisions are perceived within the RoN discourse as merely a component for achieving environmental goals, that is, a factor of production (Smith 1999: 183). There are indeed commentators who distort or commodify Indigenous cosmovisions by reducing them to a mere justification for recognizing RoN as a tool to enhance environmental protection, without fundamentally altering the view of nature as a factor of production. Without suggesting that diverse ontologies, worldviews, and cosmologies cannot offer valuable insights to one another, we must nevertheless proceed with the utmost caution and humility when attempting to replicate Indigenous cosmological thought within the framework of Western legal reasoning. Similarly, the entire idea of "postanthropocentrism," "ecocentrism," and "biocentrism" is fundamentally a Western

[25] For examples of how Indigenous people do not see nature as a totality, see Tănăsescu's (2022) case studies, collected in his chapter "The Perils of Totality: A Short Foray into Modernist Thought" (95–120).

"liberal melancholy" (Neely 2016: 6; Vizenor 1994: 14). Such "centrisms" encountered in aforementioned Western philosophies – Gaia, intrinsic value, mesh, and so on – primarily do not change the binary thinking permeating Western thought, as the center simply shifts from one category to another, that is, from human to nature (Tănăsescu 2022: 31; cf. Eze 2024: 272), but moreover, many Indigenous cosmovisions are not centered at all and instead concern deep context-specific "relations."[26]

Carl Schmitt elucidates how the practice of disregarding or appropriating Indigenous rights by Western imperial powers is not fundamentally distinct from the act of preserving or recognizing such rights. This is because, in all these performative acts, the dynamic between the imperial power and the Indigenous population persists through a form of *dominium eminens* (eminent domain). All these various possibilities may easily be mirrored in the colonial practices of land appropriations during the nineteenth and twentieth centuries (Schmitt 1950: 171–172). The making of agreements or treaties with Indigenous tribes or leaders is also an age-old feature of what Schmitt termed the *Jus Publicum Europæum*, that is, a world order imposed by European powers with Europe at its center. Non-European territories, such as Australia, were regarded as outside this legal order and viewed as *terra nullius*, which legitimized European States in asserting sovereignty over them or at least establishing an inchoate title (Schmitt 1941: 68; 1950: 189).

The recognition of Indigenous rights by a dominant Western power cannot be fully comprehended without this understanding of colonialism. This is particularly true when considering the ongoing reproduction of *terra nullius* in contemporary Australia; as Kramer (2016) notes, against the backdrop of color-blindness, racialized signifiers of *terra nullius*, capitalist logic, and legal equality are still deliberately employed to dispossess Indigenous Australians. Considering the viewpoint that the recognition of RoN is an extension of Western liberal State-centric law's ontology and epistemology, Rawson and Mansfield (2018) have coined RoN as a transnational policy network (TPN). By tracing the mobilization of RoN through TPN it becomes evident, according to Rawson and Mansfield, that the signifiers of legal recognition for nonhuman actors presents a natural global convergence, wherein Western ideas are employed to overcome the human–nature dualism and whereby Indigeneity is strategically utilized (100–101), all according to the "same schema" (Baudrillard 1972: 255).

Recognition thus originates from a specific cultural and historical context, which has become invisible due to its globally ingrained status. Recognition of legal personhood in liberal State-centered law revolves around signs that delineate the visibility of legal entities such as individuals, corporations, and States. Entities that are not legal persons lack agency, remain invisible, and are not acknowledged within

[26] According to Baudrillard (1978), a term such as "relation" also no longer belongs to the domain of the symbolic or the ritual but rather to the domain of the social: "the very terms 'rapport' and 'relation' already carry something of death, and something of death itself" (104).

judicial forums. Although the recognition of natural entities does render them as visible signs, akin to a corporation being a visible sign, the natural entity simultaneously adorns itself with a quasi-Indigenous signifier, obscuring the fact that its syntax has been wholly adapted to Western legal frameworks (Arnold 2023). According to Derrida, such concealment of Western context is idiosyncratic to Western ontology, giving concepts the semblance of universality and timelessness – a phenomenon he associated with the term "white mythology" (Derrida 1971).

Despite Western philosophers' claims that their philosophies break with the totalizing or universalist thinking of the past – as exemplified by Latour's statement about Gaia: "it is not universal" (2015: 183) – none of the examples listed in this contribution manage to escape from it: on the contrary, the very denial of theoretical totality or universality reveals a concealing mythology that provides a framework for understanding the overall ecological crisis. Although reality is indeed presented as networks, relationships, and similar concepts, the way it is depicted still reveals an underlying belief in a universal principle that governs the entirety of reality. This belief ultimately reintroduces reality as something structured by a higher, teleological purpose (Baudrillard 1977: 46). Thus, "Gaia," in Latour's case, remains something he stands in opposition to – "This is what I mean by 'facing Gaia'" (2015: 245). Latour consequently relates to this higher positivity and must acknowledge:

> I beg you not to conclude that I am disdaining the ideal of universality: I recognize, I share, I cherish this ideal. But I am seeking a realistic way to achieve it. And, to do so, we have to act as though we were certain that it has not already been realized. (245)

Latour posits Gaia as the ultimate alternative to any arbitrary deity (253), thereby endowing Gaia with the attributes of a "political religion" (Voegelin 1939). In a classic Marxist critique of environmentalist political religion, Baudrillard once remarked that such mythologization is nothing more than a new "opium of the people" (Baudrillard 1974). What is undeniably clear, once again, is that Western thought remains unable to evade its flight into abstraction, as a means of avoiding engagement with the concrete.

3.8 End Remarks: Production, Reproduction, and Sign

Unlike a purely legitimizing–philosophical perspective on RoN, the RoN discourse criticizes philosophy for being insufficiently stimulating or obstructive to its discursive strategy: "We can pose philosophical questions about this, but these are often disguised ways of expressing reluctance or discomfort. It is a way of making a fuss to avoid addressing something" (Jongepier 2024). This is a pity, as good philosophy does not merely prescribe how people should think but rather highlights how and why people's thinking is profoundly shaped. All too often, within the RoN discourse, philosophy is employed as a strategy for environmental politics, yet it frequently falls short of offering genuine alternatives for recognizing Indigenous worldviews, instead reducing them to tools that advance environmental objectives. The same applies to Indigenous symbolic and ritual orders, which are of value for RoN insofar as they align with environmental politics – a "radical negation of the sign as value" (Baudrillard 1981: 16). In this manner, the discourse overlooks that, in the production of RoN – or in the desire for its re-production – it may be destroying the very things it claims to defend, such as the institutions that have historically advanced the social (institutions like production, education, medicine, social security, and, of course, the law), which, in the same movement, produce and destroy the social itself (Baudrillard 1978: 93). Thus, if an abstract institution of the social, such as RoN, arises on the millennia-old symbolic and ritualistic edifice of Indigenous Australian communities, this institution continually produces more of the social, while also reinforcing its devouring nature on the symbolic and the ritualistic (94).

In the production of the social, however, RoN perform something semiologically quite remarkable. In contrast to old Western Law – with a capital "L" (cf. Agamben 2007) – which until the nineteenth century heavily relied on symbols and rituals, the symbolic and ritual aspects of Law gradually lost their significance in the social era of mass production and reproduction (Brigham and Schreiner 2004: 263). Under the influence of capital accumulation and mass production, Law gave way to instrumental reasoning, as seen in sociological jurisprudence and social engineering (Roscoe Pound 1907). Where once Law was defined by its aura, symbol, and ritual, it evolved into a social system founded upon reproduction.[27] "Reproduction" here emphasizes the way law becomes a system that is continuously reproduced within the larger social structure, driven by economic imperatives rather than symbolic meanings or rituals. This does not imply that there are no longer any symbolic elements in Western courts, or that rituals have disappeared entirely (Jansen 2024b). What has faded, as a result of the socialization and strategization of Law, is that judicial symbols and rituals no longer serve as signifiers (e.g., the robe, the gavel) referring to their signifieds (e.g., neutrality, authority); with this reversal, we depart from the Law and the interactions of its forms, entering the phase of (re) production, the domain of the mercantile law of value and its precise calculations (Baudrillard 1972: 172–199; 1976: 84).

Many still attribute to the grand pillars, sweeping staircases, the portrait of the head of State, the robes, and the entire courtroom setting, the very substance of justice; yet the symbol and ritual carry us away, detached from their true lack of significance. The symbol and ritual are wholly embodied in form, a judicial form stripped of substantive weight, transformed into a lifeless body (Baudrillard 1972:

[27] And later even by digitalization: Jansen and Schreiner (2023) In this article, Jansen and Schreiner take inspiration from Walter Benjamin's seminal essay on the effects of mechanical reproduction of art (1935). Paralleling Benjamin's insights, they examine how innovations such as mechanical mass (re)production and digitalization influence the legal profession as well as the concept of "aura."

274). It is the empty form that still references Western jurisprudence as its semiotic residue (Baudrillard 1981):

> Here, at the "sophisticated" borders of a triumphant market economy, one finds once again a scarcity/sign, . . ., under the banner of ecology, energy crisis, and criticism of capital, an ultimate esoteric aureole added to the triumph of an exoteric culture. (27)

The RoN discourse, in contrast to the semiotic residue, seeks to reclaim the substance of environmental justice through the gravitas of the Indigenous symbol and ritual of law. Postmodern ruse or not, the RoN are adorned with the alluring Indigenous symbol and ritual, in which the contemporary environmentalist perceives justice itself being lively embodied anew.

Acknowledgments

We would like to extend our sincere gratitude to Jessika Eichler, Mario G. Aguilera, Constantijn van Aartsen, Ronald Jeurissen, and Annida Aqiila Putri for their valuable glosses on earlier versions of this chapter.

References

Agamben, G. (2007 [2011]). *The Kingdom and the Glory*. Stanford University Press (orig. *Il Regno e fa Gloria*).

Akchurin, M. (2015). Constructing the Rights of Nature. *Law & Social Inquiry* 40(4), 937–968. https://doi.org/10.1111/lsi.12141.

Alexander, A. J., Nicholls, H., & Plater, D. (2024). Outlaws in Their Native Land, in Griffiths, C. & Korporowicz, Ł. (eds.), *English Law, the Legal Profession, and Colonialism* (pp. 139–173). Routledge. https://doi.org/10.4324/9781003315926-10.

Allott, A., & Woodman, G. R. (1985). Introduction, in Allott, A. & Woodman, G. R. (eds.), *People's Law and State Law* (pp. 1–10). De Gruyter Mouton. https://doi.org/10.1515/9783110866285.1.

Anghie, A. (2005). *Imperialism, Sovereignty, and the Making of International Law*. Cambridge University Press.

Arnold, B. B. (2023). Signs of Invisibility. *International Journal for the Semiotics of Law* 36, 457–475. https://doi.org/10.1007/s11196-022-09920-7.

Austin, J. L. (1962). *How to Do Things with Words*. Harvard University Press.

Baard, P. (2023). Are Rights of Nature Manifesto Rights? *Res Publica* 29(4), 425–443. https://doi.org/10.1007/s11158-023-09584-5.

Barthes, R. (1966). Introduction à l'analyse structurale des récits [Introduction to the Structural Analysis of Narratives]. *Communications* 8, 1–27.

Barthes, R. (1971 [1976]). *Sade, Fourier, Loyola*. University of California Press (orig. *Sade, Fourier, Loyola*. Éditions du Seuil).

Baudrillard, J. (1972). *Pour une critique de l'économie politique du signe* [*For a Critique of the Political Economy of the Sign*]. Gallimard.
Baudrillard, J. (1974). The Environmental Witch-Hunt, in Banham, R. (ed.), *The Aspen Papers*. Praeger.
Baudrillard, J. (1976). *L'échange symbolique et la mort* [*Symbolic Exchange and Death*]. Gallimard.
Baudrillard, J. (1977). *Oublier Foucault* [*Forgetting Foucault*]. Galilée.
Baudrillard, J. (1978). *A l'ombre des majorités silencieuses ou la fin du social* [*In the Shadow of the Silent Majorities or the End of the Social*]. Utopie.
Baudrillard, J. (1979). *De la séduction* [*On Seduction*]. Galilée.
Baudrillard, J. (1981). *Simulacres et simulation* [*Simulacra and Simulation*]. Galilée.
Baudrillard, J. (1983 [2008]). *Fatal Strategies*. Semiotext(e) (orig. *Les stratégies fatales*). Grasset & Fasquelle.
Baudrillard, J. (1992 [1994]). *The Illusion of the End*. Stanford University Press (orig. *L'Illusion de la fin ou la grève des événements*. Galilée).
Baudrillard, J. (2006). *Cool Memories V*. Polity.
Bellina, A. (2024). A Novel Way of Being Together? *Environmental Politics* 33(2), 321–339. https://doi.org/10.1080/09644016.2023.2209005.
Benjamin, W. (1935 [1963]). *Das Kunstwerk im Zeitalter seiner technischen Reproduzierbarkeit* [*The Work of Art in the Age of Its Technical Reproducibility*]. Suhrkamp (orig. *L'Œuvre d'art à l'époque de sa reproductibilité technique*).
Best, E. (1923). The Origin of the Māori. *Journal of the Polynesian Society* 32(1), 10–20.
Blichner, L. C., & Molander, A. (2008). Mapping Juridification. *European Law Journal* 13(1), 36–54.
Bookman, S. (2023). Rights of Nature in Comparative Perspective. *Natural Resources & Environment* 4.
Bourdieu, P. F. (1980). *Le sens pratique* [*The Logic of Practice*]. Minuit.
Bourdieu, P. F. (1986). La force du droit [The Force of Law]. *Actes de la Recherche en Sciences Sociales* 64 (Special Issue: *De quel droit?*), 3–19.
Boyd, D. R. (2017). *The Rights of Nature*. ECW Press.
Brigham, J. & Schreiner, A. T. M. (2004). The Semiotics of Digital Law. *International Journal for the Semiotics of Law* 17, 259–266. https://doi.org/10.1007/s11196-004-8643-4.
Burdon, P. D. (2011). Earth Rights. *IUCN Academy of Environmental Law E-journal* 1, 1–12.
Burdon, P. D. (2012). A Theory of Earth Jurisprudence. *Australian Journal of Legal Philosophy* 37, 28–60.
Burdon, P. D. (2013). The Earth Community and Ecological Jurisprudence. *Onati Socio-Legal Series* 3(5), 815–837.
Burke, P. (2020). The Anthropology of Indigenous Australia and Native Title Claims, in Foblets, M-C., Goodale, M., Sapignoli, M., & Zenker, O. (eds.), *The Oxford Handbook of Law and Anthropology* (pp. 94–111). Oxford University Press. https://doi.org/10.1093/oxfordhb/9780198840534.013.14.
Butler, J. (1991). Contingent Foundations. *Praxis International* 11(2), 150–165.
Cabanes, V. (2023). Rights of Nature, a New Perspective in Law, in Lamalle, S. & Stoett, P. (eds.), *Representation and Rights of the Environment* (pp. 233–58). Cambridge University Press. https://doi.org/10.1017/9781108769327.014.

Calzadilla, P. V. (2019). A Paradigm Shift in Courts' View on Nature. *Law, Environment and Development Journal* 15(1), 397–405.

Cano Pecharroman, L. (2018). Rights of Nature. *Resources* 7(1), 13–27.

Casagrande, A. & Collin, P. (2024). Juridification and the Indigenous Peoples in Brazil, in Auer, M., Duve, Th., & Vogenauer, S. (eds.), *Law and Diversity* (pp. 359–384). Max Planck Institute for Legal History and Legal Theory. https://doi.org/10.1353/book.123563.

Cicoria, M. (2022). Legal Subjectivity and Absolute Rights of Nature, in *New Legal Reality* (pp. 65–87). University of Latvia Press. https://doi.org/10.22364/iscflul.8.2.06.

Cribb, M. & Leberman, S. (2021). Te Pā Auroa Nā Te Awa Tupua, in Parsons, M., Fisher, K., & Crease, R. P. (eds.), *Decolonising Blue Spaces in the Anthropocene*. Palgrave Macmillan.

Cribb, M., Macpherson, E., & Borchgrevink, A. (2024). Beyond Legal Personhood for the Whanganui River. *The International Journal of Human Rights*. https://doi.org/10.1080/13642987.2024.2314532.

Danto, A. C. (2003). *The Abuse of Beauty*. Open Court.

Derrida, J. (1967). *De la grammatologie* [*Of Grammatology*]. Minuit.

Derrida, J. (1971). *La mythologie blanche* [*The White Mythology*]. Seuil.

Derrida, J. (1988). *Limited Inc*. Northwestern University Press.

Derrida, J. (2003). *Voyeus* [*Rogues*]. Galilée.

Evans, J. (2002). Indigenous Australians. *International Journal for the Semiotics of Law* 15, 127–141.

Eze, M. O. (2024). Decolonizing "Decolonization" and Knowledge Production Beyond Eurocentrism. *The Monist* 107, 264–278. https://doi.org/10.1093/monist/onae013.

Fanon, F. (1952). *Peau noire, masques blancs* [*Black Skin, White Masks*]. Seuil.

Fitzpatrick, P. (1992). *The Mythology of Modern Law*. Routledge.

Foucault, M. (1966). *Les mots et les choses* [*The Words and the Things*]. Gallimard.

Fuenzalida, N. Y. (2024). The Juridification of Indigenous Claims in Latin America, in Auer, M., Duve, Th., & Vogenauer, S. (eds.), *Law and Diversity* (pp. 395–416). Max Planck Institute for Legal History and Legal Theory. https://doi.org/10.1353/book.123563.

Galanter, M. (1981). Justice in Many Rooms. *Journal of Legal Pluralism* 19, 1–48.

Gilbert, J., Soliev, I., Robertson, A., Vermeylen, S., Williams, N. W., & Grabowski, R. C. (2023). Understanding the Rights of Nature. *Human Ecology* 51(3), 363–377. https://doi.org/10.1007/s10745-023-00420-1.

Gonzalez, C. (2015). Bridging the North–South Divide. *Pace Environmental Law Review* 32, 407–434. https://doi.org/10.58948/0738-6206.1765.

González-Serrano, M. X. (2024). Rights of Nature, an Ornamental Legal Framework. *The Journal of Peasant Studies*. https://doi.org/10.1080/03066150.2024.2349228.

Gover, K. (2020). Legal Pluralism and Indigenous Legal Traditions, in P. S. Berman (ed.), *The Oxford Handbook of Global Legal Pluralism* (pp. 847–75). Oxford University Press. https://doi.org/10.1093/oxfordhb/9780197516744.013.7.

Gregg, B. (2020). The Indigenous Rights State. *Ratio Juris* 33(1), 98–116. https://doi.org/10.1111/raju.12270.

Griffiths, J. (1986). What Is Legal Pluralism? *The Journal of Legal Pluralism and Unofficial Law* 18(24), 1–55. https://doi.org/10.1080/07329113.1986.10756387.

Gudynas, E. (2011). Buen Vivir. *Development* 54(4), 441–447.
Guim, M. & Livermore, M. A. (2021). Where Nature's Rights Go Wrong. *Virginia Law Review* 107(7), 1347–1419.
Habermas, J. (1981 [1987]). *The Theory of Communicative Action, Vol. 2: A Critique of Functionalist Reason.* Beacon Press (orig. *Theorie des kommunikativen Handelns. Zur Kritik der funktionalistischen Vernunft*).
Hames, E. R. (2007). The Ecologically Noble Savage Debate. *Annual Review of Anthropology* 36, 177–190. https://doi.org/10.1146/annurev.anthro.35.081705.123321.
Hanschel, D., Aguilera Bravo, M. G., Dashpurev, B., & Idris, A. K. (2022). Environmental Rights Between Constitutional Law and Local Context. *German Law Journal* 23(7), 1012–1028. https://doi.org/10.1017/glj.2022.68.
Harden-Davies, H., Humphries, F., Maloney, M., Wright, G., Gjerde, K., & Vierros, M. (2020). Rights of Nature. *Marine Policy* 122, 104059. https://doi.org/10.1016/j.marpol.2020.104059.
Harris, B. (2024). Legal Pluralism, in *Indigenous Peoples and Constitutional Reform in Australian* (pp. 143–91). Springer. https://doi.org/10.1007/978-981-99-7121-3_6.
Hart, H. L. A. (1961). *The Concept of Law.* Clarendon Press.
Heidegger, M. (1962). *Die Technik und die Kehre* [*Technology and the Turning*]. Neske.
Henrard, K. & Gilbert, J. (2018). Introducing Multidisciplinary Perspectives to the Adjudication of Indigenous Rights. *Erasmus Law Review* 11(1). https://doi.org/10.5553/ELR.000101.
Hickman, L. A. (1996). Nature as Culture, in Light, A. & Katz, E. (eds.), *Environmental Pragmatism* (pp. 50–72). Routledge.
Higgins, N. (2021). Songlines and Land Claims; Space and Place. *International Journal for the Semiotics of Law* 34(3), 723–741. https://doi.org/10.1007/s11196-020-09748-z.
Hightower, B. & Anker, K. (2016). (Re)Imagining Law. *International Journal for the Semiotics of Law* 29(1), 1–8. https://doi.org/10.1007/s11196-015-9454-5.
Holm, S. (2017). Teleology and Biocentrism. *Synthese* 194(6), 1075–1087. https://doi.org/10.1007/s11229-016-1300-0.
Jagodzinski, J. (2024). *Pedagogical Encounters in the Post-Anthropocene.* Palgrave Macmillan. https://doi.org/10.1007/978-3-031-54849-9.
Jansen, B. (2023). *The Juridification of Business Ethics.* Springer. https://doi.org/10.1007/978-3-031-39908-4.
Jansen, B. (2024a). The Ontological Indifference of Rights of Nature. *Liverpool Law Review* 45, 171–178. https://doi.org/10.1007/s10991-023-09344-8.
Jansen, B. (2024b). The Disappearance of Semiotics. *Journal on the Empirical Research on Law in Action* 45(1), 115–124. https://doi.org/10.5553/RdW/138064242024045001009.
Jansen, B. & Schreiner, A. T. M. (2023). Captured by Digitization. *International Journal for the Semiotics of Law*, 36(3), 2179–2191. https://doi.org/10.1007/s11196-022-09958-7.
Jongepier, F. (2024). Laat de Waddenzee zélf bepalen of ze boorplatformen wil [Let the Wadden Sea Itself Decide Whether It Wants Oil Rigs]. *Trouw* [Dutch newspaper], July 12.
Kahn, P. W. (2005 [2008]). *Putting Liberalism in Its Place.* Princeton University Press.
Kahn, P. W. (2011). *Political Theology.* Columbia University Press.

Kahui, V., Armstrong, C. W., & Aanesen, M. (2024). Comparative Analysis of Rights of Nature (RoN) Case Studies Worldwide. *Ecological Economics* 221, 108193. https://doi.org/10.1016/j.ecolecon.2024.108193.
Kant, I. (1790 [1922]). *Kritik der Urteilskraft* [*Critique of Judgment*]. Felix Meine.
Kauffman, C. M. & Martin, P. L. (2017). Can Rights of Nature Make Development More Sustainable? *World Development* 92(C), 130–142.
Kendon, A. (1988). *Sign Languages of Aboriginal Australia*. Cambridge University Press.
Kirsch, S. (2012). Juridification of Indigenous Politics, in Eckert, J., Donahoe, B., Strümpell, C., & Biner, Z. Ö. (eds.), *Law against the State* (pp. 23–43). Cambridge University Press.
Kleinhans, M.-M. & Macdonald, R. A. (1997). What Is a *Critical* Legal Pluralism? *Canadian Journal of Law & Society* 12(2), 25–46.
Kramer, J. (2016). (Re)Mapping *Terra Nullius*. *International Journal for the Semiotics of Law* 29(2), 191–212. https://doi.org/10.1007/s11196-015-9427-8.
Krutch, J. W. (1955). *The Voice of the Desert*. William Sloane Associates.
Krygier, M. E. (2002). The Grammar of Colonial Legality, in Brennan, G. & Castles, F. G. (eds.), *Australia Reshaped* (pp. 220–260). Cambridge University Press.
Kuhn, Th. S. (1962 [1970]). *The Structure of Scientific Revolutions*. University of Chicago Press.
Kurki, V. A. J. (2022). Can Nature Hold Rights? *Transnational Environmental Law* 11(3), 525–552. https://doi.org/10.1017/S2047102522000358.
Latour, B. (2004). *Politiques de la nature* [*Politics of Nature*]. La Découverte.
Latour, B. (2015 [2017]). *Facing Gaia*. Polity (orig. *Face à Gaïa*. La Découverte).
Latour, B. (2017 [2018]). *Down to Earth*. Polity (orig. *Où atterrir?* La Découverte).
Lévi-Strauss, C. (1962). *La pensée sauvage* [*Wild Thought*]. Plon.
Lindt, A. (2024). Law in Conflict. Doctoral dissertation, University of Bern. Transcript. https://doi.org/10.14361/9783839469699.
Lyotard, J-F. (1974). *Économie libidinale* [*Libidinal Economy*]. Minuit.
Marshall, V. (2019). Removing the Veil from the 'Rights of Nature'. *Australian Feminist Law Journal* 45(2), 233–248. https://doi.org/10.1080/13200968.2019.1802154.
Martuwarra Fitzroy River Council. (2016). *Fitzroy River Declaration*. Available at: http://majala.com.au/news/protecting-the-fitzroy-river-catchment.
Matthee, M. (2024). Law, Poetry, and the Voice of Nature, in Crawley, K., Giddens, T., & Peters, T. D. (eds.), *The Routledge Handbook of Cultural Legal Studies*. Routledge. https://doi.org/10.4324/9781003467762-16.
Matthews, D. (2019). Law and Aesthetics in the Anthropocene. *Law, Culture and the Humanities* 19(2), 227–247. https://doi.org/10.1177/1743872119871830.
Mauss, M. (1925 [2012]). *Essai sur le don* [*Essay on the Gift*]. Presses Universitaires de France.
McGregor, D. & Sritharan, M. (2023). Decolonising the Dialogue on Climate Change, in Lamalle, S. & Stoett, P. (eds.), *Representation and Rights of the Environment* (pp. 66–86). Cambridge University Press. https://doi.org/10.1017/9781108769327.005.
Mena, M. (2024). Semiotic Whitening. *Linguistic Anthropology* 34(2), 220–242. https://doi.org/10.1111/jola.12425.
Mill, J. S. (1859). *On Liberty*. J.W. Parker and Son.
Morton, T. (2010). *The Ecological Thought*. Harvard University Press.

Morton, T. (2013). *Realist Magic*. Duke University Press.
Mouffe, Ch. (2005). *On the Political*. Routledge.
Mutua, M. (2002). *Human Rights*. University of Pennsylvania Press.
Naess, A. (1973). The Shallow and the Deep, Long-Range Ecology Movement. *Inquiry* 16 (1–4), 95–100. https://doi.org/10.1080/00201747308601682.
Nash, R. (1989). *The Rights of Nature*. University of Wisconsin Press.
Neely, S. (2016). On Becoming Human in Lingít Aaní. *Environmental Philosophy* 13(1), 83–104. https://doi.org/10.5840/envirophil201642634.
Nietzsche, F. W. (1830 [1973]). Die dionysische Weltanschauung [The Dionysian Worldvision], in *Band 2 Nachgelassene Schriften 1870–1873* (pp. 43–70). De Gruyter. https://doi-org.proxy.uba.uva.nl/10.1515/9783110835304.43.
Nordlander, A. (2021). Green Purpose. *Studies in Christian Ethics* 34(1), 36–55. https://doi.org/10.1177/0953946820910672.
O'Donnell, E., Poelina, A., Pelizzon, A., & Clark, C. (2020). Stop Burying the Lede. *Transnational Environmental Law* 9(3), 403–427. https://doi.org/10.1017/S2047102520000242.
Page, J. & Pelizzon, A. (2024). Of Rivers, Law and Justice in the Anthropocene. *The Geographical Journal* 190, e12442. https://doi.org/10.1111/geoj.12442.
Petel, M. (2024). The Illusion of Harmony. *Transnational Environmental Law* 13(1), 12–34. https://doi.org/10.1017/S2047102523000262.
Petersmann, M.-C. (2024). The EU Charter on Rights of Nature, in Alvarez-Nakagawa, A. & Douzinas, C. (eds.), *Non-Human Rights* (pp. 141–63). Edward Elgar. https://doi.org/10.4337/9781802208528.00012.
Poelina, A., Bagnall, D., Graham, M., Williams, R. T., Yunkaporta, T., Marshall, C., Diop, S. A., Samnakay, N., Maloney, M., & Davis, M. (2024). *Declaration of Peace for Indigenous Australians and Nature*. Springer.
Povinelli, E. A. (2002). *The Cunning of Recognition*. Duke University Press.
Putzer, A., Lambooy, T., Breemer, I., & Rietveld, A. (2022a). The Rights of Nature as a Bridge Between Land-Ownership Regimes. *Transnational Environmental Law* 11(3), 501–523. https://doi.org/10.1017/S2047102522000334.
Putzer, A., Lambooy, T., Jeurissen, R., & Kim, E. (2022b). Putting the Rights of Nature on the Map. *Journal of Maps*, 18(1), 89–96. https://doi.org/10.1080/17445647.2022.2079432.
Rawson, A. and Mansfield, B. (2018). Producing Juridical Knowledge: 'Rights of Nature' or the Naturalization of Rights? *Environment and Planning E: Nature and Space*, 1(1–2), 99–119.
Rifkin, M. (2017). *Beyond Settler Time*. Duke University Press.
Roscoe Pound, N. (1907). The Need of a Sociological Jurisprudence. *The Green Bag* 19(10), 607–615.
Said, E. W. (1978 [1979]). *Orientalism*. Vintage.
Schmitt, C. (1941). *Völkerrechtliche Großraumordnung mit Interventionsverbot für raumfremde Mächte* [*International Law and the Great Power Order with a Prohibition on Intervention by External Powers*]. Duncker & Humblot.
Schmitt, C. (1950). *Der Nomos der Erde im Völkerrecht des* Jus Publicum Europæum [*The Nomos of the Earth in the International Law of the* Jus Publicum Europæum]. Duncker & Humblot.

Schreiner, A. T. M. (1990). *Roem van het recht [The Glory of Law]*. Doctoral dissertation, University of Amsterdam. 1001 Publishers.
Schreiner, A. T. M. (2004). Observing the Differences, in Soeteman, A. (ed.), *Pluralism and Law: Proceedings of the 20th IVR World Congress. Vol. 3: Global Problems* (pp. 87–94). Franz Steiner.
Schreiner, A. T. M. (2007). Landmarks for Aboriginal Law in Australia, in Wagne, A., Werner, W., & Cao, D. (eds.), *Interpretation, Law and the Construction of Meaning* (pp. 195–204). Springer.
Schreiner, A. T. M. (2013). How Law Manifests Itself in Australian Aboriginal Art. *Erasmus Law Review* 3(4), 167–172.
Schreiner, A. T. M. (2019). *According to Aboriginal Law* . . . 1001 Publishers.
Serres, M. (1990). *Le contrat naturel* [*The Natural Contract*]. François Bourin.
Sieder, R. (2020). The Juridification of Politics, in Foblets, M-C., Goodale, M., Sapignoli, M., & Zenker, O. (eds.), *The Oxford Handbook of Law and Anthropology* (pp. 701–15). Oxford University Press. https://doi.org/10.1093/oxfordhb/9780198840534.013.4.
Skurky, C. (2022). Toward a Decolonized Non-anthropocentric Legal System. *Georgetown Environmental Law Review* 34(2), 351–372.
Sloterdijk, P. (1983). *Kritik der Zynischen Vernunft* [*Critique of Cynical Reason*]. Suhrkamp.
Smith, L. T. (1999 [2008]). *Decolonizing Methodologies*. Zed Books & University of Otago Press.
Stone, C. D. (1972 [2010]). *Should Trees Have Standing?* Oxford University Press.
Swyngedouw, E. (2010). Trouble With Nature, in Hillier, J. & Healey, P. (eds.), *The Ashgate Research Companion to Planning Theory*. Routledge. https://doi.org/10.4324/9781315612750.
Táíwò, O. (2022). *Against Decolonisation*. Hurst.
Talbot-Jones, J. & Bennett, J. (2022). Implementing Bottom-Up Governance through Granting Legal Rights to Rivers. *Australasian Journal of Environmental Management* 29(1). https://doi.org/10.1080/14486563.2022.2029775.
Tamanaha, B. Z. (2008). Understanding Legal Pluralism. *Sydney Law Review* 30(3), 375–411.
Tănăsescu, M. (2015). Nature Advocacy and the Indigenous Symbol. *Environmental Values* 24(1), 105–122.
Tănăsescu, M. (2020). Rights of Nature, Legal Personality, and Indigenous Philosophies. *Transnational Environmental Law* 9(3), 429–453. https://doi:10.1017/S2047102520000217.
Tănăsescu, M. (2022). *Understanding the Rights of Nature*. Transcript.
Tarrdif, M-J., Rankin, T., & Deer, K. K. (2023). Traditional Indigenous Knowledge and the Relationship to Mother Earth, in Lamalle, S. & Stoett, P. (eds.), *Representation and Rights of the Environment* (pp. 147–159). Cambridge University Press. https://doi.org/10.1017/9781108769327.009.
Teubner, G. (1998). Legal Irritants. *The Modern Law Review* 61(1), 11–32.
Ugwu, I. P. (2025). Environmental Protection, Rights of Nature, and Religious Beliefs in Europe. *International Journal for the Semiotics of Law* 38, 993–1014. https://doi.org/10.1007/s11196-024-10193-5.

Valenzuela, P. (2017). The Metaphysical Bond between Natural and Human Beings. *FORUM*, 3, 299–312. https://doi.org/10.17421/2498-9746-03-17.
Vilkka, L. (1997). *The Intrinsic Value of Nature*. Rodopi.
Vizenor, G. (1994). *Manifest Manners*. University of Nebraska Press.
Voegelin, E. (1939). *Die politischen Religionen* [*The Political Religions*]. Bermann-Fischer.
Watts, O. (2016). Contemporary Indigenous Art, Resistance and Imaging the Processes of Legal Subjection. *International Journal for the Semiotics of Law* 29, 213–235. https://doi.org/10.1007/s11196-016-9464-y.
Wesche, T. (2023). *Die Rechte der Natur* [*The Rights of Nature*]. Suhrkamp.
Whittemore, M. E. (2011). The Problem of Enforcing Nature's Rights under Ecuador's Constitution. *Pacific Rim Law & Policy Journal*, 20(3), 659–691.
Willems, M., Lambooy, T., & Begum, S. (2021). New Governance Ways Aimed at Protecting Nature for Future Generations. *IOP Conference Series: Earth and Environmental Science* 690(1), 012059. https://doi.org/10.1088/1755-1315/690/1/012059.
Williams, N. M. (1987). *Two Laws*. Australian Institute of Aboriginal Studies.
Zimmerman, M. E. (1983). Toward a Heideggerian *Ethos* for Radical Environmentalism. *Environmental Ethics* 5, 99–131.
Zoettl, P. A. (2016). The (Il)legal Indian. *Social & Legal Studies* 25(1), 3–21. https://doi.org/10.1177/0964663915593412.

4

The Rights of Nature and the Right to Territory of Indigenous Peoples

Decolonizing Ecocentrism

Digno Montalván-Zambrano and Isabel Wences

4.1 Introduction

The Rights of Nature (RoN) have become one of the most discussed legal responses to the ecological crisis. The RoN framework challenges the exclusively anthropocentric approach through which the law has determined who can be considered rights-holders.[1] As David R. Boyd, former United Nations Special Rapporteur on human rights, observes, within predominant Western thought (and, therefore, in classical environmental law) "nonhuman animals and ecosystems have always been treated as things, goods intended for human use and exploitation," but, "in a spectacular evolution that encompasses the entire planet, these entities are now being recognized as legitimate subjects and rights holders" (Boyd 2017: 101). Since 2008, laws, rulings, and even a constitution have recognized nature as a whole, or specific elements thereof as subjects of rights.[2] The growing interest in RoN[3] is accompanied by a transformative potential, yet we may also feel inclined to immerse ourselves in deeper reflection on its conceptual foundations and practical

[1] While the concept of "rights," as historically developed within an anthropocentric framework, limits rights-holders primarily to certain categories of humans, emerging "non-anthropocentric ethical approaches open the possibility of non-human entities becoming right-holders" (Corrigan and Oksanen 2021: 3–4).

[2] Some examples are: in 2008, the Constitution of Ecuador recognized Nature as a subject of rights and, based on this, its Constitutional Court has declared mangroves and forests as subjects of rights. In 2010, Bolivia issued the Law on the Rights of Mother Earth. In Colombia, its High Courts have recognized rivers, the Amazon, snow-capped mountains, and mangroves as subjects of rights. In New Zealand, the Parliament enshrined rights for a river. In February 2019, the Supreme Court of Bangladesh granted legal personality to all rivers in its territory. In Spain, in 2022, a law recognized rights for a lagoon, the Mar Menor.

[3] For a quantitative study on the increase in the number of cases of recognition of the rights of Nature until 2022, see Putzer et al. (2022; 2025).

implications. Geoffrey Garver, for instance, has cautioned that, despite their intention to move beyond anthropocentric frameworks, RoN initiatives often remain entangled within them by ascribing legal personhood to nature. Such an approach, he warns, risks perpetuating a divisive, reductionist, and atomistic understanding of the human–nature relationship, thereby undermining the deeper transformative aspirations of ecological law (Garver 2021: 90). Although RoN aspires to challenge dominant legal ontologies, it continues to operate within the discursive and institutional frameworks it seeks to transform.

This conflict raises important questions about whether RoN can genuinely constitute a paradigmatic shift in legal thought, or whether it ultimately reconfigures the language of rights without fully departing from its Western anthropocentric roots. This issue becomes particularly critical when associating the RoN with Indigenous worldviews, given that "western law has long resisted creating more space for the wisdom of Indigenous legal traditions within a pluralistic understanding of law" (Garver 2021: 98). Vargas Roncancio (2021: 122) further highlights that although some RoN efforts seek to reflect Indigenous relational ontologies, they often replicate individualistic legal structures that fail to capture the deeply interconnected relationships Indigenous peoples maintain with the non-human world. Moreover, RoN frameworks risk depoliticizing environmental conflicts by abstracting rights claims from their socioecological realities, territories, lifeways, and Indigenous struggles. In this context, according to Macpherson, activism for the Rights of Nature may inadvertently overshadow the more radical Indigenous struggles for sovereignty, control, and ownership of their lands and the construction of their territories, running the risk of "repeating colonial injustices by overriding hard-won Indigenous rights" (Macpherson et al. 2021: 445–446). In the same vein, Anker warns that integrating Indigenous knowledge into ecological jurisprudence risks perpetuating the myth of the "ecological Indian," a colonial construct that idealizes Indigenous peoples as static and only ecological. Such representations obscure the political agency and evolving legal traditions of Indigenous communities, while reinforcing colonial structures by depoliticizing their knowledge systems (Anker 2021). This reveals that, although RoN initiatives represent an important step toward reimagining legal relations with the natural world, they are not free from internal contradictions and limitations.

Drawing from these conflicts, this article seeks to provide distinct insights about the relationship and the differences between the discursive framework in favor of the RoN and the one concerning the right to territory of Indigenous peoples. Although other rights of Indigenous peoples, such as the right to land or self-determination, are being associated with nature,[4] we take as our analytical

[4] In this regard, it has been argued that the jurisprudence of the Inter-American Court of Human Rights related to Indigenous peoples shows limitations by relying primarily on the right to communal property to protect their rights. This approach has been considered "not adequate to deal with the complex legal and socio-environmental issues that characterize cases concerning Indigenous and tribal peoples" (Aguilera 2023: 81, 125). It has also been emphasized that the right to self-determination has played a key role "not only for

framework exclusively the "right to territory." The right to territory, unlike other rights such as the right to land, self-determination, or even environmental rights, foregrounds the ontological and relational dimensions intrinsic to nature that are central to many Indigenous worldviews. As we explain in Section 4.3 of this chapter, while the right to land primarily safeguards the physical space where Indigenous peoples live, and the right to self-determination protects their political autonomy, the right to territory pursues a different distinct objective, that is, the protection of the profound relationships Indigenous peoples maintain with nonhuman beings and the environment itself. From their vision about territory arise the norms of relationship that Indigenous peoples maintain with "earth beings."[5]

If the underlying premise of the Rights of Nature movement is to resituate our relationship with the nonhuman world by recognizing nature as a subject with intrinsic value, then the Indigenous concept most closely aligned with this objective is precisely that of "territory." This alignment is exemplified, in the approach of the Special Jurisdiction for Peace (*Jurisdicción Especial para la Paz*, JEP) in Colombia, which in several landmark decisions involving Indigenous peoples has not declared "nature" per se as a victim of the Colombian armed conflict, but rather has recognized the *Katsa Su*, the *CxHab Wala Kile*, and the *Eperera Euja*, ancestral territories of the Awá, Nasa, and Sia Indigenous peoples, as victims and therefore subjects of rights.[6] This distinction, we consider, is crucial because although RoN proposals often emphasize the intrinsic value or preservation of nature, Indigenous conceptions of territory cannot be constrained to conservation or ownership thereof; they involve complex, reciprocal relationships with nonhuman beings and entities instead. By focusing on the right to territory, we foreground these relational ontologies and critically assess the extent to which RoN frameworks resonate with, or otherwise risk obscuring, Indigenous ways of relating to the natural world. Rather than diluting our analysis by addressing a broader array of Indigenous rights, we intentionally focus on territory, as it is precisely at this intersection – between place, identity, and relationality – that the conflicts and possibilities between RoN and Indigenous claims are most vividly revealed.

Engaging with this intersections demands a careful methodological reflection on how we understand and represent "territory." Although we will take up the words of the Indigenous peoples themselves, we distance ourselves from any essentialist view on Indigenous peoples. As authors we, on the contrary, recognize their heterogeneity, the diversity of Indigenous territorialities, their varied relationships with land and nature, and the internal debates and conflicts that may shape

guaranteeing a holistic, contextual approach of the law, but also building connections between different rights of existential value for Indigenous peoples, including physical and cultural survival" (Eichler 2024, p. 149).

[5] Following the term proposed by the anthropologist Marisol de la Cadena (2015).

[6] For an anthropological analysis of the tensions between the Rights of Nature framework and the rights of Indigenous peoples, see Viaene (2022). Regarding the specific issue of territory being recognized as a victim of the armed conflict, and its distinctions from the Rights of Nature approach, see the article co-authored by Viaene and Belkis Izquierdo the Indigenous judge of the JEP responsible for the rulings (Izquierdo and Viaene 2024).

those relationships. It would not be coherent to defend the recognition of plurality, unifying its protagonists and placing them under a static and a historically confining conceptual umbrella.

Within this context, our research objective arises; it notably consists in explaining why we consider it crucial to differentiate in terms of their discursive frameworks, between the RoN and the rights to territory or, at least, to recognize that the possible alliances between the two do not imply a complete alignment of their objectives. The different epistemic parameters based on which the RoN and the right to territory of Indigenous peoples have been claimed also reflect different political objectives. While the Western discourse on RoN is the product of a philosophical–moral, conservationist, scientific, and ius-naturalist debate, the right to territory is a claim for the construction of meanings, this is, for the exercise of the ontological and relational plurality of Indigenous peoples with their environment. Whereas RoN seek to give relevance to the interests of nonhumans in our reflections about justice, the right to territory seeks to protect the specific ways in which Indigenous peoples relate to their environment. In accounting for the differences, we do not intend to create new disjunctions, but only to clarify the terms based on which the debate takes place while fostering symmetrical dialogue and recognition. Therefore, we do not wish to downplay the importance of the search for places of encounter in the struggle against anthropocentrism. However, we consider that this should be adequately defined not so much as a single movement, but as a plural alliance of actors and proposals that find a space for connection, dialogue, and mutual influence in questioning the anthropocentric.

Based on these premises, this chapter will present, first, an interpretation of "ecocentrism," not necessarily founded, however, on "Western" scientific ecological knowledge, and will elaborate a tentative classification of the different coexisting ecocentric proposals. Second, using Indigenous voices, we will try to give an account of the meaning of territory for Indigenous peoples, its link to the decolonial ecocentric model, and the objectives behind its articulation as a right. Third, by means of examples, we will show why it is key to adequately differentiate between the predominant ecocentric frameworks of reflection, giving special emphasis to the existing distances between the claim for territory of Indigenous peoples and certain foundations of the RoN. Finally, we propose a specific interpretation of the RoN that allows us to see these as tools to discuss who should hold the representation of nature in the courts and, in this way, give way to epistemic and ontological plurality in its definition.

4.2 The Ecocentric Moment: A Historiography

A "new" ecocentric paradigm is emerging in the face of the failure of the current anthropocentric model of environmental management. This new paradigm seeks to overcome the utilitarian model concerned with the protection of ecosystems exclusively based on the benefits they can bring to human beings, and instead to give way to a model of mutual respect, whereby human beings are placed in the context of the ecosystems in which they live, from a horizontal viewpoint of mutual dependence. In other words, in the anthropocentric model, nature is an object at the disposal of human beings; in the ecocentric model, it is an "Other" deserving of respect and protection.

The ecocentric paradigm is often associated with the *deep ecology* movement. Although the visibility that ecocentric thinking has now gained, has been, in part, thanks to the philosophers, lawyers, artists, and activists who articulated around this movement, it does not capture all the ecocentric ways of living in the world. The origin of the term "deep ecology" is attributed to the Norwegian philosopher Arne Naess (1973: 95). With this expression, Naess sought to differentiate those approaches focused exclusively on the fight against pollution and the depletion of resources aimed at favoring the health and productivity of developed States – which he calls "*superficial ecology*" – from the proposals based on a relational image of human beings with nature – which he calls "*deep ecology*" (Naess 1973: 96).

In its origins, deep ecology was primarily inspired by North American naturalism and conservationism. Although it has broadened its sources to other non-Western ways of living in the world, such as Taoism, Buddhism, Hinduism, and the worldview of different Indigenous peoples (Devall and Sessions 1999: 79–108), the emergence of the deep ecology movement is clearly determined both spatially (Europe) and temporally (late 1970s and early 1980s), as it is defined by its main interlocutors, namely Western ecophilosophers. This is precisely one of the criticisms made by the ecoanarchist Murray Bookchin when he points out that deep ecology has been "formulated largely by privileged male white academics" who have sought to simplify the different ways of living in the world (1987: 4). Certainly, one of the problems with deep ecology lies in the variety of positions it seeks to unite, at the expense of diminishing their complexities and profound differences (Bookchin 1987: 6–7). Beyond the provocative tone with which Bookchin voiced his critique of deep ecology, it reveals an important issue that, in the framework of the present piece, cannot be omitted: deep ecology is a movement formed by specific actors who have interpreted other realities and spiritualties, such as the Indigenous worldviews, from their specific perspectives.

The term "ecocentrism," on the other hand, has a more inclusive potential. Although this term also originated in the West (United States, late 1980s and early 1990s),[7] unlike deep ecology, ecocentrism is not to be understood as a movement, but as a paradigm that groups together ways of seeing the world. Originally, ecocentrism was used to describe holistic environmental ethics formulated by the "West" and in which scientific discourse played a leading role.[8]

[7] The use of the term "ecocentrism" was standardized by the American philosopher J. Baird Callicott (Moore 2008: 5).

[8] J. Baird Callicott, for example, in his study of the Land Ethic proposed by the US American naturalist Aldo Leopold (1949), shows that the foundations of his ecocentric philosophy rest on three pillars: (1) evolutionary biology and (2) ecological biology in a context of (3) Copernican astronomy (Callicott 1987: 194–195). In line with this, Callicott, seeking to provide scientific arguments for his land ethic, has endeavored to establish the links between it and general evolutionary theory, evolutionary biology, mechanistic ecology and ecosystemic ecology (2013: 82–122).

However, the expansion of this approach has led to ecocentrism having opened up to the ancestral practices of Indigenous peoples and non-Judeo-Christian religions around the world.[9] In this second sense, ecocentrism has left its original framework of scientific reflection to include other forms of relationships with nature, namely horizontal ones linked to the spirituality and cosmovision of other non-Western peoples.

The ecocentric paradigm then results in three models for understanding nature (Montalván-Zambrano 2026): (1) as an object defined, with pretensions of universality, by Western scientific–ecological knowledge (*ecocentric-conservationist interpretation*); (2) as the starting point for the construction of a new ecological consciousness based on religious spirituality (*ecocentric-religious interpretation*), or (3) as the ontological foundation of a horizontal relationship where the boundaries between human and nonhuman are diluted (*decolonial-ecocentric interpretation*).[10] All ecocentric proposals share a vision of a human–nature relationship defined in horizontal terms; however, they differ in the ways in which this horizontal dialogue takes place. For an ecocentric-conservationist this dialogue will be mediated by scientific discourse; for an ecocentric-religious proponent, by the spiritual experiences produced by contact with nature; and for a decolonial ecocentrist by a cosmovision rooted primarily in identification with their territory.[11]

Each of the ecocentric approaches presented here also entails different schemes of how nature and power are being represented and what decision-making would look like. Within the *ecocentric-conservationist model*, it is the community of Western scientists who have been attributed the highest interpretive authority on the value and interests of nature. For the *ecocentric-religious model*, the value of nature is expounded by spiritual leaders or theologists who interpret and reinterpret the sacred texts of the different religions of the world, giving account of an ecocentric

[9] In this line, the US American philosopher J. Baird Callicott, in his book *Earth's Insights*, studied the possibility of constructing environmental ethics from the thought of the Indigenous peoples of Polynesia (the Maori people among them), North American Indians, Indigenous peoples of South America, African tribal peoples, and native-Australian peoples (Callicott 1997). Within this trend of widening the scope of the term ecocentrism, we can find also the book *The Great Work* (1999) by the theologian and philosopher Thomas Berry and the book *Wild Law* by the South African lawyer Cormarc Cullinan (2011).

[10] These categories are proposed and extensively developed by Digno Montalván in his book Naturalezas y Derechos: la representación de lo no-humano en el antropocentrismo, el biocentrismo y el ecocentrismo (Nature and Rights: The Representation of the Non-Human in Anthropocentrism, Biocentrism, and Ecocentrism) (Montalván-Zambrano 2026). The book is based on his doctoral dissertation, Natures and Rights: The Representation of the Non-Human in Philosophy, Politics, and Law, which was awarded the Josep Miquel Prats Canut Prize in 2024 for the best doctoral thesis in Environmental Law in Spain (2023 edition).

[11] While several authors of the Ecology and Religion school include within the category "religion" the cosmovisions of Indigenous peoples (Gottlieb 2006; Jenkins et al. 2017), we reject such an association. We do not consider that the Indigenous is limited to the spiritual. In Latin America, for example, Indigenous peoples have exercised, from various fields, an active political and resistance struggle, which, we consider, is best explained through the claim for their territories. This resistance has not only been expressed with respect to religion, but also against domination, inequality, and contempt.

vocation within them.[12] These two models follow a top-down approach in the establishment of ecocentric values: it is scientists or ecotheologists who construct the value that nature should possess. Finally, *decolonial ecocentrism* is characterized, on the contrary, by a bottom-up approach: it is the practices that local communities have built up over the years or centuries which reflect an ecocentric attitude. While in the first two, an ecocentric theory is constructed from which a practice is expected to emerge, in decolonial ecocentrism there is first a practice that is then systematized and conceptualized.

Despite these differences, the claim of RoN is often used to represent the convergence of the main elements constituting the ecocentric paradigm, in which each of the actors would share similar reflections on the importance of or reasons for changing the focus of human beings from being superior to being part of nature. On the contrary, we consider that the philosophical and scientific roots on which conservationist or religious ecocentrism are based, reveal the distance of these approaches from the decolonial ecocentrism practiced by Indigenous peoples around the world. This difference results, at the same time, from the fact that the claims of each approach are not necessarily the same and their translation into law neither pursue the same objectives.

For example, the 1972 essay, *Should Trees have Standing*, by the US American legal scholar Christopher D. Stone, is often considered the first text to engage with the idea of the RoN and, therefore, also the main influence behind the recognition of these rights in legal texts, such as the 2008 Constitution of Ecuador. Yet, this statement is not entirely true. Stone did indeed propose that trees or rivers could be represented before the courts; however, his work was not aimed at considering nature as a subject of rights. Moreover, Stone did not manifest any affinity with the Indigenous worldviews and relational ontologies that, as we shall see below, gave rise to the rights of Pachamama or of nature in the emblematic 2008 Constitution of Ecuador.

The consideration that nature is an "Other," a subject, with which we relate, is the central feature of the current definition of the RoN, but it has also been part of the relational ontologies that various Indigenous peoples of the world have practiced for centuries.[13] This, however, is not Stone's understanding of nature. In the epilogue to the third edition of *Trees*, written thirty-five years after its original publication, Stone clarified that the three original elements of legal personality to entities of nature that he proposed are:

> (1) That the claim be admitted on behalf of and in the interest of the object; (2) that the calculation of damages (or the balance in equity where damages were

[12] Pope Francis' encyclical letter *Laudato Si* provides an illustrative example of this model.

[13] Anthropology has been reporting on this for several decades. In this regard, we can see studies such as those of Brazilian anthropologist Viveiros de Castro (2010; 2014; 2015) and the French anthropologist Philippe Descola (2013) on the Indigenous peoples of the Brazilian Amazon, or those of the Colombian anthropologist Arturo Escobar on Afro-Colombian peoples (2014; 2018) and that of the Peruvian anthropologist Marisol de la Cadena on the Andean peoples (2015).

> inappropriate) include an accounting for interest or non-intrinsic value of the object (not limited to the economic market value); and (3) that the judgment be applied for the benefit of the object. (Stone 2010: 159)

As we can see, Stone never goes so far as to speak of nature in terms of being a subject of rights, and this is coherent, for Stone did not consider that natural entities such as rivers had an "interest" of their own that had to be preserved (Stone 2010: 169). At the same time, Stone's attempts to raise a new environmental consciousness are rather minor. In his view, it is more important to create institutions that protect the environment than to rely on changing people's consciousness (1974: 47). However, he did recognize that we must – albeit in the background – work for the construction of new environmental ethics that will guide our understanding of law and bring about "a radical change in our feelings about 'our' place in the rest of nature" (1974: 48). Nevertheless, he rejected, expressly, that such a new consciousness is born of Indigenous knowledge. In his words:

> I am under the impression, too, that notwithstanding the vaunted "harmony" between the American Plains Indians and Nature, once they had equipped themselves with rifles, their pursuit of the buffalo expanded to fill the technological potential. (Stone 1974: 47; 2010: 27)

The above quote from Stone gives an account of the author's ethnocentric tendencies and the critical view he had of Indigenous worldviews. This is even more evident if we consider what theoretical sources he was relying on. Citing an article by US American legal scholar Earl Finbar Murphy, Stone subscribes to the idea that neither the spiritual beliefs of the Chinese and Native Americans "in the unity between man and nature had no greater effect than the contrary beliefs in Europe in producing a balance between man and his environment" (Stone 1974: 46; 2010: 26). It is important to refer to the article cited by Stone in support of this argument, because it can give an account of the true meaning of his words. In this article, Murphy, after exposing how throughout history human beings have tended to take refuge in cities, establishes that the spiritual views of any culture when it comes to establishing harmony between "man"[14] and his environment play an irrelevant role (Murphy 1971: 477). Referring to Native Americans as "semi-primitive," he states that the goal is not to learn from past cultures, but to continue technological development inspired by Western human reason to the point where it can completely dominate nature. In his words:

> To cease present practices and become passive, or to go backward to a past pattern, even if possible, is not adequate (...) Artifice of the most technical sort will be required, rather than some emotionally predicated organicism. (Murphy 1971: 479–480)

[14] This is the term used by the author to refer to humanity.

Following Murphy's line of thought and thus a techno-optimism and a rejection that solutions lie in what non-Western cultures can teach, Stone, once again, showing certain ethnocentric tendencies, states:

> Pantheism, Shintoism, and Taoism all have myths to offer. But they are all, each in its own fashion, quaint, primitive, and archaic. What is needed is a myth that can fit our growing body of knowledge of geophysics, biology and the cosmos. (Stone 2010: 29)

As we will show later, Stone's limited interest in reshaping human–nature relationships from Indigenous worldviews underscores the deep gap between his proposal and the rights of Pachamama enshrined in Ecuador's 2008 Constitution. Whereas Stone framed nature's protection through legal representation within a Western-based, and arguably ethnocentric, perspective, the rights of Pachamama reflect a decolonial shift grounded in Indigenous worldviews that recognize nature as a living subject.

Another school of RoN that has been, in our opinion, mistakenly associated with the rights of the Pachamama of Ecuador is the call for a "*Great Law*" and a "*Wild Law.*" These are approaches that seek to implement a new nonanthropocentric Ius Naturalism in US common law. The precursor of this thinking was the US American priest, historian, and theologian Thomas Berry with his book *The Great Work*, published in 1999. In this book, Berry stated that the "Great Work" of our time was to bring about the transition from a period of human devastation of the earth to a period in which humans were present on the planet in a mutually beneficial way, a new era, which he calls "ecozoic."

Transitioning to the "ecozoic" would require, according to Berry, moving from our human center to an Earth-centered framework of understanding and assigning value to the world. This, he suggests, is the *Great Work* of our time, to make the Earth or, as Berry calls it, this "bio-spiritual planet" the source of all our knowledge, institutions, and ethics. The sources of wisdom for raising such ecological consciousness, according to Berry, are fourfold: the wisdom of Indigenous peoples, the wisdom of women, the wisdom of classical traditions, and the wisdom of science. This seems to account for a pluralistic approach in Berry's reflections. However, the role and practical importance he gives to non-Western sources of thought is not entirely clear. In his work he promotes the idea that all our mythical accounts must be transformed in the light of what observational sciences, such as ecology, establish. The natural sciences, he argues, have now moved beyond the mechanistic framework of understanding – a worldview that conceives of nature as an inert object composed of discrete parts governed by deterministic laws – recognizing that there is subjectivity in all our knowledge. For Berry, ecology should become the queen of all sciences and humanities: it would help us shape a viable world for the future through action in key sectors of society such as religion, law, education and economics (Berry 1999: 64–68, 86–91, 80–81).

Berry's approach would enter into debate with the South African scholar Cormac Cullinan and his book *Wild Law* (2011). In this work, Cullinan, following Berry, comes up with a nonanthropocentric Ius Naturalist theory of law whereby the laws of the universe dictate the origin of all rights. Specifically, he states that in order to rediscover *Earth Jurisprudence* and develop forms appropriate for our time, it is essential to begin by observing the laws dictated by the *Great Law*, that is, the fundamental principles that govern the universe. Once we align with the laws of the universe, we can formulate an *Earth Jurisprudence* (a human philosophy) that enables us to dwell harmoniously with the universe, from which appropriate legal systems can then be derived. These new laws or judicial rulings are what he calls *Wild Law*. Thus, the scheme he gives rise to would be the following: from the *Great Law* (from the laws of the universe) are born directly *Earth Rights* (natural rights for more-than-human entities), but, is also born, from our human reflection on the *Great Law*, an *Earth Jurisprudence* (a philosophy) that inspires us to create a *Wild Law* (laws in the legal-formal sense).

At the core of Cullinan's theoretical attempt, we find the *laws of the universe*, from which he derives his entire theory of law. But what are the laws of the universe? Who defines them? When are we acting for or against them? The *Great Law* does not pronounce on what the universe is in itself, but only what scientific analysis is capable of interpreting and describing the former in an approximate way. Thus, it would be "Western" science that would act as the new foundation for the granting of all rights. In Cullinan's work, all human rights, including the rights of Indigenous peoples, are derived from the laws of the universe. In this scheme, the question of who determines which Indigenous people do or do not supposedly maintain a harmonious relationship with the natural world is not a minor one. It raises critical concerns about the criteria used to assess such harmony, and more importantly, about who holds the authority to make those assessments – an issue that becomes especially sensitive in intercultural and legal contexts. If scientists, as Burdon points out (2012: 41–46), are the first ones called upon to express what the *Great Law* means in conflict scenarios, their voice would have more force than that of Indigenous peoples. This inseparable link between following the "laws of the universe" and having rights can be, in real situations, highly dangerous: because the *laws of the universe* are the source of all rights, the *Great Law* would also be the superior law, even above human rights (Cullinan 2011: 105). What Cullinan attempts to do is to associate the tradition of Western Ius Naturalism with a nonanthropocentric approach. Here, once again, there are few coincidences between his work and the relational ontologies of Indigenous rights. One might wonder how much acceptance the idea of *Wild Law* would have among the Indigenous communities themselves, knowing that it could imply the suspension of their human rights for the guarantee of that superior Right of "Nature."

To finalize the debate in this section, we must speak of the ethics of Gaia, another frequently cited source of the RoN. Gaia and Pachamama are often treated as synonyms, which is a big mistake. The Gaia ethic can be derived from the ideas developed by the former NASA worker and UK scientist James Lovelock. His Gaia hypothesis, published in 1970, is a scientific theory about biogeochemical processes, not a postulation about some new "Mother Earth." In fact, the author himself is compelled to clarify the above in his book *The Revenge of Gaia*, by defining Gaia in the following scientific terms:

> Gaia is a thin spherical shell of matter that surrounds the incandescent interior; it begins where the crustal rocks meet the magma of the Earth's hot interior, about 100 miles below the surface, and proceeds another 100 miles outwards through the ocean and air to the even hotter thermosphere at the edge of space. (Lovelock 2007: 20)

At the same time, Lovelock considers that Gaia is not to be confused with "Mother Nature." In his words:

> It is time to wake up and realize that Gaia is no cozy mother that nurtures humans and can be propitiated by gestures such as carbon trading or sustainable development. Gaia, even though we are a part of her, will always dictate the terms of peace. (Lovelock 2009: 31)

With the above, Lovelock wants to show that we are at war with Gaia – a statement far removed from the idea of harmony with the earth that nurtures Indigenous thought. In Lovelock's opinion, by changing the environment we have "unknowingly declared war on Gaia" and we have turned her into our greatest enemy (Lovelock 2007: 13). Thus, for Lovelock we must make peace with Gaia in our own interest. This makes Gaia ethics express a certain anthropocentrism. On the connection between Lovelock's Gaia and the worldviews of Indigenous peoples, we refer to the following quote from his work, which explains, by itself, why the theory of Gaia by Lovelock and the Indigenous relational ontologies do not seem to be compatible:

> The innocent among the urban intelligentsia think and talk of early humans as living in harmony with the natural world. Some of them go further and gather funds to preserve what they see as natural communities living in remote regions, such as the tropical forests. They see the modern world as clever but bad and these simple lifestyles as natural and good. They are wrong. We should not think of early humans as better or worse than we are; indeed, they were probably very little different. (. . .) Peace on you Aboriginals; you individually are no worse and no better than we are, it is just that we are power-assisted and more numerous. (Lovelock 2007: 209–210)

For Lovelock, the way to face the war that Gaia supposedly gives rise to is not to focus on the past and try to recover what, in his opinion, was a "false harmony" that the ancestral peoples supposedly had with the earth. Lovelock is a defender of science and progress. On the contrary, he believes that the only way to make peace with Gaia is to improve our technology to a point where it does not affect the state of planetary homeostasis.

4.3 From Relational Ontology and Communal Grammar to the – Decolonial – Vindication of Territory as a Right

It is important to begin this section by clarifying that, as we have stated in a different work, the conceptual categories "land" and "territory" should not be considered analogously (Montalván-Zambrano & Wences 2022). To start with, the right to land recognizes the geographic space which Indigenous peoples have ancestrally inhabited, commonly protected through the right to communal property. By contrast, the right to Indigenous territory cannot be reduced to the idea of property. Territory is a relational space in constant transformation; it is a fabric in permanent constitution and, therefore, it is not reducible to traditional cartographic representations nor static coordinates. Territory is a sociocultural and historical construction where the relational ontologies of Indigenous peoples with nature are expressed with greater forcefulness.

The category *relational ontologies* refers to modes of identification in which all beings – both human and nonhuman – are understood not as isolated entities, but as emergent from dynamic, interdependent relationships that constitute their very existence and identity. That is, they show the "constitutive relationality of everything real," accounting for the fact that "nothing preexists the relations that constitute it" (Escobar 2014: 57–61). Nature does not pre-exist as an undisputed reality, but is formed in the interaction between the biophysical, human, and supernatural worlds (Escobar 2020: 72). From this relational perspective, we consider the right to territory as the context of emergence for the decolonial ecocentrism of Indigenous peoples. Based on the above, in this section we will focus, first, on approaching the meaning that Indigenous peoples assign to territory, making, collaterally, reference to the struggle for its defense. And, in a subsequent step, we will articulate the necessary task of decolonizing its understanding to overcome its representation as a cartography or static coordinate.

We consider it appropriate to begin by recalling, as noted in the introduction, that we approach Indigenous peoples as diverse and dynamic, shaped by distinct histories, practices, and internal debates. Rather than reducing them to fixed categories or uniform representations, we emphasize that their relationships with territory are situated, evolving, and deeply embedded in relational worldviews. However, we consider that there are, in them, "social, economic and cultural configurations that show shared aspects" (Bartolomé 2006: 36). The words of Lorena Cabnal, a Mayan-Xinka Indigenous community feminist, are clarifying in this regard:

> it is necessary to share that there is a plurality of worldviews in the native peoples, there is not only one that homogenizes life and cultural practices, but there are threads that connect this plurality as founding threads, among them, their principles and sacred values, i.e. their cosmogony. (Cabnal 2010: 14)

The same author, in another text, maintains that "what for the Western world is interpreted as philosophy, for Indigenous societies is cosmogony, a concept that refers to the plural interpretation of life in the cosmos, its being and being in relation to reciprocity for life" (Cabnal 2019: 120). Within this cosmogony, territory functions as a foundational thread that weaves together material, cultural, and spiritual dimensions. Territory is much more than a form of possession and production; rather, it is to be regarded one of the pillars of their culture, their spiritual life, and their integrity, and therefore it has a sacred value.[15] In the declarations of the First Summit of Indigenous Women of the Americas held in the State of Oaxaca, Mexico, in 2002, as recovered by Sylvia Marcos, it is made clear that the universe of the sacred is closely interconnected, even fused, with land and territory – that is, a fusion "of embodied practices, with its correlate of shared community presences" (Marcos 2019: 126). Therefore, territory, emphasizes Mixtec intellectual Francisco López Bárcenas, is "where there are sacred places and relations of reciprocity. There is no desire to understand," he continues, "that when Indigenous peoples defend their territories, their sacred resources or their cultural heritage, what they are defending is their own way of life, as they understand it, with their times, their forms of organization, their holistic relationship with nature" (López Bárcenas 2015: 91).

The importance of relational ontology and, with it, the relevance of the community, also shines through the words of Pedro Garzón, a Chinanteco Indigenous person, who points out that:

> A constitutive feature of the Indigenous world is the holistic, substantial and relational conception of all the normative elements that structure the nucleus of substantial self-determination: self-government, self-rights, culture, territory, nature, etc. All these components are conceived on the same plane of normative importance, whose reading is only comprehensible from a collective grammar, that is, in relational and interdependent terms. (Garzón 2016: 255)

Comandante Tacho of the Zapatista Army of National Liberation voiced the following words during the Encounter with Peasants of the World held in San Cristóbal de las Casas, Chiapas on July 19, 2007:

> For us Indigenous Zapatistas, the struggle for land and territory is the principal basis of our peoples. It is indispensable (. . .) the defense of mother earth and territory (. . .) We Indigenous and peasant peoples historically have our roots in these territories. There we produce our food to live, there we are born, there we develop, there we multiply and coexist, with the mountains, with the rivers, with the air, with

[15] According to the words of Luis A. Yonda Yuluçx (2017), from the Nasnasa culture, the territory is cosmos, it is "spiritual projection," it is where "the Moon, the Sun, the planets, the stars, the stars, the Milky Way, that is the cosmic territory above [. . .]. But also the territory in the natural world where we are, the living beings. But there is also the territory below, (. . .) that of the depths, (. . .) there are also beings there, the nasa tusxkwe."

> the life of nature itself, with the springs; also in them live all living beings with the right to life, as well as the resources of the subsoil.[16]

In short, territory is the source of the identity of Indigenous communities and this identity is constituted by the ways of life of these communities, by the relationships they maintain, and the activities they carry out with those with whom they feel intimately linked – that is, by the "communal wefts that give rise to complex systems of exchanges that cross the ethnic and geographic borders drawn colonially," affirms the K'iche' Maya native of the Paquí canton, Chuimeq'ena', Gladys Tzul Tzul (2018: 199).

From the Indigenous voices quoted above we can extract five reflections. First, territory is indivisible. Second, territory cannot be reduced to the geographic surface of a given space. It cannot be explained with the parameters of Western science that measures everything through topology and cartography. Territory "is not areolar," but must be conceived as a fabric, as a network, as a "communal weft" (Tzul Tzul 2018); "it is a living body that feeds, reproduces itself and weaves relationships with other bodies" (Echeverri 2004: 263) and, consequently, it is in a continuous process of constitution and reconstitution. Third, territory finds itself in a "space–time interrelation with the surrounding natural world and is a constitutive part of it" (Escobar 2015: 33) – it is a dynamic and versatile realm, a reflection of "multipolar plots of social interaction" (García Hierro & Surrallés 2004: 18) of which humans and nonhumans (the organic, the nonorganic, the sacred, and the spiritual) are part of. Fourth, territory is a place of construction of meaning and of "infrastructures of reciprocity" (Tănăsescu 2022a: 115–121); territory is the foundation of existence, it is the repository of the memory of the peoples who occupy it, an "ontogenetic source of collective memory" (Melín et al. 2019: 8), and it is the seedbed of their identity. Fifth, the relationship with the territory is intimately connected with the "hermeneutics of orality" (Marcos 2014: 29) proper to Indigenous peoples where "narrative, legend, crossed conversation, mythical imagination, the orality of storytelling" and dreams are projections proper to this relationship (Martínez de Bringas 2021: 210). In the words of Yanomami shaman Davi Kopenawa: "The forest belongs to Omama." "The words of Omama and the *xapiri* [the spirits] are the ones I like best." These words "often came to visit me in dreams," "they are very old, yet the shamans constantly renew them. They have always protected the forest and its inhabitants." "I did not learn to think about the things of the forest by setting my eyes on paper skins. I saw them for real by drinking my elders' breath of life (. . .) I am not an elder and I still don't know much. Yet I had my account drawn in the white people's language so it could be heard far from the forest" (Kopenawa 2013: 13, 23, 45, 386).

Following the indigenous voices we have referred to in this section, we can conclude that the dense network of interrelationships and the communal grammar

[16] Available in Spanish at: www.jornada.com.mx/2007/08/20/oja124-pagfinal.html.

are the foundations based on which Indigenous peoples interpret and exercise territoriality. Therefore, in the face of monocultural conceptions of territory, the precept of Zapatista thought makes sense: we want *a world in which many worlds fit.*

4.4 Rights of Nature and Right to Territory: Conflicts, Encounters, and Reconciliation

The questions we wish to raise in this section are the following. How does the new recognition of RoN coexist with the historical claim of the right of Indigenous peoples to their territory? Do the RoN constitute a paradigmatic concept that can be assimilated into the right to territory? The answers to these questions are not straightforward or clear, and, moreover, they will change as the discourse on the RoN unveils its philosophical and conceptual foundations in each case. Therefore, in this section we do not intend to give an absolute answer to these considerations, but instead only disclose certain critical points about the interrelation between the two frameworks, through specific cases.

4.4.1 The Recognition of the Rights of Pachamama in the 2008 Constitution of Ecuador and the Dispute over its Theoretical Origins

Article 71 of the 2008 Constitution of Ecuador states:

> Art. 71. Nature or Pachamama, where life is reproduced and exists, has the right to exist, persist, maintain and regenerate its vital cycles, structure, functions and its processes in evolution.

In this article nature is defined as "Pachamama," being an Indigenous-Kichwa concept that has been translated as "Mother Earth." The concept expresses the spiritual relationship that Indigenous peoples maintain with their territory; the constitutional reference to it should not be overlooked, as it constitutes the specific and truly revolutionary basis for the emergence of the RoN in Ecuador.

At the beginning of the twenty-first century, some Latin American States initiated a reformist process characterized, among other issues, by the spilling over of Indigenous movements into the political–institutional arena. As a result, new forms of constitutionalism emerged in which Indigenous peoples played a central role.[17] Within this context, as Aguilera explained, Ecuador's constituent process was characterized by broad participation and an intercultural approach, where the recognition of the rights of nature could be seen "as a product of an intercultural legal translation process that represents the dialogue between the state legal system – including the language of rights – and Indigenous biocultural normative

[17] In this regard, you can see Eichler (2024: 28–29, 253), Pacari et al. (2021), Sieder and Barrera Vivero (2017), Van Cott (2002), Yashar (2005: 85–151), and Yrigoyen Fajardo (2012).

ontologies" (Hanschel et al. 2022: 1021). Therefore, in Ecuador, the initial idea to recognize RoN served as a meeting point between different social positions in the constituent debates such as those on "plurinationality," the horizontal relationship of Indigenous peoples with the natural world as well as those addressing "Buen Vivir" or "Sumak Kawsay" (Fundación Pachamama, n.d.). The Pachamama Foundation – an organization that has been working in the Ecuadorian Amazon since 1995, accompanying Indigenous peoples in the defense of their territories[18] – sought to introduce the debate on the RoN, because it saw in it a tool to promote the defense of the territory and the rights of the Amazonian peoples. The result, after a broad debate in which Indigenous peoples were protagonists, mainly through the Confederation of Indigenous Nationalities of Ecuador (CONAIE), was to recognize Pachamama as a subject of rights. The representatives of CONAIE, as reported by Fundación Pachamama:

> found inconceivable that the Pachamama had no rights up to that moment, as this collided with the Indigenous worldvision based on a harmonic coexistence with the nature. This worldvision, based on the principle of respect to the nature, enhanced and legitimated even more the proposal. (Fundación Pachamama, n.d.)

The influence of Indigenous visions on the recognition of RoN in Ecuador can also be seen in the minutes of the constituent debates: as it was stated in the majority report of the commission in charge of the elaboration of article 71 of the Ecuadorian constitution of 2008, the underlying rationale of recognizing the rights of the Pachamama was to take distance from the Eurocentrism that had hitherto governed our vision of the nonhuman world:

> The western European vision (. . .) erred crassly by considering inferior, uncivilized and even heretical the visions of the subjected peoples that now, emerge with strength, with reason and truth in their mouths, demanding a change . . . a necessary change for the respect to the mother of all, the Pachamama, and the subsistence of the species itself. (Constituent Assembly of Ecuador 2008: 2)

Similarly, in the aforementioned report of the commission it was made explicit that the inclusion of the term "Pachamama" as a subject of rights sought to "demonstrate that this new legal conception of human relations with nature was assimilated by the Andean cultures long ago" (Constituent Assembly of Ecuador 2008: 5). As can be seen, the RoN, as conceived in Ecuador, have the closest ties and find their deepest roots in the worldview of Indigenous peoples and the defense of their territory, a worldview in which nature is a subject with which they communicate. This non-Western and spiritual approach on the RoN does not seem to fit Stone's proposal of nature as an object and an ethic that can only be "Western" and scientific. Despite the above, Professor Stone included in the preface of the third edition of his book

[18] More information about the organization can be found at the following link: www.pachamama.org.ec/nosotros/.

Should the Trees Have Standing? the rights of the Pachamama as enshrined in the 2008 Constitution of Ecuador as an example of the "impact" of his work. In his words:

> Shortly after the publication of *Trees*, several correspondents raised the issue of the defense of the unborn (. . .) In 2008, Ecuador amended its Constitution to establish that nature "has the right to exist, persist, maintain and regenerate its life cycles, its structure, its functions and its processes of evolution." (Stone 2010, p. 164)

Considering Stone's express rejection of an ecological consciousness born of Indigenous relational ontologies,[19] it seems that his assertion about the influence of his book on the 2008 Constitution of Ecuador is wrong. These disputes over the foundations of the rights of Pachamama have not remained only at the theoretical level. As Aguilera has pointed out in his analysis of the ruling of the Constitutional Court of Ecuador that recognized Los Cedros Protected Forest as a subject of rights,[20] there is a tendency to represent the rights of Pachamama from an exclusively natural scientific perspective (Hanschel et al. 2022: 1022–1023). Along the same lines, Tănăsescu et al. (2024: 14–16) have noted that the impact of indigenous law and its relational ontologies on rulings recognizing the rights of natural entities in Ecuador has been minimal. This, we believe, demonstrates the importance of thinking about the RoN from its legal foundations and specific objectives in each context. We argue that sustained critical debate is essential for the conceptual development, normative refinement, and practical effectiveness of the RoN for it to be considered a truly counterhegemonic framework.

4.4.2 Te Awa Tapua and Te Urewera: The Recognition of Legal Personality for Rivers and Ecosystems in Māori Territories

Understanding the context in which the recognition of nature operates as a legal entity in New Zealand takes us back to the founding text of Aotearoa, the Treaty of Waitangi.[21] This was an agreement signed in 1840 between the British Crown and several Māori chiefs of *Aotearoa*[22] whereby the former committed to protect the Māori people from the colonizing ambitions of the French Empire over their territories. The agreement was drafted and signed in both English and Māori; however, there were important differences between the translations: whereas the Māori version recognized the sovereignty of these tribes over their territories and people, granting only certain governmental functions to the Queen, in the English version, sovereignty was vested in the British Crown and the tribes were granted only uninterfered possession of their lands and respect for their spiritual practices and customs. However, since the signing of the Treaty in 1840, the Māori have

[19] See Section 4.2 of this chapter.
[20] Constitutional Court of Ecuador, Ruling No. 1149-19-JP/21, November 10, 2021.
[21] In Maori: *Te Tiriti o Waitangi.*
[22] The Maori name for New Zealand.

lodged official complaints with the Crown for the lack of compliance with its agreements.

In this context, during the 1990s, Māori tribes living in the Whanganui-New Zealand area sued the British Crown before the Waitangi Tribunal seeking recognition, in application of their sovereignty rights over the territories guaranteed in the Māori version of the Treaty of Waitangi, notably of their right of possession and control over the Whanganui River and its tributaries (Waitangi Tribunal 1999: 1–6). At the end of the process, the Waitangi Tribunal issued a report in which it emphasized that the river was the center of life for the Māori tribes: the river (Māori: *awa*), the Tribunal said, was for them a living entity (Māori: *tapuna*) with its own personality and life force; the relationship between the people and the river is guided by mutual respect between the people and that "living being river" or, in Māori language, *tapuna awa* (Waitangi Tribunal 1999: xiii, 23, 36–48).

The most contentious issue in the negotiations between the Crown and the Māori tribes pursuant to the Waitangi Tribunal report was the recognition of the tribes' ownership of the river. The Crown argued that it was not possible for her to agree that the river was the property of the Māori, because, according to the Common Law of New Zealand, water was a public good administered by the State for the benefit of all inhabitants. Faced with this impasse, in 2010, New Zealand scholars James Morris and Jacinta Ruru published an article in which, inspired by the work of Christopher Stone, they alternatively recommended to recognize the Whanganui River as a legal person (Morris and Ruru 2010). This idea eventually reached the negotiating table and was put forward as a solution to the conflict. Thus, in 2014, the Crown and the Māori tribes signed an agreement in which they did not recognize the Māori's right to ownership over the river, but declared the *Te Awa Tupua*, that is, the Whanganui River in its entirety, including its physical and spiritual elements, a legal person with inherent rights. It was further agreed that these rights be represented by two persons whose decisions must be taken by consensus, those of one representative of the Crown and one of the Māori tribes, respectively. These persons would act as the human face of the living being water or, in Māori, as *Te Pou Tupua*.[23] In March 2017, this agreement was elevated to the status of law through the *Te Awa Tupua Act*,[24] being considered and celebrated as the first case globally speaking in which the rights of nature are applied (Boyd 2017, pp. 140–150).

The case in which *Te Urewera* was granted rights has a similar history, with the only important difference being that in that case, the Māori tribe involved, the *Tūhoe*, were one of the few tribes that in 1840 refused to sign the Treaty of Waitangi, owing to their intention to maintain absolute sovereignty over their lands. Despite the above, during the "New Zealand Wars" the Crown invaded their territory,

[23] The agreement is entitled *Ruruku Whakatupua Te Mana o te Awa Tupua*. The full text of the agreement is available at the following link: www.govt.nz/assets/Documents/OTS/Whanganui-Iwi/Whanganui-River-Deed-of-Settlement-Ruruku-Whakatupua-Te-Mana-o-Te-Awa-Tupua-5-Aug-2014.pdf

[24] Available at: www.legislation.govt.nz/act/public/2017/0007/latest/whole.html.

confiscating around 162,000 hectares of Māori land. Given the beauty and biodiversity of the area, *Te Urewera* was declared a national park in the 1950s, controlled by the New Zealand Government. After years of demanding the return of their land, in 1987, the *Tūhoe* sued the Crown before the Waitangi Tribunal. In the process, the Tribunal issued six reports between 2009 and 2015 concluding that the Crown had failed to respect the *Tūhoe*'s right to self-government and had illegally expropriated their land through the creation of national parks[25] (Waitangi Tribunal 2017 [2015]: pp. 3103, 3456–3461).

As in the previous case, these negotiations ended with an agreement that would later be elevated to the rank of law recognizing the *Te Urewera* as a legal entity with its own rights. These rights are exercised and represented by the *Te Urewera Board'*(Arts. 11, 16–20), which, during the first three years of operating was composed of eight members: four representatives of the *Tūhoe* tribes (called in Māori *Te Uru Taumatua*) and four of the Government. Subsequently, the Board would be composed of nine members: six representatives of the *Tūhoe* tribes and three from the Government (Art. 21). Thus, as Tănăsescu highlights, the constitution of *Te Urewera* as a legal entity in the context of the Treaty of Waitangi negotiations assisted in avoiding granting land ownership either to the *Tūhoe* or the Government (2022b: 80).

4.4.3 The Recognition of the Atrato River as a Subject of Rights, Biocultural Rights, and the Right to Territory of Ethnic Communities in Colombia

In 2015, those ethnic communities ancestrally inhabiting the banks of the Atrato River filed a tutela action seeking to stop the intensive and large-scale operation of various mining and logging activities that were contaminating the river, its basins, marshes, wetlands, and tributaries. In this action, the communities requested the protection of their rights to life, health, water, food security, a healthy environment, culture – and especially territory.[26] In the first instance ruling, issued on February 11, 2015, the action of protection was denied, according to which the proper way was not an action of protection but popular action. The second instance ruling, issued on April 21, 2021, overruled the previous decision. Against this backdrop, the Constitutional Court of Colombia, within the framework of its powers to review rulings,[27] on October 14, 2015, began to hear the case.

Three elements are important for understanding this case, notably, first, the application of the right to territory for Afro-Colombian populations; second, the development of what the Constitutional Court has called the "Ecological Constitution"; and third, the implementation of so-called "biocultural rights." On

[25] All the volumes of the report can be consulted at the following link: https://ndhadeliver.natlib.govt.nz/delivery/DeliveryManagerServlet?dps_pid=IE58413128.

[26] Constitutional Court of Colombia, Judgment T-622/16 of 2016, sec. 2.1–2.10. Available here: www.corteconstitucional.gov.co/relatoria/2016/t-622-16.htm.

[27] Article 241.9 of the Constitution of Colombia.

the one hand, although the text of ILO Convention 169 explicitly protects the right to territory of Indigenous and tribal peoples, the Constitutional Court of Colombia in 2003, broadly interpreting the Convention, extended its scope to also protect black communities living in Colombia.[28] Thus, the claim made by the ethnic communities of Atrato, both Afro-Colombian and Indigenous, was framed in terms of the claim for their rights to territory.

On the other hand, the Constitutional Court, since 1992, has interpreted the Colombian Political Constitution as containing the axioms of an "Ecological Constitution," postulating the protection of the environment as a "universally recognized and socially felt" need. In the case of Atrato, the Colombian Constitutional Court stated that currently the Ecological Constitution followed three approaches:

> (i) in the first place, it is based on an anthropocentric vision that conceives the present human being as the sole raison d'être of the legal system and natural resources as mere objects at the service of the former, (ii) a second biocentric point of view claims more global and solidary conceptions of human responsibility, which advocate – in equal measure – man's duties towards nature and future generations; (iii) finally, ecocentric positions have been formulated that conceive of nature as a true subject of rights and that support plural and alternative world-views to the approaches recently presented.[29]

From the ecocentric approach the Court derives what it terms "biocultural rights," mirroring the work of authors such as Sajir Bavikatte, Tom Bennett, Cher Weixia Chen, and Michael Gilmore[30] (cited in the judgment). Biocultural rights, in the words of the Court, make it possible to reconcile "the special relationship that Indigenous, tribal and other ethnic groups have towards the care or stewardship of nature and its resources."[31] Therefore, as the Court itself establishes, biocultural rights "imply that communities must maintain their distinctive cultural heritage, which is essential for the maintenance of biological diversity and the cultural diversity of the planet."[32] The ecocentric application of biocultural rights to the concrete case produced "a new socio-legal understanding in which nature and its environment must be taken seriously and with full rights. That is, as subjects of rights."[33] Thus, quoting the New Zealand precedents mentioned above, the Court determined that the Atrato River was a subject of rights.[34] To guarantee the rights of the Atrato River, the Court – drawing once again on the precedent set by the Whanganui River case in New Zealand – ordered that the guardianship of the

[28] Constitutional Court of Colombia, *Decision T-955/03*, October 17, 2003.
[29] Constitutional Court of Colombia, Judgment T-622/16 of 2016, sec. 5.6.
[30] Framework proposed, mainly, since 2014 through the following works: Bavikatte (2014), Bavikatte and Bennett (2015), and Chen and Gilmore (2015).
[31] Constitutional Court of Colombia, Judgment T-622/16 of 2016, footnote 86.
[32] Constitutional Court of Colombia, Judgment T-622/16 of 2016, secs. 5.11–5.18.
[33] Constitutional Court of Colombia, Judgment T-622/16 of 2016, sec. 9.28.
[34] Constitutional Court of Colombia, Judgment T-622/16 of 2016, secs. 9.32 and 10.2.

river be exercised jointly by a representative of the domestic government and a representative of the ethnic communities of the Atrato River, who would henceforth act as "guardians of the river."[35]

4.5 The Rights of Nature from a Decolonial Perspective

Throughout the last decades, the recognition of the RoN has emerged in different contexts, frequently in connection with Indigenous claims to territory. However, although these processes share a surface resemblance, a closer analysis reveals significant differences in their origins, theoretical underpinnings, and political consequences. The cases of the Whanganui River in New Zealand, the Atrato River in Colombia, and the constitutional recognition of Pachamama in Ecuador offer a fruitful comparative lens to explore these complexities.

Both in the Whanganui River case and in the case of the Atrato River, what began as a claim for the right to territory of Indigenous peoples was, through parliamentary and judicial channels, transformed into rights for nature. In the New Zealand case, this transformation was the result of an agreement between the Māori tribes and the Crown, which remained silent on who would be the owner of the *Whanganui River* or the *Te Urewera*; these natural entities have now become their own owners (Kauffman and Martin 2021: pp. 73–74; Tănăsescu 2021: 75). The Colombian case is more controversial, as there the transformation was not the product of a political agreement between the disputing parties, but of an innovative, unsolicited court ruling.

In both cases, the recognition of rights granted to natural entities, together with the creation of commissions of representatives or guardians to speak on their behalf, marked a notable improvement compared to the previous situation faced by the ethnic communities whose territorial rights had been violated. Nonetheless, it is crucial to critically assess the risks that accompany such forms of recognition. As Macpherson points out, advocates of RoN often emphasize the concordance between this new legal construct and Indigenous rights, but omit that their theoretical underpinnings have "firmly Western and non-Indigenous" origins. Rights of Nature activism may, moreover, overshadow attention to more radical Indigenous struggles concerning sovereignty, control, and ownership over their lands and the construction of their territories, running the risk of "repeating colonial injustices by overriding hard-won Indigenous rights" (Macpherson et al. 2021: 445–446, 461).

In the same vein, Tănăsescu warns that the recognition of RoN in New Zealand "is not a piece of legislation that recognizes Tūhoe self-determination as such" (2022b: 85). The above is not to say, however, that the *Whanganui* River case was not, to some extent, a victory for Indigenous peoples, but only that we should look with caution at its scope. Tănăsescu himself emphasizes that the decision-making

[35] Constitutional Court of Colombia, Judgment T-622/16 of 2016, sec. 10.2.

spaces that were created for the representation of these new legal persons, granted greater weight to the authority of the Indigenous peoples of the area with respect to what they had previously. The idea of granting rights to nature did not seek to consider the "Western" ecocentric perspective when attributing legal status to these natural spaces, but served a purely pragmatic and political objective: it was a third alternative, a middle ground, in the face of the existing impasse in the negotiation between the Crown and the Māori tribes over who should be the owner of these natural spaces – all this, in the context of the process of reparation for the violation of the territorial rights of these tribes (Tănăsescu 2022b: 89–94). This middle ground took the form of recognizing the Whanganui River as a legal person, thus avoiding the politically contentious question of ownership by instead assigning guardianship to both the Māori and the State.

The specific arrangements within which rights are granted to nature in New Zealand allow Tănăsescu to conclude that in this case the rights of nature meant more than the sheer – although valuable – recognition of the intrinsic value of nonhumans; instead they constituted an express political tool for negotiation between contested ontologies and rights. However, this does not seem to be what occurs in the case of the Atrato River in Colombia. In that case, the association made by the Constitutional Court between Indigenous claims and biocultural rights, the latter being a novel category that avoids addressing the right to territory in depth, is highly problematic.

While the framework of biocultural rights seems to open the space for thinking about environmental problems arising in the local contexts in which Indigenous and Afro-Colombian communities express themselves in, at the same time, it conditions the exercise of the rights of these peoples by complying with the essentialized "Western" vision of the "ecological Indigenous." This perspective is reflected in the Court's ruling that biocultural rights "imply that communities must maintain their distinctive cultural heritage, which is essential for the maintenance of the biological diversity and cultural diversity of the planet."[36]

This indissoluble association between guaranteeing the cultural rights of Indigenous peoples and maintaining their collective duty of care toward the environment is the core of the biocultural rights approach. Taking this into account, Brunet argues that, although the category of biocultural rights has the merit of attempting to resituate the law within the local configurations where it first finds expression, it also: "exposes both Indigenous and local communities and those who claim to defend them to the risk of standardizing practices and, even more, of forcing these populations to assume a burden that exceeds them: that of speaking for nature in the name of all humanity" (Brunet 2024: 124).

Conditioning the granting of Indigenous rights on the fulfillment of a duty of care for nature generates enormous problems of justice. As states Sajeva, in the framework of biocultural rights, the relationship of mutual care and protection of nature

[36] Constitutional Court of Colombia, Judgment T-622/16 of 2016, secs. 5.11–5.18.

of Indigenous peoples, "ceases to be a lifestyle choice, and, instead, becomes a legal duty and a requirement to be a rights holder," placing a burden on the most vulnerable to protect nature, "a burden that might be incorporated in their world-views and practices but that could, at times, become unfair, especially if imposed by the state according to incompatible visions and understandings of environmental sustainability" (2021: 93). It should then be remembered, as Sajeva concludes, that "Indigenous peoples' rights are recognized as Indigenous peoples because they are Indigenous, without any reference to them being environmentally sustainable" (Sajeva 2021: 88).

Escobar warned about this in 2007 when he described how the discourse of sustainable development and biodiversity was in fact colonizing Indigenous claims to territory:

> This new capitalization of nature does not only rely on the semiotic conquest of territories (in terms of biodiversity reserves and new schemes for land ownership and control) and communities (as "stewards" of nature); it also requires the semiotic conquest of local knowledges, to the extent that "saving nature" demands the valuation of local knowledges of sustaining nature (. . .) By bringing them into the politics of science, local forms of knowledge are recodified by modern science in utilitarian ways. (Escobar 1995: 204)

We can substitute the words "sustainable development" and "biodiversity" for "rights of nature" and "biocultural rights" and find the full force of Escobar's paragraph quoted above. This warns us of the risk that new conceptual frameworks, although appearing emancipatory, may ultimately reproduce schemes of control over Indigenous peoples, disguised under apparently progressive notions. Such dynamics reflect the persistence of predominant epistemological paradigms within classical legal thought, which continue to prioritize Western constructions of nature and law. Importantly, these concerns are not merely theoretical: they are increasingly being voiced by Indigenous authorities themselves. Recently, the Māori tribes of the *Whanganui* have notably expressly stated that their position was not the same as that of the movement for the RoN:

> The Whanganui River Settlement signals not only a change in attitude but an entirely new construct, Te Awa Tupua and the status of legal personhood, as such it has attracted international attention. There is a large amount of interest from both an environmental and legal standpoint into what has been created through the Te Awa Tupua status. Numerous links have been made to the "Rights of Nature" movement. However the Te Awa Tupua status isn't about nature only, it isn't about rights for people, it isn't about rights to culture – it is about obligations and duties to see and place ourselves within nature's scheme and ensure that we work with nature rather than against it.[37]

[37] Information obtained from the official website of *Te Awá Tupuá*. Available at the following link: www.ngatangatatiaki.co.nz/for-your-information/faqs/</int_u>.

On the other hand, the Ecuadorian experience demonstrates a deeper and more explicit integration of Indigenous ontologies into the legal system. Article 71 of the 2008 Constitution recognizes nature – or Pachamama – as a subject of rights, drawing directly from Kichwa and broader Andean worldviews that emphasize a relational and spiritual connection with the land. The recognition of Pachamama was framed explicitly as a rupture with Western visions of nature. As noted in the Constituent Assembly's debates, it sought to vindicate long-silenced Indigenous perspectives and challenge the modern Western separation between nature and culture. Nevertheless, postconstitutional developments reveal conflicts in that regard: there is a growing tendency to reinterpret the rights of Pachamama through a scientific lens, displacing its original Indigenous-rooted meaning. Additionally, theoretical disputes – such as Christopher Stone's claim that Ecuador's recognition of RoN reflects his Western-originated proposal – underscore the importance of maintaining a decolonial perspective when analyzing these frameworks.

Viewed together, the experiences of Whanganui, the Atrato River, and Pachamama reveal that the recognition of the RoN is neither a uniform nor an inherently decolonial process. Rather, it is a contested terrain where Indigenous struggles for territory are translated, negotiated, and at times diluted within State legal frameworks. Although these forms of recognition may open new spaces for Indigenous participation and ecological protection, they also risk reproducing colonial patterns when Indigenous worldviews are instrumentalized to serve external agendas or when environmental responsibilities are imposed as conditions for the exercise of rights. The transformative potential of the RoN thus lies not merely in recognizing nonhuman entities as subjects of law, but in sustaining a critical interrogation of whose voices are amplified, whose cosmologies are respected, and whose political projects are truly advanced through these legal innovations. Only by confronting these complexities head-on can RoN avoid becoming another form of epistemic colonization under the guise of ecological progress.

This is precisely why it becomes necessary to understand these legal innovations through the lens of vernacularization. As Destrooper mentions, "when specific struggles in non-Western societies utilize a Western liberal-legalist discourse, local understandings, practices, and symbolisms are applied to these global discourses and lead to a reinterpretation of its core concepts and ideas" (Destrooper 2018: 7). This is what Sally Engle Marry called "vernacularization," the process by which global legal concepts are translated, adapted, and reinterpreted by local actors in ways that resonate with their specific cultural logics, political struggles, and social practices. As Merry further elaborates, this process often includes a symbolic dimension known as "indigenization," which refers to shifts in meaning, particularly the framing of new ideas in terms of pre-existing cultural norms, values, and practices. Indigenization thus reflects how legal and normative changes become culturally legible, enabling global concepts to be rooted in local worldviews (Merry 2006: 39). When this process is genuinely participatory, it can serve as a tool for epistemic justice – allowing Indigenous and local communities not only to be recognized within legal systems, but to actively shape the meanings and trajectories of legal change. In this light, the RoN should not be seen merely as legal recognition of nonhuman entities, but as an opportunity to rethink law itself: to reconfigure its ontological assumptions, to pluralize its normative foundations, and to anchor it in relational, place-based ways of knowing and being. The transformative potential of RoN lies precisely in this possibility: where law becomes a space of encounter between different worlds, and vernacularization becomes a vehicle not of translation alone, but of political creativity and decolonial resignification.

4.6 The Rights of Nature through the Lens of the Indigenous Right to Territory

Getting out of the traps of uncritical assimilation when we speak of the RoN in Indigenous contexts implies seeing these rights as the result of the dynamics based on which the human–nature relationship is expressed in their territories. If we wanted to translate this into legal terms, it would mean seeing the right to territory of Indigenous peoples as the source or umbrella of the rights of nature. Although the Western discourse of RoN is the product of a philosophical–moral, conservationist, scientific, and Ius Naturalist debate, the right to territory is a claim for the construction of meanings, for Indigenous peoples to exercise ontological and relational plurality in the relation with their environment.

Given the divergent ways of interpreting ecocentrism and defining nature, the truly emancipatory role of RoN, we suggest, should lie in opening the discussion on who should speak on behalf of nature. Granting rights to nature requires that an "other" – a human being, a human collective, or a human entity – exercise its representation before the court. The question of who should represent nature in these scenarios allows, at least, to question the exclusivity that has been attributed to the State in deciding on the environment, notably through administrative environmental law or environmental criminal law. In this sense, granting rights to nature not only implies rethinking the traditional anthropocentric foundation that has traditionally been given to law, but also the spaces in which environmental decisions should be made, shifting authority from State-centered institutions to local communities acting as stewards and representatives of nature.

Rights of Nature, then, would not have to do with nature as such, but with the political relations between different groups of people (Tănăsescu 2021: 69). Thus, giving rights to natural entities necessarily directs us toward the concept of legal but also political representation. Whatever lawyers decide judicially will need to be previously decided in the political arena, that is, in a discursive competition that determines what is in the interest of nature. Moreover, in the case of natural entities with rights, these rights cannot be an end in themselves, but rather the beginning of a political process of representation (Tănăsescu 2021: 71). Within this framework,

Indigenous environmental rights play a procedural role: "as facilitators to enforce claims on behalf of non-human species, they become articulated through broader collective and intergenerational rights, or as manifestations of legal pluralism" (Eichler and Navarro 2023: 4). Although many RoN-based approaches claim inspiration from Indigenous worldviews, treating them as foundational, there is a risk that such paradigms instrumentalize Indigenous concepts to fit within Western legal categories. In doing so, they may obscure or displace a crucial element of Indigenous struggles: the right to territory. The right to territory is a relational right where the construction of Indigenous meaning is expressed with greater force and forcefulness. It is such space where both the autonomy and spiritual relationship of Indigenous peoples with the environment and (non-) human beings is expressed. In the Territory they construct their ontology, their being in the world.

Recognizing the dynamic and relational nature of territory must not be mistaken as a justification for undermining Indigenous territorial rights. On the contrary, such rights must be firmly enshrined in legal systems – including constitutional law – to ensure security, recognition, and protection. What must remain flexible is not the existence of these rights, but the capacity of legal systems to accommodate diverse and evolving understandings of territory.

In sum, Territory is not the objectivist construction of the value of nature associated with scientific knowledge or Western philosophy. It is not Anglo-Saxon conservationist ecology. Nor is it the source of a new natural law from which absolute and immutable truths of the world are derived, nor the distant, threatening, and impersonal Gaia of Lovelock's theory. On the contrary, territory is constantly being constructed and deconstructed through Indigenous social practices, historical struggles, and lived relationships. In other words, territory is not tantamount to the RoN, or at least not as such rights are understood by the West.

References

Aguilera, M. (2023). *Environmental Human Rights: New Thinking from Latin America and the Caribbean* (1st ed.). BRILL.

Anker, K. (2021). Ecological Jurisprudence and Indigenous Relational Ontologies: Beyond the "Ecological Indian"? in Anker, K., Burdon, P. D., Garver, G., Maloney, M., & Sbert, C. (eds.), *From Environmental to Ecological Law* (pp. 104–118). Routledge.

Bartolomé, M. Á. (2006). *Procesos interculturales. Antropología política del pluralismo cultural en América Latina*. Siglo XXI.

Bavikatte, S. K. (2014). *Stewarding the Earth: Rethinking Property and the Emergence of Biocultural Rights*. Oxford University Press.

Bavikatte, K. S. & Bennett, T. (2015). Community Stewardship: The Foundation of Biocultural Rights. *Journal of Human Rights and the Environment* 6(1), 7–29. doi.org/10.4337/jhre.2015.01.01

Berry, T. (1999). *The Great Work*. Bell Tower.

Bookchin, M. (1987). Social Ecology versus Deep Ecology: A Challenge for the Ecology Movement. *Left Green Perspectives*, 4–5. Available at: https://theanarchistlibrary.org/library/murray-bookchin-social-ecology-versus-deep-ecology-a-challenge-for-the-ecology-movement.pdf.

Boyd, D. R. (2017). *The Rights of Nature: A Legal Revolution that Could Save the World.* ECW Press.

Brunet, P. (2024). ¿Son los derechos bioculturales el fundamento de una relación responsable entre los seres humanos y la naturaleza? *Revista de Estudios Políticos* 204, 95–129. https://doi.org/10.18042/cepc/rep.204.03.

Burdon, P. D. (2012). A Theory of Earth Jurisprudence. *Australian Journal of Legal Philosophy* 37, 28–60.

Cabnal, L. (2010). Acercamiento a la construcción de la propuesta de pensamiento epistémico de las mujeres indígenas feministas comunitarias de Abya Yala, in *Feminismos Diversos: El Feminismo Comunitario*. ACSUR-Las Segovias. https://porunavidavivible.

Cabnal, L. (2019). El relato de las violencias desde mi territorio cuerpo-tierra, in Solano, X. L. & Icaza, R. (coords.), *En tiempos de muerte: cuerpos, rebeldías y resistencias* (pp. 113–123). Consejo Latinoamericano de Ciencias Sociales; San Cristóbal de las Casas (Chiapas), Cooperativa Editorial Retos; La Haya, Institute of Social Studies.

Cadena, M. de la. (2015). *Earth Beings: Ecologies of Practice across Andean Worlds.* Duke University Press.

Callicott, J. B. (1987). The Conceptual Foundations of the Land Ethic, in *Companion to A Sand County Almanac: Interpretive & Critical Essays* (pp. 186–217). University of Wisconsin Press.

Callicott, J. B. (1997). *Earth's Insights: A Survey of Ecological Ethics from the Mediterranean Basin to the Australian Outback.* University of California Press.

Callicott, J. B. (2013). *Thinking Like a Planet: The Land Ethic and the Earth Ethic.* Oxford University Press.

Chen, C. W. & Gilmore, M. (2015). Biocultural Rights: A New Paradigm for Protecting Natural and Cultural Resources of Indigenous Communities. *International Indigenous Policy Journal*, 6(3). https://doi.org/10.18584/iipj.2015.6.3.3.

Constituent Assembly of Ecuador (2008). Informe de Mayoría sobre los Derechos de la Naturaleza de la Mesa No. 1 de Derechos Fundamentales y Garantías Constitucionales.

Corrigan, D. P. & Oksanen, M. (2021). Rights of Nature: Exploring the Territory, in Corrigan, D. P. & Oksanen, M. (eds.), *Rights of Nature: A Re-examination* (pp. 1–13). Routledge.

Cullinan, C. (2011). *Wild Law: A Manifesto for Earth Justice* (2d ed.). Green Books.

Descola, P. (2013). *Beyond Nature and Culture.* The University of Chicago Press.

Devall, B. & Sessions, G. (1999). *Deep Ecology.* Gibbs M. Smith.

Destrooper, T. (2018). Introduction. On Travel, Translation, and Transformation, in Destrooper, T. & Merry, S. E. (eds.), *Human Rights Transformation in Practice* (pp. 1–28). University of Pennsylvania Press.

Echeverri, J. Á. (2004). Territorio como cuerpo y territorio como naturaleza: ¿diálogo intercultural?, in Surralés, A. & García Hierro, P. (eds.), *Tierra adentro: Territorio indígena y percepción del entorno* (pp. 259–276). IWGIA.

Eichler, J. (2024). *An Interdisciplinary Journey from Non-discrimination to Collective Rights: A Critique of Equality*. Springer.

Eichler, J. & Navarro, F. V. M. (2023). Proceduralising Indigenous Peoples' Demands: Indigenous Environmental Rights and Legal Pluralism in Contemporary Jurisprudence. *Legal Pluralism and Critical Social Analysis* 55(1), 5–34.

Escobar, A. (1995). *Encountering Development: The Making and Unmaking of the Third World*. Princeton University Press.

Escobar, A. (2014). *Sentipensar con la tierra: Nuevas lecturas sobre desarrollo, territorio y diferencia*. Ediciones Unaula.

Escobar, A. (2015). Territorios de diferencia: la ontología política de los derechos al territorio. *Cuadernos de Antropología Social* (41), 25–37.

Escobar, A. (2018). *Otro posible es posible: Caminando hacia las transiciones desde Abya Yala/Afro/Latino-América*. Ediciones Desde Abajo.

Escobar, A. (2020). *Pluriversal Politics: The Real and the Possible*. Duke University Press.

Fundación Pachamama (n.d.). *Recogniting Rights for Nature in the Ecuadorian Constitution*. Global Alliance for the Rights of Nature.

García Hierro, P. & Surrallés, A. (eds.) (2004). *Tierra adentro: Territorio indígena y percepción del entorno*. IWGIA.

Garver, G. (2021). Are Rights of Nature Radical Enough for Ecological Law? In Anker, K., Burdon, P. D., Garver, G., Maloney, M. & Sbert, C. (eds.), *From Environmental to Ecological Law* (pp. 90–103). Routledge.

Garzón, P. (2016). *Ciudadanía Indígena: Del Multiculturalismo a la colonialidad del poder*. Centro de Estudios Políticos y Constitucionales.

Gottlieb, R. S. (ed.). (2006). *The Oxford Handbook of Religion and Ecology*. Oxford University Press.

Hanschel, D., Aguilera Bravo, M. G., Dashpurev, B., & Idris, A. K. (2022). Environmental Rights Between Constitutional Law and Local Context: Reflections on a Moving Target. *German Law Journal* 23(7), 1012–1028.

Izquierdo Torres, B. F. & Viaene, L. (2024). Una im-posibilidad legal. E l Territorio-ser viviente, víctima del conflicto armado colombiano. Algunas reflexiones desde un diálogo colaborativo interdisciplinar. *Eunomía. Revista en Cultura de la Legalidad* 27, pp. 72–101.

Jenkins, W., Tucker, M. E., & Grim, J. (eds.). (2017). *Routledge Handbook of Religion and Ecology*. Routledge.

Kauffman, C. M. & Martin, P. (2021). *The Politics of Rights of Nature: Strategies for Building a More Sustainable Future*. The MIT Press.

Kopenawa, D. (2013). *The Falling Sky: Words of a Yanomami Shaman*. Harvard University Press.

Leopold, A. (1949). *A Sand County Almanac with Other Essays on Conservation from Round River*. Oxford University Press.

López Bárcenas, F. (2015). *¡La tierra no se vende! Las tierras y los territorios de los pueblos indígenas en México*. Centro de Orientación y Asesoría a Pueblos Indígenas, TOSEPAN, IMDEC.

Lovelock, J. (2007). *The Revenge of Gaia*. Penguin.

Lovelock, J. (2009). *The Vanishing Face of Gaia: A Final Warning*. Basic Books.

Macpherson, E., Borchgrevink, A., Ranjan, R., & Vallejo Piedrahíta, C. (2021). Where Ordinary Laws Fall Short: 'Riverine Rights' and Constitutionalism. *Griffith Law Review* 30(3), 438–473.

Marcos, S. (2014). Feminismos en camino descolonial, in Millán, M. (coord.), *Más allá del feminismo: caminos para andar* (pp. 15–34). Red de Feminismos Descoloniales.

Marcos, S. (2019)."Espiritualidad indígena y feminismos descoloniales, in Muñoz, K. O. (coord.), *Miradas en torno al problema colonial. Pensamiento anticolonial y feminismos descoloniales en los sures globales* (pp. 119–134). Akal.

Martínez de Bringas, A. (2021). Metodologías indígenas y derechos humanos. Enfoque relacional de los saberes en la construcción de los derechos. *Utopía y práxis latinoamericana*, 26(93): 207–224.

Melín, M., Mansilla, P., & Royo, M. (2019). *Cartografía cultural del Wallmapu. Elementos para descolonizar el mapa en territorio mapuche.* Lom Ediciones.

Merry, S. E. (2006). Transnational Human Rights and Local Activism: Mapping the Middle. *American Anthropologist* 108(1), 38–51. https://doi.org/10.1525/aa.2006.108.1.38.

Montalván-Zambrano, D. (2026). Naturalezas y derechos: La representación de lo no-humano desde el antropocentrismo, el biocentrismo y el ecocentrismo. Tirant lo Blanch.

Montalván-Zambrano, D. & Wences, I. (2022). Hacia una interpretación descolonial del derecho al territorio de los pueblos indígenas en el Derecho Internacional de los Derechos Humanos: más allá de la propiedad y la cartografía. *Ius et Praxis* 28(3), 61–84.

Moore, B. L. (2008). *Ecology and Literature.* Palgrave Macmillan.

Morris, J. D. K. & Ruru, J. (2010). Giving Voice to Rivers: Legal Personality as a Vehicle for Recognising Indigenous Peoples' Relationships to Water? *Australian Indigenous Law Review* 14(2), 49–62.

Murphy, E. F. (1971). Has Nature Any Right to Life. *Hastings Law Journal* 22, 467–484.

Naess, A. (1973). The Shallow and the Deep, Long-range Ecology Movement. A Summary. *Inquiry* 16(1–4), 95–100.

Pacari, N., Macas, L., Chancosa, B., Churuchumbi, G., Gualinga, P., Simbaña, F., Juncosa, J., & Astudillo, J. (2021). *Proceso constituyente y buen vivir 2007-2022: A quinceaños del inicio de la Asamblea Constituyente* (F. H. Flor, Ed.). SIPAE.

Putzer, A., Lambooy, T., Jeurissen, R., & Kim, E. (2022). Putting the Rights of Nature on the Map. A Quantitative Analysis of Rights of Nature Initiatives across the World. *Journal of Maps* 18(1), 89–96.

Putzer, A., Cook, J., & Pollock, B. (2025). Putting the Rights of Nature on the Map. A Quantitative Analysis of Rights of Nature Initiatives across the World – Second Edition. *Journal of Maps*, 21(1).

Sajeva, G. (2021). Environmentally Conditioned Human Rights a Good Idea? In Corrigan, D. P. & Oksanen, M. (eds.), *Rights of Nature: A Re-examination* (pp. 84–100). Routledge.

Sieder, R., & Barrera Vivero, A. (2017). Legalizing Indigenous Self-Determination: Autonomy and Buen Vivir in Latin America. *The Journal of Latin American and Caribbean Anthropology* 22(1), 9–26. https://doi.org/10.1111/jlca.12233.

Stone, Christopher D. (1974). *Should Trees Have Standing?: Toward Legal Rights for Natural Objects.* William Kaufmann.

Stone, C. D. (2010). *Should Trees Have Standing? Law, Morality, and the Environment* (3rd ed.). Oxford University Press.

Tănăsescu, M. (2021). The Rights of Nature as Politics, in Corrigan, D. P. & Oksanen, M. (eds.), *Rights of Nature: A Re-examination* (pp. 69–84). Routledge.

Tănăsescu, M. (2022a). *Ecocene Politics*. Open Book Publishers.

Tănăsescu, M. (2022b). *Understanding the Rights of Nature: A Critical Introduction*. Transcript.

Tănăsescu, M., Macpherson, E., Jefferson, D., & Torres Ventura, J. (2024). Rights of nature and rivers in Ecuador's Constitutional Court. *The International Journal of Human Rights*, 1–23. https://doi.org/10.1080/13642987.2024.2314536.

Tzul Tzul, G. (2018). *Sistemas de gobierno comunal indígena. Mujeres y tramas de parentesco Chuimeq'ena'*. Instituto Amaq', Bufete para Pueblos Indígenas y Libertad bajo palabra.

Van Cott, D. L. (2002). Constitutional Reform in the Andes: Redefining Indigenous–State Relations, in Sieder, R. (ed.), *Multiculturalism in Latin America: Indigenous Rights, Diversity, and Democracy* (pp. 45–73). Palgrave Macmillan.

Vargas Roncancio, I. D. (2021). Conjuring Sentient Beings and Relations in the Law. Rights of Nature and a Comparative Praxis of Legal Cosmologies in Latin America, in Anker, K., Burdon, P. D., Garver, G., Maloney, M., & Sbert, C. (eds.), *From Environmental to Ecological Law* (pp. 119–134). Routledge.

Viaene, L. (2022). Can Rights of Nature Save Us from the Anthropocene Catastrophe? Some Critical Reflections from the Field. *Asian Journal of Law and Society* 9(2), 187–206. https://doi.org/10.1017/als.2022.2.

Viveiros de Castro, E. (2010). *Metafísicas caníbales: Líneas de antropología postestructural*. Katz.

Viveiros de Castro, E. (2014). *La mirada del jaguar: Introduccion al perspectivismo amerindio; entrevistas*. Tinta Limón.

Viveiros de Castro, E. (2015). *The Relative Native: Essays on Indigenous Conceptual Worlds*. HAU Books.

Waitangi Tribunal. (1999). *The Whanganui River Report*. GP Publications. https://forms.justice.govt.nz/search/Documents/WT/wt_DOC_68450539/Whanganui%20River%20Report%201999.pdf.

Waitangi Tribunal. (2017). *Te Urewera*. Legislation Direct.

Yashar, D. J. (2005). *Contesting Citizenship in Latin America: The Rise of Indigenous Movements and the Postliberal Challenge*. Cambridge University Press.

Yonda Yuluçx, L. A., Drexler, J., & Tocancipá-Falla, J. (2017). Kwesx kiwes peykanha fxiçenxi yuwe: Hacia una comprensión intercultural de la lucha por la madre tierra, el territorio y la cosmovisión político religiosa en los nasasa. *Tabula Rasa* 27, 429–458.

Yrigoyen Fajardo, R. (2012). Pluralismo jurídico y jurisdicción indígena en el horizonte del constitucionalismo pluralista, in Ahrens, H. (ed.), *El estado de derecho hoy en América Latina: Libro homenaje a Horst Schönbohm* (pp. 171–193). GIZ, Deutsche Gesellschaft für Internationale Zusammenarbeit.

5

Rights of Nature

The Biocultural Approach and Indigenous Customary Law in Latin America

Laura Calle-Alzate and Nurys Esperanza Silva-Cantillo

5.1 Introduction

The dominant development model, grounded in the logic of unlimited economic growth, has led to widespread environmental degradation. This model, often identified as "neoliberal capitalism," operates not only through economic liberalization but also through the imposition of a Western-centric paradigm that commodifies nature and reconfigures society–nature relations (Escobar 1995; Harvey 2003). As a result, extractivism has become a central mechanism of accumulation, deepening socioenvironmental conflicts and reinforcing colonial patterns of dispossession (Gudynas 2015; Svampa 2019). Scholars such as Latouche (2008) critique the ideology of growth as a culturally constructed imperative that underpins this model, whereas Escobar (1995) situates it within broader neoliberal and extractivist dynamics that reproduce colonial forms of domination. Global challenges such as climate change, global warming, and water scarcity have intensified social conflicts and deepened historical injustices – particularly in the Global South, where these issues intersect with legacies of colonialism and economic exploitation (Harvey 2005; Piketty 2014). These impacts are disproportionately borne by vulnerable communities with minimal historical responsibility for the climate crisis Tetreault et al. 2013.

In response, Latin American social movements – such as those advocating for the Rights of Mother Earth in Bolivia and Ecuador, and more recently the biocultural rights of the Atrato River and the Amazon in Colombia (Pico 2019) – have demanded the protection of local ways of life against extractivist pressures. These mobilizations challenge the ecological and social injustices of the capitalist model, giving rise to legal innovations such as the recognition of the Rights of Nature (RoN), which seek to overcome the limitations of anthropocentric legal frameworks – incapable of addressing both exogenous (human-made) and endogenous (natural) socioenvironmental impacts – by introducing nature as a legal subject (Acosta 2012; Bebbington 2011; Boyd 2017; Gudynas 2011; Stone 1972).

The global environmental crisis, which endangers biodiversity and human survival, calls for more than technical responses. It requires a human rights-based approach (HRBA) and a firm commitment to environmental justice (Knox 2017; Martínez-Alier 2002). This includes addressing systemic inequities and ensuring fair distribution of environmental benefits and burdens, particularly for communities with sustainable life strategies that support ecological diversity.

The recognition of the RoN, notably in Ecuador and Bolivia, signals a paradigm shift toward ecocentric governance (Kauffman and Martin 2018). However, these legal innovations often face implementation challenges due to entrenched political and economic interests (Escobar 2015). The urgency of rethinking nature's role in legal systems is heightened by the ecological footprint of capitalism, which reveals a fundamental tension between the pursuit of economic growth and the responsible management of finite natural resources (Portela and Sanabria 2019). This crisis is inseparable from fossil-fuel-driven greenhouse gas emissions and the commodification of ecosystems, as well as the dualistic view of nature as either a resource to be exploited or a passive reserve for future use (Bakker 2007; Espinosa 2015).

Beyond the economic model, environmental degradation also stems from a political and cultural paradigm that views nature dualistically – either as a resource to be exploited or as a passive reserve to be preserved for future use. This anthropocentric worldview, historically spread through colonialism and reinforced by neoliberal globalization, separates humanity from nature and denies its agency (Bakker 2007). In contrast, Indigenous ontologies in Latin America sustain relational worldviews in which nature is a social actor and member of an extended community (Descola 2012; Duchesne 2019; Escobar 2015). These life systems, often found in regions with high linguistic and biological diversity, represent some of the strongest forms of resistance to the totalizing logic of neoliberal capitalism (Bartra 2008 in Espinosa 2015; Maffi and Woodley 2010).

The Indigenous and Afro-descendant peoples' worldview offers an alternative approach to the environmental crisis by reconfiguring nature not as an object, but as a relational subject of social life (Escobar 2015). This perspective has gained increasing recognition in international environmental law, especially in Latin America, where legal personhood is being granted to rivers, forests, and other ecosystems (Kauffman and Martin 2018). Customary Indigenous legal systems have significantly influenced these developments, positioning both RoN and biocultural rights within global legal debates. This chapter explores the possibilities and limitations of legal frameworks in addressing the structural drivers of environmental injustice, especially within contexts shaped by enduring colonial and neoliberal logics.

This chapter opens with reflections on the theoretical and methodological foundations of the study, followed by a conceptual introduction. It then explores the legal and political implications of RoN, arguing that their effective implementation requires a transition from anthropocentric to ecocentric models. The third section addresses biocultural rights, which interlink biodiversity with cultural diversity and Indigenous sovereignty. Finally, the chapter examines legal pluralism and Indigenous customary law as critical tools to challenge dominant paradigms and promote contextual, relational understandings of nature–culture relations.

5.1.1 Theoretical and Methodological Considerations

Building on the call for a paradigmatic shift outlined in the introduction, this chapter adopts a theoretical–methodological framework grounded in *political ontology* and the *biocultural approach* to examine the challenges surrounding the implementation of the RoN. These perspectives illuminate how Indigenous, Afro-descendant, and peasant communities articulate alternative lifeways and legal imaginaries amid the socioenvironmental crisis. The political ontology approach examines the interactions and power dynamics between ontological systems (Blaser 2019); an ontology refers to a world construction based on the attributions humans make toward nonhumans (Descola 2012). Through symbolic representations of other beings, relationships and practices are formed, shaping and animating reality. As Blaser (2019: 207) explains, "an ontology is a way of world-making, it is a form of enacting reality." In this view, conflicts in culturally diverse contexts do not arise from "different points of view about the same world" clashing, but rather from the fact that the actors involved fail to recognize that each is representing – and assuming – different worlds (Blaser 2019; Ruíz and Del Cairo 2016; Silva and Calle 2025).

The modern dichotomy between nature and culture not only represents an epistemological perspective but an ontology that may contradict the relational ontologies of Indigenous peoples (Ruíz and Del Cairo 2016). The biocultural approach criticizes this modern dichotomy, which artificially separates humans from the natural world. Instead, it posits that local communities, especially indigenous and rural ones, possess an integrated understanding of their territories, rooted in both ecological knowledge and cultural practices developed over centuries (Toledo and Barrera 2008).

From a decolonial perspective, political ontology emphasizes the importance of recognizing, thereby legitimizing the knowledge systems and lifeways of colonized peoples, rather than imposing colonial power relations and related categories upon them (Ruíz and Del Cairo 2016). This requires creating space for alternative understandings of nature, society, and power, such as those found in Indigenous and Afro-descendant cosmologies – perspectives historically marginalized or rendered invisible (Escobar 2015). In a decolonial context, the biocultural approach likewise values these knowledges and practices, recognizing that colonialism sought to sever the ties between nature and culture through resource exploitation and the imposition of extractivist economic models (Coronil 2000; Escobar 1995; Lander 2000; Quijano 2014). Both the specific political ontology discussed, and the biocultural approach align with decolonizing objectives by challenging the universality of Western knowledge systems and their corresponding systems of justice. They notably advocate for a plurality of epistemologies and ontologies and for a more integrated, respectful relationship with nature and culture, countering the colonial legacy of imposing a singular worldview. Together, such political ontology and the biocultural approach facilitate the recovery of diverse ways of knowing and living that have been silenced or subordinated by colonial logics (Duchesne 2019). In doing so, they promote epistemic and socioecological justice.

This analysis is grounded in a theoretical reflection on the normative developments of the RoN in Latin American States and the cultural concepts embedded in Indigenous customary law. It is informed by empirical research conducted with Indigenous communities facing territorial and socioenvironmental conflicts. Fieldwork was conducted in the Andes with the Nasa (2017), Muisca (2005–06, 2012, 2014–15), and Embera (2008) peoples in Colombia and the Kichwa (2012) nation in Otavalo, Ecuador; in the northern Colombian Amazon with the Carijona (2018–24) people; in the Orinoquía region with the Sikuani, Piapoco, and Sáliba (2004–24) peoples; in the Caribbean with the Wayúu peoples (2017–24); and in the border region of Misiones Province, spanning Argentina, Paraguay, and Brazil, with the Mbyá Guaraní (2019). The analysis centers on issues related to the exploitation of nature as a resource, its conservation as a reserve, and its use based on traditional knowledge.

5.2 The Rights of Nature: Conceptual Origins and Influences

Rights of Nature have emerged as a response to escalating environmental crises and as a legal–political articulation of demands by local populations defending their territories and traditional ways of life. Rooted in grassroots mobilizations and Indigenous worldviews, RoN propose a redefinition of legal subjectivity to include ecosystems and natural entities – such as mountains, rivers, or forests – as rights-bearing subjects (Acosta 2012; Gudynas 2011; 2015). This shift departs from traditional legal paradigms in which nature is treated as property, proposing instead an ecocentric perspective grounded in reciprocity and interdependence.

Although initially rooted in Latin American constitutional innovations, the RoN framework has gained increasing attention among Euro-American legal scholars, who consider it a potential antidote to the legal inertia surrounding environmental protection (Viaene 2024). In the face of accelerating environmental breakdown – exemplified by the record global warming levels reported in the 2023 UN Emissions Gap Report – RoN represent a rupture with anthropocentric legal orders and a step toward systemic transformation.

This legal–political framework resonates with broader critiques of extractivism and development (e.g., Gudynas, 2011 and Svampa, 2019), which argue for alternative models grounded in the defense of ecological diversity and social justice. The recognition of nature's rights thus becomes both a legal innovation and a political project – one that challenges dominant economic models and reconfigures the boundaries between law, nature, and society.

The current debate around RoN is interdisciplinary and dynamic, involving contributions from environmental law, political ecology, conservation biology, and environmental anthropology. It also extends well beyond academia, engaging a wide range of actors including civil society organizations, Indigenous movements, legal practitioners, and local communities (Gudynas 2015). Although the conceptual roots of RoN can be traced back to Christopher Stone's landmark 1972 essay *Should Trees Have Standing?*, which advocated for the legal personhood of nature, its contemporary relevance lies in its capacity to rethink law in times of socioecological crisis – not as a technocratic instrument, but as a space of contestation and imagination.

Subsequently, "Deep Ecology" principles emerged, promoting biospheric egalitarianism and asserting the intrinsic value of all living beings, independent of their utility. Later, the concept of animism was reformulated to advocate for the dissolution of the boundary between persons and nonpersons, based on the idea that nature shares the same vital spirit. This approach treats humans, other living beings, and nonhuman entities as subjects, drawing inspiration from indigenous interactions with nature (see the work of Descola, Bird-David, Viveiros de Castro, Ingold, and Latour). These currents are related to James Lovelock's "Gaia Hypothesis" and Thomas Berry's "Earth Jurisprudence" (Laszlo and Combs 2011). The Gaia Hypothesis posits that Earth functions as a self-regulating system in which living and nonliving components interact to maintain life-supporting conditions. According to this hypothesis, life itself contributes to stabilizing the planet's environment, thus preserving its habitability. Earth Jurisprudence highlights the interconnectedness of all elements – both living and nonliving – and advocates for a legal framework that acknowledges the rights of the Earth as a whole, focusing on the common good of the entire ecological system (Burdon 2012).

The paradigmatic shift from an anthropocentric perspective to biocentric and ecocentric frameworks in the recognition of RoN introduces alternative ethical and legal paradigms for valuing nature, each bearing distinct normative implications. The biocentric perspective emphasizes the intrinsic worth of all living beings, asserting that each organism, regardless of species or individual attributes, deserves moral consideration and protection simply by virtue of its existence. However, it excludes nonliving entities from ethical consideration. In contrast, the ecocentric approach advocates a holistic perspective, recognizing the Earth as an interconnected system (Nash 1993). It thus promotes a more inclusive notion of environmental ethics, extending moral and legal rights to the entire natural world.

Contemporary debates on the human–nature relationship revolve around anthropocentric, biocentric, and ecocentric paradigms. The conventional rights system, which traditionally conceptualizes nature as an object of use, is rooted in the anthropocentric model. However, reducing this debate to a dichotomy between anthropocentrism (= nature as object) and biocentrism or ecocentrism (= nature as subject) is an oversimplification. Indeed, nature's rights can be justified from within any of these frameworks. The following sections examine each of these perspectives in greater detail.

Anthropocentrism holds that only human interests merit moral and legal protection, and can be categorized into three strands (Sánchez et al. 2021). *Radical anthropocentrism* denies rights to nonhumans, justifying environmental protection solely by human benefit (Burdon 2011). *Moderate anthropocentrism* supports environmental rights instrumentally, to safeguard future generations (Guzmán and Ubajoa 2020). *Ethical anthropocentrism*, influenced by Singer and Regan, extends moral consideration to nonhuman animals based on sentience or rationality (Regan 2004; Singer and Cavalieri 1993). The RoN movement draws on diverse ethical foundations to advocate for the legal recognition of nonhuman entities – including inanimate elements, flora, fauna, biomes, and ecosystems – giving rise to theoretical frameworks such as Deep Ecology, Earth Jurisprudence, Ecofeminism, Earth System Law, and Ecological Constitutionalism (Sánchez et al. 2021).

From biocentric and ecocentric perspectives, RoN is rooted in the recognition of the intrinsic value of all life forms, and has progressively influenced international, constitutional, and judicial frameworks.[1] These developments reflect a growing trend toward the legal recognition of nature's rights, often accompanied by the appointment of legal guardians for their protection.

Differing views on RoN consider them idealistic and inconsequential, whereas others see them as transformative, challenging modernity's legal and economic models. Since the late 2000s, however, the paradigm of RoN has been proposed as a response to economic and governance models that have led to excessive exploitation of natural resources (Abate 2020; Cullinan 2011; Gudynas 2015). This debate has become increasingly polarized: while some see RoN as a profound legal shift capable of deconstructing Western paradigms – even "saving the world," as Boyd (2017) suggests – others emphasize its limitations and potential risks, including concerns about its practical implementation and unintended consequences (Clavijo-Ospina 2020; García 2020).

Rights of Nature have emerged as a new "legal trend" (Viaene 2024: 302) in courts, which may contribute to depoliticizing communities' struggles to defend

[1] Key international milestones in the institutionalization of the Rights of Nature include: the *World Charter for Nature* (UN, 1982); Ecuador's 2008 Constitution – the first to grant legal personhood to nature; Bolivia's Law 71 and constitutional reforms (2010); the Colombian Constitutional Court ruling T-622/2016, which recognized the biocultural rights of the Atrato River; New Zealand's *Te Awa Tupua Act* (2017), granting personhood to the Whanganui River; and the 2022 ruling by the High Court of Murcia, which recognized the Mar Menor lagoon as a legal subject.

their territories and obscure local contexts. In Colombia, the existing legal framework continues to reproduce asymmetrical power relations and fails to challenge the extractivist model (González-Serrano 2025; Melo-Ascencio 2024). For instance, despite the Atrato River being granted legal personality in 2016 – a recognition explicitly linked to the collective rights of Indigenous and Afro-descendant communities – implementation has been slow, and illegal mining continues unabated. Similarly, the 2018 ruling recognizing rights for the Amazon has failed to curb deforestation due to insufficient State action and funding. These cases illustrate the limitations of RoN jurisprudence when it is not accompanied by structural changes in resource governance and allocation. In other words, without addressing the underlying power dynamics and colonial legacies, risks perpetuating the same exploitative structures it seeks to dismantle.

To fully realize the transformative potential of RoN, a shift away from anthropocentric models – and the socioeconomic systems that sustain them – is essential. This approach responds to the crisis of the modern colonial world-system (Lander and Arconada 2020), recognizing that well-being cannot be based on material accumulation and unlimited economic growth. Overcoming colonial and Eurocentric frameworks is therefore central to addressing this socioenvironmental crisis (Acosta 2012). As anthropologist Arturo Escobar notes, this multifaceted crisis challenges the very model of existence and society we live in, highlighting the need for a socioecological transition to restore the fabric of life (Escobar 2022).

5.2.1 Contextualizing the Rights of Nature: Modern Capitalism and the Demands of "Development"

Despite the global resonance of RoN achieved through recognition processes, their implementation faces significant challenges; normative advancements have not translated into structural changes supporting their recognition and practice. The modern capitalist ontology, grounded in a conception separating nature from culture, reinforces socio-economic and political structures that objectify nature and obstruct its recognition as a subject of rights. The epistemological foundation of the capitalist view of nature derives from the Judeo-Christian creation myth, which posits a split between nature and society. The expulsion from paradise following the first sin severs ties with nature – now wild, fallen – and the divine, relegated to a transcendent realm. Humanity is condemned to exploit nature for survival (Lander 2000). Capitalism intensifies this relationship of separation, exploitation, and subordination, treating nature as an inexhaustible resource (Acosta 2012). This relentless pursuit of profit and continuous growth conflicts with the earth's finite capacity for sustainability. This contradiction raises a fundamental question: how can nature be simultaneously treated as a subject of rights and as an object of exploitation?

Historically, capitalist modernity has been expanding globally through colonial processes, appropriating nature and labor to generate profits, impoverishing and subordinating colonies while enriching certain centers of power. In the case of

Latin America, during the Spanish and Portuguese colonization, resources such as gold and silver were intensely exploited for the benefit of European metropolises at the expense of local indigenous peoples and the environment. This exploitation continued after the independence of the republics (Coronil 2000; Quijano 2014). In the Amazon, the rubber boom during the first half of the twentieth century involved slavery, inhumane working conditions, torture, and the death of indigenous peoples to satisfy international latex demand (Hettler and Plotkin 2019; Pineda 2000; Reyes 2018). Colonialism not only entailed economic exploitation but also political and cultural domination (Quijano 2014). It perpetuated imaginaries of subordination, where territories and local populations were regarded as "savage," whereas the colonizers were regarded as "civilized." This legacy of exploitation has profoundly impacted the economic, sociocultural, and environmental structures of many regions. Although independence movements have been interpreted as the end of colonialism and the beginning of modern States, coloniality persists under neoliberal capitalism through global geopolitics, the subalternation of populations, their ways of life, and the ongoing exploitation of nature (Quijano 2014; Spivak 1988).

In modern States, the discourse of development has perpetuated differential classifications of States based on ethnocentric notions of economic and social progress. Notably, Rostow (1960) proposed a linear theory of development, suggesting that societies must pass through stages of economic growth to reach the status of an industrialized State. This approach assumes that underdevelopment is a transitional phase that States must overcome, creating a classification that distinguishes between "developed" States or those in the "first world" and "developing" States in the "third world." This developmental perspective constituted yet another tool of domination and coloniality, imposing economic and cultural models on communities foreign to local realities (Escobar 1995). Thus, development is not a neutral process but a discursive construct that legitimizes the intervention of so-called developed States in the Global South.

5.2.2 The Empirical Side of the Rights of Nature: Extractive Industries, Carbon Credits, and Traditional Conservationism

In Latin America, multiple cases illustrate the inherent tensions between development agendas, environmental rights, and the rights of Indigenous peoples. These tensions are particularly salient in a region characterized by exceptional biodiversity and a long history of Indigenous marginalization, which together intensify the socioenvironmental conflicts at stake. Emblematic cases from Colombia and Ecuador expose the structural contradictions between progressive constitutional frameworks and the socioecological realities encountered in practice. Diverse forms of "development" – ranging from conventional extractive industries to market-driven models of sustainable development and conservation – operate within a shared epistemological paradigm. This paradigm, predicated on the nature–culture divide, ultimately reinforces colonial legacies and reproduces global asymmetries.

Case Study: Coal Exploitation in La Guajira

Despite the recognition of Colombia's ethnic and cultural diversity in the 1991 Constitution and the prioritization of water use for human subsistence (Law 99 of 1993, Articles 1, 5), the exploitation of one of the largest open-pit mines in the world in the semi-arid region of La Guajira, home to the Wayúu indigenous people, has persisted in the name of development. The extraction of this mineral serves as an energy source for the Global North and generates royalty revenues for Colombia.

However, the mine's operation has led to the displacement of approximately eighteen ethnic communities; the desiccation, diversion, and contamination of fifteen water sources; the appropriation of agricultural land; as well as air and water pollution (García et al. 2022). Existing regulations do not sufficiently guarantee the rights of the Wayúu people, who faced the deaths of nearly 4,770 children due to malnutrition between 2008 and 2015 as a result of hunger and drought (Procuraduría 2016: 26).

In consequence, the Wayúu peoples have had to seek judicial recourse to claim their rights to water, food, health, prior consultation, and cultural integrity (Judgment SU698 of 2017, Constitutional Court). In the past decade, an indigenous community opposed the diversion of the Arroyo Bruno proposed by the multinational company Glencore for the advancement of coal extraction. This water source was vital for community sustenance. The Constitutional Court of Colombia ordered the suspension of extractive activities near the Arroyo Bruno until uncertainties regarding the guarantee of their rights had been resolved. In response, Glencore sued Colombia for USD $489.2 million before an international arbitration tribunal over the court's decision to suspend extraction activities in parts of the mine (CIADI Case No. ARB/21/30). This case exemplifies the structural tensions between extractive capitalism and the effective realization of environmental and Indigenous rights.

Case Study: Oil Exploitation in Yasuní National Park

The ongoing oil exploitation in Ecuador's Yasuní National Park, even after it was declared a World Biosphere Reserve in 1989 (UNESCO, n.d.), illustrates the conflicts between development initiatives and rights guarantees. Extractive activities have impacted the ecological connectivity of one of the most biodiverse regions in the world, affecting the territory of

(cont.)

the Waorani and indigenous peoples in voluntary isolation. Despite the recognition of RoN in the Ecuadorian Constitution, an "oil moratorium" was declared to suspend extractive activities in Yasuní while maintaining 20 percent of the State's oil reserves underground in exchange for a 50 percent financial contribution from the international community and the Ecuadorian State. After 2013, exploitation resumed due to the need to contribute to economic development through oil revenues (Stoessel and Scarpacci 2021).

In 2023, a historic referendum affirmed the necessity of maintaining reserves underground. Nevertheless, petroleum exploitation has continued unabated (Olmo 2024). Although instruments such as the Ecuadorian Constitution and ILO Convention 169 formally recognize the RoN and Indigenous rights, their implementation remains compromised by dominant economic agendas.

Case Study: Carbon Credits and Indigenous Rights

Carbon credits present a revealing case that exposes the fundamental contradictions between development paradigms and Indigenous peoples' rights, despite being conceived under the notion of sustainability. Under the Kyoto Protocol (1998), entities with higher emissions are required to compensate for the environmental harm caused. This has led to the emergence of carbon credits as a market-based solution, enabling companies, organizations, or individuals to offset their carbon footprint voluntarily. In some instances, these credits allow entities to surpass the emission limits set by international agreements.

According to a study conducted by the SINCHI Institute (2022) in the Colombian Amazon, the carbon credits market has adversely affected territorial rights, social fabric, and the livelihoods of indigenous peoples. Seventy-eight communities signed contracts without being able to exercise their right to prior consultation and without a clear understanding of the implications. Some contracts were signed in English, a language not understood locally; others were signed by individuals not representing the communities. One of the concerning aspects involves the commitment to reduce 30 percent of the area of "chagras" (subsistence gardens), recognized for their compatibility with forest conservation. Reducing the chagras of

(cont.)

seventy-eight communities would undermine traditional subsistence systems and forest use, contradicting social and environmental safeguards (ICANH 2023; SINCHI 2022: 41).

Case Study: Conservation and Displacement – Tayrona National Park

Finally, the case of Tayrona National Natural Park (Colombia) illustrates how natural area conservation proposals are intricately intertwined with violence and the violation of community rights. This case demonstrates how conservation paradigms, despite their purported environmental objectives, can function as mechanisms of territorial dispossession. Conservation discourses led to the disregard for local ways of life of farmers and fishermen in the name of the environment, security, and development (Bocarejo and Ojeda 2016). They were represented in public discourse as environmental predators and invaders of the protected area, serving as a justification for their criminalization and subsequent violent dispossession. Inhabitants who relied on local resources for subsistence and tourism were evicted under the guise of conservation, only for the area to be concessioned to Aviatur, an international tourism company. This case demonstrates how conservation efforts, far from being neutral, can function as instruments to suppress cultural practices and exclude local populations.

In these cases, the violation of Indigenous rights in the name of conservation is part of a broader global phenomenon in which communities in the Global South face structural power imbalances in negotiations. The expansion of capitalism into new territories is accompanied by the discourse of sustainability, ultimately facilitating new forms of capital accumulation rather than genuinely protecting biodiversity (Harvey 2003; Lang et al. 2023). The cases of La Guajira, Yasuní, carbon credits, and Tayrona National Park reveal a systematic pattern wherein both traditional extractivism and purported "sustainable" alternatives share the same colonial matrix that subordinates Indigenous epistemologies and ecological integrity to the capitalist paradigm. Whether through direct exploitation (coal, oil), market mechanisms (carbon credits), or exclusionary conservationism (displacements in Tayrona), an instrumental separation between nature and culture persists, facilitating new forms of accumulation. Paradoxically, even legal frameworks that formally recognize the RoN remain incapable of transcending these contradictions while trapped within hegemonic development logics. This confirms the importance of situating the effective guarantee of RoN "outside the epistemic boundaries of capitalist modernity" (Tamayo-Álvarez 2023: 23).

5.3 Indigenous Biocultural Rights: Integrating Nature, Culture, and Collective Sovereignty

Biocultural rights have emerged as a robust framework to integrate protections for Indigenous territorial rights, ecosystem integrity, and ontological self-determination (Bavikatte and Bennett 2015). Although aligned with territorial rights and RoN, this approach challenges the nature–culture divide by highlighting the intrinsic link between biological and cultural diversity (González-Morales 2023). Its central aim is to safeguard ancestral knowledge, cultural practices, and the lifeways of Indigenous peoples and local communities, intrinsically linked to territorial biodiversity. Often described as a "basket" of indeterminate rights, biocultural rights aim to uphold and promote community-based lifeways as key to biodiversity conservation (Bondia 2013).

Within this context, biocultural rights provide a valuable lens through which to address tensions between the RoN and Indigenous territorial rights. Although legal systems such as those in Ecuador and New Zealand recognize both RoN and Indigenous collective rights, their implementation reveals both synergies and conflicts. For instance, in New Zealand, the *Te Awa Tupua* (Whanganui River Claims Settlement) Act 2017 granted legal personhood to the Whanganui River, recognizing it as an indivisible and living whole while also affirming the rights and governance role of the Whanganui Iwi (a Māori tribe) (Charpleix 2018). This case illustrates how Indigenous worldviews can be embedded within legal frameworks in ways that simultaneously reinforce ecological integrity and cultural preservation.

Nevertheless, rather than endorsing the RoN as codified in State law, many Indigenous peoples advocate for ontological frameworks that better reflect their relational worldviews. In Ecuador, the Sarayaku People advocate for the concept of *Kawsak Sacha* (Living Forest), which surpasses legal RoN by asserting nature as a sentient, interconnected life-sustaining space (Sarayaku 2018). This perspective challenges normative frameworks that, although recognizing nature's rights, often constrain Indigenous land use or disregard their governance autonomy. Given these complexities, legal frameworks must reconcile ecological preservation with social justice while respecting Indigenous ontologies and safeguarding self-determination. Unlike technocratic conservation models that prioritize resource management via metrics like "carrying capacity" and "pollution thresholds," biocultural rights promote holistic conservation linking biodiversity and community well-being. Biocultural rights are part of a deep and enduring trend that promotes the localization and contextual adaptation of legal concepts – a movement deeply informed by the social sciences, particularly anthropology (Brunet 2024). This trend is rooted in a robust critique of expertocracy and a corresponding shift toward grassroots-oriented approaches.

The concept of "biocultural diversity" serves as an analytical lens through which the functioning of biocultural rights can be understood by examining the interactions between human and nonhuman entities and their interdependent relationships (Thornton et al. 2020). These relationships, in turn, are anchored in "biocultural memory," which reflects the coevolutionary ties between local communities and ecosystems. Through their social structures, traditional knowledge systems, and everyday practices, local communities serve as long-term stewards of biodiversity, aligning their livelihoods with environmental cycles (Toledo 2002; Toledo and Barrera 2008). "Biocultural heritage" further integrates natural and cultural elements, including Indigenous knowledge and community-based practices within complex socioecological systems (Ekblom et al. 2019; Gavin et al. 2015).

The biocultural rights perspective has gained increasing traction in legal developments and jurisprudence such as the Colombian Constitutional Court's ruling T-622/2016, which recognizes the Atrato River as a subject of rights to ensure its conservation. The ruling defines biocultural rights as "the rights of ethnic communities to administer and exercise autonomous guardianship over their territories and natural resources, according to their own laws and customs, where they develop their culture, traditions, and way of life, based on their special relationship with the environment and biodiversity" (5.11). This decision illustrates how legal recognition can simultaneously uphold cultural practices and ecological integrity within a unified biocultural framework. Nevertheless, as noted earlier, the realization of these rights in practice has been uneven, exposing a persistent gap between normative recognition and institutional implementation – one that is further compounded by the enduring extractivist economic model and ongoing violence in the territory. These structural barriers not only hinder effective enforcement but also threaten the biocultural foundations of Indigenous and local communities' relationships with their environments.

The displacement of Indigenous populations in the name of conservation would result in the abandonment of ecosystems they have historically managed through sustainable practices. Thus, safeguarding the rights of Indigenous peoples and local communities, including their worldviews that inform environmental stewardship, is essential. This biocultural perspective highlights the profound connection between biodiversity and cultural diversity, reinforcing the imperative to protect and respect life practices that foster enduring and sustainable relationships with the environment. The equilibrium of ecosystems is critical for the subsistence and well-being of these communities. Furthermore, it has been compellingly argued that the cultural and physical survival of Indigenous peoples is inseparable from the ecological integrity of their territories, with any ecological disruption directly threatening their continued existence (Maffi and Woodley 2010).

While biocultural rights acknowledge the pivotal role of communities in territorial management, they often operate primarily as mechanisms of self-defense rather than tools for catalyzing transformative shifts in prevailing sociolegal paradigms. For instance, although legal frameworks have recognized biocultural rights for Indigenous communities in countries such as Colombia and India, extractivist economic models and State-centric policies continue to prioritize large-scale development over Indigenous governance. These rights anchor communities to their lands and ecosystems via traditional territorial governance mechanisms, such as those employed by Indigenous groups like the Maasai in Kenya and Tanzania, the Kichwa in Ecuador, and the Nasa in Colombia. Such mechanisms enable ethnic communities to exercise autonomous governance over their territories in accordance with their customary legal systems. The Nasa peoples, for example, resist dispossession and displacement through the "Liberation of Mother Earth" – a political–ecological strategy of reclaiming ancestral lands by mobilizing territorial defense against chemical contamination and monocultural agriculture (Vargas and Ariza 2019).

Although often promoted as a means of protecting the interdependence between communities and their environment, some scholars argue that biocultural rights may circumvent the recognition of Indigenous peoples' rights to autonomy and self-determination (Sajeva 2022). Critics contend, moreover, that such frameworks reinforce state control over natural resources rather than enabling Indigenous governance. Additionally, by prioritizing cultural practices and traditional knowledge, these legal mechanisms often fail to guarantee effective control over ancestral territories, potentially facilitating the co-optation of Indigenous knowledge and resources by external actors (Reyes-García and Martí 2017). The abstract nature of biocultural rights may also hinder their capacity to address the territorial realities and power asymmetries Indigenous communities face, thereby limiting the exercise of self-determination (Anquet and Girard 2022).

Nevertheless, in Colombia, where our research has long engaged with Indigenous peoples, many communities and organizations have strategically leveraged biocultural rights as legal and political tools to defend their territories against extractive industries and other threats. This pragmatic approach reveals the situated and contested nature of implementing biocultural rights within broader struggles over territory, recognition, and autonomy. In this context, understanding how Indigenous, peasant, and Afro-descendant communities engage with and reinterpret legal frameworks requires a shift toward analytical tools that account for ontological plurality and legal heterogeneity. In this sense, political ontology and legal pluralism are key to unpacking these dynamics and situating rights discourses within diverse cosmopolitical configurations.

5.3.1 Political Ontology and Legal Pluralism

"Political ontology" and the "biocultural approach" contest the Western imposition of a singular ontological framework by affirming the legitimacy of multiple worldviews rooted in distinct cosmologies. The biocultural approach – eschewing essentialism – integrates situated knowledge, territorial memory, and socio-ecological practices (Sánchez et al. 2021). It fosters dialogue between these ontologies and dominant legal and political frameworks, exposing the tensions marginalized communities face under State-centric legal systems.

Political ontology illuminates how ontological divergence generates conflicts in territorial and environmental governance. For instance, many Indigenous peoples privilege customary legal systems that embody relational ontologies of land, life, and community, in contrast to the State's naturalistic governance models. The tension between State-centric naturalism and Indigenous multinaturalism on the other hand underscores the political stakes of these ontological differences. "Political ontology" is crucial for analyzing power dynamics in territorial struggles across Latin America, advocating for the recognition of a "pluriverse," which acknowledges the existence of multiple, coexisting worlds (Blaser 2019; Escobar 2015). This framework disrupts the colonial nature–culture binary, promoting a more integrated legal and social framework that respects diverse ontological realities.

However, although "political ontology" and the "biocultural approach" stress the importance of recognizing diverse worldviews, conflicts may arise when these perspectives intersect with legal frameworks like RoN: the prevailing formulation of the RoN, which individuates natural entities and reconstitutes them as legal subjects, stands in contrast to Indigenous ontologies that conceive nature as a collective and relational being. This systemic and sacred relationship, which is central to Indigenous cosmologies, often clashes with those legal frameworks that emphasize nature's intrinsic ecological value, potentially undermining the broader cultural and spiritual dimensions involved (Gómez 2015; Shaquiñan – Ministry of the Environment 2012).

As we will explore further, Indigenous customary law plays a key role in regulating these cultural, social, and territorial norms. Grounded in principles of reciprocity and ecological equilibrium, Indigenous customary law reveals the structural limitations of State-centric protections of Indigenous rights and territorial claims. In a legally pluralistic context, the integration and true recognition of Indigenous customary law within domestic legal systems is vital to ensuring these communities' autonomy, self-governance, and collective self-determination. The notion of biocultural diversity advances rights-based approaches to environmental stewardship, highlighting the protective role of Indigenous and local communities in their territories.

However, its implementation poses significant challenges, such as the perpetuation of the "noble ecological savage" myth, the difficulty of reconciling divergent nature–culture ontologies, the commodification of nature, and the instrumentalization of biocultural rights by dominant power structures. Biocultural rights lack the political weight typically associated with collective rights, rendering them less threatening to States and their economic agendas (Bavikatte and Bennett 2015). This depoliticized form presents both risks and opportunities, prompting critical questions as to whether States engage with these rights primarily as tools for managing power asymmetries between economic and political centers and marginalized populations, rather than as a genuine commitment to fostering relational care between nature and culture.

Indigenous and local communities have strategically engaged with legal mechanisms for biocultural protection, using the concept of biocultural heritage to formalize previously unrecognized relationships. This is reflected in the development of Biocultural Community Protocols, asserting collective values, rights, and responsibilities concerning ancestral knowledge and biological and genetic resources, combining customary law with domestic and international legal systems. Notable examples include the Black Communities of Alto San Juan (Colombia, 2011), the Chipaya and Tapacari Communities (Bolivia, 2009), the A'i Kofan Indigenous Communities (Ecuador, 2016), the Oxlaju Ajpop Mayan Communities (Guatemala, 2012), the Lafkenche Mapuche Communities (Chile, 2012), and the Capadálpam Community (Mexico, 2018) (Sánchez et al. 2021).

Although these protocols reflect Indigenous peoples' proactive assertion of authority over their biocultural heritage and territories, they simultaneously reveal underlying tensions in the conceptualization of their relationship with nature. In many cases, the legal frameworks that support such protocols can unintentionally reinforce the erroneous assumption that Indigenous peoples are inherently conservationist. This perception stems from stereotypes constructed by capitalist modernity, particularly the notion of the "noble savage." A historical reading of Western discursive constructions of Indigeneity reveals a significant epistemic shift. Under colonial logics, Indigenous peoples were construed as inherently entwined with nature, thereby justifying their exploitation as both instruments of production and targets of evangelization, aimed at redeeming their so-called "animality." This resonates with dominant republican ideas, which portrayed Indigenous peoples as "savages" or "minors" lacking what was expected at the time. These colonial tropes continue to inform contemporary imaginaries, such as the notion of the "ecological native" (Ulloa 2004), a form of environmentalist renaturalization that echoes this trope. Within this discourse, Indigenous populations are often framed through a deterministic and reductive vision that assigns them a singular or limited role in environmental conservation. This framing risks naturalizing specific duties and behaviors, positioning them as the guardians of humanity's shared natural heritage.

At the international level, however, Indigenous peoples have increasingly emerged as key interlocutors in articulating a shared environmental agenda, as reflected in instruments such as the UN Declaration on the Rights of Indigenous Peoples (UNDRIPS) and the Convention on Biological Diversity (CBD). These instruments recognize Indigenous peoples not merely as stewards of biodiversity, but as central political actors whose knowledge systems contribute to shaping international environmental governance. Although critiques of biocultural rights highlight the risks of essentializing Indigenous identities, such legal instruments also furnish critical avenues through which Indigenous peoples assert their rights and influence global sustainability policies.

At the domestic level, some States have taken steps to formalize Indigenous environmental governance. In Colombia, for instance, Decree Law 1275 – enacted jointly by the Ministry of Environment and the Ministry of the Interior – formally recognizes the environmental competencies of Indigenous authorities. This development marks a pivotal shift, reinforcing their agency in decision-making processes concerning their territories. However, under the persistent framing of the "ecological native," Indigenous peoples are disproportionately burdened with responsibilities imposed by dominant society, whereas that same society continues to overexploit natural resources to maintain high-consumption lifestyles. Although society demands, for instance, that Indigenous peoples protect the Amazon rainforest, it remains largely unwilling to alter urban practices that contribute to environmental degradation. A striking example of this dynamic is meat consumption: the Amazon is being deforested to create pasture for cattle, yet urban populations remain largely resistant to reducing meat consumption (Olaya et al. 2022). This asymmetry fosters an imaginary in which Indigenous peoples are presumed to be nature's protectors and are disproportionately penalized when they engage in resource use.

This dynamic was evident in our fieldwork with the Sikuani in the Orinoquía region of Colombia (2023–24), where we documented how Cormacarena, the regional environmental authority institution, imposes sanctions on Indigenous peoples for digging small wells to access water, while large agribusiness and oil companies continue operating with relative impunity despite significant environmental impacts. Likewise, Indigenous peoples often face legal restrictions or criminalization for engaging in subsistence agriculture, in contrast to the impunity enjoyed by corporate actors responsible for extensive deforestation (Fieldnotes: Calle 2023–2024).

The stereotype of Indigenous peoples as inherently ecological can obscure their broader struggles for autonomy and cultural survival, independent of environmental preservation agendas. At the same time, it can divert attention from the root causes of environmental degradation, thus legitimizing hegemonic development paradigms (Assies 2003). In this context, legal frameworks offer limited transformative capacity (Hale 2020) as they offer inadequate tools for Indigenous and local communities, who are simultaneously expected to comply with legal requirements and bear the burden of environmental stewardship. This imposed burden reflects a broader conflict between Western and Indigenous worldviews on nature and human–nature relationships. Whereas Western paradigms tend to bifurcate economic extraction and conservation, Indigenous perspectives are rooted in a fundamentally different understanding of nature's role within their communities: rather than being viewed as passive resources, natural elements are integral participants in a reciprocal relationship with humans, sustaining both symbolic and material life.

In many Indigenous worldviews, nature is not merely a resource but an active agent in the social and spiritual life of communities, possessing rights and responsibilities akin to human beings. Among the Wayuu, for instance, natural elements such as the Bruno stream are regarded as sentient beings imbued with spiritual significance, governed by norms of exchange and reciprocity. Disruptions to these natural systems, such as the diversion of the Bruno stream, are understood not solely as environmental harm but as violations of the cultural and spiritual relationships that sustain life and social harmony (Duchesne 2015; Escobar 2014; Silva and Calle 2025).

This relational ontology underpins a broader understanding of justice, in which environmental harm constitutes a breach of the normative systems governing human-nature interactions. Such perspectives expand legal subjecthood to encompass nonhuman entities, urging a rethinking of existing categories of justice and rights. Grounded in reciprocity and interdependence, Indigenous notions of justice pave the way for exploring legal pluralism, where diverse normative systems, including Indigenous law, coexist and interact with State-centric legal frameworks.

5.4 Perspectives from Legal Pluralism and Indigenous Customary Law

While the exercise of Nature's Rights poses a challenge to capitalist modernity, this is not necessarily true for justice systems embedded in societies where the human–nature relationship is not fragmented. From a biocultural perspective, the nature–culture bond is an integral part of the worldview of Indigenous peoples who resisted colonization by seeking refuge in areas that required greater ecological knowledge, such as rainforests, highlands, wetlands, and vast savannas. In these regions, they established ways of life dependent on their daily interactions with the land, water, and forests. These interactions informed their conceptions of well-being and justice, which stand in contrast to the segmented and anthropocentric logic of modern capitalism.

In Latin America, in particular, the recognition of cultural diversity within States has evolved in parallel with the acknowledgment of legal pluralism. The formal recognition of Indigenous legal systems has been essential to affirming their status as distinct peoples and enabling the exercise of collective autonomy and self-determination (Gabbert 2003: 128).

The path toward legal pluralism, however, has not been linear. It has emerged from historical struggles involving legal parallelism, persistent Indigenous claims, and the development of international legal instruments, such as ILO Convention 169 (1989), which affirms Indigenous rights (Gómez 2015; ICANH 2017). Additionally, historical treaties and agreements between States and Indigenous nations have significantly influenced the configuration of legal pluralism. For instance, in Chile, the Mapuche signed agreements with both the Spanish Crown and the Chilean State that recognized their territorial autonomy. In New Zealand, the Treaty of Waitangi (1840) established a foundational – albeit contested – framework for Indigenous–State relations.

Gómez (2015: 19–20) argues that legal pluralism arises from legal parallelism, emphasizing that during colonization and the formation of republics, States lacked comprehensive control over law and social life in regions where Indigenous resistance persisted. He notes: "this parallelism accounts for why many Indigenous communities have historically – and often still – handled intra-ethnic conflicts through their own rules, norms, and customs, operating independently of, or in opposition to, colonial and later republican law" (Gómez 2015: 32).

This enduring parallelism has generated a historical dialectic between State law and Indigenous justice systems. The geography of resistance shaped colonial strategies, which prioritized domination in zones of economic exploitation. Consequently, areas requiring greater ecological knowledge often became refuges for Indigenous, Afro-descendant, and marginalized peasant populations, where traditional forms of social organization and ecological relationships endured (Herrera 2007; ICANH 2017). In such regions – those that evaded colonial control – cosmologies grounded in alternative ontologies persisted. For many Indigenous communities, humans are believed to descend from animal or plant species regarded as deities, reflecting a profound interconnectedness among the spiritual, natural, and human realms.

Similarly, laws were not solely the product of human-written documents but were understood as pre-existing principles inherent to the natural and social order. These principles could be accessed through the memory of the peoples and by learning to read nature's "signs" (Silva 2024). Such principles are not abstract laws, but empirical norms directly observed in relation to inhabited territory (Silva and Calle 2025). The "Law of Origin," a term adopted by several Indigenous peoples to describe the foundational principles of their customary legal systems, refers to the natural laws that sustain life for both human and nonhuman beings. For instance, the Wayuu Normative System establishes a form of self-governance that not only encompasses representation norms but also enables dialogue with the spiritual and physical elements of the territory. Some concepts embedded in the customary legal systems of Andean–Amazonian peoples illuminate the connection between nature and culture that governs their approach to natural laws: these include "universality," "complementarity," "community," "reciprocity," and the interrelation between territory and memory (ICANH 2017; Shaquiñan – Ministry of the Environment 2012: 32).

Each principle merits closer examination. "Universality" asserts that all beings are governed by the laws and dynamics of "Father Sun" and "Mother Earth." Comparable to a family, all beings who emerge within the cycles of the Sun and the Earth have the right to a place and territory. "Complementarity" holds that the world requires the existence of opposites that, like day and night, come together in time and space. In their exchange and complementarity, they make life possible, manifesting itself both in balance and movement. "Community" suggests the impossibility of thinking of human and nonhuman beings in isolation; no-one can exist without being interdependent on other beings (ICANH 2017; Shaquiñan – Ministry of the Environment 2012: 32).

"Reciprocity," or Payacua, is the principle learned from "Mother Earth": "Giving and receiving is what we learned from Mother Territory, so if I receive water, I cannot return fire; if I receive appreciation, I cannot return offense. The hands that give receive, the hands that sow reap; one cannot expect fruit if one has not sown. (. . .) Giving more than is received is the symbol of payacua, which is why there is yapa extra" (Shaquiñan – Ministry of the Environment 2012: 32), representing the land's generosity. The land always gives more than it is offered: a small seed is planted and fertilized, and in return, the land provides trees and fruits that nourish. Therefore, Payacua is the symbol of abundance. From this perspective, reciprocity is not merely a compensation system, but a system of gifts, payments, and additional offerings to ensure the continuity of life (ICANH 2017; Shaquiñan – Ministry of the Environment 2012). Consequently, capitalist extraction inherently represents the path to scarcity. According to local voices, "if you take and don't put back, soon the harvest runs out" (Silva Cantillo, Fieldnotes, 2018). Even perspectives on sustainable capitalism that seek environmental compensation are limited compared to the land's laws of Payacua, which always teach to give more than one receives. Simple compensation does not enable continuity, but halts reciprocity dynamics, which weave a fabric between humans and between nature and culture.

Governance and justice cannot be fully understood as democratic if they are limited to *dēmos* (people) and *kratos* (power), which rely on an exclusively human practice. In response, Andean–Amazonian peoples have proposed the concept of *cosmocracia* (cosmocracy) to describe social relations between human and nonhuman entities (Shaquiñan – Ministry of the Environment 2012). From Indigenous perspectives, nature as a subject arises from a worldview centered on reciprocity and exchange, rather than the Western notions of production. This "South American animist cosmopraxis" challenges capitalist alienation by framing human and nonhuman relationships on the same ontological plane (Duchesne 2015: 200) – unlike the capitalist mode of production, in which nature holds value only through human modification. In contrast, non-Western societies view nature as an active subject, sustaining life through reciprocal and symbiotic relationships. An Achuar woman does not "produce" plants in the conventional Western economic sense; rather, she forms a personal bond with them, viewing them as adopted children, speaking to them and offering guidance. In this context, production is less about material output and more about cultivating relationships and negotiating with both human and non-human entities (Duchesne 2015: 204).

This notion of South American *animist cosmopraxis* also proposes an alternative normative orientation in which reciprocity between beings is essential for existence. This perspective underpins *cosmocracia*, a form of governance grounded not in human-centric democracy but in the laws of the cosmos – nonhuman, territory-specific normative systems that sustain life through dynamic equilibrium and reciprocal exchange. These laws precede human norms and are not codified in writing, but rather are inscribed in landscapes and revealed through origin stories, memory, and natural signs (Shaquiñan – Ministry of the Environment 2012; Silva 2024). Unlike the notion of ecocentric democracy – which extends human decision-making processes to include the intrinsic value of nonhuman Nature (UN 2016) – *cosmocracia* is not about extending democracy to nature, but about recognizing a form of governance rooted in the earth itself, where authority derives from the relational fabric between humans and the more-than-human world.

In this sense, customary legal systems do not rely on the punitive notion of payment for a wrong but instead embrace the notion of restoring harm. This concept is key to understanding the impossibility of compensating for environmental damage with capital and the need to restore natural orders and nature–culture relations as the ontological foundation of Indigenous customary law (Gómez 2015). For many Amazonian and Caribbean peoples, norms are defined by the spirits of each territory, not by humans. As such, codifying these laws in written form is often meaningless, as they are known through origin stories and natural signs (Silva and Calle 2025). Moreover, these laws are also specific to each territory, neither general nor abstract. Similarly, humans do not own the land; instead, rivers, forests, animals, and plants have spiritual owners with whom coexistence must be negotiated according to Indigenous cosmologies. For instance, the Wayuu recognize *Pulowi̇̈* as the spiritual owner of water (Silva, Fieldnotes, 2017–2024) while the Carijona acknowledge *Itutari̇̈* as the guardian of the forest (Silva, Fieldnotes, 2018–2024). These beings regulate access to resources and demand respect to prevent disease or scarcity.

Although RoN are often framed as an initiative involving Indigenous peoples and other sectors to transform exploitative dynamics, this narrative is not universally accepted. In fact, some Indigenous groups reject RoN, arguing that they impose legal constructs that do not align with their own normative systems or territorial governance practices (Sánchez et al. 2021). While Indigenous leadership has been instrumental in shaping global debates on RoN, including in United Nations (UN) specialized mechanisms, these critiques highlight the need to consider diverse Indigenous perspectives on the matter. Such critiques raise concerns about potential conflicts between RoN and Indigenous interests, especially for societies without formal legal systems. For instance, the Māori see RoN not through Western legal lenses, but as a pragmatic tool to protect their social structures against external impositions. This example underscores the complexities of applying RoN universally, as it may depoliticize local struggles (Espinosa 2019; Valladares and Boelens 2019). While RoN can promote environmental justice, it is crucial to assess whether such approaches risk reinforcing the colonial structures they aim to dismantle.

This tension challenges Western legal approaches, highlighting Indigenous societies' unique relations to nature and governance. For many Amazonian and Caribbean peoples, laws are created by spiritual entities, not humans (Silva and Calle, 2025). Their legal systems stem from origin stories and natural signs, tied to specific landscapes. Unlike modern, abstract law, these norms are place-based and spiritually grounded. Rivers, forests, animals, and plants have their own spiritual owners with whom coexistence must be negotiated. Imposing Western legal models risks erasing these localized and nuanced interpretations of rights. Whereas some Indigenous groups draft laws to bridge different worldviews and interact with State institutions, the individualization of natural entities as rights-bearing subjects by RoN approaches may generate conflicts by disregarding Indigenous systemic and relational cultural perspectives, upon which their nutrition, health, subsistence, and way of life depend. The RoN thus represent not the sole response to the social demands that motivated their creation.

Other legal arrangements, particularly those recognizing Indigenous customary law, are more inclusive and culturally attuned. Indigenous societies view nature as a living entity with inherent rights, rather than a mere resource. Their relationship with nature is based on reciprocity, which stands in stark opposition to extractivist practices. Through their ancestral knowledge and spiritual ties, Indigenous peoples are positioned as effective stewards of ecosystems. This perspective challenges capitalist notions of property, which prioritize individual ownership and the exploitation of resources. These capitalist legal constructs often conflict with Indigenous customary laws that emphasize collective stewardship and reciprocal obligations. By recognizing the rights of nature alongside human rights, the legal approach seeks to challenge extractivist models and promote normative systems that reflect relational ways of living. Although the approach aligns with sustainability discourses, it also advocates for a reconceptualization of dominant models of sustainability, incorporating Indigenous ecological knowledge and governance systems.

5.5 Conclusions

In conclusion, the recognition of RoN as a legal development represents an important response to contemporary environmental crises. While granting legal personhood to nature brings with it a potential shift in legal paradigms, its transformative capacity is shaped by broader legal, epistemological and power structures, some of which remain influenced by capitalist modernity. This, however, is not a uniform reality, as certain legal regimes – such as biodiversity protection laws – operate under distinctly different logics. These environmental conservation and biodiversity protection norms are situated within power relations that position them in a diametrically opposed direction to capital production mechanisms, creating a complex field of legal and economic contestation. As a result, legal, economic, and social systems maintain a form of objectification and commodification of nature, reinforcing practices that drive environmental degradation. A fundamental shift toward biocentric or ecocentric worldviews is therefore necessary to address the root causes of these crises.

This chapter has explored the "biocultural approach" and Indigenous legal systems as alternatives to dominant Western epistemologies, advocating for a relational ontological model of human–nature interaction. Biocultural rights offer a compelling alternative paradigm, notably by accommodating Indigenous sovereignty, cultural diversity, and environmental protection, and by recognizing the intrinsic connection between biodiversity and Indigenous cultural practices. These rights highlight the critical role of Indigenous knowledge systems and community stewardship, offering a corrective to the limitations of Western conservation models. Likewise, Indigenous legal systems, rooted in historical resistance to colonialism, present normative orders based on reciprocal relationships between people and nature. Far from being a mere set of rules, these systems embody holistic philosophies of life. In some Latin American States, their integration into State legal systems has challenged extractive capitalist logics by promoting principles of reciprocity and fostering a symbiotic relationship with the environment. However, this approach is not uniform across the region, as legal recognition and implementation vary significantly between domestic contexts.

Ultimately, addressing global environmental challenges requires accommodating diverse normative systems, particularly those of Indigenous peoples. While RoN represents a significant legal development, Indigenous legal traditions – grounded in reciprocity, stewardship, and the inseparability of humans and nature – stand as robust normative orders in their own right, introducing perspectives that can also complement existing legal models. By valuing Indigenous knowledge, cultural practices, and spiritual connections to the land, a more inclusive and culturally sensitive approach to environmental protection can be achieved – one that promotes not only ecological sustainability but also justice for Indigenous peoples. In this way, the integration of biocultural perspectives and legal pluralism represents a pathway toward genuine sustainability and ecological justice.

References

Abate, R. (2020). *Climate Change and the Voiceless: Protecting Future Generations, Wildlife, and Natural Resources*. Cambridge University Press.

Acosta, A. (2012). La Naturaleza con Derechos: Una propuesta para un cambio civilizatorio. Available at: www.garn.org/wp-content/uploads/2021/09/Acosta_DDN_2012.pdf.

Anquet, R. & Girard, F. (2022). Biocultural Community Protocols and the Ethic of Stewardship: The Sovereign Stewards of Biodiversity, in Girard, F., Hall, I., & Frison, C. (eds.), *Biocultural Rights, Indigenous Peoples and Local Communities: Protecting Culture and the Environment* (pp. 271–313). Routledge.

Assies, W. (2003). Territorialidad, Indianidad y Desarrollo: las cuentas pendientes, in *Tercera Semana de la Cooperación y de la Solidaridad Internacionales*. Tolosa.

Bakker, K. (2007). The "Commons" versus the "Commodity". *Antipode* 39(3), 430–455.

Bavikatte, K. & Bennett, T. (2015). Community Stewardship: The Foundation of Biocultural Rights. *Journal of Human Rights and the Environment* 6(1), 7–29.

Bebbington, A. (2011). Extractive Industries, Socio-environmental Conflicts and Political Economic Transformations in Andean America, in Bebbington, A. (ed.), *Social Conflict, Economic Development and the Extractive Industry: Evidence from South America* (pp. 3–26). Routledge. https://doi.org/10.4324/9780203639030.

Blaser, M. (2019). Reflexiones sobre la ontología política de los conflictos medioambientales, in Tobar, J. (ed.), *Diversidad epistémica y pensamiento crítico* (pp. 197–214). Universidad del Cauca.

Bocarejo, D. & Ojeda, D. (2016). Violence and Conservation: Beyond Unintended Consequences and Unfortunate Coincidences. *Geoforum* 69, 176–183.

Bondia, D. (2013). La reivindicación de los derechos humanos emergentes bioculturales: Los logros del Protocolo de Nagoya, in Pons, X. (ed.), *Alimentación y Derecho Internacional. Normas, instituciones y procesos* (pp. 1–22). Marcial Pons.

Boyd, D. (2017). *Rights of Nature: A Legal Revolution that Could Save the World.* ECW Press.

Brunet, P. (2024). ¿Son los derechos bioculturales el fundamento de una relación responsable entre los seres humanos y la naturaleza? *Revista de Estudios Políticos*, 204, 95–129. https://doi.org/10.18042/cepc/rep.204.03.

Burdon, P. (2011). Earth Rights: The Theory. *UICN Academy of Environmental Law e-Journal Issue*, no. 1: 1–12.

Burdon, P. (2012). A Theory of Earth Jurisprudence. *Australian Journal of Legal Philosophy* 37, 28–60.

Calle, L. (2023–2024). Fieldnotes: Indigenous Ancestral Territories Project. Anthropological fieldnotes, Orinoquía region, Colombia.

Clavijo-Ospina, F. (2020). Una revolución llamada derechos de la naturaleza / A Rights Revolution for Nature, in Castro, J. & Robayo, C. (eds.), *Emergencia climática: Prospectiva 2030 – XXI Jornadas de Derecho Constitucional.* Universidad Externado.

Charpleix, L. (2018). The Whanganui River as Te Awa Tupua: Place-based Law in a Legally Pluralistic Society. *The Geographical Journal* 184(1), 19–30. https://doi.org/10.1111/geoj.12238.

Coronil, F. (2000). Naturaleza del poscolonialismo: del eurocentrismo al globocentrismo, in *La colonialidad del saber: eurocentrismo y ciencias sociales. Perspectivas latinoamericanas.* CLACSO.

Cullinan, C. (2011). *Wild Law: A Manifesto for Earth Justice.* Chelsea Green Publishing.

Descola, P. (2012). *Más allá de la naturaleza y la cultura.* Amarrortu Editores.

Duchesne, J. (2015). *Caribe, Caribana: cosmografías literarias.* Ediciones Callejón.

Duchesne, J. (2019). La cosmopolítica como ampliación de la ecología, in Tobar, J. (ed.), *Diversidad epistémica y pensamiento crítico* (pp. 215–232). Editorial Universidad del Cauca.

Ekblom, A., Shoemaker, A., Gillson, L., Lane, P., & Lindholm, K. (2019). Conservation through Biocultural Heritage – Examples from Sub-Saharan Africa. *Land* 8(1), 5.

Escobar, A. (1995). El desarrollo sostenible. Diálogo de discursos. *Ecología política* 9(1), 7–25.

Escobar, A. (2014). *La invención del Desarrollo* (2nd ed.). Translated by D. Ochoa. Universidad del Cauca.

Escobar, A. (2015). Territorios de diferencia: la ontología política de los "derechos al territorio". *Cuadernos de Antropología Social* 41, 25–38.

Escobar, A. (2022). Ambiente, bienes públicos y cambio climático', diálogo magistral en la 9ª Conferencia Latinoamericana y Caribeña de Ciencias Sociales. In *Tramas de las desigualdades en América Latina y el Caribe. Saberes, luchas y transformaciones*. CLACSO.

Espinosa, M. (2015). Cambio Climático: las contradicciones del capitalismo contemporáneo en la producción de maíz en México. *Polis, Revista Latinoamericana* 14(40), 351–376.

Espinosa, C. (2019). Interpretive Affinities: The Constitutionalization of Rights of Nature, Pacha Mama, in Ecuador. *Journal of Environmental Policy & Planning* 21(5), 608–622.

García, M. (ed.). (2020) *Reconocimiento de la naturaleza y de sus componentes como sujetos de derechos*. Universidad Externado de Colombia. https://publicaciones.uexternado.edu.co/gpd-reconocimiento-de-la-naturaleza-y-de-sus-componentes-como-sujetos-de-derechos.html.

García, M., López Pushaina, M., Peláez Ortiz, C., Ipuana, R., Sierra Frías, E., Sierra Frías, C., Sierra Frías, L., Arregocés, E.E., Arregocés Pérez, S. S., Socarrás Ipuana, L. M., Socarrás, M. Jr., López Pushaina, A., Ipuana, I., & González Paz, C. J. (2022). *Minería a gran escala y Derechos Humanos*. CINEP.

Gabbert, W. (2003). La interacción entre derecho nacional y derecho consuetudinario en América Latina, in Pérez Galán, B. & Díetz, G. (eds.), *Globalización, resistencia y negociación en América Latina* (pp. 127–139). Los Libros de la Catarata.

Gavin, M., McCarter, J., Mead, A., Berkes, F., Stepp, J., Peterson, D., & Tang, R. (2015). Defining Biocultural Approaches to Conservation. *Trends in Ecology & Evolution* 30(3), 140–145.

Gómez, H. (2015). *Justicias indígenas de Colombia : reflexiones para un debate cultural, jurídico, político: pueblos Kogui, Arhuaco, Wiwa, Kankuamo, Nasa, Misak, Yanacona y Camëntsá*. Consejo Superior de la Judicatura.

González-Morales, V. (2023). Derechos bioculturales: perspectiva filosófica. *Naturaleza y Sociedad. Desafíos Medioambientales* 5, 117–142. https://doi.org/10.53010/nys5.06.

González-Serrano, M. X. (2025). Rights of Nature, an Ornamental Legal Framework: Water Extractivism and Backbone Rivers with Rights in Colombia. *The Journal of Peasant Studies* 52(2), 322–242. https://doi.org/10.1080/03066150.2024.2349228.

Gudynas, E. (2011). Los derechos de la naturaleza en serio, in Acosta, A. & Martínez, E. (comps.), *La naturaleza con Derechos. De la filosofía a la política* (pp. 239–286). AbyaYala y Universidad Politécnica Salesiana.

Gudynas, E. (2015). *Derechos de la naturaleza: Ética biocéntrica y políticas ambientales*. Tinta Limón.

Guzmán, L. & Ubajoa J. (2020). La personalidad jurídica de la naturaleza y de sus elementos versus el deber constitucional de proteger el medio ambiente, in del Pilar García Pachón, M. (ed.), *Reconocimiento de la Naturaleza y sus Componentes como Sujetos de Derechos*. Universidad Externado de Colombia.

Hale, C. R. (2020). Using and Refusing the Law: Indigenous Struggles and Legal Strategies after Neoliberal Multiculturalism. *American Anthropologist*, 122(3), 618–631.

Harvey, D. (2003). *The New Imperialism*. Oxford University Press.

Harvey, D. (2005). *A Brief History of Neoliberalism*. Oxford University Press.

Herrera, M. (2007). *Ordenar para controlar. Ordenamiento espacial y control político en las llanuras del Caribe y en el Andes centrales Neogranadinos, Siglo XVIII*. CESO-ICANH-La Carreta Editores.

Hettler, B. & Plotkin, M. (2019). *Los Viajes Amazónicos de Richard Evans Schultes*. ACT – Banco de la República.

ICANH. (2017). Informe: *Justicias indígenas en Colombia y los desafíos de coordinación con la justicia ordinaria. Análisis comparativo de los conceptos presentados al Consejo Superior de la Judicatura por el ICANH*. ICANH.

ICANH. (2023). *Bonos de Carbono y pueblos indígenas de la Amazonia colombiana. Respuesta del ICANH a la Corte Constitucional Auto de Decreto y práctica de pruebas del 2 de junio de 2023*. ICANH.

Kauffman, C. M. & Martin, P. L. (2018). Constructing Rights of Nature Norms in the US, Ecuador, and New Zealand. *Global Environmental Politics*, 18(4), 43–62.

Knox, J. H. (2017). *Framework Principles on Human Rights and the Environment*. United Nations OHCHR.

Kyoto Protocol (1998). Protocol to the United Nations Framework Convention on Climate Change, Kyoto, December 11, 1997. Available at: https://bit.ly/3B20m0s.

Lander, E. (2000). *La colonialidad del saber: eurocentrismo y ciencias sociales. Perspectivas latinoamericanas*. CLACSO.

Lander, E. & Arconada, S. (2020). *Crisis civilizatoria: experiencias de los gobiernos progresistas y debates en la izquierda latinoamericana*. FLACSO Ecuador.

Lang, M., Bringel, B., & Manahan, M. A. (2023). Introducción. Transiciones lucrativas, colonialismo verde y caminos hacia una justicia ecosocial transformadora, in Lang, M., Bringel, B., & Manahan, M. A. (eds.), *Más allá del colonialismo verde: justicia global y geopolítica de las transiciones ecosociales* (pp. 15–48). CLACSO.

Laszlo, E. & Combs, A. (eds.) (2011). *Thomas Berry, Dreamer of the Earth: The Spiritual Ecology of the Father of Environmentalism*. Inner Traditions.

Latouche, S. (2008). *La apuesta por el decrecimiento: ¿Cómo salir del imaginario dominante?* Icaria Editorial. Colección Antrazyt, no. 273.

Maffi, L. & Woodley, E. (2010). *Biocultural Diversity Conservation. A Global Sourcebook*. Earthscan.

Martínez-Alier, J. (2002). *The Environmentalism of the Poor: A Study of Ecological Conflicts and Valuation*. Edward Elgar.

Melo-Ascencio, D. A. (2024). A Postcolonial Marxist Critique of the River-as-Subject: Situating the Atrato River in Its Development Aporias. *Antipode*, 56(5), 1754–1774. https://doi.org/10.1111/anti.13052.

Nash, J. (1993). The Case for Biotic Rights. *Yale Journal of International Law* 18(1), 235–249.

Olaya, C., Daza Niño, N., & Annear Camero, C. (2022). *¿Carne deforestadora? Cuellos de botella en el control de las cadenas de suministro de carne bovina en Colombia*. Editorial Dejusticia.

Olmo, G. (2024). Por qué Ecuador sigue explotando petróleo en el Parque Yasuní un año después del histórico referendo en el que se votó a favor de prohibirlo. BBC. 26 de septiembre. www.bbc.com/mundo/articles/cvgw4y122z4o.

Pico, J. (2019). El papel de los movimientos sociales en la adjudicación de derechos de la naturaleza y su difusión internacional (2008–2019). Maestría en Ciencia Política, Universidad de los Andes.

Piketty, T. (2014). *Capital in the Twenty-First Century*. Harvard University Press.

Pineda, R. (2000). *Holocausto en el Amazonas: una historia social de la Casa Arana*. Planeta.

Portela, H. & Sanabria O. (2019). Los estudios bioculturales en la era del antropoceno. Simposio. In *Congreso Colombiano de Antropología*. ICESI.

Procuraduría General de la Nación. (2016). *La Guajira: pueblo Wayúu, con hambre de dignidad, sed de justicia y otras necesidades insatisfechas*. PNG.

Quijano, A. (2014). Colonialidad del poder, eurocentrismo y América Latina, in *Cuestiones y horizontes: de la dependencia histórico-estructural a la colonialidad/descolonialidad del poder* (pp. 337–377). CLACSO.

Regan, T. (2004). *The Case for Animal Rights*. University of California Press.

Reyes, A. (2018). El fin de la esclavitud cauchera en el Amazonas. *El Espectador* 30 November.

Reyes-García, V., & Martí, S. (2017). Indigenous Peoples' Knowledge and Sustainable Development. *Annual Review of Environment and Resources* 42, 173–197.

Rostow, W. (1960). *The Stages of Economic Growth: A Non-Communist Manifesto*. Cambridge University Press.

Ruíz, D. & Del Cairo, C. (2016). Los debates del giro ontológico en torno al naturalismo moderno. *Revista de Estudios Sociales*, 1(55), 193–204.

Sajeva, G. (2022). The Legal Framework Behind Biocultural Rights: An Analysis of Their Pros and Cons for Indigenous Peoples and for Local Communities, in Girard, F., Hall, I., & Frison, C. (eds.), *Biocultural Rights, Indigenous Peoples and Local Communities: Protecting Culture and the Environment* (pp. 165–181). Routledge.

Sarayaku (2018). Kawsak Sacha: El Bosque Viviente. Propuesta del Pueblo Originario Kichwa de Sarayaku para la protección de la vida. https://sarayaku.org

Sánchez, Á., Morales, P., & González, V. (2021). *Derechos de la Naturaleza y Derechos Bioculturales: escenarios de posibilidad ante la degradación de la naturaleza*. Centro Sociojurídico para la Defensa Territorial Siembra.

Shaquiñan – Ministerio de Ambiente (2012). Agenda Ambiental en el territorio del Nudo de la Wuaka o de los Pastos para la permanencia de la vida y la cultura – Shaquilulo. Convenio no. 054.

Silva, N. (2018–2024). Fieldnotes: The Lost Bonds – Carijona People's Ecological Knowledge in the Context of the Illicit Crop Eradication Program through Aerial Spraying with Glyphosate (PECIG). Amazon Region, Colombia.

Silva, N. (2017–2024). Fieldnotes: Impacts of the Bruno Creek Channel Diversion Project on the Fundamental Rights of the Wayúu People. Judgment T-698 of 2017 by the Constitutional Court of Colombia. Caribbean Region, Colombia.

Silva, N. (2024). Los vínculos perdidos: conocimientos del pueblo Carijona sobre la naturaleza frente al programa de erradicación de cultivos ilícitos mediante aspersiones aéreas con Glifosato PECIG. Tesis doctoral no publicada. Doctorado en Etnobiología y Estudios Bioculturales, Universidad del Cauca.

Silva, N. & Calle, L. (2025). Desafíos de diálogo intercultural en la consulta previa: el pueblo Wayuu y el desvío del arroyo Bruno en la Guajira Colombia. *Revista de Antropología Iberoamericana* 20(1), 43–65. https://doi.org/10.11156/aibr.200103.

SINCHI. (2022). *Conflictos asociados a la ejecución de proyectos REDD+ en el gran resguardo del Vaupés*. SINCHI.

Singer, P. & Cavalieri, P. (1993). *The Great Ape Project: Equality Beyond Humanity*. St. Martin's Press.

Spivak, G. C. (1988). Can the Subaltern Speak?, in Nelson, C. & Grossberg, L. (eds.), *Marxism and the Interpretation of Culture* (pp. 271–313). University of Illinois Press.

Stoessel, S. & Scarpacci, M. (2021). Disputas en torno al desarrollo y el territorio: el caso de Yasuní-ITT durante el Ecuador de la Revolución Ciudadana. *Territorios*, 45, 1–21. https://doi.org/10.12804/revistas.urosario.edu.co/territorios/a.8382.

Stone, C. (1972). Should Trees Have Standing? – Towards Legal Rights for Natural Objects. *Southern California Law Review*, 42, 450–501.

Svampa, M. (2019). *Las fronteras del neoextractivismo en América Latina. Conflictos socioambientales, giro ecoterritorial y nuevas dependencias.* CALAS.

Tamayo-Álvarez, R. (2023). Los derechos de la naturaleza y el principio del buen vivir como un giro decolonial en la gobernanza ambiental internacional. *Revista Derecho del Estado*, 54, 19–54.

Tetreault, D., Ochoa, H., & Hernández, E. (2013). *Conflictos socioambientales y alternativas de la sociedad civil.* ITESO.

Thornton, S., Koyo, K., Dudin, Y., Harrison, M., Page, S., & Upton, C. (2020). Towards Biocultural Approaches to Peatland Conservation: The Case for Fish and Livelihoods in Indonesia. *Environmental Science and Policy* 114, 341–351.

Toledo, V. (2002). Ethnoecology: A Conceptual Framework for the Study of Indigenous Knowledge of Nature, in Stepp, J. R., Wyndham, F. S., & Zarger, R. K. (eds.), *Ethnobiology and Biocultural Diversity. Proceedings of the 7th International Congress of Ethnobiology, Athens, Georgia, USA, October 2000* (pp. 511–522). International Society for Ethnobiology.

Toledo, V. & Barrera, N. (2008). *La memoria biocultural: la importancia ecológica de las sabidurías tradicionales.* Icaria editorial.

Ulloa, A. (2004). *La construcción del nativo ecológico. Complejidades, paradojas y dilemas de la relación entre los movimientos indígenas y el ambientalismo en Colombia.* ICANH.

UNESCO. (n.d.). *Yasuní Biosphere Reserve, Ecuador.* UNESCO Man and the Biosphere Programme. Available at https://en.unesco.org/biosphere/lac/yasuni.

United Nations (2016). Harmony with Nature: Note by the Secretary-General (1 August). UN Doc A/71/266.

Valladares, C. & Boelens, R. (2019). Mining for Mother Earth: Governmentalities, Sacred Waters and Nature Rights in Ecuador. *Geoforum* 100, 68–79.

Vargas, B. & Ariza, R. (2019). Liberación de la Madre Tierra: Resistencia del pueblo nasa en el Norte del Cauca. *Estudios Socio-Jurídicos* 22(1), 203–231. https://doi.org/10.12804/revistas.urosario.edu.co/sociojuridicos/a.7641.

Viaene, L. (2024). La moda de los derechos de la naturaleza: consideraciones críticas. *Revista de Estudios Políticos* 204, 299–326. https://doi.org/10.18042/cepc/rep.204.10.

PART III

Decolonizing the Law

What Place for (Transformative) Legal Pluralism?

6 Mapuche Law (*Az Mapu*), Legal Pluralism, and Transmodernity

Possibilities and Limitations of Contextual Environmental Justice

Ricardo Salas Astrain and Cristian Pacheco Huaiquifil

6.1 Problematization and Study Context

In studies of Indigenous environmental law, concepts such as Indigenous customary law, the law of Indigenous peoples, and Mapuche own law, *az mapu* (Antona 2014; Cloud 2012; Melin et al. 2016), are frequently used to denote a set of norms and values that do not correspond to the meanings and symbolic representations attributed to law in the West, which has prevailed in the legal systems of countries emerging since the nineteenth century. These concepts clearly refer to a Mapuche ontological worldview, which function as a device that challenges and contradicts the traditions of hegemonic liberal law and its monocultural Western tradition (Yrigoyen Fajardo 2017). The commonly used concept of law invites critical reflection from a decolonial perspective that is consistent with the objectives of this study. In this way, we will highlight multiple theoretical frameworks related to the rights of nature and the issue of environmental justice (Gudynas 2015; Leff 2021a), as well as the challenges of transmodernity (Dussel 2003). We will consider studies by Mapuche intellectuals that account for the conflictive colonial situations currently affecting the territories of Wallmapu (Mapuche Indigenous territories in Chile and Argentina) and will refer to some concrete experiences.

Mapuche communities in Wallmapu and throughout Abya Yala (Indigenous America) are experiencing socioenvironmental conflicts with large multinational corporations (Reding and Salas 2024; Svampa 2017), which are aggravated by the impact of mega-fires and the desertification of territories. The forestry, mining, and oil exploitation of the Amazon, for example, creates socioenvironmental disasters that primarily affect Indigenous peoples by destroying natural ecosystems. In Indigenous America, social, cultural, and economic conflicts are intensifying between government-led development projects and Indigenous peoples, who are among the most impoverished and vulnerable sectors of society. This global crisis has been exacerbated by the magnitude of global climate change and the dominance of a neoliberal extractivist development model (Bachmann and Navarro 2021).

In this context, the methodology of this study was developed through a documentary and bibliographic review concerning Indigenous Peoples. The main objective is to triangulate and interconnect the information gathered to subsequently analyze it in relation to fieldwork based on the demands of the Mapuche communities and social movement, while maintaining alignment with the study's principal goals. This work is not limited to theoretical documentary research; rather, it is an ethical–political endeavor aimed at developing a critical and pluralistic conception of law that accounts for the complex situation of interethnic territories (Salas 2022). It is not, therefore, about the creation of knowledge from the outside, by researchers the sociolegal problems of Indigenous Peoples, but rather a form of legal thinking that is affectively committed, which embraces the resistance struggles of Indigenous peoples and is attuned to the sustained rise in Mapuche demands across Wallmapu (Antona 2014; Le Bonniec and Salas 2015) and in other territories. It also critically engages the tragedy of the selective assassination of dozens of environmental and Indigenous leaders in the interethnic territories of America. In Abya Yala, we highlight, for example, the role assumed by the Aymara scholar Silvia Rivera in the defense of human rights and the rights of Indigenous Peoples (Rivera 1997). Through her theoretical and practical activist work within universities, and particularly beyond them, she has built visible sociopolitical commitments with vulnerable communities. She has become a key reference and a source of inspiration for women, feminists, sexual dissidents, academics, Indigenous and non-Indigenous activists, and for social movements more broadly. Similarly, the feminist academic Rita Segato has made significant contributions through her intellectual and practical efforts to promote women's rights and address the effects of patriarchy in contemporary society.

6.2 Decoloniality: Theoretical Approaches

In order to address the issue of the environmental rights of the Mapuche people, situated within the sociopolitical processes of global capital, it is necessary to develop a new theoretical framework that responds to the emerging and complex problems of planetary degradation in an era where the current challenges of capitalism place increasing strain on global dynamics (Antona 2014; Richards 2016). It is well understood that different forms of capitalism exist today on a global scale and should not be conflated. However, in all cases, it is essential to assess how these systems shape their relationships with Indigenous populations, and, above all, to determine how such economic models impact territories – whether through the specific consequences of forced integration into national economies or the systematic and arbitrary devastation of ecosystems. Decolonial studies by scholars such as Claudia Briones, Enrique Dussel, Maristela Svampa, Walter Mignolo, Rita Segato, Boaventura De Sousa Santos, Silvia Rivera Cusicanqui, Arturo Escobar, Enrique Leff, Judith Butler, and Philippe Descola, among others, demonstrate how systematic destruction of vital human and nonhuman ecosystems (plants, rivers, rocks, minerals, oceans, air, hills, volcanoes, animals, insects, water, spirits, among other beings of nature) have disastrous results for life on the planet. In this section, we position *az mapu* as a legal system and explore how it dialogues with other sources of law, in such a way that decoloniality helps to clarify environmental issues. This approach reveals how Indigenous law can integrate an Indigenous perspective that aligns more closely with environmental challenges and goals, including those within Western ontologies and epistemologies. It stirs the conscience of members of both Indigenous and non-Indigenous cultures, compelling us to critically rethink the unsustainable project of technoscientific "civilization" constructed at a global level and arbitrarily imposed on Indigenous territories (Mignolo and Walsh 2018). This project disregarded and denied the corporeal, epistemic, and ontological pre-existence of Indigenous peoples and, consequently, their cultural, social, religious, healing, educational, political, economic, ecological, and normative frameworks, where part of Indigenous customary law was neutralized and rendered invisible, as occurred in the Mapuche case with *az mapu* or Mapuche law in Wallmapu.

We thus present a set of theoretical and practical issues that afflict hegemonic societies, and the communities and individuals belonging to Indigenous peoples. This calls for the adoption of a transmodern lens and one of pluralistic dialogue that questions the familiar forms of radical capitalism in interethnic territories and, in turn, challenges dominant legal monism. The situation concerning the rights of Indigenous Peoples cannot simply be coupled with Western legal concepts to develop counterhegemonic responses within the framework of positive law to which they are coercively subjected. The concept of "legal pluralism" helps move us in this direction, as it "consists in recognizing the existence of more than one legal system within the same geopolitical space (the State) [a legal device that] does not challenge the unity of law, provided that mechanisms for coordination between Indigenous and ordinary justice are established" (De Sousa Santos and Grijalba Jiménez 2012: 21). As Raquel Yrigoyen Fajardo points out, a model of legal pluralism that meaningfully incorporates Indigenous rights is characterized by the following underlying assumptions: first, it is based on the principle of the equal dignity of peoples and cultures; second, it entails processes of decolonizing the relations of superiority/inferiority between peoples and cultures, and between the State and Indigenous peoples; third, it assumes that peoples have "control over their ways of life and institutions," as recognized by ILO Convention 169; and fourth, regarding the competencies of Indigenous jurisdiction, these are a function of their own law and social and cultural needs, and therefore cannot have neocolonial limits that are not even included in the Constitution or constitutional law.

The development and productivity of decolonial studies are reflected in a range of issues rooted in lived worlds and in the struggles of ethnic and social movements. In particular, we observe that in the process of Indigenous peoples' decolonization struggles, specific features emerge that underscore the relevance we assign to sociohistorical contexts in rethinking sociocultural and economic interactions and frictions, beyond dominant economic paradigms.

In relation to environmental issues, we are now a different global stage, where the political problem of economic power becomes much more explicit, bringing into play the delimitation of rights safeguarded within investment projects, where new sociocultural and environmental interactions converge (Salas 2019). Consequently, the relationship between economy, politics, and Indigenous rights requires reassessment through a theory of recognition that is also applied to understanding the dynamics of the facticity of power and environmental rights. In particular, it is necessary to acknowledge the experiences of injustice of Indigenous peoples and the ecological niches of the territories, which are hinted at in expressions such as "cognitive injustice," "epistemic violence," and "epistemicide." These concepts correspond to efforts aimed at fostering a potential dialogue of knowledges, a justice among knowledges, to safeguard nature in all its dimensions (De Sousa Santos and Méndez 2017; Leff 2021b). Such categories invite us to embrace the pluriform gestation of knowledges among peoples and cultures, and to deepen the critique of environmental sciences that adhere to the guidelines of a "hegemonic science" (Fornet-Betancourt 2017). Moreover, the proposed pursuit of justice among knowledges has, in a sense, become embedded within the scholarly foundation of contemporary environmental studies.

As Price (2023) points out, "epistemicide" refers to the dominance of scientific knowledge and the suppression, or erasure, of other forms of knowledge. This scientific hegemony and the privileging of a single epistemology have a long history. It began in a structural and systematic way in the seventeenth century, although its roots took hold earlier. Nonetheless, it did not achieve the effects anticipated by elites and missionaries, as the traditional knowledges of ancestral peoples were not entirely extinguished.

The issue of epistemicide raised here brings about two central questions for this work: (1) what are the political implications of this debate on universal science and communitarian cultural knowledges for revisiting a universalist and hegemonic vision of Indigenous science that fails to account for the growing deterioration of living ecosystems?; and (2) what is the ethical–political significance of the resistance struggles led by Indigenous peoples, as they insist on ways of relating to living beings that allow for the preservation of the sustainability of territories and support the preservation of the planet for future generations? It is along this path that we recognize the value of Mapuche justice, or *az mapu*. Indigenous science is increasingly centered in epistemic dialogues, as it is now acknowledged to contain patterns allowing for its systematic elaboration. Ancestral knowledges such as Mapun Kimün and Mapuche Rakizuam embody research questions, specific methodologies, and forms of internal validation within the culture.

6.3 The Proposal of Transmodernity

This section is based on the work of the liberation philosopher E. Dussel, widely recognized for his contribution to understanding the sociopolitical and cultural processes experienced by peoples in achieving their sociopolitical and cultural emancipation (Dussel 2012). The historical and political perspective developed by Dussel, particularly his references to 1492 as part of the process of the Invasion of America, is linked to the decolonial turn he describes in his works from the last two decades. His critique of the misnamed "Discovery of America" is central to understanding the notion of transmodernity (Erazo and López 2024). Dussel proposed a thesis on what occurred in 1492 from a world-historical perspective, a contribution that proves significant for grasping the philosophical, epistemological, and ethical–political implications of today's global environmental crises. His thesis of the concealment of the Other(s) prompts a re-examination of the other side of modernity, forged against the newly "discovered" peoples and marked by structural imposition of economic, political, and cultural domination that are part of that "dark" side of modernity. Dussel's decolonial thought provides clarity regarding the complex horizons of the current epistemic moment concerning the rights of nature, particularly in the face of the emergence of Western scientific reason as the epistemic guarantor of an abstract universality, defining the political and legal process that, to this day, underpins technoscientific action. This scientistic dominance has ignored the critical forms abundant in that tradition.

The modern movement defines both a political and a legal framework, bringing about an epistemic and political discussion on the emerging meanings of contextual law found in the works of J.J. Faundes and S. Ramírez. Thus far, modern law has been justified by its references to a monadic vision, expressed in individual rights, which overlooks the communitarian elements embedded in the sociocultural parameters of Indigenous peoples. This legal approach is understood as a way of rethinking rights through the protagonism of the communities themselves, taking shape in tension with the legal structures inherited from Ibero-colonial domination. "Contextual law" refers to the recognition of peoples' rights through an interpretation and application of the law that considers the social, historical, and cultural context in which it develops. This implies understanding legal norms not only from a formal perspective, but also taking into account social realities, people's needs, and the power dynamics that influence how the law is applied (Faundes and Ramírez 2020). This contextual turn in law opens up possibilities for a legal pluralism that articulates a society's own normative frameworks along with those of other societies. It can then be considered that "Legal pluralism refers to the existence of multiple normative or legal systems, coexisting in the same social and political space. This means that law is not only that which emanates from the State, but also that other normative sources may also exist, such as the uses and customs of Indigenous peoples, or community norms, which are recognized and implemented by social groups" (authorized interpretation).

Furthermore, this decolonial thinking compels us to propose a political–legal thought that confronts the enormous difficulties of social coexistence and the excesses of interactions between humans and nonhumans, demanding that we define perspectives for the new horizon of the Mapuche *az mapu* in relation to the phenomena of life on an exhausted planet.

In the Düsselian context, transmodernity is defined as follows:

> Transmodernity, from its genesis, is conceived as a global meta-narrative of liberation and a realisable planetary pluriverse. (Dussel 1992)

To clearly define the transmodern proposal and bring it into closer alignment with the concrete practices of Indigenous peoples, in search of its material viability, Dussel (2017) outlines six diachronic stages. These stages are: the relationship between modernity and coloniality, the emergence of awareness of modern/capitalist structures of domination, the archaeological reconstruction of cultural and popular memory, the vital flourishing of postcolonial cultures, and the consolidation of the transmodern project itself (another age of world/action). Dussel contends that modernity is not the outcome of a purportedly autopoietic supremacy or an exclusively European achievement, but rather the result of the fortuitous (and unplanned) invasion of 1492. Therefore, modernity emerges from the colonization of other territories (across the Americas), the negation of (analogical) alterity, and the imposition of a univocal worldview (Erazo and López 2024). For Dussel, Eurocentric modernity amounts to the erasure or disregard of an earlier or Hispanic modernity – an erasure compounded by the reductionism produced by the rationalization and mathematization of life ushered in by Descartes (Dussel 1993). This, in turn, has led to the current crisis of instrumental reason, now manifested in technoscience. These dangers will remain unresolved so long as exteriority continues to be denied and the fundamental ethical (and philosophical) questions of the fifteenth and sixteenth centuries are left unaddressed: "What right does the European have to occupy, dominate, and administer the recently discovered cultures, militarily conquered, and now colonized cultures?" (Dussel 1998: 59).

Stated schematically, modernity presupposes coloniality, as it is inaugurated in 1492 with Europe's turn toward the Atlantic (in search of a connection with the East) and the unexpected appearance of the Americas. Modernity is sustained by the coloniality of power, as it entails the erasure of the Other, the denial of alterity, and the subsumption and domination of the cultures and Indigenous peoples of the "New Continent" – as well as the subsequent enslavement of African men and women. Modernity is thus neocolonialism and capitalism; it is slavery and the extraction of wealth, the theft of knowledge and technologies, the exploitation of labor, and the plundering of food from the colonies and neocolonies (Dussel 2017).

On the other hand, within this theoretical framework, it is crucial to understand intercultural dialogue as a utopian horizon of encounter and mutual learning, a symmetrical form of communication that enables engagement with other languages and cultures, other values and principles, and alternative economies and political systems, beyond the Western paradigm (although not excluding it). Accordingly, it must unfold in all possible directions: South–South, South–North, North–North. Each of these is briefly described below (Dallmayr 2023).

The affirmation of disdained exteriority: This initial stage alludes to the two previously outlined hypotheses and can be understood as the reconstruction of the legacy and value of diverse peoples or the strengthening of identity.

Critique or self-critique of one's own traditions: The prior affirmation of self-worth must pass through the desubstantialization of a culture, a process that results from critique grounded both in the assumptions of one's own culture and in those of others (including modernity).

Strategies of resistance: Dussel (2003) begins this section by asserting that "to resist, one must mature" (p. 22). Resistance, therefore, must have a foundation. One cannot fall into mere, insubstantial reaction, or blind and unfounded activism. Cultural resistance must stem from critical and self-critical consciousness, although in the case of Indigenous peoples, we maintain that cultural resistance constitutes a right in itself, in light of their historical struggles and demands for justice (Dussel 2007).

Finally, the strategy of liberatory growth: This strategy involves a translation or synthesis that enables cross-fertilization of knowledge, upon which the strategy of liberating growth is designed. This stage integrates the four preceding phases and opens up the idea of a broader liberation project. Appearing in Dussel (2003, 2006, and 2012), this point becomes the penultimate diachronic stage for understanding transmodernity in Dussel (2017).

From this point on, the definition of transmodernity becomes clearer. Since its inception (Dussel 1992), transmodernity has essentially been conceived as a future-oriented project, a global metanarrative of liberation. The prefix "trans," which once indicated the outside, now points to what comes *after* modernity – its overcoming. In this sense, transmodernity addresses postcolonial concerns that must be specified (Salas 2016).

On the other hand, the concept of pluriverse highlights the existence of other realities. As articulated by Arturo Escobar (2018: 29):

(a) The Pluriverse is grounded in the concept of diversity within the entire terrestrial system, a multiplicity of worlds and peoples coexisting on the planet.
(b) The Pluriverse also signifies the incessant nature of life, its constant flow and transformation, which arises from the interdependence of all aspects of living due to the interdependence of all aspects of living systems.

(c) The Pluriverse has no beginning or end, only continuous ebbs and flows. This is the natural state. Human intervention that obstructs or destroys this self-organizing dynamic is a source of much suffering and instability.
(d) The concept of the Pluriverse compels us to think in terms of multiple possible worlds, as well as the circularity of life, a perpetual flow, and the "radical interdependence" of all living beings.

Within this conceptual framework, we maintain that transmodernity and the pluriverse, although distinct, intersect in their analyses of ontological and epistemological dimensions shaped by radical differences. These differences crystallize historical suffering and trauma produced by hegemonic, scientific, and capitalist thought in Abya Yala, while also opening up possibilities for relational forms of survival from, rooted in and with nature, and grounded in the recognition of the rights of Indigenous peoples and of *ixofijmogen* (all that lives).

6.4 E-Communitarism and Legal Pluralism in Chile in the Era of Global Capital

Within a framework aligned with Dussel's proposal, the e-communitarian perspective of the Uruguayan–Brazilian philosopher Sirio López Velasco (De la Fuente and Salas 2021) helps deepen our understanding of the situation faced by Indigenous peoples across the Americas. According to López, with regard to the lack of respect for nature, what is happening to the Mapuche people does not radically differ from what occurs in other interethnic territories in the Americas. The Mapuche territory has lived, suffered, and resisted the consequences of being located in a country that, since the beginning of the Military Government in 1973, has served as a laboratory of global neoliberalism. It is essential to understand the individualism that permeates the micro-, meso-, and macroeconomics of deregulated productive and distributive systems, and particularly in relation to traditional ways of life. At the same time, expressions of racism and discrimination, constructed by the nationalist imaginary of the Chilean elite, remain present in Chilean society, disproportionately targeting disenfranchised and Indigenous communities that organize to claim their rights (Richards 2016). This group and its belief system reject legal pluralism, as evidenced by the Chilean constituent processes over the last five years.

These conceptual engagements with legal pluralism created possibilities for the recognition and reinterpretation of the legal systems of Indigenous peoples, whose frameworks have been denied by conservative elites and often reduced to simplistic notions based solely on Indigenous beliefs, customs, and customary law. Such oversimplifications obscure the broader social, cultural, economic, and political dimensions embodied in Indigenous peoples' own concepts of justice, and these are precisely the dimensions we aim to highlight in this article concerning *az mapu*, Mapuche law. Our analysis centers on explaining the concepts *kimün*, *mapun*, *inatuzugun*, *as mogen*, *ixofij mogen*, *mapun kimün*, and *mapun rakizuam* in relation to the framework of e-communitarism.

Legal pluralism was intensely debated in Chile during the constitutional process that took place between 2019 and 2023. Through that process, albeit in a somewhat biased manner, its scope and limitations were examined in a complex sociopolitical context. Despite the presence of Indigenous Peoples and human rights defenders, this public discourse was dominated by racist, neoliberal political forces that both directly and indirectly contributed to the systematic and categorical rejection of the concept.

Within this context, legal pluralism was caricatured by the Chilean elite and publicly portrayed as a threat to colonial and neoliberal models of Western development. Through hegemonic media outlets, it was framed as a concept radically opposed to Chile's prevailing monocultural rule of law. This rule of law, as we have pointed out, was de-facto reconstructed by the military regime in 1980 through the Political Constitution of the Republic under dictator Augusto Pinochet and the Chilean and US elites, the latter having been instrumental in promoting neoliberalism throughout Latin America. In this sense, there were national and international expectations in this post-dictatorship constitutional process, resulting from the social uprising of October 18, 2019. Ideally, legal pluralism would be seen as a means to institutionalize the rights of Indigenous Peoples through the mechanics of binding participation, as set forth by the ILO 169 and the United Nations Declaration on the Rights of Indigenous Peoples. This institutionalization was tied to the right of Indigenous and Tribal Peoples to self-determination and, consequently, to Indigenous law that predates positive law and the formation of the State. Furthermore, legal pluralism would provide tools to resolve interethnic and intercultural conflicts, especially those associated with land tenure and usurpation, and the exploitation of natural resources by transnational corporations. Ultimately, legal pluralism would serve as a tangible and effective mechanism for Indigenous Peoples, migrant communities, and Afro-descendant populations.

In practical terms, however, the implementation of these rights remains permeated and constrained by ontological and epistemological disputes imposed by actors aligned with hegemonic, neocolonial, and neoliberal capitalist interests. Some of these actors would block the exercise of Indigenous Peoples' rights at any cost. This has become increasingly evident in recent years in Chile. Despite having a progressive center-left government led by President Gabriel Boric, who publicly declares respect for human rights and the rights of Indigenous Peoples, in practice, as his term nears its end, there has been little to no progress in implementing constitutional reforms or legislative changes to address the conflicts affecting southern Chile. In early May 2025, President Boric received a report from the "Peace and Understanding" commission, whose proposals should be subject to Indigenous Consultation according to ILO Convention 169.

The concept of legal pluralism could be articulated with other normative dimensions that are gaining relevance in Chile, such as: the Indigenous Law, the

Framework Law on Climate Change, the Law on Environmental Crimes, the Biodiversity Law, and the Escazú Agreement, which has emphasized the protection of environmental rights and the rights of nature defenders, among others (Valle Franco 2023).

Although the investments of multinational corporations are subject to review by environmental tribunals and the Committee of Ministers in Chile, they consider the rights of Indigenous communities in a restricted manner, as seen with the dams built by ENDESA on the BíoBío River, which led to questioning of the very Indigenous law generated by the Chilean State (Namuncura 1999). Furthermore, the macroeconomic model stretching from Mexico to Chile is primarily governed by a pattern of megaproject investments by multinational corporations (Reding and Salas 2024) in mining, forestry, and energy (dams and wind farms). These projects have had a significant impact on Indigenous communities, destabilizing the norms and rules that govern the communal relationship to economic and cultural processes (Olivé 2004). The Peruvian scholar R. Yrigoyen Fajardo has demonstrated the same concerns for the rights of the Achuar People. Mexican researcher Ana Luisa Guerrero has likewise shown how Indigenous rights are not sufficiently defended by international organizations (Guerrero 2021). Particularly in the socioenvironmental arena, the capitalist investment model directly and indirectly violates the human and environmental rights of Indigenous peoples, causing interference in their traditional and contemporary cultural practices, especially through the extractive uses of nature and the systematic denial of Indigenous ontologies and epistemologies.

To understand a significant part of the new rules and structures that define this complex intersection between the logic of dominant economic rationality and the logic derived from the traditional wisdom of the Mapuche, it is necessary to examine the frictions and conflicts, the contexts of rupture, and the possibilities for founding an autonomous project grounded in old and new rights of the Peoples of the Earth. It is within this framework that we consider the "e-communitarian"[1]

[1] E-communitarianism is a theoretical–practical philosophical proposal developed by the philosopher Sirio López Velasco. At its core, as the author himself states: "we propose that the individual changes each person can and must carry out within themselves should be combined with a collective effort (community-based, environmental, political) to transform the Way of Life throughout Nuestramérica. This must take place through struggles and transformative processes as part of an E-communitarian journey, ranging from the local to the global community – passing through regional, national (for as long as countries and States continue to exist), and continental communities – aiming to live according to the principles of E-communitarianism. From each according to his abilities and to each according to his needs, respecting ecological balances and interculturality. These include: E-communitarian Environmental Education (that challenges assumptions and is socially widespread, in both formal and non-formal settings); an ecological, community-based, and cooperative Economy (which applies, in the economic realm, the overarching guiding principle of E-communitarianism, to be outlined below); Politics by and for all (preferably based on practices of direct democracy through assemblies, plebiscites, and referendums); horizontal and symmetrical Communication (which transfers ownership and management of all media to the communities); Liberation Aesthetic (which encourages and educates everyone to create and enjoy the arts); and non-militant Atheism (which, while promoting the unity of believers and non-believers in the struggle to move beyond capitalism toward E-communitarianism, also fosters a long-term, patient dialogue to overcome

proposal put forward in the work of S. López Velasco. The territorial demands of the Mapuche people are valued because they continue to defend, to this day, their own ancestral ways of understanding their rootedness to ancestral lands and their traditional methods of production (Salas 2019). Although it has been swiftly quieted by the Chilean State, in recent decades, the Mapuche social movement has raised a strong critique of the instrumental and short-term model of multinational corporations that exploit, excessively and rapidly, the limited natural resources of the territory (Namuncura 1999).

As illustrated by the interpretative conflict regarding the dams on the BíoBío River, an issue that has sparked debate among settlers and various regional and national interest groups, the conflict between the Chilean State, society, and the Mapuche Nation has been increasingly interpreted through the lens of these competing perspectives. This is evidenced by the works of the Mapuche History Community (CHM) and articulated in the Report of the Commission for Peace and Understanding presented to the President of the Republic in May 2025. Some interpret this as an "interethnic conflict" that, by the late twentieth century, had become part of both the regional and national political agendas due to the issue of sustainable economic development. However, the contentious processes regarding development models and the recovery of Mapuche lands have been consistently neglected by Chilean authorities across successive governments since 1989. This neglect has been especially evident among the political and corporate elites based in Chile's capital, as well as among regional landowners, whose responses have tended to be defensive. Within this context, protests were criminalized, and the rights of corporate projects were unilaterally prioritized, without consideration for the economic, political, cultural, and environmental rights of Indigenous peoples (Guerrero 2021). Therefore, a conflict has existed since the 1990s regarding the type of development needed in order to appropriately align with the Mapuche identity. In recent decades, some members of the Mapuche social movement, nongovernmental organizations (NGOs), and a number of academic studies have proposed concepts to help shape these relationships, such as "development with identity," "ethnodevelopment," and the notion of "co-development." Other alternative proposals have also emerged in Ngulumapu. However, the dominant approach systematically conflicts with the rights of the Mapuche people, as it is shaped by asymmetric power relations rather than by mutual socioeconomic collaboration. In practice, this has rendered the Mapuche little more than spectators to the unilateral decisions made by Chilean elites regarding natural "resources," which, as we know, have historically been tied to Indigenous territories.

Today, the Mapuche movement no longer advocates only for recovering ancestral lands but also seeks to reconstruct and reorganize inhabited territories from an endogenous perspective. Since 1995, the issue of culture and development has

religious alienation, alongside the overcoming of secular forms of alienation that prevail under capitalism)." www.aporrea.org/internacionales/a339915.html.

remained points of contention. In Chile and other Latin American countries, political sectors on the center-right, as well as left-wing extractivist factions and corporate conglomerates, have converged in promoting a pro-market model, within which poverty alleviation policies have failed to address the increasing impoverishment of Indigenous communities. The environmental consequences of large-scale investment projects (in forestry, hydroelectricity, and mining) reveal economic gains that are not distributed equitably among the population while simultaneously having undeniably contributed to environmental degradation (Namuncura 1999). Although Indigenous peoples agree broadly with the goals of State policies to eradicate poverty (education, health, roads, etc.), they question the ways these policies are carried out, dismantling traditional cultural foundations and modes of production. This type of international investment is considered responsible for territorial, environmental, and cultural consequences as it promotes development projects and business models that do not provide relevant benefits for the inhabitants of the territory (Silva and Guerra 2017), nor do they safeguard cultural and spiritual heritage. The critical issue here is that a business-driven economic model does not respect Indigenous ways of life or their approaches to meeting basic needs, what the Mapuche community term "Good Living" (*Küme Mogen* in the Mapuche language). There is widespread awareness that the Mapuche concept of well-being is holistic and centered on a worldview of respect for all life, both human and nonhuman. Considering this, the most significant gap in current government discourse is its avoidance of a plurinational framework, which would allow for the constitutional and legal recognition of Indigenous peoples. It is argued that "development" is a fundamental objective of the State; thus, recognizing Indigenous rights is seen as a challenge to the economic projections of the State. The value of plurinational rights in Latin America has been widely endorsed by Indigenous peoples, particularly in the constitutions of Bolivia and Ecuador, where these concepts continue to be central to political debate.

In general, when considering the current neoliberal economic context, there is little room for alternative approaches: development is understood exclusively in productive and quantitative terms. What is increasingly clear is that when development is conceived in this way, it does not result in tangible benefits for those living in the affected territories. Therefore, if we hope to move toward a meaningful dialogue, we must fully embrace the demands of *Küme Mogen* (Quidel Lincoleo 2023). International instances of having embraced alternative notions of development in their constitutions, such as "Sumak kamaña" in Bolivia and "Sumak Kawsay" in Ecuador, provide opportunities to critically examine possible idealizations, essentialisms, contradictions, and cultural clashes between modernity and Indigenous ontologies. In this regard, the debate between S. López and Choquiwanca in Bolivia exemplifies the political controversies between E. Morales and Arce.

The Mapuche concept of Good Living, *Küme Mogen* (Antona 2014; Quidel Lincoleo 2023), is key to deepening human rights that are not merely reduced to cultural identity, as is sometimes done in a multicultural interpretation of Indigenous rights that fall short of the demands made by recognition-based theories. This proposal refers fundamentally to a comprehensive set of economic, political, social, and environmental rights that are central to the proposal of human rights and the rights of Indigenous peoples. Certainly, as Alberto Acosta points out, there is a discrepancy between the so-called right to economic growth, promoted by States and multinational corporations, versus a broader set of interests and rights that are meaningful to all human beings. Ultimately, as Gudynas states, "debates on Good Living (understood in its original versions) have advantages for this task [as] they compel the recognition of ecological limits given their mandate by the rights of Nature" (Gudynas 2019: 275).

The debates regarding the friction between human and Indigenous rights lie in the fact that this tension is not resolved by the policies of the States of Chile and Argentina, which do not recognize customary law (*az mapu*). In their traditional guidelines, Indigenous communities have cultural, economic, political, and legal clarity regarding how to produce and distribute their goods and resources to meet their human needs. However, it is acknowledged that since the arrival of conquerors, landowners, and settlers, the economy has been understood through purposes not intrinsic to the Indigenous world. Thus, goals of enrichment or profitability, let alone rapid gains, do not enter into traditional Indigenous knowledge.

The current point of discussion is that Indigenous peoples understand these economic practices within strictly communitarian and religious–symbolic matrices, where the concept of individual right from liberalism and capitalist modernity is set aside (De la Fuente and Salas 2021). However, this also intersects with cultural hybridity, whose dynamics have altered traditions and introduced exogenous practices into Indigenous ontologies where capitalist modernity has both a significant place and, in some Indigenous communities, a degree of acceptance.

Traditional economic activities carried out by Indigenous communities resemble those undertaken by rural communities more broadly, but they are embedded in different patterns of reciprocity. Indigenous enterprises, specifically, are not sufficiently recognized by the development agencies of the States of Chile and Argentina. Their specific institutions for promoting rural activities and traditional economic strategies are viewed as obstacles to achieving high-impact productive growth. This could be described as a case of failed State management, as it both reduces the possibility of increasing transnational capital and also infringes upon the right of Indigenous peoples to self-determination, denying their agency, autonomy, and decision-making regarding their own potential economic development.

Nevertheless, throughout this long history of conflictive sociocultural and economic relations between said States and the Mapuche people inhabiting both sides of the Andes, there have been consequences, particularly systems of asymmetrical economic subordination. Agricultural products from these communities are often devalued because they do not meet the standards imposed by the market. Even though Mapuche communities have consistently asserted the patterns of their identity and their persistent cultural traits, the local and regional markets tend to limit their products to those with folkloric appeal, where purchasing power remains controlled by the dominant society. Consider the case of the various Dialogue Commissions that exist in Chile. The hegemonic power in negotiation is defined by sectors of hegemonic society rather than by Indigenous representatives, creating a markedly asymmetrical relationship. Numerous official documents show a profound lack of knowledge about the Mapuche people, their culture, their language, their spirituality, and the constant struggle they have faced for five centuries to defend their ways of life (*az mogen*).

For half a century now, interethnic discussions on the issue of Indigenous development have acknowledged the role of worldviews. For the Mapuches, this includes the strong influence of their spirituality, political organization, and the current and effective presence of ancestors in the territories and in their modes of production. In the alliances formed among lineages, the complex relations within the *ixofijmongen*, and the productive practices and economic life of the *lof*, State policies continue to reduce economic relations to a form of instrumental and neoliberal economic planning. Overall, the State's vision excludes the intricate network of Mapuche modes of production and their enduring connection to spiritual, social, and practical dimensions grounded in *mapun kimün* and *mapun rakizuam*.

The concepts of *mapun kimün* and *mapun rakizuam* underscore the importance of the holistic nature of the discussion around different perspectives of development, as in the understanding of how the distinct spiritual, cognitive, social, and practical dimensions come together to generate a more complete worldview and a particular method of knowledge construction (*kimün*). The notion of *mapun* implies grounding and situating knowledge, from the Mapuche territorial perspective, as a way of knowing and understanding reality, including the natural and social world, as well as a particular way of doing things. In this sense, it includes the construction of knowledge from a distinct rationality about the world and its phenomena. The notion of *kimün*, meanwhile, refers to the idea that knowledge is created through a reflective process, expressed along a specific, unique path (*inatuzugun*) (Quidel Lincoleo 2023: 59–88).

6.5 Mapuche Knowledges (*Mapun Kimün*) and its Ecological Dimensions

Between 2018 and 2019, through a knowledge-sharing experience as part of a mixed commission in Temuco, academics, professionals, and Mapuche authorities came together to discuss various aspects of Mapuche culture, ecology, society, and language within a co-development framework. Through this experience, it was widely agreed that academic studies and research almost always have a reductionist approach, and that such studies follow a fragmented, compartmentalized logic that reflects the structure of modern disciplines and professions. In other words, six years later, we concur with the academic and *lonko* José Quidel Lincoleo that many studies show little commitment to the current vitality of the Mapuche people, as they are more closely oriented toward academic production and the standards required by the current science and technology system. As a result, the construction of Mapuche knowledge is distorted and undermined through this process of imposed categorizations, often only superficially addressing pressing issues such as extractivism, socioenvironmental controversies, the exploitation of nature, the dispossession of land and territory, and the criminalization of communities in resistance, to name a few. This ultimately indicates academic extractivism.

Through this shared dialogue, it was also acknowledged that certain topics had been scarcely analyzed and that it is essential to continue working toward an ecodevelopment model based on a genuine dialogue of knowledges, with a link to Maristella Svampa's concept of the "ecoterritorial turn" (2017). In this knowledge dialogue experience, nine central themes were identified as points of intersection between both socioeconomic and cultural systems. Below are those elaborated by Mapuche academics José Quidel and Gabriel Llanquinao, and can be expressed in the Mapuche language, *mapuzugun*, as follows:

(1) *Mapun gijañmawün ka mapun azgünewün mapunche rakizuam mew* – Spirituality and autonomy from Mapuche thought
This dimension speaks to the Mapuche worldview – the relationship of the mystical, ethereal world and all dimensions of life, ancestral wisdom, spirituality, and the Mapuche religion.

(2) *Mapuche mapu Zugu* – Mapuche territory and lands
This dimension addresses the territory historically linked to the Mapuche people, from prehistory and principal settlements through to the military occupations of the nineteenth and twentieth centuries. It also includes processes understood through Mapuche *Wajontu Mapu*, reflecting on the territories of their ancestors as interpreted by the social movement, requiring the examination of specific records concerning the dispossession of lands across distinct territorial identities (Nangche, Lafquenche, Huilliche).

(3) *Az mapu Zugu* – Mapuche law
This dimension analyzes legal and legal-political forms, conceptions, and the use of Indigenous law declared in international law and its implications for Mapuche law (*az mapu*).

(4) *Kalewerpun ka reyülerpun mapun azmogen fantepu* – Transformations of the Mapuche economic system
The fourth dimension highlights how the Mapuche economic system has been forced to adapt to a hegemonic development model. The objective is to consider whether these conditions have fragmented and impoverished the Mapuche economy and the ancestral knowledge on which it is based, or whether they have favored a new economic model.

(5) *Mapuche bawentuwün Zugu* – Mapuche medicine
This domain is the privileged sphere of interaction between Mapuche spiritual knowledge and practical social therapeutic knowledge. It is probably the most specialized knowledge field in the complex Mapuche cultural repertoire. Here, the focus is on the observation of healers, practices, and their relationship with Western allopathic medicine, offering a potential for knowledge dialogue from practical, ideological, and cosmological perspectives, while also considering environmental relationships and food sovereignty.
(6) *Wigka chijkatun zugu mapuche mapu mew* – Impact of schooling on Mapuche life
It is a controversial field that seeks the constitution of a Mapuche school education model that legitimizes vernacular culture as the *sine qua non* resource for educational achievement.
(7) *Koneltual güneltun Zugu mew* – Foundations for Mapuche political participation
This theme is key to establishing Mapuche autonomy, governance, participation, and relations with the State.
(8) *Mapunzugun ñi wirigen ka kake xoytugen* – Writing of *mapuzungun* and its diverse manifestations
Together with the first dimension (*Mapun gijañmawün ka mapun azgünewün mapunche rakizuam mew*), this is present in all other dimensions while also possessing its own distinct character. Language is one of the most persistent cultural traits and has provided cohesion to the Mapuche people. It is present in each and every cultural expression: from the spiritual and cosmological, where it serves as an expression of ancestral knowledge, to its everyday use in all spheres of daily life.
(9) *Fijke az, azentun, azkan mapunche mogen mew* – Expressions of art and design in the Mapuche world
As the complexity of the Indigenous world becomes increasingly evident, so do the artistic works that emerge from different spaces and scenarios to denounce, transmit, and enhance their own aesthetic ways of understanding the world.

To understand each of these themes and dimensions, it is necessary to start by seeking guidance from what Mapuche colleagues call *Mapün Kimün*. This notion can be translated as Mapuche thought, and here we will understand it as Mapuche wisdom. Among the central themes outlined in the previous paragraphs, we can affirm that *Ixofijmogen*, as both a material and immaterial Indigenous conception of nature, emerges as a transcendental dimension in each of the points mentioned. In our understanding, it defines, both ontologically and epistemologically, the natural and supernatural habitat in which Mapuche society as a whole has existed since time immemorial. In this sense, the concept semantically places Indigenous humans, species, spirits, and all forms of life inside of and together with nature, where they become part of a relationship and interdependence. This notion of *Ixofijmogen* also connects with the spiritual dimension of territory, as it allows us to see how those principles extend into the ecological, not in an instrumental sense, but as part of a holistic understanding of Cosmic Life and Planetary Life.

6.6 *Az Mapu*, Mapuche Law

Referring to *az mapu* as Mapuche law may well unsettle some thinkers from the Western legal tradition, given that the notion of law crystallizes a strictly Western ontological conception, with its meaning understood through positivist disciplines that interpret and construct concepts aligned with homogenizing and monocultural normative systems. This stands in contrast to other frameworks that shape the understanding of Mapuche law, such as *az mapu*, whose meaning is ascribed to the *mapuzugun* language and the ancestral epistemology of *mapun kimün*. However, it is worth noting that "the word 'law' cannot be literally translated into *mapuzugun*. Works by Mapuche researchers refer to the concept of *Az Mapu* as the source of norms and laws governing Mapuche territories" (Cloud 2012: 504).

On the other hand, mapuzugun is an ancient language spoken by the Mapuche people, still in use today in Wallmapu. *Mapun kimün* constitutes the body of knowledge and wisdom that sustains the Mapuche people, which, despite colonial and republican processes of ethnocidal and ecocidal traits, maintains notable vigor within Mapuche communities. It remains highly relevant in the twenty-first century, as *kimche* (Mapuche wise men and women) transmit their wisdom to the next generations, who are responsible for reinterpreting and translating them into the contexts of transmodernity and decoloniality. These socioeducational and pedagogical processes are regulated by *az mapu*, representing a normative system that governs and administers the fundamental elements of society: economy, politics, and culture, while also regulating, through the Mapuche language, the domains of spirituality and work (Lloredo 2024).

Az mapu enables the recognition of other forms of rationality that seek justice from their own ontological standpoints. It represents a contextual justice, rooted in local and regional struggles and resistance, allowing for an understanding of how communities have influenced and continue to influence the sociocultural development of the historical territories inhabited by the Mapuche people. It is an Indigenous legal tradition that predates Western positivist law, which, despite the limitations imposed by the capitalist and transmodern model, survives and resists within Wallmapu and across the geopolitical borders of Chile and Argentina. These scenarios inevitably condition neoliberal globalization, as the capitalist economic model operates under an instrumental logic that dismisses the substantive dimensions of Mapuche knowledge (Pichinao et al. 2022). Its short-term logic fails to integrate the ontological dimensions of the realm of the living. Although not officially recognized by the State, *az mapu* organizes, manages, controls, safeguards, benefits, and sanctions both the members of the Mapuche people and all living beings of *ixofijmogen* (nature), constituting a tangible and intangible model of anticolonial justice.

> According to Mapuche cosmo-philosophy, the state of equilibrium and harmony of the cosmos corresponds to a natural law, a logical and self-regulated natural order,

> established by divinities and expressed by the concept of *Az Mapu*. It is common to hear Mapuche people entrust the regulation of certain situations of imbalance to *Az Mapu*: The *Az Mapu* works; the *Az Mapu* will take care of it and restore order. (Cloud 2012: 505)

It is possible that *az mapu* as Mapuche law could gain greater visibility in Chile once constitutional recognition is given to legal pluralism and, consequently, to the rights of Indigenous Peoples as set out in international law. These frameworks were recognized by the State but deliberately avoided incorporating into Chilean law and, therefore, into the functioning of the judiciary. As long as constitutional recognition does not exist, *az mapu* will lack institutional status and will continue to operate in the margins of the State, functioning intraculturally within Mapuche communities and through traditional and contemporary discourses and practices rooted in the broader vision of self-determination (González et al. 2022).

6.7 Existence and Re-existence of *Ixofijmogen*

Dialogue with the theoretical perspective of philosopher Sirio López Velasco, along with inspiration from these Mapuche notions, allows us to specify the starting point that should guide us in a genuine learning process of intercultural and interethnic dialogue. In what the Mapuche call *Mapün Kimün* there exists a set of ethnocultural notions and categories that refer to the profound, real, and symbolic spiritual relationships between the Earth (*Mapu*), the people who inhabit it (*che*), and the entirety of all living beings (*ixofijmogen*). In Western languages, we might refer to this concept as the collection of animals, plants, and inanimate beings.

The keyword in this socioenvironmental sense, as we have already indicated, is *Ixofijmogen*. It is an emblematic expression that Mapuche knowledge has employed long before the Western "concern" for the environment arose due to the deterioration of planetary life. Expressions in *mapuzungun* such as "*wenu mapu*," "*newen*," and "*Ixofijmogen*" are not easily translated into modern languages, and it is here, perhaps, where the possibilities lie for what Panikkar called the dialogue of cotranslators as part of a genuine dialogue of knowledges (Leff 2021a, chapter 4). The notion of "*Ixofijmogen*" could be translated as the complex whole of life or the interaction of all existing beings. For the Mapuche world, it is about accounting for being in the semantic field of the flow of all living things (*Mogen*). In this Mapuche ontology, there is no ontological separation between the diverse types of living beings, which would imply the nonseparation of humans and nonhumans (Pichinao et al. 2022). This relationship is also found in other Indo-American languages, with notable expressions that demonstrate the richness of knowledges rendered invisible by Western sciences and academic philosophy.

This typical distinction, between human and nonhuman life, can be seen as either universal or contextual. According to what we have indicated, we view it from a biocentric ethic and from biocultural contexts, and it is in these interstices that our dialogue with López Velasco's e-communitarian proposal would be situated. To put it more emphatically, in nonhumans there are vital forms and dynamic forces that define and characterize us in our very humanity. Ancestral wisdoms, and not only those of the Mapuche communities, reveal that within what we term as "animals" there exists not only conscious and unconscious life, but also internal differentiation, sensibilities, and distinct behaviors within a single species. Indigenous wisdom traditions link all living beings (human and nonhuman) into one flowing, living whole. This link never occurs in a univocal way but instead is articulated through a set of symbols and metaphors that are intelligible in Indigenous languages. These languages make it possible to transmit all the ecological knowledge that has endured to this day. Therefore, the identitary imaginaries recognized throughout humanity's long history are related to biocultural contexts and thus respond to different places of enunciation that can never be fully extended to other territories. Related to this idea, Sirio López says:

> The human being is part of nature and (as Indigenous cultures have always known), without non-human nature, there is no human being. That is why the e-communitarian perspective is irrefutably socioenvironmental, as demanded by the three fundamental ethical norms on which it is based; the third, in particular, forces us to watch over the health of human and non-human nature. (López Velasco 2017: 134)

From this perspective, the ecological norm converges with *Mapün Kimün*, centered on that key expression, *Ixofijmogen*, understood as the intrinsic interrelation of life in its holistic magnificence. In short, the term describes the shared destiny of all living nature and of all human beings to be persons, "*che*" (Quidel Lincoleo 2023). Mapuche and other Earth-based knowledge systems underscore the crucial role that animals and inanimate beings play, through processes of perception, responsiveness, and action, in shaping how humans live within and relate to the land. They question the hegemonic knowledge of Western sciences that has hidden the potential of myths to account for experiences and coexistences that we are only just beginning to glimpse in all their real and symbolic dimensions.

In this way, we can connect the ideas of Sirio López with those of the Canadian philosopher James Tully, who recalls that Indigenous knowledge conceptualized, long before our era, the human interconnection with the earth as relationships of gift and reciprocity. These forms of knowledge propose models so that the social relationships of non-violent citizenship practices include relationships with the nonhuman world. Tully maintains that *Homo sapiens* should see themselves as civic citizens interdependent on the ecological relationships in which they live, breathe, and exist. As such, they have the responsibility to care for and maintain these ecological relationships which are themselves interdependent with humans (Tully 2019).

6.8 Conclusions

Az mapu is presented and examined in this article first as an alternative proposal for justice, relating to legal pluralism, analyzed from decolonial perspectives rooted in the field of transmodernity. It then crystallized as a form of Mapuche law that predates positive law and the dynamics of a modern State, and as a legal system associated with ontological, epistemological, cultural, social, political, ecological, and both traditional and contemporary Mapuche elements. In this transmodern and decolonial sense, *az mapu* as a legal system is constrained by the normative definitions imposed by the Chilean and Argentine States regarding Indigenous territories (Faundes 2023).

In both discursive and practical terms, *az mapu* operates within a broader set of legal and ethical systems embedded in intracultural and intercultural contexts situated within and outside the borders of Wallmapu, where its ontological and epistemological structures systematically regulate human, nonhuman, natural, and spiritual behavior. At the same time, it responds to a complex network of tensions and conflicts ascribed to hegemonic Western, ethnocentric, and anthropocentric reasonings regarding the human–nature relationship. These frameworks fragment and reduce knowledge of both humanity and nature, constructing a radical epistemic divide in which humans subordinate nature, thereby ontologically breaking with the life vision historically upheld by *az mapu* and by emerging categories such as legal pluralism, transmodernity, and decoloniality (Leff 2020).

In this context, *az mapu* is understood as a porous and holistic sociolegal body whose dimensions in the practices of its actors shape interpretations of the symmetric/asymmetric, objective/subjective relationship between the human *che* and nature *ixofijmogen*. Therefore, our work analyzed the social and historical processes marked by colonialism, patriarchy, structural racism, land dispossession, exploitation, and the emergence of legal and environmental pluralism. While we acknowledge that our discussion may focus heavily on the protection economic, social, and cultural rights of majorities, as well as the violations of the collective rights of Indigenous Peoples, our experience and reflection demonstrate that currently, these groups continue to be the most impoverished and vulnerable groups on the continent. This includes the assassination of Indigenous peoples' leaders who champion environmental struggles. Certainly, these Peoples of the Earth are not opposed to poverty eradication policies that appear in government discourse, but effectively, no improvement in their socioeconomic situation is seen. However, their socioeconomic conditions show no meaningful improvement, on the contrary. Instead, what is needed is the formulation of poverty eradication policies aligned with development approaches that address the specific needs of marginalized populations, grounded in a human rights framework that includes the rights of Indigenous Peoples. In this regard, ECLAC (CEPAL) has produced substantial work, criticizing the culture of privilege embedded in discrimination and calling for the implementation of public policies that ensure equity. Unfortunately, this cannot be said for most government reports, which remain trapped in the logics of growth and extractivism (Tsosie 2017).

The asymmetrical relationship between human and nature reflects dominant meanings embedded in modernity, which permeate behaviors that contrast with the human–nature relationship envisioned by the Mapuche and thus subscribed to *az mapu*, with anthropocentrism and androcentrism being an installed hegemonic narrative. Conversely, symmetry is a guiding principle of *az mapu* and is justified through a strict ontological and epistemological perspective that understands the relational as an emancipatory and revolutionary option. Consequently, the socio-cultural clashes between the traditional and the modern expose complex issues such as politicization, essentialisms, culturalisms, disputes over ontological and epistemological meanings, and performances of authenticity, among others. These are the elements that currently shape *az mapu* within the context of modernity and plural dialogue. These perspectives point to a unified connection of all that is living, and not only in the sense of what we typically consider living beings, but of all entities that inhabit the Cosmos, suggesting a dynamic of relative equilibriums that sustain ecological niches and make it possible for our planet to support Life.

Finally, in the theoretical portion, our approach to legal pluralism includes a series of decolonial implications, to which academics such as Dussel, Rivera, Walsh, and other authors contribute. Particularly valuable were the reflections of two Mapuche colleagues regarding their own legal system, *az mapu*, and other sources of international law. In this framework, the decolonial perspective is articulated with environmental demands, showing how Indigenous law can incorporate an environmental vision into ontologies and epistemologies, and into the debates of Western policy regarding Indigenous peoples. It is worth emphasizing that in the field of social sciences, it is both timely and necessary to make visible and reinterpret the Mapuche legal system *az mapu* and its relationship with legal pluralism in academic and professional work – while also strengthening its political dimension within social movements. Furthermore, debates around the existence and persistence (*re-existence*) of ancestral Mapuche justice are intensifying in response to the impositions and constraints of monocultural *winka* (Western) positive law and its neocolonial dimensions. It is the effects of this power that paradoxically enable the emergence and resurgence of demands for the recognition of Mapuche pre-existing rights still in force across Wallmapu.

References

Antona, J. (2014). *Los derechos humanos de los pueblos indígenas: El az mapu y el caso mapuche*. Ediciones Cátedra Bartolomé de las Casas. https://ediciones.uct.cl/content/uploads/2021/06/Bustos_2015.-Los-derechos-humanos-de-los-pueblos-indigenas-El-az-mapu.pdf.

Bachmann, R. & Navarro, V. (2021). Derechos de la naturaleza y personalidad jurídica de los ecosistemas: nuevo paradigma de protección medioambiental. Un enfoque comparado. *Revista Internacional de Pensamiento Político* 16, 357–378.

Cloud, L. (2012). Az Mapu, derecho "invisible" o derecho mapuche. *Thule. Rivista italiana di studi americanistici*, 26(29): 501–544.

Dallmayr, F. (2023). *Dialogue and the New Cosmopolitanism*. Lexington Books.

De la Fuente, J. & Salas, R. (2021). *Introducción al Ecomunitarismo y a la educación ambiental*. Ariadna Ediciones.

De Sousa Santos, B., Grijalva Jiménez, A. (eds.) (2012). *Cuando los excluidos tienen Derecho: Justicia indígena, plurinacionalidad e interculturalidad en Ecuador*. Editorial El Conejo. https://estudogeral.uc.pt/bitstream/10316/44230/1/Cuando%20los%20excluidos%20tienen%20Derecho_justicia%20ind%C3%ADgena.pdf.

De Sousa Santos, B. & Mendez, J. M. (eds.) (2017). *Demodiversidad. Imaginar nuevas posibilidades democráticas* (pp. 59–92). Ediciones Akal.

Dussel, E. (1992). *1492: el encubrimiento del otro: hacia el origen del mito de la modernidad*. Editorial Nueva Utopía.

Dussel, E. (1993). *Apel, Ricoeur, Rorty y la Filosofía de la Liberación*. Universidad de Guadalajara.

Dussel, E. (1998). *Ética de la liberación en la edad de la globalización y de la exclusión*. Editorial Trotta.

Dussel, E. (2003). Transmodernidad e interculturalidad (Interpretación desde la Filosofía de la liberación). *Erasmus* 5(1–2), 65–102. www.icala.org.ar/erasmus/Archivo/2003/Erasmus-5-1-2-2003.pdf.

Dussel, E. (2006). *Filosofía de la cultura y la liberación: Ensayos*. UACM, Universidad Autónoma de la Ciudad de México.

Dussel, E. (2007). *Materiales para una política de la liberación*. UANL/Plaza y Valdés.

Dussel, E. (2012). *Obras selectas. En busca del sentido. Sobre el origen y el desarrollo de una Filosofía de la liberación*. Docencia.

Dussel, E. (2017). Analogía y comunicación (interpelación, diálogo intercultural hacia la transmodernidad). *Cuadernos Filosóficos*, 14, 66–101. https://doi.org/10.35305/cf2.vi14.31.

Erazo, C. & López, G. (2024). Lo pedagógico crítico en el proyecto transmoderno de Enrique Dussel. Lecturas y rupturas para fundamentar una nueva pedagogía, in Pincheira, L. & López, G. (eds.), *Decolonialidad e Interculturalidad crítica. Teoría y praxis desde los territorios en Latinoamérica* (pp. 27–49). Ariadna Ediciones.

Escobar, A. (2018). Adiós al desarrollo. *Great Transition Initiative* (February 2018), http://greattransition.org/publication/farewell-to-development.

Faundes, J. J. (2023). *El Derecho Humano a la identidad cultural en el Derecho Internacional*. Tirant le Blanche.

Faundes, J. J. & Ramírez, S. (2020). *El Derecho a la identidad cultural. Abordajes plurales desde América Latina*. RIL Editores.

Fornet-Betancourt, R. (2017). *Elementos para una crítica intercultural de la ciencia hegemónica*. Wissenschaftsverlag Mainz.

González, L., Belemmi, V., Gumucio, C., Mansuy, N., & Burdiles, G. (2022). Hacia una Constitución Ecológica Derechos de la Naturaleza en la Nueva Constitución. www.fima.cl/wp-content/uploads/2022/01/informe-derechos-de-la-naturaleza-1.pdf.

Gudynas, E. (2015). *Extractivismos. Ecología, economía y política de un modo de entender el desarrollo y la naturaleza*. Centro Latino Americano de Ecología Social.

Gudynas, E. (2019). Desarrollo y límites al crecimiento económico: una polémica persistente, in García, P., Ordoñez, J., & Munck, R. (eds.). *Desarrollo, Sociedad, Alternativas*. UTPL & Glasnevin Publishing. https://gudynas.com/wp-content/uploads/GudynasDesarrolloLimitesCrecimientoPolemica19.pdf.

Guerrero, A. L. (coord.) (2021). *Las empresas transnacionales y los derechos humanos: debates desde América Latina*. UNAM.

Le Bonniec, F. & Salas, R. (2015). *Les Mapuche à la mode. Modes d'existence et de résistance au Chili, en Argentine et au-delà*. L'Harmattan.

Leff, E. (2020). *El conflicto de la vida*. Siglo XXI Ediciones.

Leff, E. (2021a). *Political Ecology. Deconstructing Capital and Territorializing Life*. Palgrave Mac Millan. https://doi.org/10.1007/978-3-030-63325-7.

Leff, E. (2021b). 'Racionalidad y Justicia Ambiental: La Elusiva Injusticia de la Vida'. Historia Ambiental Latinoamericana y Caribeña (HALAC). *Revista de la Solcha* 11(3), 19–38. https://doi.org/10.32991/2237-2717.2021v11i3.p19-38.

Lloredo, A. L. (2024). Derechos de la naturaleza y bienes comunes naturales: análisis de algunas tensiones conceptuales a la luz del caso chileno. *Revista de Estudios Políticos* 204, 241–275. https://doi.org/10.18042/cepc/rep.204.08.

López Velasco, S. (2017). *Contribuição à teoria da democracia: uma perspectiva ecomunitarista*. Editora Fi.

Melin, M., Coliqueo, P., Curihuinca, E., & Royo, M. (2016). AZMAPU. Una aproximación al Sistema Normativo Mapuche desde el Rakizuam y el Derecho Propio. https://bibliotecadigital.indh.cl/items/1f7f7e07-709f-404f-9268-3a0a3e66d214.

Mignolo, W. D. & Walsh, C. E. (2018). *On Decoloniality: Concepts, Analytics, Praxis*. Duke University Press. https://doi.org/10.2307/j.ctv11g9616.

Namuncura, D. (1999). *Ralco: ¿Represa o pobreza?* Ediciones LOM.

Olivé, L. (2004). *Interculturalismo y Justicia social*. UNAM.

Pichinao, J., Melico, F., & Huenchulaf, E. (2022). *La forma mapunche de pensar y practicar la socialidad religiosa en Gülu y en Puwel Mapu*. Ediciones UC Temuco.

Price, J. (2023). *Translation and Epistemicide. Racialization of Languages in the Americas*. University of Arizona Press.

Quidel Lincoleo, J. (2023). *La noción mapuche de che (persona)*. Pehuén.

Reding, S. & Salas, R. (2024). *Exponer al peligro o conjurar la crisis: desafíos ético-políticos ante el neoliberalismo en América Latina*. UNAM.

Richards, P. (2016). Racismo. *El modelo chileno y el multiculturalismo neoliberal bajo la Concertación 1990–2010*. Pehuén.

Rivera, S. (1997). La noción de "derecho" o las paradojas de la modernidad postcolonial: indígenas y mujeres en Bolivia. *Temas Sociales* 19, 27–52.

Salas, R. (2016). Reconfigurations identitaires, décolonialité critique et capitalisme global en Amérique du sud, in Gómez-Müller, A. (ed.), *Le post-colonial en Amérique latine. Débats contemporains* (pp. 93–116). Editions Kimé.

Salas, R. (2019). Contexto, Justicia y Universalidad en la Filosofía Política Actual. Algunas Críticas y Aportes a la Teoría de la Justicia de Habermas. *Estudios Políticos Medellín* 55, 163–181.

Salas, R. (2022). Justicia contextual, derechos indígenas y empresas multinacionales en Ngulumapu (Chile), in Guerrero, A. (ed.), *Empresas Transnacionales y Derechos Humanos. Debates desde América Latina.* UNAM.

Silva, H. & Guerra, F. (2017). *Derechos Humanos y pueblos indígenas en Chile hoy: las amenazas al agua, a la biodiversidad y a la protesta social.* Observatorio Ciudadano.

Svampa, M. (2017). *Del cambio de época al fin de ciclo. Gobiernos progresistas, extractivismos y movimientos sociales* (pp. 79–106). Edhasa.

Tsosie, R. (2017). Indigenous Peoples, Anthropology, and the Legacy of Epistemic Injustice, in *The Routledge Handbook of Epistemic Injustice* (pp. 356–369). Taylor and Francis. https://doi.org/10.4324/9781315212043.

Tully, J. (2019). Life Sustains Life 1: Value: Social and Ecological, in Bilgrami, A. (ed.), *Nature and Value.* Columbia University Press.

Valle Franco, A. (2023). Los Bienes Comunes y los Derechos de la Naturaleza en Debate: análisis de la dicotomía de objeto /sujeto de derechos. *Cadernos Eletrônicos Direito Internacional Sem Fronteiras* 5(1), e20230104. https://doi.org/10.5281/zenodo.7749144.

Yrigoyen Fajardo, R. (2017). '¿Qué es el Pluralismo Jurídico Igualitario?'. *Revista Alertanet en Litigio Estratégico y Formación en Derechos Indígenas.* (ABC 5. pp. 10–15). https://issuu.com/iids/docs/revista_alertanet_2017.

7

The Religious Dimensions of Indigenous Environmental Rights: Disputes Over Land and Pathways Forward

Núria Reguart-Segarra

7.1 Introduction

In the course of recent decades, Indigenous voices have increasingly been gaining importance in the broad multilateral dialogue around international human rights protection. They have become powerful social actors capable of fostering group mobilization, creating transnational networks, and joining forces for a common goal: make their human rights be respected, so that they can be effectively enjoyed. The so-called global Indigenous movement has achieved that these peoples' claims and concerns have eventually been paid well-deserved attention from international human rights bodies, State and non-State actors, academia, and beyond.[1] Nevertheless, they are still subject to gross human rights violations. Most of them are in close connection to the peaceful possession of their ancestral territories, which are in turn being severely impacted by environmental degradation processes that aggravate vulnerabilities and social injustices (Mearns and Norton 2010).

Whereas the negative impacts of environmental degradation on ecosystems seem to be widely known, this is not the case for the disproportionate implications it will have, intergenerationally, for Indigenous livelihoods and cultures (IUCN 2008),[2]

[1] Indigenous peoples have received particular attention within the United Nations (UN) system, which has established specialized mechanisms, such as the UN Permanent Forum on Indigenous Issues, the mandate of the Special Rapporteur on the Rights of Indigenous Peoples, or an Expert Mechanism. All these efforts culminated in the adoption, by the UN General Assembly, of the UN Declaration on the Rights of Indigenous Peoples (UNDRIPS) on September 13, 2007 (A/RES/61/295). See generally Charters and Stavenhagen (2009).

[2] See also the report prepared by the Special Rapporteur in the field of cultural rights, Karima Bennoune, of August 10, 2020 (A/75/298).

who tend to care profoundly about their homelands not only because of their spiritual attachment, but also because their own lifestyles and identities as peoples are often at stake (UNPFII 2007: 5).

In this context, their traditional ecological knowledge (TK) appears as the most effective means in their power to avoid the deterioration of their territories, and it is being increasingly valued and recognized as key to combat the environmental crisis. This TK is an inextricable, constituent part not only of their right to a healthy environment, but also of their fundamental right to freedom of religion or belief (FoRB), all of which shows that traditional practices, knowledge systems, and belief systems are deeply interrelated in their worldviews. In spite of this, there is a worrying lack of understanding and operationalization of these peoples' FoRB, which hinders, in turn, the full, genuine, and ultimately rights-holder-oriented realization of their environmental rights.[3] With that in mind, and through an inductive approach, this chapter aims at exploring this nexus from an analytical and theoretical perspective, while assessing the severe threats Indigenous religious identities and cultural survival are currently exposed to as a consequence of environmental degradation, so as to provide critical guidelines on possible ways forward, which must necessarily build on securing the full and effective participation of Indigenous peoples in environmental action and policy-making.

7.2 Decolonizing the Right to Freedom of Religion or Belief through Its Application to Indigenous Peoples' Claims

Although the general recognition of the fundamental right to FoRB is appreciated in virtually every international instrument on the protection of human rights,[4] its adaptation to the particular circumstances that surround Indigenous peoples has long been a critical issue that needed to be addressed. This section aims at succinctly determining the essential substance of FoRB as understood by Indigenous worldviews, which will prove decisive in decolonizing this right's traditional conception. It also underlines how international actors have only lately begun to pay attention to

[3] The concept of environmental rights on which this research is based builds on the definition provided by Knox, who describes them as those basic rights related to the environment, which can in turn be classified as *substantive* environmental rights – whose enjoyment is particularly vulnerable to environmental degradation – and *procedural* environmental rights – whose exercise better supports environmental policy-making. See the Report of the Independent Expert on the Issue of Human Rights Obligations Relating to the Enjoyment of a Safe, Clean, Healthy and Sustainable Environment, John H. Knox, "Preliminary Report" of December 24, 2012 (A/HRC/22/43), para. 17.

[4] See, for instance, Article 18 of the Universal Declaration of Human Rights, Article 18 of the International Covenant on Civil and Political Rights (ICCPR), Article 9 of the European Convention on Human Rights, Article 12 of the American Convention on Human Rights (ACHR), or Article 8 of the African Charter on Human and Peoples' Rights.

the key position this right is afforded by indigenous peoples, despite the fact that the UN Human Rights Committee declared, as early as 1993, that this human right is far-reaching and profound and that its application is not limited to "traditional religions or to religions and beliefs with institutional characteristics or practices analogous to those of traditional religions" (UNHRC 1993), as in the present case.

7.2.1 The Essential Substance of Indigenous Worldviews

It is deemed an irrefutable fact that an Indigenous community without religious beliefs has never been found (Corry 2014: 286). In fact, Indigenous peoples' religious beliefs represent their quintessential defining element. Such beliefs must be understood as those that emanate from their deep spiritual connection with their ancestral territories (Reguart-Segarra 2021: 292) and that encourage them to venerate their natural habitat as inherently sacred (Westra 2008: 20). This bond is central to their collective identity and to their physical and spiritual well-being,[5] as it sustains the material and spiritual foundations of their cultural identities (Williams 1990: 689).

Indigenous peoples have maintained, since time immemorial, a particular way of living, of conceiving their relation with nature, with the supernatural and their community, which is integrated into an eminently spiritual system of beliefs (Vilella-Flores 2009: 465). Within its core, the land is understood as "the basis of their life, the condition for their subsistence and the reason for their community organization" (Osorio-Calvo 2017: 191), meaning that the sacred bond they share with it represents "the path and meaning of their existence" (Camarero-Suárez 2018: 26). It is the nuclear spiritual element for their religious practice, which involves that damaging it would in turn imply violating their very spirituality (Iglesias-Vázquez 2017: 468; Sonkar 2023), because both concepts make up an inseparable unit. This is notwithstanding the fact that, at the same time, territory and spirituality should also be understood and recognized as the object of two distinct, autonomous rights to be safeguarded, as will be argued below.

It is precisely the centrality land holds in the Indigenous forms of religiosity that has traditionally not allowed such beliefs to be considered under the concept of religion that prevails in Western ontologies (Fonda 2011: 1; Loftin 1989: 6; Masferrer-Kan 2002: 152), on the basis of which land constitutes a material means of production that lacks religious significance (Camarero-Suárez 2024: 128). Sacrality has often been solely attributed to those buildings designated as sacred spaces by major religious denominations, which has led to the notion of religion being conceived in a rather restrictive way (Beaman 2002: 145). This has in

[5] This has been also supported by the Inter-American Court of Human Rights (IACtHR) case law. For instance, see IACtHR Judgments on: *Case of the Mayagna (Sumo) Awas Tingni Community v. Nicaragua* (Series C, No. 79), of August 31, 2001, at 148; *Case of the Kichwa Indigenous People of Sarayaku v. Ecuador* (Series C, No. 245), of June 27, 2012, at 149; among others.

turn caused the delegitimization of Indigenous religious beliefs, which have been deemed inferior and unworthy of protection (Reguart-Segarra 2021: 291).

In spite of the above, as a result of the axiological intensity of Indigenous beliefs, these are legitimately protected by the right to FoRB and by all the instruments that enshrine it at the domestic and international level,[6] as they represent, in community members' lives, their highest standards of behavior. Their legitimacy and validity make them worthy of the special legal protection granted by international law, not only due to their particular status as Indigenous peoples, but also because they are collective holders of FoRB. Hence, the decolonization of this right necessarily involves protecting Indigenous beliefs, because all forms of religiosity that pursue the moral improvement of human beings must receive the recognition and effective protection they deserve, as already affirmed by Special Rapporteur Martínez-Cobo in his authoritative Study of the Problem of Discrimination against Indigenous Populations (1983: 279).

7.2.2 The Growing Attention to Its Treatment by International Actors

International attention to Indigenous peoples' FoRB (hereinafter, IPFoRB) has been exponentially growing in the past few years. While, for decades, international human rights bodies had focused their efforts on ensuring these peoples' rights to their collective land property (Aguilera 2023; Gilbert 2006), to free, prior, and informed consent (Eichler 2019), and to a dignified life (Reguart-Segarra 2019b), among others, they have only recently started to pay attention to their FoRB, albeit the existence of a comprehensive legal status which would allow for it.[7] The first relevant approach to the full understanding and operationalization of IPFoRB by international actors came with the thematic report submitted by the UN Special Rapporteur on FoRB to the General Assembly in 2022,[8] which for the first time completely revolved around Indigenous peoples' right to FoRB. This marked the beginning of a valuable conversation within the UN system, after which the current mandate holder has continued to pay attention to Indigenous peoples in subsequent reports.[9]

Following this international trend in human rights policy, the United States Commission on International Religious Freedom issued the 2023 report *Religious Freedom for Indigenous Communities in Latin America*. It concluded that the enforcement of legal provisions related to the protection of IPFoRB often falls

[6] See note 4.

[7] There has long been a positive trend toward the explicit recognition of Indigenous spiritual values. In particular, the UNDRIPS, in clear harmony with Article 18 ICCPR, proclaims their FoRB in Article 12, which bets on the express recognition of the collective facet of this right.

[8] Interim report of the Special Rapporteur on freedom of religion or belief, Ahmed Shaheed, of October 10, 2022 (A/77/514).

[9] Report of the Special Rapporteur on freedom of religion or belief, Nazila Ghanea, "Landscape of freedom of religion or belief," of January 30, 2023 (A/HRC/52/38).

short in practice, pointing out that clear and established legal mechanisms should be strengthened. In the European continent, the most relevant attempt by domestic authorities to address this issue is represented by the *3rd Report of the German Federal Government on the Global Situation of FoRB*, which devotes a whole chapter to analyzing IPFoRB. It reaches the conclusion that Indigenous spiritualities and the connection between these peoples and their ancestral territories must be understood much more strongly as part of FoRB and should be more firmly anchored in foreign and development policy.

In reference to regional human rights bodies, the Inter-American Commission on Human Rights (IACHR) has also recently established Inter-American Standards on FoRB, in which, for the first time, it explicitly establishes a direct relation between Indigenous peoples and their specific, autonomous right to FoRB regarding disputes over land and the environment,[10] by stating that "any limitation to the collective property of indigenous or Afro-descendant tribal peoples, or the destruction of the resources found there, has great repercussions on the exercise of their own religion."[11]

A detailed analysis of the Inter-American Court of Human Rights (IACtHR) land-grabbing case law reveals that this judicial body has mainly examined the existence of Indigenous peoples' collective right to land property.[12] In such cases, the spiritual link they share with their traditional lands has been considered as a determining factor by the Court.[13] However, neither the Inter-American Commission nor the Court have ever analyzed this spiritual connection under the protection of their FoRB, hitherto being exclusively articulated under the right to collective property, and more recently under their right to cultural identity (Aguilera 2023: 77). This has meant that the violation of Indigenous peoples' FoRB as a consequence of land-grabbing practices have not been analyzed as such in the Inter-American System, which means the latter has traditionally overlooked the singularity of this long-standing human right (Reguart-Segarra 2021: 298). This evident weakness surprisingly contrasts with the treatment afforded by the African bodies of human rights protection, which have expressly acknowledged the violation of IPFoRB in cases of this sort,[14] specifying that in indigenous societies, "the

[10] IACHR, Study on Freedom of Religion or Belief. Inter-American Standards (OEA/Ser.L/V/II, of 10 September 2023), pp. 99–110.

[11] Ibid., para. 208.

[12] This is despite the fact that Indigenous representatives have also alleged the violation of other related rights, such as the right to cultural identity, for instance (Aguilera 2023: 42).

[13] For instance, see IACtHR Judgments on: *Case of the Yakye Axa Indigenous Community v. Paraguay* (Series C, No. 125), of June 17, 2005, at 118; *Case of the Lhaka Honhat (Our Land) Association v. Argentina* (Series C, No. 400), of February 6, 2020, at 93; *Case of the Maya Q'ecqchi' Agua Caliente Indigenous Community v. Guatemala* (Series C, No. 488), of May 16, 2023, at 198.

[14] In particular, see the decision of the African Commission on Human and Peoples' Rights on the case of *Centre for Minority Rights Development (Kenya) and Minority Rights Group International on behalf of Endorois Welfare Council v. Kenya (App. No. 276/03)*, of February 2, 2010; and the May 26, 2017, and June 23, 2022, Judgments of the ACtHPR on the case of the Ogiek of Kenya (App. No. 006/2012).

freedom to worship and to engage in religious ceremonies depends on access to land and the natural environment. Any impediment to, or interference with accessing the natural environment, including land, severely constrains their ability to conduct or engage in religious rituals with considerable repercussion on the enjoyment of their freedom of worship."[15]

Nevertheless, this detrimental trend has been reversed in one of the latest land-grabbing cases decided by the IACtHR, *U'wa Indigenous Peoples v. Colombia*, in which three concurring Judges have claimed the autonomous violation of these peoples' FoRB. The judges pointed out that, based on the facts of this case, apart from constituting a violation of the right to cultural identity protected by Article 26 ACHR, also represented a violation of FoRB guaranteed by Article 12 ACHR, inasmuch as these rights have an autonomous content deserving of protection: although cultural identity protects, inter alia, religious systems as such, FoRB protects the right to choose a religion or belief and to manifest it freely. In their opinion, the autonomous violation of the latter should have been acknowledged in this case.[16] The work carried out by the concurring Judges in delimitating the content of this human right in cases of this sort must undoubtedly serve as a paradigm for its inclusion in subsequent rulings of the IACtHR that establish a necessary jurisprudential precedent.

The positioning of the European Court of Human Rights (ECtHR) as regards Indigenous rights negatively deviates from that of its correlatives, as it has not dealt with Indigenous rights in accordance with international standards when they approached their control mechanism.[17] In land-grabbing cases under its jurisdiction, the Court has focused its assessment on the traditional conception of the protection of property,[18] as enshrined in Article 1 of the First Additional Protocol to the European Convention on Human Rights and Fundamental Freedoms, and has failed to evaluate the existence of a religious factor that could rightfully be protected under FoRB (Reguart-Segarra and Camarero-Suárez 2023: 43). However, the ECtHR cannot miss out on the legal opportunity provided by modern international law, that is, to strictly align with common standards on the rights of Indigenous peoples that would strengthen their claims in future cases of this sort.

[15] May 26, 2017 Judgment of the ACtHPR on the case of the Ogiek of Kenya (App. No. 006/2012), at 164.

[16] IACtHR Judgment on the *Case of the U'wa Indigenous Peoples and their members v. Colombia* (Series C, No. 530), of July 4, 2024. Concurring opinion of Judges Mudrovitsch, Ferrer Mac-Gregor and Pérez Manrique.

[17] In this vein, it cannot be forgotten that most European States have not ratified ILO Convention 169, all of which might suggest a negative trend toward the protection of Indigenous peoples' rights in this continent.

[18] In this regard, see the ECtHR Judgments on the cases of *Johtti Sapmelaccat Ry. and others v. Finland* (App. No. 42969/98), of January 18, 2005; *Hingitaq 53 and others v. Denmark* (App. No. 18584/04), of January 12, 2006; *Handölsdalen Sami village and others v. Sweden* (App. No. 39013/04), of March 30, 2010.

7.3 Exploring the Intrinsic Connection between Indigenous Environmental Rights and Their Freedom of Religion or Belief

7.3.1 Preliminary Considerations

The formal recognition by the UN General Assembly in 2022 of the right to a clean, healthy, and sustainable environment as a human right[19] marked the beginning of a new era in socioenvironmental justice, fostering a human rights-based approach which had previously been deemed not only helpful but also essential to this end.[20] Whereas such an approach to environmental protection encompasses all human rights, among Indigenous environmental rights, the rights to a healthy environment, to cultural identity, and to land must occupy a central position. Nevertheless, it should not be ignored that these rights are deeply intertwined with Indigenous peoples' right to FoRB, whose lack of understanding and operationalization by relevant human rights bodies is capable of hindering the full realization of the former rights, as will be shown shortly.

To begin with, the effective enjoyment by Indigenous peoples of their collective right to land property has often been regarded as a first step[21] in order that they could also effectively enjoy other human rights (Iglesias-Vázquez 2016: 289). More recently, this role has been attributed to the collective right to cultural identity, which, according to Aguilera (2023: 77), "is the ontological condition for recognizing Indigenous and tribal peoples as distinct social and political actors with the right to collectively enjoy certain rights." In this respect, the subsequent enjoyment of their right to a healthy environment requires that Indigenous peoples be recognized as such and retain possession of their ancestral lands, which makes the connection between these rights more than evident. However, it cannot be forgotten that land and natural resources lay at the core of Indigenous peoples FoRB, to the extent that, without them, this right would end up being devoid of substance. Needless to say, although the concept of religion might also be deemed a manifestation of culture,[22] this cannot imply that FoRB must not be claimed as a self-standing human right to be protected, as will be discussed in the next subsections.

In spite of the above, much of the land occupied by Indigenous peoples is not legally recognized as belonging to them (Sarmiento-Barletti 2018), which clearly benefits all those State and non-State actors that have a financial interest in

[19] Resolution adopted by the UN General Assembly on July 28, 2022 (A/RES/76/300).

[20] Report of the Special Rapporteur on the issue of human rights obligations relating to the enjoyment of a safe, clean, healthy, and sustainable environment, David Boyd, "Right to a Healthy Environment: Good Practices," of December 30, 2019 (A/HRC/43/53).

[21] See generally IACtHR Judgments on the *Case of the Mayagna (Sumo) Awas Tingni Community v. Nicaragua* (Series C, No. 79), of August 31, 2001.

[22] Rather than representing a series of isolated manifestations or hermetic compartments, culture must be seen as "an interactive process whereby individuals and communities, while preserving their specificities and purposes, give expression to the culture of humanity" (UNCESCR 2009).

exploiting them. Moreover, insecure land tenure results in conflict situations, environmental degradation, and scarce social–economic development, as well as in severe cultural and spiritual damage (IUCN 2008: 7; Stevens 1997: 3). Within the past few years, Indigenous rights advocacy worldwide has borne fruit by achieving an increase in the percentage of land legally owned by these groups, which is now slightly higher than 11 percent (RRI 2023).[23] However, this has not stopped "development" projects from being carried out in their territories in violation of their rights, whether operated by transnational corporations with purely economic purposes[24] or in the name of conservation. In the latter case, it should be noted that conservation used to be carried out by erasing human presence in all protected areas, which led to cultural destruction and large-scale displacement (Giacomini 2023: 510). This is despite the fact that safeguarding Indigenous peoples' land rights has typically led to improved protection for ecosystems and biodiversity, while their exclusion from Indigenous territories with conservation purposes has normally resulted in failure (Schuster et al. 2019). That is why respect for human rights ought not to be seen as contradictory, but rather complementary, to the protection of Mother Earth.[25] In this vein, it has also been demonstrated that ancestral territories over which Indigenous communities have legal rights have been substantially better conserved than adjacent lands.[26]

7.3.2 Beyond Western Science: The Intersection between Traditional Knowledge and Indigenous Spirituality

One of the most critical and effective tools Indigenous peoples have in their power in order to give meaning and to fulfill their right to a healthy environment is the TK they have been gathering over generations.[27] Indigenous peoples, recognized for their significant contributions to environmental protection (IPCC 2021), have increasingly been acknowledged as essential actors in climate action and policy-making. This recognition comes despite the fact that they are among the human groups most directly experiencing the severe impacts of the ongoing climate crisis (ILO 2017). This can only be understood by taking into account the close spiritual relationship first peoples keep with their ancestral lands and natural resources, upon

[23] The study analyzes seventy-three countries, covering 85 percent of global land area.

[24] For a thorough analysis on the complicated relationship between economics and human rights, see Gómez-Isa (2020).

[25] Report of the Special Rapporteur on the issue of human rights obligations relating to the enjoyment of a safe, clean, healthy and sustainable environment, John Knox, of January 19, 2017 (A/HRC/34/49).

[26] Report of the Special Rapporteur of the Human Rights Council on the rights of indigenous peoples, Victoria Tauli-Corpuz, "Rights of Indigenous Peoples," of July 29, 2016 (A/71/229).

[27] The first approaches to this line of research were carried out at the Strathclyde Centre for Environmental Law and Governance, through a three-month research stay supervised by Professor Elisa Morgera, current UN Special Rapporteur on Human Rights and Climate Change, to whom the author would like to express deep gratitude.

which their TK was originally built, and which encourages them to keep engaging in ecological traditional practices.

It should be noted that, even though there is no general agreement on the definition of TK in international law, scholars have frequently used Berkes' definition as a starting point, which describes it as "a cumulative body of knowledge, practice and belief, evolving by adaptive processes and handed down through generations by cultural transmission, about the relationship of living beings (including humans) with one another and with their environment" (Berkes 2012: 7). However, first peoples regard their knowledge as much more than just a "body of knowledge." They generally consider it as a holistic way of life that emanates from their deepest spirituality. It represents an integral part of their worldviews that is closely linked to their lands, culture, social, political, and economic systems, and traditional institutions (Verma 2005: 766). Unlike Western researchers, Indigenous peoples view "the people, the knowledge and the land as a single, integrated whole" (McGreggor 2004: 79) and, therefore, spirituality cannot be deemed an isolated aspect of TK.

This conception is in line with Indigenous worldviews and their characteristic all-pervasiveness (Bullock 2023). That is why they do not share the "dichotomous occidental worldview" (Winter 2022) according to which the material and the spiritual, nature and culture, humankind and other forms of life are clearly differentiated. In this regard, Indigenous peoples believe the boundaries between the secular and the spiritual, the empirical and the sacred, are completely permeable and, thus, all of them complement and enrich each other, leaving aside competition or contradiction (Nakashima and Roué 2002: 1–2). In consequence, the protection of TK, rather than constituting an independent subject matter, should be integrated into the overall protection of communities' lifestyles and cultures (Verma 2005: 766).

7.3.3 Indigenous Knowledge from a Human Rights-Based Approach

Indigenous spirituality represents the cornerstone of Indigenous worldviews and, subsequently, of their systems of knowledge (Camacaro 2012). Traditional knowledge has proven to be an inextricable part not only of their right to a healthy environment, but also of their FoRB, all of which shows how in their worldviews traditional practices and knowledge systems are intertwined with belief systems (Colding and Folke 1997). Although TK finds its deepest origin in the spiritual value systems of its holders, international human rights law (IHRL) has traditionally not considered TK as being included under the scope of protection of FoRB. Rather, it has frequently protected it under the coverage of the more generic right to culture (Savaresi 2016: 30). This is because the right to culture comprises, inter alia, ways of life, religion or belief systems, rites and ceremonies, methods of production or technology, arts, customs and traditions through which individuals and communities express their humanity and give meaning to their existence, and build their worldview accordingly (UNCESCR 2009), all of which clearly cover TK (Chiarolla and Savaresi 2016: 11).

In the particular case of Indigenous peoples, human rights bodies have explicitly acknowledged their right to maintain, control, protect, and develop their cultural heritage, TK and traditional cultural expressions (Xanthaki et al. 2017), as well as the manifestations of their sciences, technologies and cultures (UNCESCR 2009). However, it is worth emphasizing that TK is not only a cultural expression, but, most importantly, it is a manifestation of their religious beliefs and worldviews. This conception of life represents one of the elements that each community identifies with and that are expressed through beliefs, customs, and traditions transmitted by their ancestors that ultimately constitute their own culture, of which their religious beliefs are an intrinsic part. Such beliefs guide individual and collective behavior on a mandatory basis and, therefore, fall under the scope of protection of FoRB, the object of which is precisely constituted by the activities carried out in the exercise of this freedom (Reguart-Segarra 2019a: 24). Protecting Indigenous knowledge through the right to FoRB of its holders would vest these peoples' fight with a much greater protection, benefiting from the vast array of human rights instruments that recognize this right as a self-standing, autonomous human right, which has been traditionally considered as the first freedom of all (Jellinek 1908), both from a chronological perspective, as well as from an ontological one, since all other freedoms emanate from it (Souto-Paz 1999: 143).

In the strictly normative field, the freedom to manifest religion and beliefs through worship has been said to extend to "ritual and ceremonial acts giving direct expression to belief, as well as various practices integral to such acts" (UNHRC 1993). Hence, the traditional skills, practices, and knowledge that emanate from Indigenous deepest spirituality clearly represent a manifestation of their FoRB. This is reaffirmed in other human rights instruments, such as ILO Convention 169,[28] which, albeit not containing an explicit protection clause on TK, indirectly safeguards TK through the protection it affords to rights over lands and natural resources as a consequence of the deeply rooted religious links these peoples share with each other,[29] inasmuch as these rights are prerequisites for generating and preserving TK (Meyer 2001: 43). As regards the UNDRIPS, the core provision in relation with TK lies in Article 31,[30] which expressly acknowledges the right of Indigenous peoples to "maintain, control, protect and develop their cultural heritage, traditional knowledge and traditional cultural expressions, as well as the manifestations of their sciences, technologies and cultures [...]," thus protecting

[28] Adopted on June 27, 1989, entered into force on September 5, 1991.

[29] See Articles 4, 5, 7, and 13–15.

[30] Apart from it, further implicit allusions to TK in relation to Indigenous spirituality can be found in this instrument. For instance, see Articles 11, 12, 29, and 34.

the Indigenous "proper way of life."[31] Also, Article 7.13 of the Escazú Agreement[32] promotes "regard for local knowledge, dialogue and interaction of different views and knowledge, where appropriate." This recognition implies that TK holders can also be considered as "epistemic authorities or experts," whose contributions are part of a notion of knowledge which extends beyond Western science (Aguilera 2023: 295).

Finally, in the American Declaration on the Rights of Indigenous Peoples (ADRIPS),[33] the main set of provisions regarding TK relates to their rights to cultural identity.[34] In this system, the IACtHR underscored the interconnection between cultural and environmental rights in *Lhaka Honhat v. Argentina*,[35] the first contentious case brought before it in which it expressly recognized a violation of the right to a healthy environment as included in the rights derived interpretatively from Article 26 ACHR. Such interconnection reflects in the acknowledgment that rights to adequate food, water, and cultural identity also derive from this article. This in turn stems from the close link between the environment and human rights, which implies that the effective protection of the former often depends on the free exercise of the latter.[36] Going one step further, in the *Case of the Maya Kaqchikel Indigenous Peoples of Sumpango v. Guatemala*,[37] the IACtHR established a direct connection between the right to participate in cultural life and the right to freedom of thought and expression, attributing an instrumental character to this freedom in such a way that its effective guarantee appears as essential to take part in the cultural life of an Indigenous community.[38]

Notwithstanding the undeniable relevance of the IACtHR's role in delineating the rights Indigenous peoples are entitled to (Iglesias-Vázquez 2021: 228), the pattern of recognition of rights it follows in its land-grabbing case law tends to overlook the singularity of Indigenous peoples' freedom of religion or belief as a separate, autonomous right to be safeguarded. In this vein, this Court has strictly protected the essential content of this right[39] through the rights to culture and to cultural identity, as well as to collective land property. This is despite acknowledging, at the same time, that the inherent religiousness of the deeply rooted connection

[31] On the intricacy around the "ecologically noble Indian" stereotype, see Nadasdy (2005).

[32] Regional Agreement on Access to Information, Public Participation and Justice in Environmental Matters in Latin America and The Caribbean (adopted on March 4, 2018, entered into force on April 22, 2021).

[33] Adopted on June 15, 2016, AG/RES. 2888 (XLVI-O/16).

[34] See Articles XIII and XIV.

[35] *Case of the Lhaka Honhat (Our Land) Association v. Argentina* (Series C, No. 400), IACtHR Judgment of February 6, 2020.

[36] See IACtHR Advisory Opinion OC-23/17, of November 15, 2017, at 51 and 54. This has been more recently reiterated in the *Case of the Rama and Kriol Peoples, Black Creole Indigenous Community of Bluefields and Others v. Nicaragua* (Series C, No. 522), IACtHR Judgment of April 1, 2024, at 427.

[37] Series C, No. 440, of October 6, 2021.

[38] Ibid., at 128. This follows a first approach to the issue by the Court in the *Case of Norín Catrimán et al. (Leaders, members and activist of the Mapuche Indigenous people) v. Chile* (Series C, No. 279), Judgment of May 19, 2014, at 370–378.

[39] See Section 7.2.1 of this chapter.

first peoples share with their surrounding natural environment compels them to treat their habitat in a way that respects its intrinsic sacredness and to keep developing their TK in a manner that is consistent with their religious beliefs.[40] This is a crucial fact that is nevertheless being eventually recognized in human rights policy on Indigenous peoples' FoRB,[41] and which is expected to continue to gain recognition over the upcoming years, following the emerging trend outlined above.

7.3.4 The Fundamental Role of Traditional Knowledge in Environmental Action and Policy-making

The main obstacle Indigenous peoples have had to face regarding their TK is that of its recognition as a valuable and dynamic system of knowledge capable of playing a vital role in environmental action, as it has traditionally been underestimated by Western scientists due to the cultural and religious forms in which it is recorded and transmitted (Durning 1992: 29; Morgera 2015: 806). Nevertheless, TK is nowadays recognized as a form of "rational and reliable" knowledge and can rightfully be considered as part of science (Mauro and Hardison 2000: 1263). This has been recently supported by the Special Rapporteur in the field of cultural rights, Alexandra Xanthaki, who has advocated for the decolonization of scientific knowledge by emphasizing the importance of an inclusive approach to the right to science and by recalling the evolution of the meaning of science, which now encompasses all scientific approaches, including Indigenous science.[42] As vital and active contributors to many ecosystems, first peoples can actually help to enhance their resilience by drawing on their TK so as to react to climate change impacts in creative ways, which may in turn help society in a broad way to cope with these changes (Salick and Byg 2007: 4).

It should first be noted that the increasing recognition TK has been gaining in climate change mitigation and adaptation policy formulation and implementation began only a few decades ago, when world leaders realized the spiritually based TK was the reason Indigenous peoples had survived all sorts of environmental changes over the years (IUCN 2008: 11). In fact, it was not until 2007 when the Intergovernmental Panel on Climate Change (IPCC) recognized, for the very first time, the usefulness of this knowledge in understanding Indigenous peoples' response strategies and adaptive capacity. Since that first mention, the allusions to Indigenous peoples' knowledge in the reports published by the IPCC have only increased, both in terms of quantity and quality (Reguart-Segarra 2022: 210).

First, mitigation actions, which aim at controlling the accumulation of greenhouse gases in the atmosphere, are necessary for restraining the degree and

[40] *Case of the Kaliña and Lokono Peoples v. Suriname* (Series C, No. 309), IACtHR Judgment of November 25, 2015, at 34–35.

[41] See Section 7.2.2.

[42] Report of the Special Rapporteur in the field of cultural rights, Alexandra Xanthaki, "Right to Participate in Science," of February 21, 2024 (A/HRC/55/44).

magnitude of climate change (Brugnach et al. 2017: 19). In this respect, reforestation, sustainable forest management, and reduction of deforestation have been pointed out as some of the most coeffective mitigation options (IPCC 2014a: 24). Based on their spiritual values, Indigenous peoples are committed to creating original solutions, such as reducing emissions through traditional fire control systems, using renewable energy on their lands, and implementing resource management projects that reduce pressure on natural resources and increase local adaptation capacity (Ramos-Castillo and Galloway McLean 2012). At the same time, it has been proven that the recognition of their legal rights on the territories they have traditionally inhabited is essential for lowering carbon dioxide emissions and deforestation (Stevens et al. 2014: 3), which means that climate action should go hand in hand with the strengthening of communities' rights over lands and forests.

As for adaptation, although some believe that the deeply rooted cultural values first peoples have clearly represent an obstacle to adapting to the new circumstances created by the impacts of climate change, others suggest adaptation strategies should also draw on the cultural aspects of TK.[43] Here lies the significance of delving into Indigenous spirituality and worldviews, as the isolated study of TK without framing it in its wider context would be limited and partial and would ultimately lack a critical component. By its very nature, TK involves "coping with and adapting to changeable and changing environments" (Naess 2013: 100), which comprises a reflective way of learning that places a key relevance in decolonizing scientific knowledge (Datta et al. 2024). Although traditionally TK has not been used in adaptation strategies, the IPCC has acknowledged that it is a "major source for adapting to climate change." For that reason, the combination of TK with existing practices would increase the effectiveness of such strategies (IPCC 2014b: 26). In its last thematic report, the IPCC also recognized the value of diverse forms of knowledge,[44] such as Indigenous knowledge, in understanding and assessing climate adaptation processes and actions to reduce human-induced climate change risks (IPCC 2022: 7).

The Intergovernmental Science–Policy Platform on Biodiversity and Ecosystem Services has also taken significant steps forward in this regard. Its Global Assessment Report on Biodiversity and Ecosystem Services released in 2019 based its finding not only on scientific sources, but also on Indigenous knowledge, and revealed that, despite the growing pressure under which nature managed by Indigenous peoples is, it is generally declining at a lower speed than in other lands. Consequently, the recognition of Indigenous knowledge, innovation, and practices, and their participation in environmental decision-making processes is

[43] Report prepared by the Special Rapporteur in the field of cultural rights, Karima Bennoune, of August 10, 2020 (A/75/298).

[44] In this context, the notion which is being developed and gaining importance is that of "knowledge dialogue," which expresses an interest in building relations of respect, horizontality, and collaboration between actors with different knowledge systems so as to achieve common goals with a social mission (Pérez-Ruiz and Argueta-Villamar 2022).

urgently needed, as this will enhance both their quality of life and nature conservation in the interest of the broader society (IPBES 2019).

The progressive recognition of TK value in the scientific field has been paralleled with that afforded in the normative one. At that level, the Convention on Biological Diversity (CBD)[45] is deemed the primary instrument by which Indigenous peoples have the possibility of expressing their demands for the protection of their TK in relation to biological resources (Meyer 2001: 41). Among the Rio Conventions, it contains the most advanced set of obligations relating to TK and, accordingly, international biodiversity law is considered to be at an "advanced stage of regime strengthening" in this respect (Savaresi 2016: 13). This stands in stark contrast with the notable absence of any reference to TK in the primary legal instruments that form the foundation of international climate change law.[46] This deficiency was finally compensated by the adoption of the Paris Agreement,[47] which recognized, in its Article 7.5, the need for adaptation to climate change to be inspired by the TK of Indigenous peoples. The Decision approving this Agreement simultaneously opened the door to the establishment of a platform for the exchange of experiences and best practices on mitigation and adaptation strategies in a holistic and integrated manner, which has become to be known as the Local Communities and Indigenous Peoples Platform and which already has its own Facilitative Working Group (FWG), whose task is to achieve its full operationalization.[48]

Although it is evident that the progress made in recent years in these areas of the international environmental regime is abundant, the remaining challenges are also considerable. The fact that Indigenous peoples have eventually seen their rights and their decisive role in environmental action recognized is highly satisfactory, but this must necessarily translate not only into the greater visibility they already enjoy, but, above all, in a greater real role in policy-making on equal terms and conditions to all the other stakeholders (Jones 2024). Structural problems such as inequalities in power relationships still weigh on them, which hinder, in practice, everything they have been formally achieving by claiming, with perseverance and tenacity, that their knowledge is essential to ensure the future of humankind. That is why their current claims focus on achieving that the recognition they have already obtained at a formal level is reflected in their effective participation, on a basis of substantive equality, and with due respect to their human rights, in this broad multilateral dialogue on the environmental crisis (Reguart-Segarra 2022: 210). Within the CBD regime, a major step forward was taken in COP16 through the creation of

[45] Adopted on June 5, 1992, entered into force on December 29, 1993. See Article 8(j). As for the interlinkage between the CBD and other international instruments, see generally Campins-Eritja and Fajardo del Castillo (2021).

[46] See the UN Framework Convention on Climate Change (adopted on May 9, 1992, entered into force on March 21, 1994) and the Kyoto Protocol (adopted on December 11, 1997, entered into force on February 16, 2005).

[47] Adopted by Decision 1/CP.21, of December 12, 2015.

[48] See Decision 2/CP.24, of December 2, 2018.

a subsidiary body on Article 8(j) and the acknowledgment of the unique role of Indigenous peoples and local communities and their TK in the implementation of the Convention and its Protocols.[49] In this same vein, COP29 took a decisive step toward increasing the full and effective participation of Indigenous peoples in the United Nations Framework Convention on Climate Change (UNFCCC) process through the renovation of the FWG mandate and the adoption of the Baku Workplan, which is aimed at promoting knowledge exchange, building engagement capacity, and incorporating diverse values and knowledge systems into climate policies and actions.[50]

7.4 Responding to the Current Threats to Indigenous Religious Identities and Cultural Survival: Keys to Path the Way Forward

The current threats Indigenous peoples' religious identities and cultural survival are being exposed to, which in turn stand as clear obstacles to the effective realization of their human rights, and especially, of their FoRB, are mainly based on two proven circumstances affecting both their territories and ways of living. On the one hand, the ambitious plans transnational corporations aim at carrying out in their ancestral territories, often with the complicity of State actors, not only have a severe environmental impact, but also lead to land grabs that are accompanied by terrible human rights violations (Cotula 2014; Del Valle Calzada 2024). This phenomenon clearly conceals an excessive desire to control the natural resources of the Global South (Camarero-Suárez and Zamora-Cabot 2016). Land grabs might obey purely economic reasons or may be the consequence of "green" policies that overlook the rights of the Indigenous inhabitants of the lands on which they are going to be implemented (Blomley et al. 2013). In both cases, land-grabbing practices imply the forced displacement of the Indigenous community affected. Given the intrinsic sacredness attributed to their territories, FoRB extends beyond the protection of specific sacred sites to encompass the entirety of their ancestral lands, which are fundamental to their cultural survival. Such displacement thus prevents Indigenous peoples from fully enjoying their environmental rights and their FoRB.

Along with land-grabbing, the other major threat that endangers Indigenous religious identities and cultural survival with increasing intensity and imminence is climate change, as Indigenous peoples are placed in a situation of particular vulnerability to its worst effects (IPCC 2023). Extreme meteorological phenomena – such as floods, hurricanes, earthquakes, along with the rise of sea levels,

[49] See "Institutional arrangements for the full and effective participation of Indigenous peoples and local communities in the work undertaken under the Convention on Biological Diversity," Draft decision submitted by the Chair of Working Group I, of October 30, 2024 (CBD/COP/16/L.6).

[50] UNCC News (2024). "COP29 Adopts Baku Workplan to Elevate Voices of Indigenous Peoples and Local Communities in Climate Action." https://unfccc.int/news/cop29-adopts-baku-workplan-to-elevate-voices-of-indigenous-peoples-and-local-communities-in-climate.

desertification, or draughts – are becoming increasingly frequent (IPCC 2022), to the extent that some Indigenous peoples are already being forced to leave their homelands or expect this will become a reality in the near future (Borràs-Pentinat 2020: 26; Felipe-Pérez et al. 2019: 21). The impact of such climate-induced displacements will be devastating (Nicholson and Mayer 2023), as they will irretrievably disintegrate Indigenous peoples at an intergenerational level. This is because their interdependence with the land and natural resources is so deep that forced displacement would imply losing the focal point around which their systems of spiritual beliefs are built, in turn infringing the enjoyment of other human rights while exacerbating conditions of vulnerability and marginalization (Aguilera 2023: 39).

The degree to which such impact will affect Indigenous identities will vary depending on the duration of the displacement, which may be temporary, circular, or permanent. Although predicting such duration with due precision is complex, temporary and seasonal displacements predominate in the short term, but once climate impacts worsen, they tend to become permanent (Felipe-Pérez 2019: 74). This latter case represents the most significant challenge to Indigenous religious identities as a consequence of climate change.

All in all, every action that might lead to the forced displacement of Indigenous peoples from their traditional territories is not only prohibited by international law,[51] but would also pose a serious threat to their religious identities and cultural survival as distinct communities, while also violating the various human rights outlined above. Hence, the effective guarantee of Indigenous peoples' FoRB in all its dimensions is the cornerstone around which the two great challenges Indigenous peoples face today revolve – that is, land-grabbing and climate change – and, thus, it should be further operationalized. In order to path the way forward, and as outlined in this chapter, there needs to be a better understanding of this right from a decolonial approach and how it applies to the particular case of Indigenous peoples, who enjoy *at least* the same protection any other individual or group has, not only on the basis of the specific international instruments on their rights (UNDRIPS, ILO Convention 169, ADRIPS), but also of international human rights standards applicable to all.

Given the scenario presented, although the environmental degradation of their territories may appear inevitable and irreparable, it should not be forgotten that Indigenous peoples possess vital strategies for coping with it. It is urgent that the governments of the States in which Indigenous peoples reside implement efficient plans to alleviate the worst effects of environmental degradation not only on their ancestral territories, but also on their culture and religiousness. To this end, governments should assess Indigenous lands at risk and collaborate with communities to determine how to preserve cultural and religious identity factors and to design effective economic development plans accordingly (Zafar 2020).

[51] See Article 10 UNDRIPS; Article 16 ILO Convention 169.

This should be strongly promoted by international human rights bodies, who cannot turn a blind eye on State practices that overlook the most basic rights Indigenous peoples have so firmly fought for. The already well-defined IHRL on Indigenous peoples must be applied without hesitation in every case, given the evidence that their very survival might be at stake. This is particularly important on the part of other key stakeholders – transnational corporations (Morgera 2020) – which must be formally urged to start implementing due diligence plans in accordance with recent international standards in this field,[52] by taking account of the potential socioenvironmental and cultural impacts of their projects on Indigenous lands.

7.5 Concluding Remarks

As has been shown, the religious dimensions of disputes over lands and the environment are the key around which current threats to Indigenous cultural survival revolve. Indigenous beliefs undoubtedly fall under the scope of protection of their most primary right to freedom of religion or belief, whose full recognition and free enjoyment cannot be taken for granted. Indeed, land and natural resources lay at the core of Indigenous peoples' FoRB, to the extent that, without them, this fundamental human right would end up being devoid of substance. Denying its key relevance would imply depriving Indigenous peoples' fight for their territories from its essential meaning – their *raison d'être*. That is why decolonizing the traditional conception of FoRB has proven to be critical to understanding the key role Indigenous beliefs play in their traditional practices, being at the forefront of the advocacy for their rights.

As a consequence of Indigenous worldviews' inherent holism, this right is deeply intertwined with their environmental rights, among which the rights to a healthy environment, to cultural identity, and to land occupy a central position. For their full realization, FoRB needs to be further operationalized and promoted in line with new trends in international law. Human rights institutions, whether universal or regional, must lead the way in this process, which has only recently started to receive attention in academia and beyond. At the same time, their TK, which gives meaning to their right to a healthy environment and which is protected by their FoRB, must undoubtedly lie at the very core of institutional policies aimed at environmental conservation and climate change mitigation and adaptation. At the domestic level, respectful forms of collaboration and coordinated action of Indigenous communities and the States where their territories are located are of critical importance to ensure their socioeconomic, cultural, and religious survival, which implies that

[52] On May 24, 2024, the Council of the European Union completed the adoption process of the EU Corporate Sustainability Due Diligence Directive, aimed at fostering sustainable and responsible corporate behavior with a particular focus on human rights and environmental impacts.

public policies must expressly provide for Indigenous peoples' full and active participation, in accordance with recent developments observed in the international environmental regime.

Although the human rights violations Indigenous peoples are still suffering spread far beyond their FoRB, this cannot belittle its indisputable uniqueness. The historical tradition of this freedom, along with its fundamental role in the consolidation of our plural societies, immeasurably strengthens the claims of Indigenous peoples and gives them, in turn, an unquestionable strength and consistency. Hence, guaranteeing the effective enjoyment of Indigenous peoples' right to FoRB in all its dimensions constitutes the most effective action to ensure their very survival. For this to be achieved, its interlinkage with Indigenous environmental rights must be respected and very carefully taken into consideration, so that the emerging holistic regime around them can reach its full potential by creating effective synergies between not so different realities.

Acknowledgments

This research has been funded by Project CIGE/2022/63 "Opportunities and challenges in the implementation of business due diligence standards with regard to human rights and the environment" (23I206.01/1), granted by the Generalitat Valenciana.

References

Aguilera, M. G. (2023). *Environmental Human Rights. New Thinking from Latin America and the Caribbean*. Brill.

Beaman, L. G. (2002). Aboriginal Spirituality and the Legal Construction of the Freedom of Religion. *Journal of Church and State* 44(1), 135–149.

Berkes, F. (2012). *Sacred Ecology* (3rd ed.). Routledge.

Blomley, T., Roe, D., Nelson, F., & Flintan, F. (2013). 'Land Grabbing': Is Conservation Part of the Problem or the Solution? International Institute for Environment and Development. *JSTOR*, www.jstor.org/stable/resrep01526.

Borràs-Pentinat, S. (2020). *El cuidado de la vida. Las personas en movimiento forzado en tiempos de emergencias ecosociales*. Foro Transiciones.

Brugnach, M, Craps, M., & Dewulf, A. (2017). Including Indigenous Peoples in Climate Change Mitigation: Addressing Issues of Scale, Knowledge and Power. *Climatic Change* 140, 19–32.

Bullock, C. (2023). Indigenous Ecological Knowledge Is Essential in the Management of Forests and the Seafloor. *Cultural Survival*. www.culturalsurvival.org/news/indigenous-ecological-knowledge-essential-management-forests-and-seafloor.

Camacaro, O. (2012). El lugar de la espiritualidad indígena en tiempos de globalización. *América Latina en Movimiento*. www.alainet.org/es/articulo/158701.

Camarero-Suárez, V. (2018). Acaparamientos de tierras y aguas: impacto sobre los pueblos indígenas y sus convicciones religiosas. *Anuario de Derecho Eclesiástico del Estado* 34, 23–73.

Camarero-Suárez, V. (2024). La defensa de las creencias de grupos vulnerables en el ámbito de las empresas y los derechos humanos. *Revista Española de Empresas y Derechos Humanos* 3, 123–143.

Camarero-Suárez, V. & Zamora-Cabot, F. J. (2016). El derecho humano al agua y al saneamiento y las empresas multinacionales: casos seleccionados. *Papeles El Tiempo de los Derechos* 2, 1–13.

Campins-Eritja, M. & Fajardo del Castillo, T. (eds.). (2021). *Biological Diversity and International Law: Challenges for the Post 2020 Scenario*. Springer.

Charters, C. & Stavenhagen, R. (eds.). (2009). *Making the Declaration Work: The United Nations Declaration on the Rights of Indigenous Peoples*. IWGIA.

Chiarolla, C. & Savaresi, A. (2016). Indigenous Challenges Under IPBES – Embracing Indigenous Knowledge and Beyond. In Hrabanski, M. & Pesche, D. (eds.), *The Intergovernmental Platform on Biodiversity and Ecosystem Services (IPBES): Meeting the Challenge for Biodiversity Conservation and Governance* (pp. 190–210). Routledge.

Colding, J. & Folke, C. (1997). The Relations Among Threatened Species, Their Protection, and Taboos. *Conservation Ecology* 1(1), 1–17.

Corry, S. (2014). *Pueblos indígenas para el mundo del mañana*. Editorial Círculo Rojo.

Cotula, L. (2014). Addressing the Human Rights Impacts of 'Land Grabbing'. European Parliament (EXPO/B/DROI/2014/06, PE 534.984).

Datta, R., Chapola, J., & Acharibasam, J. B. (eds.). (2024). *Indigenous Land-Based Knowledge and Sustainability*. Routledge.

Del Valle Calzada, E. (2024). *El acaparamiento de tierras como amenaza en auge para los derechos humanos*. Tirant lo Blanch.

Durning, A. T. (1992). *Guardians of the Land: Indigenous Peoples and the Health of the Earth*. Worldwatch Institute.

Eichler, J. (2019). *Reconciling Indigenous Peoples' Individual and Collective Rights. Participation, Prior Consultation and Self-Determination in Latin America*. Routledge.

Felipe-Pérez, B. (2019). *Las migraciones climáticas ante el ordenamiento jurídico internacional*. Thomson Reuters Aranzadi.

Felipe Pérez, B., Iglesias Márquez, D., & Villavicencio Calzadilla, P. (2019). Migraciones climáticas: el papel de los derechos humanos para superar el persistente vacío jurídico. *Revista Latinoamericana de Derechos Humanos* 30(1), 15–46.

Fonda, M. V. (2011). Are They Like Us Yet? Some Thoughts on Why Religious Freedom Remains Elusive for Aboriginals in North America. *The International Indigenous Policy Journal* 2(4), 1–15.

Giacomini, G. (2023). Human Rights Violations in the Name of Environmental Protection: Reflections on the Reparations Owed to the Ogiek Indigenous Peoples of Kenya. *Ordine Internazionale e Diritti Umani* 3, 508–20.

Gilbert, J. (2006). *Indigenous Peoples' Land Rights under International Law: From Victims to Actors*. Transnational Publishers.

Gómez-Isa, F. (2020). Economic, Social, and Political Costs of the (Non-)Realization of Human Rights: Towards a New Social Contract, in Wouters, J., Lemmons, K., Van Poecke, T., & Bourguignon, M. (eds.), *Can We Still Afford Human Rights? Critical*

Reflections on Universality, Proliferation and Costs (pp. 220–240). Edward Elgar Publishing.

Iglesias-Vázquez, M. A. (2016). La protección de los derechos de las comunidades indígenas en la jurisprudencia de la Corte Interamericana de Derechos Humanos. *Revista Principia Iuris* 13(26), 261–298.

Iglesias-Vázquez, M. A. (2017). El hecho religioso en las comunidades indígenas y la jurisprudencia de los tribunales regionales de protección de los derechos humanos. Especial referencia a Europa. *Anuario de Derecho Eclesiástico del Estado* 33, 461–494.

Iglesias-Vázquez, M. A. (2021). Los pueblos indígenas y la protección del medioambiente: la indigenización del derecho internacional, derechos bioculturales y derechos de la naturaleza. *Cadernos de Dereito Actual* 16, 216–240.

International Labour Organization (ILO). (2017). *Indigenous Peoples and Climate Change. From Victims to Change Agents through Decent Work*. ILO.

Intergovernmental Panel on Climate Change (IPCC). (2014a). *Climate Change 2014: Mitigation of Climate Change. Working Group III Contribution to the Fifth Assessment Report*. Edenhofer, O. et al. (eds.). Cambridge University Press.

IPCC. (2014b). *Climate Change 2014: Impacts, Adaptation and Vulnerability. Working Group II Contribution to the Fifth Assessment Report*. Field, C. B. et al. (eds.). Cambridge University Press.

IPCC. (2021). *Climate Change 2021: The Physical Science Basis. Working Group I Contribution to the Sixth Assessment Report*. Masson-Delmotte, V. et al. (eds.). Cambridge University Press.

IPCC. (2022). *Climate Change 2022: Impacts, Adaptation and Vulnerability. Working Group II Contribution to the Sixth Assessment Report*. Pörtner, H.-O. et al. (eds.). Cambridge University Press.

IPCC. (2023). *Synthesis Report. Summary for Policymakers*. Lee, H. & Romero, J. (eds.). IPCC.

Intergovernmental Science-Policy Platform on Biodiversity and Ecosystem Services (IPBES). (2019). Summary for Policymakers of the Global Assessment Report on Biodiversity and Ecosystem Services (IPBES/7/10/Add.1, of May 29, 2019).

International Union for Conservation of Nature (IUCN). (2008). Indigenous and Traditional Peoples and Climate Change. Issues Paper. Macchi et al. (eds.). IUCN.

Jellinek, G. (1908). *La Declaración de los Derechos del Hombre y del Ciudadano*. Librería General de Victoriano Suárez.

Jones, N. (2024). *Self-Determination as Voice. The Participation of Indigenous Peoples in International Governance*. Cambridge University Press.

Loftin, J. D. (1989). Anglo-American Jurisprudence and the Native American Tribal Quest for Religious Freedom. *American Indian Culture and Research Journal* 13(1), 1–52.

Martínez-Cobo, J. (1983). Study of the Problem of Discrimination Against Indigenous Populations. Final Report (E/CN.4 Sub.2/1983/21/Add.8). Chapter XXI, 'Conclusions'. United Nations.

Masferrer-Kan, E. (2002). Los derechos religiosos de las comunidades indígenas, in González-Galván, J. A. (ed.), *Constitución y derechos indígenas* (pp. 147–164). UNAM.

Mauro, F. & Hardison, P. D. (2000). Traditional Knowledge of Indigenous and Local Communities: International Debate and Policy Initiatives. *Ecological Applications* 10(5), 1263–1269.

McGregor, D. (2004). Traditional Ecological Knowledge and Sustainable Development: Towards Coexistence, in Blaser, M., McRae, G., & Feit, H. (eds.), *In the Way of Development: Indigenous Peoples, Life Projects and Globalization* (pp. 72-91). International Development Centre.

Mearns, R. & Norton, A. (eds.). (2010). *Social Dimensions of Climate Change: Equity and Vulnerability in a Warming World.* World Bank.

Meyer, A. (2001). International Environmental Law and Human Rights: Towards the Explicit Recognition of Traditional Knowledge. *RECIEL* 10(1), 37–46.

Morgera, E. (2015). Fair and Equitable Benefit-Sharing at the Crossroads of the Human Right to Science and International Biodiversity Law. *Laws* 4(4), 803–831.

Morgera, E. (2020). *Corporate Accountability in International Environmental Law.* Oxford University Press.

Nadasdy, P. (2005).'Transcending the Debate over the Ecologically Noble Indian: Indigenous Peoples and Environmentalism. *Ethnohistory* 52(2), 291–331.

Naess, L. O. (2013). The Role of Local Knowledge in Adaptation to Climate Change. *WIREs Climate Change* 4, 99–106.

Nakashima, D. J. & Roué, M. (2002). Indigenous Knowledge, Peoples, and Sustainable Practice, in Munn, T. (ed.), *Encyclopedia of Global Environmental Change* (pp. 314–24). Wiley and Sons.

Nicholson, C. & Mayer, B. (2023). *Climate Migration. Critical Perspectives for Law, Policy and Research.* Hart Publishing.

Osorio-Calvo, C. A. (2017). Religiosidad e identidad: la lucha indígena como resistencia territorial desde la espiritualidad. *Revista Kavilando* 9(1), 184–203.

Pérez-Ruiz, M. L. & Argueta-Villamar, A. (2022). Descolonización, diálogo de saberes e investigación colaborativa. *Utopía y Praxis Latinoamericana* 27(98).

Ramos-Castillo, A. & Galloway McLean, K. (2012). Climate Change Mitigation with Local Communities and Indigenous Peoples: Practices, Lessons Learned and Prospects. Proceedings of the Expert Workshop on Climate Change Mitigation with Local Communities and Indigenous Peoples held on 26–28 March 2012 in Cairns, Australia.

Reguart-Segarra, N. (2019a). La protección del conocimiento tradicional indígena a través del derecho a la libertad religiosa: un nuevo frente en la lucha contra el cambio climático. *Revista General de Derecho Canónico y Derecho Eclesiástico del Estado* 49, 1–32.

Reguart-Segarra, N. (2019b). Business, Indigenous Peoples' Rights and Security in the Case Law of the Inter-American Court of Human Rights. *Business and Human Rights Journal* 4(1), 109–130.

Reguart-Segarra, N. (2021). *La libertad religiosa de los pueblos indígenas. Estudio normativo y jurisprudencial de su relevancia en la lucha por sus tierras.* Tirant lo Blanch.

Reguart-Segarra, N. (2022). El papel decisivo de los pueblos indígenas en la mitigación y adaptación al cambio climático: evolución y retos pendientes. *Anuario de la Facultad de Derecho de la Universidade Autonóma de Madrid* 26, 183–214.

Reguart-Segarra, N. & Camarero-Suárez, V. (2023). Freedom of Thought, Conscience and Religion under the European Convention on Human Rights: New Approaches, in

Paladini, L. & Iglesias-Vázquez, M. A. (eds.), *Protection and Promotion of Freedom of Religions and Beliefs in the European Context* (pp. 21–52). Springer Nature.

Rights and Resources Initiative (RRI). (2023). *Who Owns the World's Land? Global State of Indigenous, Afro-descendant, and Local Communities Land Rights Recognition from 2015–2020* (2nd ed.). RRI.

Salick, J. & Byg, A. (2007). *Indigenous Peoples and Climate Change*. Tyndall Centre for Climate Change Research.

Sarmiento-Barletti, J. (2018). Securing Rights of Indigenous Peoples and Local Communities May Curb Global Warming. *Forests News*. https://forestsnews.cifor.org/58147/securing-rights-of-indigenous-peoples-local-communities-may-curb-global-warming-reaction-to-ipcc-report?fnl=en.

Savaresi, A. (2016). Doing the Right Thing with Traditional Knowledge in International Law: Lessons for the Climate Regime. *BENELEX Working Paper* 8, 1–49.

Schuster, R., Germain, R. R., Bennett, J. R., Reo, N. J., & Arcese, P. (2019). Vertebrate Biodiversity on Indigenous-Managed Lands in Australia, Brazil, and Canada Equals That in Protected Areas. *Environmental Science & Policy* 101, 1–6.

Sonkar, S. (2023). Balancing Faith and Equality: Examining the Adequacy of the Doctrine of Essential Religious Practices from Gender Perspectives in India. *Oxford Journal of Law and Religion* 12(1), 121–138.

Souto-Paz, J. A. (1999). *Comunidad política y libertad de creencias: introducción a las libertades públicas en el Derecho comparado*. Marcial Pons.

Stevens, C., Winterbottom, R., Springer, J., & Reytar, K. (2014). *Securing Rights, Combating Climate Change: How Strengthening Community Forest Rights Mitigates Climate Change*. World Resources Institute.

Stevens, S. (1997). *Conservation Through Cultural Survival: Indigenous Peoples and Protected Areas*. Island Press.

United Nations Committee on Economic, Social, and Cultural Rights (UNCESCR). (2009). *General Comment No. 21. Right of Everyone to Take Part in Cultural Life*, art. 15, para. 1 (a), of the International Covenant on Economic, Social and Cultural Rights), adopted at the 43rd Session of the Committee on Economic, Social and Cultural Rights (E/C.12/GC/21, of 21 December 2009).

United Nations Human Rights Committee (UNHRC). (1993). *ICCPR General Comment No. 22 on Article 18*, adopted at the 48th Session of the Human Rights Committee (CCPR/C/21/Rev.1/Add.4, of 30 July 1993).

United Nations Permanent Forum on Indigenous Issues (UNPFII). (2007). Report on the 6th Session held on 14–25 May 2007 (E/2007/43-E/C.19/2007/12).

Verma, S. K. (2005). Protecting Traditional Knowledge: A *Sui Generis* System and Answer? *The Journal of World Intellectual Property* 7(6), 765–805.

Vilella-Flores, S. L. (2009). Cosmovisión indígena, in*Estado del desarrollo económico y social de los pueblos indígenas de Guerrero* (pp. 465–507). UNAM.

Westra, L. (2008). *Environmental Justice & the Rights of Indigenous Peoples. International and Domestic Legal Perspectives*. Taylor & Francis.

Williams, R. A., Jr. (1990). Encounters on the Frontiers of International Human Rights Law: Redefining the Terms of Indigenous Peoples' Survival in the World. *Duke Law Journal* 1990, 660–704.

Winter, C. J. (2022). *Subjects of Intergenerational Justice: Indigenous Philosophy, the Environment and Relationships*. Routledge.

Xanthaki, A., Valkonen, S., Heinämäki, L., & Nuorgam, P. K. (eds.). (2017). *Indigenous Peoples' Cultural Heritage: Rights, Debates, Challenges*. Brill Nijhoff.

Zafar, Z. (2020). Protecting Indigenous Communities in Cases of Climate-Forced Migration. *Oxford Human Rights Hub*. https://ohrh.law.ox.ac.uk/protecting-indigenous-communities-in-cases-of-climate-forced-migration/.

INDEX

Printed in the United Kingdom by TJ Clays Ltd.